Florida

Contents

The Principal Sights at a Glance

N.B. The above list includes only the more important places of touristic interest in Florida which are worth seeing either for themselves or for other attractions in the vicinity. In addition there are many other notable sights which are designated by one or two asterisks within the text of each entry.

Preface

This guide to Florida is one of the new generation of Baedeker guides.

These guides, illustrated throughout in colour, are designed to meet the needs of the modern traveller. They are quick and easy to consult, with the principal places of interest described in alphabetical order, and the information is presented in a format that is both attractive and easy to follow.

The subject of this guide is the American Federal State of Florida, consisting of the peninsula of the same name with its numerous sights, the so-called panhandle, together with the offshore islands, including the Florida Keys.

The guide is in three parts. The first part gives a general account of the state and its topography, its climate, flora and fauna, environmental problems and nature conservation, population, government and society, economy, history, famous people, art and architecture. A brief selection of quotations and a number of suggested routes provide a transition to the second part, in which the places of tourist interest – towns and villages, scenery and natural features – with their individual sights are described. The third part contains a variety of practical information. Both the sights and the practical information are listed in alphabetical order.

How to use this book

Following the tradition established by Karl Baedeker in 1844, sights of particular interest and hotels and restaurants of particular quality are distinguished by either one ★ or two ★★ stars.

To make it easier to locate the various sights listed in the "A to Z" section of the Guide, their co-ordinates on the large city map are shown in red at the head of each entry, e.g. ★Miami Beach K 15.

Only a selection of hotels and restaurants can be given; no reflection is implied, therefore, on establishments not included.

The symbol   on a town plan indicates the local tourist office from which further information can be obtained. The post-horn symbol indicates a post office.

In a time of rapid change it is difficult to ensure that all the information given is entirely accurate and up to date, and the possibility of error can never be completely eliminated. Although the publishers can accept no responsibility for inaccuracies and omissions, they are always grateful for corrections and suggestions for improvement.

Facts and Figures

Arms of
Florida

The Sunshine State of Florida is one of the world's top tourist destinations, especially when it comes to family holidays. It attracts nearly 40 million visitors a year from home and abroad, more than a million of them from the United Kingdom alone, with its broad white sandy and shelly beaches, its primeval swampland, still home to the alligator and the Florida panther, crystal-clear spring-fed pools and coral reefs teeming with colourful marine life, famous theme parks such as Walt Disney World, Busch Gardens, Universal Studios and Sea World and, of course, Spaceport USA at NASA's Kennedy Space Center on Cape Canaveral. In fact, there are so many interesting places to visit in the State of Florida that this guide has had to confine itself to a selective choice of some of them.

CT = Connecticut ; DE = Delaware ; MA = Massachusetts ; MD = Maryland ; NH = New Hampshire ; NJ = New Jersey ; RI = Rhode Island ; VT = Vermont ; WV = West Virginia

General

Florida forms the south-eastern tip of the mainland United States, reaching further south than any other state. It lies between 80° and 88° of longitude west and is in the same latitudes – between 24° and 31° north – as Egypt and the northern Sahara. The Florida Keys, at only 62 miles/100km from the Tropic of Cancer, are virtually in the tropics. The state territory consists of the "panhandle" in the north-west – a narrow strip of the flat coast of the Gulf of Mexico – and the Florida peninsula, and is bounded by the States of Georgia and Alabama in the north, the Gulf of Mexico in the west, and the Atlantic in the east, while its southern tip, Key West, is only 90 miles/145km from Cuba, and the Bahamas are about 62 miles/100km out to the west.

◄ In the Everglades

The 22nd largest of the states, Florida covers an area of about 58,560sq.miles/151,714sq.km, and 4424sq.miles/11,458sq.km of its surface area is water. It has about 1790 miles/2880km of coastline, although this could amount to well over 4350 miles/7000km if all the bays and river estuaries are included.

The Florida peninsula is some 435 miles/700km from top to toe, and averages about 124 miles/200km across. No town is more than 62 miles/100km from the sea.

Population growth and economic prosperity

Thanks to its pleasant climate and its economic potential this corner of the United States has experienced phenomenal population growth, soaring from barely 35,000 in 1830, when this was virtually virgin territory, to the present figure of well over 13 million. The origins of this population explosion can be traced back to just after the Second World War, when Florida's population numbered no more than 2.7 million, and the advent of leisure tourism, together with the location here of NASA and its associated hi-tech industries. The giant theme parks that sprang up in the 1960s and 1970s brought in yet more tourists, while the state also became a haven for the elderly and the retired, wanting to live out their lives in the Florida sunshine, with sun-seekers from the chilly north, who came down here to spend the winter.

The area around Miami has undergone particularly dynamic development, becoming one of the USA's financial strongholds while assuming considerable importance both as a crossroads for communications between North and South America on the one hand and a gateway to Europe on the other.

Topography

The Florida Peninsula is a flat plain made up of sedimentary deposits, rock layers of limestone and large areas of swampland, with a range of landscape features that includes a proliferation of lakes, many of them formed into sinkholes, an eastern coastline fragmented by bays, spits and inlets, mangroves fringing the south and south-east, and coral reefs on the shoreline.

Geology

Palaeolithic, Mesolithic

At the end of the Palaeolithic era, about 250 million years ago, Florida still formed part of Gondwanaland, the great continent in the southern hemisphere which encompassed parts of Africa and South America. Gondwana eventually split asunder, owing in part to intensive volcanic fission, during the Mesolithic period 230 to 65 million years ago. The fact that these landmasses were earlier joined together is borne out by matching rock formations and a magnetic anomaly stretching to Florida from Senegal and Gambia. Florida, like the islands of the Caribbean, was an island group of volcanoes.

Tertiary

The land began sinking into the sea in the Tertiary era, about 65 million years ago. Massive sediment deposits, mainly chalk but also sand and clay, formed to depths of up to 13,128ft/4000m on the rock base which sank still further under their great weight, and then in the late Tertiary era, about 20 million years ago, the sea retreated. The peninsula is relatively young, geologically speaking, and was the last part of the continental USA to rise above sea level.

Ice Ages

The eustatic changes in sea level throughout the world during the ice ages 1.5 million years ago meant that at times Florida was twice its present size, as great expanses of ice extended it in the north. The various shelfs are an indication of what the sea levels were in the different ice ages, in some cases as much as 328ft/100m below the present level. As the sea retreated, so broad tracts of the seabed dried out and the land was shaped by the twin forces of wind and water as winds and rivers dumped vast quantities of sand on what had become plains of dry land, as much as 124 miles/200km across.

With the melting of the glaciers 12,000 years ago at the end of the last ice age the sea flooded over the dry flatlands again. Wind and waves distributed the sand along the coasts, creating sandbanks and dune systems, while also forming a long chain of constantly shifting sandy islands separated from the mainland by the lagoons that today form the intracoastal waterway. In the warm shallow salt water sedimentation, evaporation and various organisms combined to make oolite and other limestone formations, while corals created reefs and islets in the clear and highly oxygenated water, the coral islands that were to become the Florida Keys, curling around the tip of the peninsula.

Post Ice Age, the present

Along the shallow water coastlines around the river estuaries in north Florida vast swamplands grew up, with flats and saltmarsh, providing habitats for a rich diversity of flora and fauna.

Around the southern tip of Florida grew a belt of mangroves whose dense root systems shielded the hinterland from tidal waves. Groundwater seeped into the porous limestone inland, dissolving it into a carbonic acid solution that ate into the rock and formed vast cave systems and countless sinkholes. Many of these craters filled with water, thus helping to create a lakeland landscape, while the pressure exerted on the groundwater often caused springs to gush forth from the limestone and form pools with their sometimes copious outflow.

The Florida peninsula of today owes its appearance to erosion by rain, wind and wave action, with the karst nature of the limestone bedrock raised only just above sea level lending itself to a whole variety of geomorphological forms.

The Different Habitats and their Morphology

Mainland USA's most southeasterly state is generally speaking so flat as to be considered monotonous. Its highest natural point above sea level – in Walton County in the north of the state – is only a mere 345ft/105m.

This lack of relief makes it quite difficult to differentiate in morphological terms between landscapes, so no special importance need be attached to the rather vague albeit official breakdown of Florida into a number of regions.

Northwestern Florida's "Panhandle" is a gently undulating plateau landscape, broken up by many rivers.

Panhandle

Central Florida is mostly quite flat, but slightly hilly in some places. The scenery is dotted with lakes, sinkholes and watercourses. The ridges running down its edges are presumably the remains of former shorelines.

Central Florida

Large parts of South Florida are covered in the swamp and grasslands of the Everglades, a unique ecological system that as it gets further south imperceptibly merges into marsh and mud flats, with their most striking feature the "mangle" forests formed by thousands of mangroves. Here too, in the Everglades, can be traced the former shorelines running parallel with the coast.

Everglades

Florida's coastline can be divided into six parts: the north-east and south-east Atlantic coasts, with the man-made zone of Greater Miami considered to be in a category of its own, and on the Gulf Coast the coastal strip of the Panhandle, the west coast of the Florida peninsula, and the mangrove coast of the Everglades (see below).

Coasts

Topography

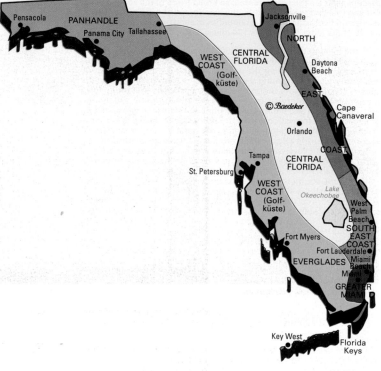

Florida Keys

Strung out into the ocean like a string of pearls, the Florida Keys are also in a category of their own.

Continental Shelf

The seabed around Florida forms a continental shelf at depths of up to about 656ft/200m before falling away steeply to 3282ft/1000m–6564ft/2000m.

Swamps

Since Florida is so flat and low-lying it has great tracts of swampland, especially south of Lake Okeechobee, where the landscape is one of cypress and grassland swamps, dotted with the tree-islands formed by the hardwood hammocks. Since 1880 there have been plans to drain this area, and as these have become reality, mostly to win land to grow cereals, fruit and vegetables, the ecosystems have suffered irreparable damage. The southern part of the actual Everglades – a saw-grass marsh, in a freshwater current up to 50 miles/80km wide flowing gently south from Lake Okeechobee – still retains its original form and is designated a National Park, although some areas on its margin are still drainage projects.

Hammocks

Hammocks, the tree-islands rising out of the swamp and grassland, owe their name to the Indian word for "garden place", and are small, relatively dry, stands of hardwoods, varying in size, and composed of palmetto and vines, cypresses, mahogany, magnolia, the occasional live oak, etc.

Source water of Wakulla Springs

The drier parts of Central and North Florida have large tracts of pines which have given rise to a flourishing lumber business, producing turpentine as well as timber.
Pinewoods

Sinkholes (also called "dolines") are craters that have resulted from the collapse of underground caverns in the limestone strata. Depending on where they are they can be large or small, shallow or deep, dry or filled with water, making many of them into ponds and lakes.
Sinkholes

Needless to say, the fact that the bedrock of the Sunshine State is formed of limestone plays an important part in its ecology. The caverns that have been formed where the limestone formations rise up above groundwater level have produced their typical stalagmites and stalactites ("the mites go up, the tites come down"), the most impressive being those in the Florida Caverns at Marianna in the north of the state.
Caverns

Atlantic (east) Coast:
Florida's east coast, on the Atlantic, is laced with sandy beaches, spits, lagoons, and bays, and the land level here appears to be still rising. The twice daily tides have a fall of between 1½ft/0.5m and about 3ft/1m.
Coasts

Florida's straggling spits often end up as islands, and the bays taper down to narrow lagoons. These spits have fine beaches on the seaward side, but can be very muddy on the landward side, with the dunes, behind them running inland.

Gulf (west) Coast:
Florida's west coast, on the Gulf of Mexico, is a mass of creeks and inlets – an indication of where the land has sunk – and has offshore spits in some parts. Its many estuaries are the product of the mixing of fresh and saltwater and the action of the tides. These are once daily and also have a fall of between 1½ft/0.5m and 3ft/1m.

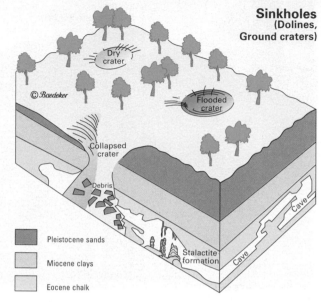

Sinkholes
(Dolines,
Ground craters)

- Pleistocene sands
- Miocene clays
- Eocene chalk

Beaches

Along Florida's coastline almost 1367 miles/2200km of beaches slope gently down to the sea. While the Atlantic beaches are mostly relatively hard coral sand, the northern Gulf coast has fine-grained quartz sand and the southern Gulf coast has rather less firm beaches of shell as well as coral sand.

Florida Keys

In Florida's deep south, where the mainland United States dips slowly into the sea, this chain of large and small coral and limestone islands run further south for another 100 miles/160km, towards the Antilles.

Mangroves

Large sections of Florida's southern coastline are under the protection of fast-growing mangroves. Typical of the tropics, they perch on stilt-like roots that enable them to adapt to the vicissitudes of the tides, and provide the habitat and nursery for a rich variety of creatures. In the course of time the mud trapped by their dense root systems will become land in its own right.

Around the coast the continental shelf extends underwater for an average of about 62 miles/100km.

Water systems

Aquifers

Unlike clay and marl, which stop groundwater running away, aquifers are strata through which water can travel. Chief among these is limestone, which can be quite porous and can collect water. Limestone is the main bedrock underlying Florida, thus providing it with an enormous underground freshwater reservoir that feeds many lakes and springs.

Aquifers may or may not be artesian. Where they are artesian, the groundwater that is under pressure will break through at weak points on the surface, so long as it is not blocked by impervious clay strata, and gush forth as a spring. Where the aquifer is not artesian the water level will rise and fall spontaneously.

Beach on the Gulf Coast

Most of Florida is covered by the Florida Aquifer, which is artesian and rich in minerals. A limestone bedrock formed in the Ezoic, Oligocene and Miocene eras between 53 and 7 million years ago, it is topped by massive layers of sediment to a depth of hundreds of feet.

Florida Aquifer

The Biscayne Aquifer, which runs through a smaller area of south-eastern Florida, is not artesian. The strata, up to 427ft/130m thick, were laid down in the Miocene and Pliocene epochs. The porous limestone is protected from saltwater penetration by relatively impermeable layers of clay and loam. However, seawater penetration into the rock from an easterly direction is only prevented by the pressure of the freshwater flow, and drainage for farming and human habitation has had a disastrous effect on this delicate balance, making it easier for the saltwater to intrude into the rock.

Biscayne Aquifer

The vast sand and gravel aquifer, up to 558ft/170m deep, in the extreme west of Florida, is also not artesian. Dating from the Miocene and Pliocene epochs, it consists mainly of fine to coarse quartz sand.

West Florida Aquifer

Florida is full of springs, although they are particularly abundant in the north of the state. Again, these may or may not be artesian. Those that are artesian are where water has collected in limestone fissures or in subterranean channels, and then gushes forth under pressure, sometimes springing up over a distance of 98ft/30m. More than a couple of dozen of these springs produce a copious outflow of over 12,729 gallons/57,917 litres a second.

Springs

Florida's relative flatness means that nearly all its rivers are quite slow-moving. They are particularly concentrated in number in the north, and some of them also have sections where they flow underground. There are also a few rivers in Central Florida, but the south of the state is largely swampland.

Rivers

Climate

Florida has three types of river. Most of them run black because of the high amount of humus leaching into them from swamps and pine-woods on their banks, while the alluvial rivers are a muddy brown because of all the sediment they are carrying. In fact the only clear water is to be found in those rivers that are fed by springs.

Lakes
About 15% of Florida is under water, covered by lakes large and small. The state's largest area of water, and the fourth biggest natural lake in the United States, is Lake Okeechobee (750sq.miles/1943sq.km), the remains of a former shallow inland sea.

Water levels
The water level of a large number of Florida's lakes depends on the amount of precipitation, and when there is no rain many of them dry up. Much of the stagnant water is in sinkholes, while some pools are fed by artesian springs. Others have been created by wind erosion as craters have had the sand that filled them blown away by the wind to be replaced by water.

Florida Straits
The Florida Straits are to be found between the Florida Keys and the Caribbean island of Cuba. About 106 miles/170km across, the straits link the Gulf of Mexico with the Atlantic Ocean.

Florida current
The warm Florida current flows through the Florida Straits as part of the Gulf Stream (see below) at a relatively high speed (2½ to 3 knots), moving great masses of water in a north-easterly direction. The force of the current and the water movements that go with it result in much displacement of the beaches all up and down Florida's east coast. Since the discovery of the West Indies the Spanish navigators, and then those of the other European colonial powers, have used the Florida current to set their vessels on course for home. Tropical storms off the Keys caused the wreck of many a treasure galleon, and it is these coral-encrusted wrecks that are so enticing for the divers of today.

Gulf Stream

The Gulf Stream plays an important part in the world's weather system, and is of particular significance for weather conditions in western and central Europe. Warm surface seawater flows out of the Gulf of Mexico, in the form of the Florida current, through the Florida Straits (see above), to merge off the east coast of Florida with the equally warm Antilles current from the West Indies to form the Gulf Stream. Averaging 31 miles/50km across and up to 3282ft/1000m deep, this warm current first flows northwards up America's east coast then turns north-east towards Europe, carrying with it as much as 19.4 million cu.ft/55 million cu.m of seawater a second.

The Gulf Stream was first described by Ponce de Leon (see Famous People) in 1513, and the Spaniards used it to get their vessels back home to Spain from the West Indies.

Climate

Florida is actually situated in the latitudes of the desert belt, but no deserts could possibly form there because it is surrounded by water.

In fact the state is one of the regions of the USA with particularly high rainfall. Its latitude and the fact that the Florida peninsula runs from North to South put Florida into two main climate zones.

Zones
Northern Florida is part of the sub-tropical warm temperate zone, while the southern half of the state is already part of the damp and change-able tropical zone, with the transitional area between the two in the

Climate Table Miami Beach	Temperature in °C		Hours of Sunshine per day	Days with precipitation	Precipitation in mm
Month	Average maximum temperature	Average minimum temperature			
January	23.4	17.7	7.5	5	52
February	23.8	17.9	8.5	5	47
March	24.8	19.1	8.7	5	58
April	26.4	21.2	9.3	6	99
May	28.0	23.3	9.1	8	164
June	29.7	24.8	8.5	10	187
July	30.6	25.4	8.4	12	171
August	31.0	25.6	8.3	12	177
September	30.0	25.1	7.3	15	241
October	28.3	23.2	6.8	12	209
November	25.8	20.7	7.5	7	72
December	24.1	18.3	6.9	6	42
Annual	27.1	21.9	8.1	103	1518

intermediate section between Tampa, Orlando and Daytona Beach in the north, and Fort Myers, Lake Okeechobee and West Palm Beach in the south. While North Florida has rain all year round, South Florida has a dry season of between three and five months without rain in the winter. The warm seas around Florida and the high rate of evaporation and air humidity help to create oppressively high humidity from late spring through to the autumn.

Seasons

From the point of view of climate, the best time to visit Florida is in the sunny and rarely humid winter months from November to April. January and February are the coldest months, when average maximum daytime temperatures are just on 64.4°F/18°C in northern Florida and about 73.4°F/23°C in the south. The average minimum temperatures are between 42.8°F/6°C and 46.4°F/8°C in the north and north-west, and between 55.4°F/13°C and 64.4°/18°C in the south.

November to April

The temperature can fall below freezing anywhere in the state apart from the Florida Keys, which are free of frost all year round. Cold fronts can push the thermometer down below 10.4°F/−12°C and even cause slight frosts in the Everglades. These frosts have disastrous consequences for the citrus groves and vegetable crops.

Cold fronts

The month of May is the brief and still quite pleasant transition period leading into the rainy season.

May

The rainy season between June and mid-October brings heavy and muggy rainfall combined with frequent storms and the threat of hurricanes and tornadoes. In a few months Florida can be subjected to as much rainfall (58in./620mm) as some Western European cities get in a whole year. At the height of the rainy season there is likely to be no more than two to six days of fine weather a month.

June to October

The weather in late July and early August, is particularly unpleasant. It is extremely close and throughout the state average maximum temperatures exceed 93°F/32°C. The top temperature on the coast can be 98.4°F/36°C, and inland it can reach 107.6°F/40°C, cooling down at night to 71.6°F/22°C in the north and 77°F/25°C–80.6°F/27°C in the south.

Hot and humid

Climate

Tornadoes, waterspouts

Particularly bad storms and passing hurricanes can lead to tornadoes over land and waterspouts over water. Florida averages up to 20 tornadoes a year, most of them in April, May and June. These violent local whirlwinds happen when there is instability in the air masses. The cyclonic rotation during a bad storm can become so strong that the acceleration caused by the air pressure balances out the centrifugal momentum. The internal pressure, which can be as much as 100 millibars, can form itself into a whirling funnel of cloud, creating a "twister" or a waterspout. The suction within the funnel also picks up heavy objects, so that a tornado, which can last up to half an hour, will leave a dreadful trail of destruction in its wake, but in the eye of this kind of whirlwind – no more than a quarter of a mile across – the air will be absolutely still with no wind at all.

Hurricane season

Between May and November, and more particularly from mid August to mid October, there is quite a big risk of encountering a hurricane. During the season there can be as many as seven of this kind of tropical cyclone, with winds reaching galeforce 12 (73mph/118kph) and above. The actual field of the hurricane can extend over between 62 miles/ 100km and 124 miles/200km, while the whole area of the storm can cover as much as 124 miles/200km–311 miles/500km, with gale forces of 8 to 11, and windspeeds of over 124mph/200kph or in some cases even 186mph/300kph. Hurricanes move at relatively low speeds, seldom exceeding 19mph/30kph. In the eye of a hurricane – in this case about 12 miles/20km across – air pressure falls to below 950 millibars. The high degree of atmospheric pressure creates very high windspeeds and cloud funnelling on a massive scale.

What makes a hurricane

The tropical cyclones which grow into the kind of devastating hurricane that can threaten Florida mostly build up over the warm parts of the north Atlantic close to the Equator.

There needs to be abnormal atmospheric pressure around 5° of latitude north which gets taken up by the Coriolis force, the deflective effect of the rotation of the earth. In addition the surface water temperatures must be well above 77°F/25°C and the atmospheric conditions must be favourable, with weak winds blowing on a fixed tack within the first 7 miles/12 kilometres of the meteorologically active troposphere.

The initial sparkpoint usually comes when cold north winds trigger off sandstorms over the Sahara and the particles fan out over the open sea towards the Equator.

The actual hurricane is often set in train by a gathering of "hot towers", high-rising stormclouds that then begin slowly to rotate. The energy input comes from the warm surface of the sea. The evaporating water ascends as vapour, condenses and releases heat, generating the

Hurricane

(diagram)

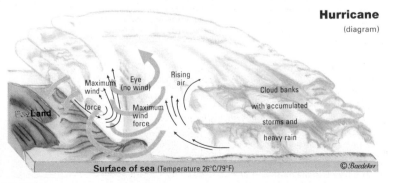

Maximum wind force · Eye (no wind) · Rising air · Maximum wind force · Cloud banks with accumulated storms and heavy rain · Land

Surface of sea (Temperature 26°C/79°F)

© Baedeker

Hurricane "Andrew" over southern Florida (1992)

energy that more or less drives the hurricane. Although the main body of the hurricane enclosing the eye is formed of rising air rotating in a clockwise direction, with the accompanying heavy rainfall, in the eye itself, where the air is descending, there are no clouds and no wind.

Tropical cyclones from the Atlantic follow a parabolic course, initially moving north-west and then arching north-east over the West Indies or off Florida. While they are over warm areas of water they can keep on regenerating, but once they reach land they lose their watery motive force and the storm breaks up.

The cyclones that come out of the Caribbean or the Gulf of Mexico to hit the American mainland, including Florida, wreak such havoc because the damage caused by the high windspeeds can be accompanied by catastrophic flooding owing to the tidal waves and torrential rainfall that follow in their wake.

The National Hurricane Center in Miami operates a warning system which uses the data gathered by satellites and aircraft to provide pretty reliable information about a hurricane's strength, course, and location, and evacuation routes are signposted throughout the state, showing how to reach safety in an emergency.

The heat and humidity die down in the second half of October and on through November, as brighter and milder days lead into the dry winter season. **October/ November**

Fog can occur in some places at night and early in the morning.

The wind in winter is mainly from the north, and in summer mainly from the south, and March and April are particularly windy months. The winds on the coast are from the land or the sea depending on the time of day. The differences in land and sea temperatures mean that there is a seawind during the day and a wind off the land at night. This is because the sun heats up the land during the day, causing the hot air **Wind conditions**

17

to rise. Its place is taken by cold air coming in from the sea, hence the seawind. Convection currents then bring the hot air down again as it cools, thus completing the circular movement. This process is reversed at night when the sea supplies the warmth and the land cools down faster.

Flora and Fauna

Anyone flying over Florida on a clear day can soon see that it is not so very long ago since the peninsula was largely covered by forests and grassy swamps. This is borne out by some of the large tracts of woodland and wetlands that still exist as nature conservation areas, such as the Ocala and Apalachicola National Forests, Big Cypress National Preserve, and the Everglades. About half the state has since been covered by farming of various kinds or been built on. Although a warning note has since been sounded loud and clear about what is happening, many greenfield sites continue to be devoured by development. The land is drained and ploughed up to make way for holiday homes, retirement projects, industrial zones, recreational complexes and grandiose road schemes that spread in cancerous fashion into the habitats of the wonderfully rich variety of animal and plantlife.

Vegetation

Woodland

A striking feature of Florida is the transition from pinewoods to tropical vegetation. North and Central Florida still have quite large areas of the woodland that was exploited in the past as a source of timber and turpentine. These pinewoods contain a variety of different species, and are relatively light and airy, with an undergrowth of palmetto.

Palms become increasingly more common further south. Florida has over a hundred varieties, the most widespread being the coconut, date and dwarf palms, with here and there larger stands of the majestic Royal palm.
The live-oaks, with thick brushwood, are particularly impressive and their branches, like those of the occasional cypress, are draped with Spanish Moss, a kind of bromeliad.

Grasslands and swamps

Further south Florida's woods give way to grasslands and wetlands. Many tropical plants grow here too, including such typical vegetation as the many varieties of cypress, grasses, epiphytes, ferns, liana and orchids, as well as bromeliads and creepers such as the strangler fig. The swamps themselves hold innumerable sedges, rushes and reeds, flags and waterlilies, together with the everpresent water hyacinth, while here too the expert will be able to find a whole array of delicate tropical orchids.

Hammocks

The hammocks scattered through northern Florida's woods and its southern swamps are tree-islands of hardwoods such as palms, live oak, mahogany, magnolia and gumbo limbo, where palmetto and other sabal palms mingle with various creepers to form an impenetrable undergrowth.

Mangroves

Around south and south-west Florida, where the mainland gradually sinks below sea level, there are forests of mangrove fringing the shoreline. This is such a highly specialised plant that it only has a few varieties, chief among them being the red mangrove which turns the water red with its tannin and is also used as a textile dye.

The large areas of black and white mangrove are also capable of tolerating salt. They too have thick evergreen leaves and tend to form

Spanish moss   Key lime

zones of their own, in a kind of amphibian jungle where they sustain themselves through their roots and aerial breathing tubes.

Florida is famous the world over for its citrus fruit, and for its oranges in particular. Together with grapefruit, tangerines, etc. these are grown in great plantations on the Indian River, in Central Florida, and along the Gulf Coast. Most of the fruit is processed into juice and concentrates.

Citrus fruit

The Key lime is a Florida speciality. The tart juice from this greenish yellow, relatively thin-skinned citrus fruit is used in cooking, while the peel is a source of volatile oils.

Key lime

Wildlife

Despite all that Man has done to ruin the ecology of the Florida peninsula, there are still a few havens where it is possible to get some idea of how rich the variety of wildlife here must originally have been. This is borne out in the works of such pioneering naturalists as Muir and Audubon (see Famous People).

Florida has a particularly rich birdlife with hundreds of different breeding species. Particularly good sites for birds include Merritt Island at Cape Canaveral, the mangroves of the south and south-west, and the still relatively undisturbed wetlands and swamps. The Everglades in particular are still a stronghold for herons such as the great white and the great blue, the Louisiana heron and the great and snowy egret, as well as brown and white pelican, anhinga, wood stork (America's only stork), roseate spoonbill, some of the few remaining wild flamingo, various woodpeckers, and vultures, here confusingly called buzzards. Osprey, quite a common raptor in Florida, are often to be seen catching fish, and an occasional bald eagle – the actual American eagle of the

Birds

A racoon

An alligator comes ashore

United States coat of arms – can be seen soaring over the bays and swamps. The more expert bird watchers will also be able to spot double-crested cormorant, purple gallinule, limpkin, white ibis, and the occasional screech owl.

Alligators

Florida's million or so alligators are very much at home in its swamps and countless small waterways, and can be seen in the channels of the Space Center at Cape Canaveral, as well as the Everglades. They also frequent gardens and golf courses, not to mention the odd gator at night ambling along the highway.

Crocodiles

The American saltwater crocodile, almost hunted out of existence, can still be seen, but only just, around Florida Bay in the Everglades, the one place in the world where crocodiles and alligators co-exist.

Tortoises and turtles

Also threatened with extinction are several of the once common species of tortoise and turtle. This is true not only of the Florida soft-shelled species but also of a whole range of sea turtles, as the sandy beaches where they lay their eggs are ruined by the encroachment of tourism.

Snakes

The palmetto undergrowth of the hammocks and other dryer habitats are favourite haunts for the venomous, and sometimes quite aggressive, diamondback rattlesnake and ground rattler. Water moccasins, coral snakes and, in northern Florida especially, copperheads also pose a deadly danger to the unwary. Florida has a great many non-venomous snakes as well, including colubrids such as the garter snake and the yellow rat-snake.

Mammals

Florida's woods, grasslands, wetlands and mangroves hold quite a few mammals, although some of these too are very much under threat. The ones most frequently encountered include raccoons, some wild cats, such as the red lynx, white-tail deer and roebuck, as well as coyotes, foxes, peccary, mink and armadillo, the last increasingly a victim of the sharp rise in road traffic.

South Florida holds the last few remaining cougar in the eastern United States. These big cats, or Florida panther as they are known locally, live in the remoter parts of the Everglades and Big Cypress Reserve, under increasing threat of extinction despite their protected status.

Florida panther

The opossum, a marsupial rather similar to a rat, is still quite common. The female can carry up to a dozen youngsters in her capacious pouch.

Opossum

Another threatened Florida species – only a few hundred are left – is the manatee, or sea cow. These large yet endearing creatures live in the shallow coastal waters, waterways and freshwater lakes, feeding on the great rafts of waterplants, moving inland as their habitat cools down in winter to the relatively warmer waters of the sloughs and springs.

Manatees

Florida's dolphins can be seen in the wild as well as in captivity, and are often to be sighted in the coastal waters off the southern and south-western parts of the state, occasionally accompanying pleasure boats and delighting photographers with their flying leaps and other watery acrobatics.

Dolphins

Tiger sharks are among the large number of sharks that frequent the waters around the Florida peninsula, so water sports enthusiasts should be on their guard.

Sharks

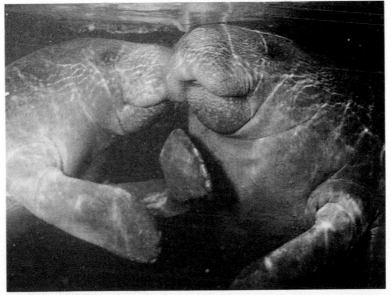

Comical manatees in a warm pool

21

Stingrays

Stingrays pose a particular danger to people walking on the beach and to swimmers, especially in summer when the rays travel to the shallow waters along bays and beaches to produce their young and bury themselves in the sand and mud, with just their eyes and tail exposed. Treading on one can result in very nasty injuries being inflicted by their poisonous spines.

Insects

In the hot humid summer months time spent out of doors can be made a misery by the swarms of flies and mosquitoes that abound in the parts of Florida which are still relatively undisturbed, where they plague the life out of man and beast.

Ticks, as well as hosts of fleas and spiders, add to the discomfort, and the occasional encounter with a scorpion cannot be ruled out.

Environmental problems and Nature conservation

Greenhouse effect

Fluctuations in sea level are not just a thing of the past. Man's ongoing industrial pollution of the atmosphere will have the effect of heating up both the sea and the air about us, setting in chain the melting of the polar ice caps and glaciers, pushing up sea levels and destroying all kinds of creatures. The growing ferocity of the hurricanes is also thought to be connected with this manmade greenhouse effect. Large parts of Florida are already in serious danger from flooding, and this could mean dramatic changes in Florida's coastline in the decades to come.

Dying coral

The coral around Florida is dying off at an alarming rate, in some parts as much as 10% a year. If this continues a large part of the coral reef around the peninsula will have been lost almost beyond recall by the turn of the century. Marine biologists cite a number of factors that are speeding up the death of the coral, with foremost among them the harmful effects of human activity. Careless divers, snorkellers, and fishermen, together with sailing and pleasure boats, all play a particular part in damaging this extremely sensitive biotope. This is combined with deterioration in seawater quality owing to global warming and to the sewage, fertiliser and other pollutants spewed out by the holiday playgrounds and intensively farmed hinterland. Every year thousands of tons of damaging substances float out into the coastal waters, including large amounts of pesticides and other dangerous chemical residues. The big drainage projects inland, entailing the diversion of a great deal of fresh water, are seriously affecting the salt content of the sea water that washes around the coral reefs. Destructive lumbering and farming and the insidious advance of urbanisation have massively reduced many species of plants and animals that crucially need to be present in large numbers for the healthy growth of the corals. Large sectors of the coral, already very much under pressure and weakened by environmental stress factors, are also falling prey to disease that only a few years ago appeared sporadically and on a strictly localised basis.

Diversity of species on land also affected

Thanks to its long hours of sunshine Florida can produce fruit and vegetables on a grand scale for the markets of America's northern states, but only with the proper irrigation. The high rate at which this has depleted the sources of fresh water has led to the lowering of the water table, with disastrous consequences for what is left of the natural swampland, and the Everglades in particular. Irrigation systems, lowering of the water table, greater pesticide inputs — some of it floated in the groundwater — and a general expansion of the area under cultivation have caused farming activity to be regarded with suspicion by anyone who is concerned with preserving what is left of the original natural habitat. Many birds, mammals and freshwater fish have already been seriously contaminated.

Extension of the road network, local people's passion for building on yet more land, and questionable leisure practices are helping to ensure that more and more species of plants and animals are threatened with extinction.

One example of this are the manatees, of which only a few are left. Many of them get injured by fishing hooks and nets, or by the propellers of the boats that roar through their watery domain. Their habitat is being reduced by water management projects, and the deterioration in water quality is contributing to their decline as well.

The Florida panther is in a similar situation. Its dramatic drop in numbers can be largely attributed to a constantly dwindling food supply, overhunting, and the ever heavier traffic on the roads cutting through the areas to which these big cats have retreated.

Also at great risk are the sea turtles who come up to lay their eggs on beaches which are also claimed by tourism. In some places a start has been made on giving parts of the beach protected status.

The basic food supply for a whole host of creatures has also been disrupted by the aerial spraying with pesticides that goes on over farmland and the fast-spreading built-up areas in the summer.

As all this goes to show, Florida's original flora and fauna are very much under threat, if not already partly destroyed. The likes of John Muir and John James Audubon (see Famous People) were among the first to seek to preserve the natural landscape, and small nature conservation areas were already being set up in the late 19th c. In 1947 the Everglades were finally designated a National Park.

Nature conservation

Growing pressure for development, and acknowledgement of the fact that Man was in the process of destroying the basic fundamentals of his own habitat, led to revision of Florida's Nature Conservation laws in 1989/1990. The first result of this was an extension of the Everglades National Park, with further land acquisition due to follow.

Many of Florida's sensitive habitats are designated nature preserves, administered and watched over either by the National Parks Service or the state's Department of Resources. Wetlands like the southern Everglades and forests such as Ocala are protected, as are large sections of the Gulf Coast in North Florida and the Atlantic coast at Cape Canaveral, and parts of the Florida Keys. This protection has also recently been extended to individual natural monuments, recreation areas, paths and trails, as well as historically important sites.

National Parks, State Parks (see Practical Information)

Each with their own parks service, these national and state parks are supervised by park rangers, who ensure the observance of the now much tighter conservation laws. They can also provide information about their own preserves and arrange various natural history excursions.

All the major parks have visitor centres where visitors can obtain leaflets, maps, and other information, and learn about the specific issues in that area from audiovisual programmes, illustrated talks and exhibitions.

Many of the parks, most of which charge for admission, have visitor facilities such as campsites and catering and, in some cases, even motels and lodges. Descriptions of the major parks can be found in the A to Z section, while all the national and state parks and forests are listed, with a map, in the Practical Information section.

Population

In 1991 the population of the state of Florida, living in an area of 58,560sq. miles/151,714sq.km, exceeded 13 million. Over a quarter of the people of Florida live along the south-eastern coast in and around Greater Miami, Fort Lauderdale and West Palm Beach. Other densely populated areas are around Tampa, St Petersburg and Pinellas Suncoast, with about 2 million, Orlando (900,000), and Jacksonville (700,000).

Population growth

The gradual opening up of Florida in the 19th c. brought about a rapid influx of population, pushing up the number of people living there from just on 35,000 in 1830 to well over 100,000 in the 1850s, and up to half a million at the turn of the century. This growth continued and by 1950 the population stood at 2.8 million, then shot up to nearly double that in 1960, when it was 5 million. By 1970 the figure was 6.8 million, in the early 1980s it climbed to over 10 million, and currently Florida's population is approaching 14 million. Virtually all this increase has been due to people moving into the state.

In terms of size of population Florida comes fourth after California, New York and Texas, although so far as rate of population growth is concerned it has averaged third place over the past 15 years.

The latest prediction is that Florida's population will continue to expand and in the next three decades will probably exceed 20 million, growing as it does at the rate of just about 900 a day.

Average age

It is mainly the elderly who come in great numbers to live in this land of sunshine, as the many retirement homes and mobile home parks testify. They can live more cheaply here than anywhere else, under a tax system that is the most favourable of any state, and also save on the cost of heating and insulation. Nevertheless, Florida is trying to rid itself of its pensioner paradise image, and is increasingly attracting a younger age group as a place in which to live, work and relax. Florida's population is still an ageing one, however, and the average age has risen from 34.7 in 1980 to the present figure of 37.

Distribution

Population distribution within the state has undergone an interesting change. In 1900 66% lived in north Florida, 29% in central Florida and only 5% in the south. Nowadays only 20% are in the north of the state, as compared with 43% in the centre and 37% in the south. Four fifths of Florida's citizens live either on the coast or no more than an hour's drive away. The most marked population growth is now on the southeast Atlantic coast and the central Gulf Coast.

Urban population

In 1860 Florida had just two towns with a population of over 2500, then around the turn of the century every fifth person lived in one of the 12 towns. Currently over four fifths of the population live in towns and urban areas.

Ethnic composition

Florida's population, although predominantly white and Englishspeaking, is very varied nevertheless. Immigrants from Canada and Europe constitute less than 10%, mainly Britons, Germans, Italians, Russians and Poles.

New Yorkers

About a fifth of the people living in the counties between Palm Beach and Miami are from New York, and these ex-New Yorkers actually form the majority of newcomers to this part of Florida.

Latinos (Hispanics)

Latinos, or Hispanics as they are also known, are the Spanish-speaking emigrants from Cuba, various Central American countries, Brazil and other parts of South America. They live mainly in and around Miami and Fort Lauderdale (about a million of them in 1991), as well as in the Tampa/St Petersburg area (150,000), Jacksonville (200,000), Orlando (100,000) and around Boca Raton and West Palm Beach (70,000).

Asians

Several thousand Asians – mostly Philippinos, Vietnamese, Chinese and some Thais and Japanese – have also settled in Florida.

Afro-Americans form about a fifth of Florida's population. Their numbers have been swollen in recent times by newcomers from several of the overcrowded islands of the Lesser Antilles and by boat people fleeing from Haiti. Many of them eke out a wretched existence because of poor pay and bad living and working conditions.

Afro-Americans

After falling to their lowest in the 1950s the numbers of American Indians have started to recover and currently stand at around 35,000. This is mainly due to Amerindians coming here from other parts of the United States in search of a better living. The descendants of the Seminoles and Miccosukees, some 3000 of them, are not simply confined to reservations in the Everglades and Big Cypress Reserve. Having adapted to the good old "American way of life", they also merge into the background in various Florida towns and cities.

Amerindians

Florida's six main religious communities are Roman Catholics (30%), Baptists (30%), Methodists (15%), Jews (12%), Presbyterians (just on 7%) and Anglicans (about 5%). In recent years there has been a sharp increase in the numbers of Muslims, Jehovah's Witnesses and adherents of the natural religions.

Religion

State and Society

Florida joined the Union of the United States of America in 1845. The state capital is Tallahassee, which is also the seat of the Governor, who heads the administration. As at Federal level, the state has a Congress consisting of the Senate (40 members) and the House of Representatives (120 members). Both meet in the State Capitol building in Tallahassee which is modelled on that of Washington. Although the position of Governor is of political importance he or she is bound by the decisions of the State Congress. This is reflected in, for example, the right of Congress to have a voice in the appointment of officials. The Governor's veto on a Congress resolution can be overturned by a simple majority. However, a significant exercise of the Governor's power has been on the number of occasions when it has been used in times of civil unrest to call out the National Guard to reinforce the State Police. Compared with their equivalents in European federal nation states, American States have powers that are much more far-reaching, as can easily be seen in Florida. Anyone travelling there will soon be struck by examples of this in daily life, where it is the State of Florida that determines speed limits, use of seatbelts, alcohol limits, disabled parking, etc., as well as liquor laws, police rules, voting rights and schools legislation.

State of Florida

The State of Florida has its own constitution, originally drawn up in 1885 and then revised in 1968.

Constitution

Florida is represented in the federal capital by two Senators and 15 Congressmen.

Representation in Washington

The state is divided up into 66 counties.

Counties

Florida's Indians administer their own reservations and pay no taxes. Most of the descendants of the original native peoples have adapted to modern living conditions, but everywhere there are signs of the reawakening of their national consciousness.

Indian reservations

Many consider the Sunshine State a model example of the multicultural society, where people of different colour and vastly different origins, with all kinds of cultural and religious backgrounds, live alongside one another to form one of life's richest patterns.

Multicultural society

Federal State of Florida

Counties

1 Escambia
2 Santa Rosa
3 Okaloosa
4 Walton
5 Holmes
6 Jackson
7 Washington
8 Bay
9 Calhoun
10 Gulf
11 Liberty
12 Gadsden
13 Leon
14 Jefferson
15 Wakulla
16 Franklin
17 Madison
18 Taylor
19 Hamilton
20 Columbia
21 Baker
22 Nassau
23 Duval
24 Clay
25 Union Bradford
26 Suwannee
27 Lafayette
28 Dixie
29 Gilchrist
30 Alachua
31 Putnam
32 St. Johns
33 Flagler

34 Levy
35 Marion
36 Volusia
37 Citrus
38 Sumter
39 Lake
40 Seminole
41 Orange
42 Hernando
43 Brevard
44 Indian River
45 Pasco
46 Pasco
47 Pinellas
48 Hillsborough
49 Polk
50 Manatee
51 Hardee
52 Highlands
53 Okeechobee
54 Sarasota
55 Desoto
56 Charlotte
57 Glades
58 Lee
59 Hendry
60 Collier
61 St. Lucie
62 Martin
63 Palm Beach
64 Broward
65 Monroe
66 Dade

Economy and Transport

The coming of the railroad in the late 19th c. triggered off a dynamic rate of development for Florida, making it possible for its tourism potential to be exploited and giving its agricultural produce speedier access to the nation's markets in the north.

The part played by America's armed forces in the state's economic development should not be underestimated. Thousands of troops from the rest of the States passed through Florida's training camps during the two world wars, or worked in its armament industries. Their presence had a multiplier effect for the commerce of the Sunshine State, helping to stimulate the tourist trade of Northerners heading south for holidays in the sun.

Economic development after the Second World War was made particularly dynamic by the building of the US Space Center at Cape Canaveral, which was probably the major single impetus for many new industries to establish themselves here, while mammoth projects such as Walt Disney World, Sea World and Busch Gardens, all quite literally conjured up out of nothing, also helped to swell the tourist ranks.

Economy

Florida has a whole host of mineral resources in the sediment layers   Minerals
deposited in its coastal areas by rivers and the action of the tides. It is
one of the leading states for the production of titanium and zircon,
found mainly in the sandy dunes of the east and north-east coasts.

In terms of non-metallic resources, Florida has considerable quantities of limestone, phosphates (about a third of world production) and
high-quality argillaceous earth. There is phosphate mining on a large
scale from the miocene and pleiocene strata in western Central Florida,
and the vast amount of limestone supplies a significant cement industry. Coquina, the soft limestone consisting mainly of fossil shells and
corals, was already being used as building material by the Spaniards.

Offshore drilling is used to exploit the oil and natural gas fields off
Florida's south-west coast.

The waters around the peninsula abound in fish and shellfish of all   Fisheries
kinds. Florida has important oyster, crab, and shrimp fisheries, and
thousands of tons of fish for the table are also landed every year.
Diving for sponges is still carried on by the descendants of the Greek
immigrants who were the first to become aware of the wealth of
sponges in Florida's waters. There are important inland fisheries too.

In addition to commercial fishing, angling as a pastime also plays a
very major role in the local economy, whether it be inland sportsfishing or in one of the boats specially equipped for big game and
deepsea fishing.

Visitors to north and south-west Florida cannot fail to notice its wealth   Forestry
of timber, and commercial forestry in fact covers more than 17.3
million acres/7 million hectares. Most of the pines and cypresses go for

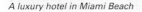

A luxury hotel in Miami Beach   *Citrus fruit ready for despatch*

27

paper and cellulose, while turpentine extraction, begun by the oldtime "crackers", is still carried on to some extent. The amount of hardwood, on the other hand, especially oak, has dwindled considerably over the years. Big afforestation programmes have been going on since the late Twenties in order to satisfy industry's demands for timber, and roughly 4 billion trees have been planted since 1928.

Citrus fruit

Citrus-growing is the most important sector of Florida's agriculture. A billion dollar crop of oranges (5 million tonnes), grapefruit (2 million tonnes), tangerines and lemons is harvested every year, mainly in the central and eastern part of the state and around Indian River especially, producing about 120 million 88lb crates of fresh fruit, although most fruit goes for processing into juice and concentrate. Citrus orchards currently take up an area of about 740 acres/300 hectares. Cold snaps have brought serious problems in recent winters, causing substantial losses for some growers despite their costly and large-scale heating schemes for the citrus groves.

Vegetables

Another traditionally important sector is the growing of winter vegetables – celery, cabbage, green beans, cucumber, tomatoes, radishes, melons, squashes, etc. – for the populous north-eastern states. These crops, which are grown on some 494,000 acres/200,000ha, have also been hard hit by frosts in recent years.

Sugar cane

Florida ranks third in the United States (after Hawaii and Louisiana) as a grower of sugar cane, with fields covering 247,000 acres/100,000ha. These make an impressive sight for many miles around Clewiston and Belle Glade in the area of Lake Okeechobee, where the lake has been dammed and the swamps and reedbeds drained.

Livestock

Livestock farming has expanded considerably in recent years. More and more land is being given over to grazing and pig-farming, with dairy cattle now around 10% and pigs 15% of the 2 million head of stock. Much of this increase in cattle-farming is due to success in cross-breeding sturdy Holsteiners with European breeds and Indian zebus. Another recent development is Florida's success with horses, particularly the rearing of Arab bloodstock.

Industry

In the past industry never played a very big part in Florida's economy, apart from food processing and tobacco. At the turn of the century there were 100 cigar factories in Tampa alone, but now there are no more than a couple of dozen in the whole state. Needless to say industries based on citrus growing still figure prominently, and Florida has many major manufacturers of citrus fruit products, with enormous modern plants packing and canning the fruit, and turning out juice, concentrate and jams. A number of specialised sectors have also grown up around the citrus industry to make oils and additives from the peel and other by-products.

Local resources also provide the base for lumbering, paper and cellulose, cement and some of the state's chemical and metals industry.

The siting of America's space travel programme at Cape Canaveral has also brought with it a host of brand new hi-tech businesses in electronics, space technology, etc., so that, for example, all the major aircraft and machinery manufacturers and computer companies have subsidiaries in Florida. The booming space industry has also spawned innumerable highly specialised ancillary services.

Financial institutions

An increasing number of financial institutions have been encouraged to establish themselves in Florida as more and more of the wealthy have been lured here by the winter sunshine, with the added attraction of nearby tax havens such as the Bahamas and Cayman Islands and the upturn in the industrial base over the past three decades. Miami has also become a top international high finance centre, as the gleaming façades of its glitzy banking emporia testify.

EPCOT Center, a place of pilgrimage for tourists

"They came with a T-shirt and a 20 dollar bill and never changed either of them", according to the old wisecrack about the early vacationers in the Roaring Twenties, who ventured here in their decrepit buses and jalopies to spend the winter in a Florida that was then still largely the back of beyond and off the beaten track for the rest of America. Several museums have photos, replicas and some of the originals of these ancient vehicles, which were often converted into forerunners of the modern camper.

Tourism is nowadays very much one of Florida's basic industries. An official study was clearly gratified by its findings that well over 90% of American and Canadian holidaymakers wanted to return to spend their vacation in Florida. In 1992 over 40 million people enjoyed a vacation in the Sunshine State. One in five overseas visitors to the USA spent all or part of their holiday in Florida, with at least 400,000 of them coming from the United Kingdom. Even the French have stepped up their holiday visits from some 45,000 in 1987 to 60,000 in 1990. Factors contributing to this upsurge in tourism to the state included visitor highlights such as Miami, the Everglades, the Space Center at Cape Canaveral, Walt Disney World, the EPCOT Center, MGM Studios, Universal Studios, and Sea World at Orlando, and Busch Gardens in Tampa, as well as the beaches on the Atlantic and the Gulf Coast. The present favourable exchange rate has also been a contributory factor and it is now a fact that 1.7 million jobs are dependent directly or indirectly on tourism, with the "white industry" earning the state an income of 31 billion dollars in 1992.

Florida has long been a favourite place to spend the winter, and many have elected to retire here or make it their second home. These have included Thomas Edison the famous inventor, automobile manufacturer Henry Ford, tyre mogul Harvey Firestone and the fabulously

Tourism

Winter residents, second homes

29

wealthy Rockefellers (see Famous People), who have been among the many wealthy and not so wealthy attracted here by the climate of the sunshine state from the colder and less healthy climes of the north-eastern United States.

In the winter months enormous mobile home encampments spring up throughout the state for the less well off, while those with a little more capital purchase their own mobile homes on one of the many permanent sites or buy a share in a high-rise condominium on the beach. Those at the top of the scale can acquire a smart house with its own garden and mooring, while the likes of Elizabeth Taylor, Don Johnson, and Edward Kennedy have luxury villas in the Miami area, on Biscayne Bay, in Palm Beach, and St Petersburg, or on Amelia, Sanibel and Marco Island, etc.

Retirement homes
The elderly who choose to retire here or spend their winters and long vacations in Florida are playing an increasingly important part in the economy of the state, a development due in part to the many building projects and complexes favoured by Florida's legislation on behalf of the older and less able generations. A great many of the retired and other pensioners live in and around the Atlantic Coast in Miami Beach, Lake Worth, Palm Beach and Ormond, and on the Gulf Coast around St Petersburg Beach, Bradenton, Sarasota, Venice and Englewood.

Transport

By air
Florida's main international airport at Miami handles more than 22 million passengers a year, making it one of the leading destinations for American and international flights. The state's other airports at Tampa, Hollywood/Fort Lauderdale, Orlando and Palm Beach are also growing in importance, thanks to their scheduled and charter flights for nearby tourist destinations such as the Space Center and Walt Disney World.

In addition Florida has a further 250 plus regional and local smaller airports, 170 of them in private hands.

By sea
About 4 million passengers a year pass through one or other of Florida's four Atlantic coast ports on cruise liners. Most of them embark on their cruises at the Port of Miami, while Port Everglades, the new modern cruise port further north, already ranks second in terms of passengers, and Port Lauderdale nearby regularly takes cruise ships from over a dozen lines. Port Canaveral, not far from the Space Center, is becoming increasingly popular as well, with Tampa and Key West also joining the number of favourite cruise destinations. The top ports for cargo handling are Tampa, Jacksonville, Pensacola and Miami.

By rail
The decisive factor in opening up Florida as a leading area for trade and tourism was undoubtedly the building of the railroad in the late 19th c. The ambitious schemes of rail barons such as Flagler and Plant (see Famous People) both boosted tourism and stimulated the flow of goods between the south-east and America's northeastern states. Florida currently has around 4350 miles/7000km of track and although now there is only a limited number of passenger trains the main lines to Miami and Tampa continue to benefit significantly from carrying passengers.

Greater Miami in particular has come to recognise the fact that rail travel can make an important contribution to solving the problems of local and regional mass transport. Its Tri-Rail service operates between Miami and West Palm Beach, linking all the communities along the coast and the three big international airports. There is also talk of a high-speed service linking Miami with the other main centres.

Florida has an excellent road network, with well over 62,000 miles/99,758km of highway ensuring the virtually unimpeded flow of traffic to the tourist centres of the Sunshine State. It has particularly fast freeways running North to South in the Florida Turnpike (tolls), Highway 95 on the east coast, Highway 75 on the west coast, and US Highway 1 down to Key West. The main east/west routes are Highway 10 from Jacksonville to Pensacola via Tallahassee, Highway 4 from Daytona to Tampa via Orlando, Alligator Alley, the tollroad on Highway 75 from Naples to Fort Lauderdale, and the Tamiami Trail, Highway 41, from Tampa to Miami.

By road

History of Florida

c. 10,000 to 8000 B.C.	Hunters and gatherers move into the Florida peninsula where they can find clear springs, good fishing in the lakes and rivers, shallow lagoons and bays full of fish and shellfish, woods with plenty of game, and pleasant living conditions all year round.
c. 5000 B.C.	The beginnings of permanent settlement in a number of Indian villages where tribes from the north are joined by others from the Caribbean islands and central America, with their own culture and styles of cultivation.
c. 2000 B.C.	Florida's north-eastern Indians develop pottery and begin growing crops on a regular basis. Evolution of more complex economic and social structures.
6/5th c. B.C.	Establishment of cult centres. Formation of shell mounds.
5th c. B.C.	Groups of Indians start cultivating maize around Lake Okeechobee.
c. A.D. 1500	European navigators begin charting Florida's coastal waters. A Spanish map of 1502 shows the outline of a peninsula that resembles Florida.
1513	Juan Ponce de León becomes the first European to set foot on Florida, probably landing on the east coast halfway between where St Augustine is today and the mouth of the St John's River. He claims the territory for the King of Spain and names his discovery "La Florida" after "Pascua Florida", the Spanish feast of flowers at Easter, the date of his arrival. Florida's native population at this time is estimated to be between 35,000 and 100,000.
1528	Pánfilo de Narvaez lands in Tampa Bay to set off on his doomed expedition in search of Florida's fabled riches, getting as far as where the state capital, Tallahassee, stands today.
1539	Hernando de Soto lands at Tampa with over 600 men and initially follows the route taken by Narvaez, encountering Juan Ortiz, a soldier from the earlier expedition who has survived capture by the Indians with the help of an Indian princess and is able to act as interpreter. Instead of meeting with rich cities of gold and silver De Soto's legendary march leads him through more than 3730 miles/6000km of America's southern wilderness. After several skirmishes with hostile Indians he reaches the Mississippi in 1541.
1559	The Spaniards are determined to found a settlement on Pensacola Bay but the expedition under Tristan de Luna soon founders after losing ships and supplies in a storm.
1562	Jean Ribault lands at St John's River with a small band of French Huguenots and claims Florida for France.
1564	René de Laudonnière builds Fort Caroline at the mouth of the St John's River.
1565	Pedro Menéndez de Avíles of Spain drives out the French intruders. As his base he founds what is now St Augustine and destroys Fort Caroline in a surprise attack, renaming it San Mateo. At the same time,

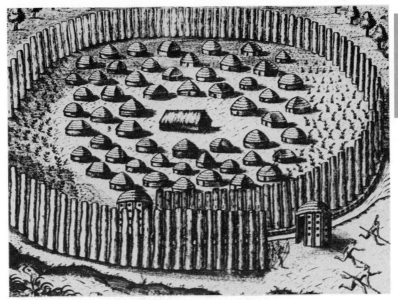

An Indian settlement in the 16th century

the French fleet under Admiral Ribault, summoned as reinforcements, is wrecked in a storm. The shipwrecked French on Anastasia Island are butchered by the Spaniards, whose remote military outpost of St Augustine is to become the United States' oldest permanent settlement.

Jesuits start their missionary work.	1566
British buccaneer Sir Francis Drake captures and sacks St Augustine.	1586
The 17th c. sees Spain stepping up its attempts at colonisation. Hostile Indians and England's awakening interest in Florida lead to the building of the first large fortifications.	17th century
Construction of Fort San Marcos de Apalache at the meeting of the Wakulla and the St Marks River.	1679
The British march into Florida led by James Moore, Governor of South Carolina. The Spanish town of St Augustine – but not the fort – is captured after a siege lasting 52 days.	1702
The French win in Pensacola.	1719
England's General James Oglethorpe marches to Florida from Georgia and takes several Spanish outposts, but the siege of St Augustine has to be abandoned because of lack of supplies.	1740
The English occupy Havana, Cuba, during the Seven Years' War between Britain and Spain. Spain surrenders Florida to Britain in 1763 in return for Havana. Wealthy Britons start up plantations in Florida.	1756–63
Florida stays loyal to Britain in the American War of Independence.	1776–80

History of Florida

1783   Florida is returned to Spain in exchange for Gibraltar and the Bahamas. Thousands of British loyalists leave.

1785–1821   Spanish-American border disputes lead to Spain's gradual withdrawal from Florida. In 1803 the Americans lay claim to western Florida at the time of the Louisiana Purchase. In 1813 America's General Andrew Jackson temporarily seizes Pensacola which had long been used by the British to support their operations against the Americans.

1817/18   First Seminole War: increasing pressure from white settlers trying to get into Florida, and the efforts of plantation owners from Georgia and Carolina to recover their runaway slaves, who often found sanctuary with the Seminoles, result in clashes with the Seminoles living in northern Florida.

General Andrew Jackson mounts a number of punitive raids between Pensacola and the Suwannee River, once more penetrating into Spanish territory and this time destroying Indian villages and carrying off their stores and livestock. Most Indians are either killed or taken prisoner. Having overcome the Seminole resistance he turns on the Spanish settlers as well in his efforts to take Florida for America.

1821   After two years of negotiations Spain cedes Florida to the United States for 5 million dollars. Andrew Jackson becomes the first Governor of the territories of east and west Florida.

1822   Florida becomes US territory, with a Governor – William Duval from Kentucky – and a Council of 13.

1824   After failure to decide on whether St Augustine or Pensacola should be the State capital, the choice falls on Tallahassee, about halfway between the two. Florida's legislative assembly meets for the first time in a hastily erected blockhouse close to the site of the present State Capitol.

1830   Start of the first land boom. American settlers flood in by steamer. Within ten years the population has grown from 15,000 to 34,000. The Indians are forced into a reservation in central Florida but are soon clashing with the land-hungry settlers. President Andrew Jackson's policy of Indian removal requires the Seminoles to be moved out west of the Mississippi.

1835–42   Second Seminole war: in 1835 Mayor Dade and two companions are ambushed near what is now Bushell by Seminoles resisting removal. Despite being heavily outnumbered, the Indians carry on a bitter guerilla war with the American army. Their leader Osceola is captured in 1837 when he presents himself for peace talks. He dies the following year in Fort Moultrie in South Carolina.

The only major battle takes place at Lake Okeechobee, Christmas 1837. The United States declare an end to what is for them an unwinnable war in 1842. More than 3800 Indians and their black allies are sent down "the Trail of Tears" to Arkansas. About 300 Seminoles stay on in Florida, retreating to the depths of the Everglades.

1838   Florida's first constitution is drafted in St Joseph.

1841   A major outbreak of yellow fever hits Florida.

1845   Florida is the 27th state of the Union and has a population of 66,500.

1849/50   Charting of the coastline. The General Land Office designates new land for settlement.

1855–58   Third Seminole War against the few remaining Indians under Billy Bowlegs. They wage a bitter guerilla war around their homes in the swampland. In 1858 the exhausted Indians give in and are deported. Billy Bowlegs and about 120 of his followers take the trail out West. A few others manage to stay hidden deep in the swampland.

Completion of the first railroad between Florida's east and west coasts, linking Fernandina with Cedar Key. — 1860

American Civil War: Florida sides with the South and joins the Confederate States, but Fort Tylor (Key West), Fort Jefferson (Dry Tortugas) and Fort Pickens (Pensacola) remain in the hands of the Union forces. — 1861–65

Florida and its ports play a major role in keeping supplies going to the southern states. In 1864 the Confederates defeat the Union forces at the battle of Olustee, and secure the supply lines in central Florida. The Civil War ends in 1865 in victory for the Union side. Slavery is abolished and Florida gets a military regime.

Start of Cuban wars of independence. The first Cuban refugees begin flooding into Florida. Vicente Martinez Ybor transfers his Cuban cigar factory to Key West in 1869. — 1868

Florida has a population of 188,000. — 1870

The forces of democracy in Florida regain the upper hand. Federal troops are withdrawn. — 1876/77

Enormous phosphate deposits are discovered in the Peace River valley. — 1881

Beginning of the great railroad era. Henry B. Plant's West Coast Railroad reaches Tampa, Henry M. Flagler presses on further south down the east coast. Both magnates build luxury hotels for their customers. — 1883–85

The arrival of Flagler's railway is celebrated

The building of the railroad provides the crucial impetus for the economic development of the state in general, and for tourism in particular.

1886	Ybor moves his cigar-making to Tampa; founding of Ybor City.
1888	The latest yellow fever epidemic leads to the setting up of the state health service.
1890	Florida has a population of just on 400,000.
1894/95	The flowering citrus groves are hit by severe frosts, and the orange plantations are moved further south. Mrs Julia Tuttle, who owns land in south-east Florida, persuades Flagler to extend his railway to Miami.
1898	Spanish-American War. Army bases are sited in Tampa, Miami and Jacksonville. American troops occupy Cuba. They return home to the north with fond memories of Florida's climate.
1904–12	Flagler undertakes a massive bridge-building programme to extend his railroad out over the keys to Key West, linked by a rail ferry to Havana, Cuba.
1905	Further education in Florida is dealt with in the Buckman Act. Gainesville becomes the centre of the University of Florida and Tallahassee the base for the Florida State College for Women and the Florida Agricultural and Mechanical College.
	Designation of the Everglades Drainage District is intended to provide the means for allowing development, through drainage, of the great swamplands of Central and South Florida.
1908	The Ocala and Choctawhatchee forests are declared areas worthy of conservation.
1910	Florida has a population of over 750,000.
1914–18	During the First World War thousands of Americans pass through Florida's training camps or are employed on shipbuilding here.
1920	Florida's population approaches a million. Wild land speculation leads to a massive building boom, particularly in the south of the state. Tourists flock to "the Sunshine State" in ever increasing numbers.
1926	A hurricane devastates the Miami region and the area around Lake Okeechobee.
1927	Sugar-cane is beginning to be grown on an extensive scale around Clewiston, south of Lake Okeechobee.
1928	Opening of the Tamiami Trail from Tampa to Miami, the first east–west route through the Everglades. The south of the state is hit by another bad hurricane. Hundreds of people are drowned when Lake Okeechobee bursts its banks. Following this disaster the decision is taken to build the Hoover Dike around the lake.
1930	Florida's population already exceeds 1.5 million.
1935	The central Florida Keys are hit by a hurricane claiming nearly 400 victims. Rebuilding the destroyed stretch of railway line to Key West is too costly so a road is built on the existing bridgeheads.

During the year Florida is visited by some 2.5 million tourists.   1940

The United States enters the Second World War. Florida gets more   1941
training camps again. There is a revival of the war industry involving
shipbuilding, engineering, etc. The army builds military hospitals and
convalescent homes.

President Truman orders the preservation of the Everglades by its   1947
designation as a National Park.

Florida has a population of over 2,771,000. Production of citrus fruit   1950
concentrate becomes an important industry.

The 15½ miles/25km of the Sunshine Skyway over Lower Tampa Bay   1954
are opened to traffic.

Work begins on building the Florida Turnpike to take the increasing   1955
flow of traffic from north to south.

NASA – the National Aeronautics and Space Administration – starts   1958
operating at Cape Canaveral Air Force Station.
  Explorer I, the first US satellite, is shot into space from Cape
Canaveral.

Fidel Castro comes to power in Cuba. Thousands of Cuban exiles   1959
subsequently settle in south-east Florida.

Florida now has a population of just on 5 million. Hurricane Donna   1960
wreaks havoc on the Florida Keys and further inland.

America's first manned space flight takes off from Cape Canaveral   1961
under Commander Alan B. Shepherd.
  In the years that follow Cape Canaveral and the nearby Kennedy
Space Center are to become the base for American space exploration,
and the launchpad of the successful Mercury, Gemini, Apollo and
Skylab missions.

Astronaut John Glenn, in his Mercury capsule, is the first American to   1962
complete three earth orbits.

Cape Canaveral is renamed Cape Kennedy.   1963

Hurricane Cleo leaves a trail of massive damage in its wake.   1964

First "soft" moon landing by a space vehicle launched from Cape   1966
Kennedy. Building starts on Walt Disney World at Orlando. Hurricane
Ines rages over Florida and the Caribbean.

Three astronauts die in a fire on board Apollo I.   1967

Richard Nixon is nominated Presidential candidate at the Republican   1968
convention in Miami Beach.

Apollo 11 astronauts Neil Armstrong and Edwin Aldrin become the   1969
first men to walk on the moon.

Despite the growing oil crisis, and a petrol shortage at the start of the 1973
winter season, Florida has a record number of 25.5 million visitors.
  In the summer famous treasure seeker Mel Fisher discovers the
wreck of the Spanish galleon "Nuestra Señora de Atocha", sunk off the
Florida keys in 1622 laden with fabulous treasure.

Joint USA/USSR space ventures, then a six-year moratorium on   1975
manned space flight. Crisis in the labour market as unemployment

rates soar to new heights. Hurricane Eloise hits north-west Florida and thousands of people are made homeless.

1977   Citrus and vegetable crops are badly hit by a severe cold spell.

1980   With a population of almost 10 million, Florida is America's seventh most populous state, although only just under a third of its population has actually been born in its territory.

A freighter rams the Sunshine Skyway over Tampa Bay. 35 people are killed when part of the bridge collapses.

Serious rioting erupts when a black insurance agent's murder is linked with the activities of a number of ex-policemen. Miami experiences a wave of violence with muggings and gang wars. The National Guard are called out but 16 people are killed and hundreds of others badly injured. The effects of all this are still being felt today.

Mass exodus from Cuba. Over 140,000 Cubans come to South Florida. This is not without its problems. Besides the bona fide relatives of other exiles and the political opponents of Castro among the "marielitos", as these Cuban exiles are called (after Mariel, the place where they come ashore), there are also thousands of criminals and mental patients whom Castro wants to expel.

1981   January frosts destroy a fifth of the citrus crop. The USA makes a comeback in manned space travel with the successful flight of the Columbia space shuttle. Growing numbers of boat people fleeing from Haiti are turning up along the coast of Florida.

1982   Devastating January frosts cause disastrous citrus crop losses.

1983   A police move against blacks in Miami unleashes days of rioting.

Sharp frosts at Christmas wipe out almost a third of the fruit and vegetable crop.

1985   A cold air front again results in serious crop losses. A tornado wreaks havoc in Venice. Several counties are ravaged by dreadful forest fires.

1986   Challenger disaster: an explosion shortly after the launch from the Kennedy Space Center of the Challenger space shuttle kills all seven astronauts on board. All manned space flight is cancelled for the next two and a half years.

Its population of just on 12 million puts Florida in fifth place among the US states.

1988   Kennedy Space Center prepares to resume manned space flight. The space shuttle Discovery is shot into orbit. Torrential rainfall in September causes flooding in large parts of North and Central Florida.

1989   More serious riots in Miami, especially in the mostly black parts of town. A cold snap at Christmas brings disastrous weather conditions, closing roads and airports and causing protracted power cuts throughout the state.

1990   Manuel Noriega, former Panama chief of state, is brought to Miami for trial on drugs charges. Iraq's invasion of Kuwait results in the call up of army reservists and the National Guard is put on emergency alert.

1991   Lawton Chiles becomes the State of Florida's 41st Governor in January. Queen Elizabeth II visits Tampa and Miami, and decorates General Norman Schwarzkopf following his Gulf War victory. Florida's population exceeds 13 million.

1992   At the end of April the race riots which erupt in Los Angeles spread to Florida, especially to Tampa and Miami, but on a much smaller scale.

Hurricane Andrew roars over South Florida in August. 24 people are killed and about 250,000 made homeless. The damage is estimated at 20 billion dollars.

During the course of the year ten foreign tourists are set upon and killed by criminals.

In March a blizzard sweeps across Florida. In its wake a series of tornadoes cause localised damage.

1993

The USA, Mexico and Canada join together to form NAFTA (the North American Free Trade Association) with a population of 360 million people. Florida's economy is expected to derive particular benefit from the fall of trade barriers.

The World Cup football competition is held in the USA with Orlando in Florida providing one of the match venues.

1994

Famous People

Neil Armstrong,
astronaut
(b. 1930)

On July 20th 1969, as part of the Apollo 11 mission launched from Cape Canaveral, American astronaut Neil Armstrong became the first man on the moon.

Born in Wapakoneta, Ohio, Armstrong was a pilot in the Marines during the Korean War. He later studied flight engineering at Purdoe University in Indiana and then worked as a test pilot for NASA before becoming an astronaut in 1962. His first space flight was in 1966 as part of the Gemini 8 mission. As Commander he was in charge of the first docking by two spacecraft. Since 1971 he has been a lecturer in space technology.

John James
Audubon,
artist and
ornithologist
(1785–1851)

This famous American artist and ornithologist was born the son of a French plantation owner in San Domingo, now Haiti. He came to America in 1805 and settled in Philadelphia where he tried his hand, with little success, as a tradesman and storekeeper.

Audubon was a talented artist, however. His engravings and portfolio of paintings of birds and other wildlife won him great acclaim. "Birds of America" was compiled between 1827 and 1838. Many of his plates are based on notes from two collecting trips to Florida around the Keys and St Augustine. As a writer, in his five-volume "Ornithological Biography" (1839), he also provided the first life history and scientific description for many of Florida's birds.

America's oldest nature conservation organisation, the National Audubon Society founded in 1905, is named after this great artist.

Al "Scarface"
Capone,
Chicago gangster
(1899–1947)

Al(fonso) Capone was a Neapolitan who grew up in New York's Brooklyn slums. In 1920 he moved to Chicago where he became a much feared underworld figure. As boss of the local Mafia syndicate he presided over gambling, bootlegging and prostitution, and had part of the Chicago police force in his pay as well. Although responsible for many a brutal slaying he was not brought to court for fear of gangland reprisals. He managed to amass an immense fortune, and was eventually in 1931 sent to jail for eleven years for income tax evasion. Part of his sentence was served in San Francisco's notorious island prison of Alcatraz.

Securing an early release in 1939 on grounds of ill health, Capone retired to Deerfield Beach in Florida. He died in Miami in 1947.

Truman Capote,
writer
(1925–84)

Truman Capote spent much of his time in Key West. Like his fellow-author and friend Tennessee Williams, he too hailed from the deep South, having been born in New Orleans. He began writing short stories at an early age. His first novel, "Other Voices, Other Rooms", was published in 1948. He achieved international fame with probably his best known novel "Breakfast at Tiffany's" (1958). "In Cold Blood" (1965) was a masterly account of an actual murder, written in documentary style, as was "Thanksgiving Visitor" (1968).

Walt Disney,
master of the
cartoon movie
(1901–66)

Born in Chicago, Walt Disney began his career in Kansas City in 1919 as a commercial artist. His first attempts at film animation in 1922 were a failure but in 1928 he was successful with his Mickey Mouse cartoons, going on to make such famous cartoon features as "Snow White" (1937), "Pinocchio" (1938), and "Bambi" (1942). He also produced adventure films ("Treasure Island"), prize-winning wildlife documentaries ("The Living Desert", 1953), family entertainment movies ("Davy Crockett", 1955, "Mary Poppins", 1965), and, in 1961, the first TV series in colour.

In 1955 he opened "Disneyland", his immensely popular theme park at Anaheim in California, and started planning "Walt Disney World", his entertainment and leisure complex at Orlando in Central Florida, but did not live to see its opening in 1971.

Thomas Edison, born in Milan, Ohio, was one of the world's greatest inventors. As a youngster he was encouraged by his mother into making early experiments and discoveries in various fields of technology. Although self-taught, in the course of fifty years he applied for well over a thousand patents. In 1877/78 he developed the carbon microphone and his long interest in telegraphy led him to build a phonograph, the precursor of the gramophone (patented 1878). In 1879 he succeeded in assembling the carbon filament light bulb and eventually was responsible for the first public electricity plant, the first underground power network and the nickel-iron battery.

Thomas Edison, inventor (1847–1931)

In 1891 he invented the kinetoscope and pioneered a cast concrete process which was to herald prefabricated building. He was also the discoverer of the Edison Effect which first made possible the development of the electron tube. Another of his processes was the production of synthetic rubber, which primarily benefited his friend Harvey Firestone.

In the winter of 1884, while holidaying in Florida for the sake of his health, Thomas Edison came across Fort Myers, a remote spot on the Gulf Coast, where he decided to build himself a winter home on the Caloosahatchee River. He came to spend an increasing amount of his time there, and worked on his pioneering inventions in its laboratory. Besides Harvey Firestone he also counted Henry Ford among his friends and neighbours.

Harvey Firestone founded his Firestone Tire & Rubber Company in 1900, acting as managing director and then Chairman of the Board. He made sure of his raw materials by putting down rubber plantations in South America and the Philippines. In the 1930s he embarked on a massive project to develop Liberia by planting 96sq.miles/250sq.km of land with rubber trees. His business expanded rapidly, buying up existing companies and setting up subsidiaries overseas.

Harvey Samuel Firestone, industrialist (1868–1938)

In the Twenties and Thirties Firestone lived for a time in Miami Beach in a Georgian style mansion on the site of what is now the Fontainebleau Hilton. He often stayed on the Gulf Coast with Thomas Edison who also helped him with his inventions.

In 1865 Henry Flagler, together with John D. Rockefeller, was one of the founders of Standard Oil. He invested his profits in building railroads which, in the 1890s, made a substantial contribution to opening up Florida. His Florida East Coast Railway, begun in 1886, went as far as St Augustine then, in 1895, was extended to Miami. He built luxury hotels along the way and spent the winter himself on his estate in Palm Beach. Eventually he decided to extend the line down along the Florida Keys on a series of great bridges. Key West was reached in 1912 and became the point of departure for train ferries to Havana, Cuba. For twenty years this was the quickest way to get from New York to Key West and then on to Cuba. The opening of the Panama Canal in 1914 lent added attraction to this route. In 1935 a terrible hurricane struck the Keys, destroying the railway bridges, and signalling the end of this stretch of line, which was never rebuilt.

Henry Morrison Flagler, entrepreneur (1830–1913)

Originally a humble machine-shop apprentice in Detroit, Henry Ford was born in Dearborn, Michigan. By dint of his own efforts he became an engineer and built his first car in 1892. In 1903 he founded the Ford Motor Company in Detroit, where he pioneered the assembly-line technique that made it possible to mass-produce the first cheap car of any quality. His workers were well paid for working comparatively

Henry Ford, car manufacturer (1863–1947)

Edison

Flagler

Hemingway

short hours, but he refused to deal with the unions. He won worldwide fame with his Model T Ford, selling 15 million "tin Lizzies" between 1908 and 1927. He kept the management of the business in the family until well into the Thirties. The Ford Foundation was established in 1936; it uses its great wealth to benefit the American education system and to fund technical aid programmes in the Third World.

Henry Ford was a friend of Thomas Edison and shared his love of Florida, becoming a neighbour of his in Fort Myers in 1916.

Ernest Hemingway, writer (1899–1961)

Ernest Hemingway was born in Oak Park, Illinois. He served as a volunteer with an ambulance unit on the Italian Front in the First World War, and went on to work as a reporter in the Middle East, the Spanish Civil War and the invasion of France in the Second World War. He is considered one of the major figures of the "lost generation", who sought to express the mood of disillusion that followed the First World War.

His writings revolve around such themes as love and war, man the sportsman and the hunter, many of them set in southern Florida or around the Caribbean, most notably "The Old Man and the Sea" (1952). In 1954 he was awarded the Nobel prize for literature.

His roving lifestyle left its mark in many places. He first visited Key West in 1928, with his second wife Pauline Pfeiffer. Three years later he bought a house on Whitehead Street. Until 1939, when he and his wife separated he spent much of the year there, indulging his passions for writing (including "For Whom the Bell Tolls"), deep-sea fishing, and heavy drinking. His favourite pub was Sloppy Joe's Bar, and many of its regulars appear in his stories. Hemingway took his own life in 1961 in Ketchum, Idaho.

Zora Neale Hurston, anthropologist and writer (1903–60)

Zora N. Hurston was born and raised in Eatonville, near Orlando. She was one of the very few writers in the Twenties and Thirties to recognise the cultural richness of their black origins, and to build their work around it. Until 1926 she studied at New York's Barnard College under the famous ethnologist Franz Boas. A scholarship helped her to become the major collector of afro-american folklore, and she was closely connected with the Harlem Renaissance, seeking to enshrine the afro-american perspective in literary prose.

Coming as she did from a black community where race was less of a burning issue, Zora Hurston's books tended to centre on the ordinary lives of her characters against a background of rural Florida. Her most important works are "Mule and Men" (1935), "Their Eyes Were Watching God" (1937, probably her best novel, and set in Eatonville), "Seraph on the Suwanee" (1948, the only novel with a white heroine), and her autobiography "Dust Tracks on a Road". She died in Fort Pierce, Florida, in 1960.

A lawyer and plantation owner from Waxhaw, South Carolina, Andrew Jackson became a judge in the Supreme Court of Tennessee in 1798. Fame came with his appointment as General and his successful defence of New Orleans against the British in January 1815, which he followed up with expeditions against the Seminoles and what was then Spanish Florida, capturing the town of Pensacola in 1817/1818. Although his precipitate action led to tension with Britain and Spain – to the Seminoles he was known as "the Devil" – he found important people to speak up for him in the American government. In 1821 Andrew Jackson became the first governor of the territories of both east and west Florida.

Three years later he failed in his first attempt to become a presidential candidate, but eventually succeeded in the elections of 1828 and 1832. As American President he tended to represent the little man, taking the liberal view and siding against big business. Despite growing unease about his policy of Indian removal and the fact that he unleashed a serious financial crisis with the suppression of the all-powerful National Bank, Andrew Jackson enjoyed considerable respect during his lifetime.

General Andrew Jackson,
7th President of the United States
(1767–1845)

De Laudonnière first sailed to Florida to found a French colony here in 1562. He then spent some time back in France before returning with three ships and another 300 colonists in 1564. His first colony had been abandoned, but he laid the foundation stone of a new settlement, Fort Caroline, at the mouth of the St John's River. This colony was also doomed to failure, as the new settlers found themselves unable to cope with not having enough labour, lack of supplies, and constant fighting with the Spanish and the Indians. In 1565 the Spanish destroyed the settlement and massacred its "heretical" inhabitants. De Laudonnière managed to escape and returned to his estates in France.

René Goulaine de Laudonnière, coloniser
(d. 1582)

De Menéndez began his career in the fight against the pirates. In 1554 he was made Commander of the Spanish fleet in the West Indies and between 1555 and 1563 undertook three voyages to the New World. In 1565 Philip II commanded him to found a settlement in Florida to counter the growing French influence.

That same year he laid the foundation stone for what is now St Augustine, the first European settlement in Florida. A short time later he attacked the French settlement of St Caroline. The French fleet which had put out to sea to fight the Spaniards was caught in a storm and every vessel wrecked, and Menéndez made sure that any ship-wrecked mariners who had survived the storm were killed, together with all of Fort Caroline's French settlers, whom he regarded as heretics. He returned to Spain in 1567 but undertook further voyages to America. These included carrying settlers to Chesapeake Bay, where they were soon killed by the Indians.

Pedro de Menéndez de Aviles, Spanish Admiral
(1519–74)

The son of a white settler and an Indian mother, Osceola Nickanochee was born in northern Georgia. When he was four his mother fled with him to Florida to escape growing discrimination from the white Americans. Osceola became one of the principal Seminole leaders. In 1812 and 1818 he fought against Andrew Jackson, refusing to sign any treaty with the whites. His attacks on army patrols and white settlers were one of the causes of the outbreak of the Second Seminole War, when the guerilla tactics of the Indians robbed the American army of any military success.

During peace talks in 1837, in an attempt to negotiate a settlement, Osceola was taken prisoner with his family and some of his supporters, despite the promise of safe conduct. He died of malaria in Fort Moultrie, South Carolina, a year later.

Osceola, Seminole leader
(c. 1800–38)

Famous People

Osceola

Plant

Ponce de León

Henry Bradley
Plant,
(1819–99)

Henry Plant came from Branford, Connecticut, and was President of a number of railroad and shipping companies. The railway line that he opened in 1884 ran down Florida's Gulf Coast as far as Tampa. New settlements grew up along the railroad, which also benefited the locally important timber trade. Like Flagler (see above), Plant calculated on the tourist potential of the Sunshine State and built luxury hotels as well.

Juan Ponce
de León,
discoverer
of Florida
(1460–1521)

Ponce de León was the first Spanish Conquistador to set foot on the soil of North America when he landed there on Easter Monday ("pasqua de flores" in Spanish) in 1513. Acting on orders from the King of Spain he founded the colony "La Florida", which reached up to Labrador from the swamps of the Gulf of Mexico. Ponce de León was also the first to discover the Gulf Stream.

He had been with Columbus on his second voyage to America in 1493, and from 1502 to 1504 had taken part in the capture of Higuey on Hispaniola in the Caribbean. From 1509 to 1512 he was governor of the neighbouring island of Puerto Rico.

In 1513 he set out on the first expedition to what is now Florida. His landing was somewhere near today's Ponte Vedra Beach and he thought he had discovered another large island.

In 1521 he embarked on another expedition to Florida, this time in search of the spring of eternal youth. While investigating one of the many water sources he was hit by a poisoned arrow in an Indian attack. Ponce de León died on the voyage back to the Caribbean and lies buried in San Juan Cathedral, Puerto Rico.

Marjorie Kinnan
Rawlings,
writer
(1896–1953)

Marjorie Kinnan Rawlings was born and brought up in Washington DC, studied in Wisconsin, then worked as a reporter in Kentucky and New York. While vacationing with her husband she fell in love with Florida. They sold their property in New York and bought a farm on Cross Creek, Central Florida, now Marjorie Kinnan Rawlings State Historic Site. When her marriage broke up Marjorie Rawlings stayed on alone at the farm. In 1841 she married a St Augustine hotelier and proceeded to divide her time between the coast and up country, increasingly devoting herself to her writing. Her first Florida stories appeared in 1931 but what made her famous was "The Yearling", published in 1938 (and subsequently filmed with Gregory Peck and Jane Wyman in the main roles). This won her the Pulitzer Prize in 1939. She wrote about the life of the "crackers", the pioneers and the simple settlers in rural Florida. Her other well known works include "South Moon Under" (1933), "Golden Apples" (1935), "When the Whippoorwill" (1940), and "Cross Creek" (1942, something of an autobiography).

Rawlings

Ringling

De Soto

"The Sejourner" came out in 1953 followed, posthumously, by "Secret River" in 1955. A keen hunter and angler, her guests included other famous authors such as Ernest Hemingway, F. Scott Fitzgerald, Margaret Mitchell and Wallace Stevens.

At the age of 16 this son of a German immigrant was already part of a versatile musical act with his brothers, playing the classics as well as putting on the Comic Concerts that were successful enough for them to set up their own circus in 1884. The seven Ringling brothers were a success, and audiences flocked to see their show. They were soon able to buy up the competition, Barnum & Bailey, and their combined Ringling Brothers and Barnum & Bailey Circus became famed the world over.

John Ringling, circus owner (1866–1936)

John Ringling had a passion for European culture which he shared with his wife Mable, the daughter of a good family whom he married in 1905. On their many trips to Europe together they were always buying furniture and objets d'art.

Ringling was also in the oil business and an investor in real estate. He bought an island near Sarasota which he transformed into an elegant estate, complete with country mansion. In 1927 his circus moved into new winter quarters at Sarasota, where they could save on heating costs and the artistes could enjoy better tryout conditions as well.

Business problems and the tragically early death of his wife Mable made him decide to leave the running of the circus to others. He retired and devoted himself to his art collection in Sarasota.

John D. Rockefeller, born in Richford, New York, was the founder of one of the most famous dynasties in American business and philanthropy, and amassed an enormous fortune in oil and steel. He founded Standard Oil (now Exxon) in 1870, and by 1882 had acquired a controlling interest in virtually the whole of the American oil business. His fellow oilmen included Henry M. Flagler (see above). He retired early from business life in 1896 to devote himself to his Rockefeller Foundation (mainly concerned with the advancement of medicine). He had a holiday home in Florida and died at Ormond Beach in 1937.

John Davison Rockefeller, industrialist (1839–1937)

Several members of the Rockefeller family have homes in the exclusive part of Palm Beach, or spend at least as much time in the state as they do in New York.

After studying at Spain's University of Salamanca Hernando De Soto served under Governor Pedrarias Davila in Central America from 1519 to 1532. In 1532/33 he took part in the conquest of Peru and the capture of Atahualpa, the last ruler of the Incas. After falling out with Pizarro in

Hernando De Soto, Spanish Conquistador (c. 1500–42)

1535 he returned to Spain, a rich man, where he married Pedrarias' daughter.

In 1537 he was appointed Governor of Cuba and King's Envoy to Florida. On May 25th 1539 he landed with about 600 men at what is now Charlotte Harbor. He then spent the months that followed on a fruitless quest for Florida's riches. On his march northwards through the swamplands he came across Juan Ortíz, a survivor of the doomed Spanish expedition under Narvaez. He had been captured by Indians and escaped death only through the intercession of a chief's daughter. He acted as De Soto's interpreter on his progress through what are now the southern states of the USA, a journey that provided the Spaniards with a great deal of useful information about this part of America. De Soto's scouts penetrated as far as Carolina and Tennessee but de Soto himself turned south in Alabama, getting back to the Gulf of Mexico at Mobile, where he waited in vain for supply ships. In 1541 during his march westward, he crossed the Mississippi where Memphis, Tennessee, stands today, and overwintered at Fort Smith in Arkansas. He returned to Florida in April 1542, and, worn out by constant Indian attack, fever, and the disappointment of failing to find any treasure, died the same year.

Isaac Bashevis Singer, writer (1904–91)

Born the son of a rabbi in Radzymin, Poland, after graduating from Warsaw University Isaac Singer elected to become a journalist. He emigrated to New York in 1935 and wrote many of his novels, short stories and plays in Yiddish before they were translated into English. Among his best known works are "The Family Moscat", "Satan in Goray", "The Magician of Lublin", and "Yentl", "Yeshiva Boy", etc.

Winner of the 1978 Nobel Prize for Literature, Singer provides a lively and often humorous insight in his work into the lives of Polish Jewry.

He lectured for a time at Miami University and spent many winters at Surfside, Miami Beach, where, in what he called this "city of the future", he wrote about "a vanished world".

Art and Architecture

Mention the word Florida and the images that spring to mind are of Miami Vice and Universal Studios, Cape Canaveral and Kennedy Space Center, Disney World and EPCOT, Sea World and Busch Gardens. In terms of culture as such, however, the Sunshine State also has much to offer – just think of its Mediterranean Revival and Art Deco. Apart from its Amerindian art, such as the famous patchwork and weaving of the Miccosukee, the artists who took Florida as their theme from the 16th c. onwards tended to be first painters and then photographers. The earliest pictures of Florida were by Jacques le Moyne de Morgues (1533–88), a French artist who accompanied Laudonnière's expedition in 1564. His interest, however, was not so much artistic as scientific, but what engaged the painters and photographers of the 19th and early 20th c. was primarily the romantic vision of a landscape full of hidden charms. There are several landscapes by Boston artist Winslow Homer (1836–1910). Walker Evans, the photographer, also worked in Florida, particularly between 1928 and 1941. Artists and photographers delighted in depicting the natural beauties of the Everglades and charming views of St Augustine, the oldest town on the American mainland, with its lovely 18th c. buildings. Views of St Augustine and the Niagara Falls were for many decades the most popular decoration on the walls of the American living room.

St Augustine's buildings are not the only ones to show the impact of the Spanish influence on Florida's architecture. Many other 19th and even 20th c. buildings with historic pretensions show Mediterranean, especially Spanish, influences. In many places, even today, Mediterranean architecture is still what marks the townscape. Particularly impressive examples are to be found not only in Coral Gables, Coconut Grove and Miami Beach in Greater Miami, but also in Palm Beach, Naples and Tampa. In Miami Beach there was even the development – as a kind of southern version of New England's Colonial Revival – of the Mediterranean Revival style of building, with its characteristic Spanish, Italian and Moorish decorative features, much of it in coral limestone.

Mediterranean influences

Nowadays the particular interest for any art lover visiting Florida is its Art Deco, and its concentration in the architecture of Miami Beach. Collecting this theatrical, and sometimes rather kitsch Jazz Age art form became very fashionable in the late Seventies and early Eighties. It was taken up by artists and yuppies alike, not to mention personalities such as Andy Warhol and Barbra Streisand, encouraging artists, gallery owners and other aficionados to campaign for the preservation of many of Miami Beach's Art Deco buildings. Well over 600 of these now enjoy protected status. Many have since been well renovated, particularly along main promenades such as Ocean Drive, Collins Avenue and Espanola Way.

Art Deco

Miami Beach now has the greatest concentration of Art Deco buildings in North America, even though New York examples like Radio City and the Chrysler Building enjoy much greater fame than the hotels and apartment blocks of South Florida. Since this style of building took off in cosmopolitan New York somewhat earlier than in the more provincial Sunshine State, it is not so surprising that influences from New York should have had an impact here too. Henry Hohauser (1895–1963), one of Miami Beach's chief architects, came from New York where he had received his training. Many other creators of Miami Beach's Art Deco District were only known locally, or at the most across

Examples of Art Deco . . .

. . . in Miami Beach

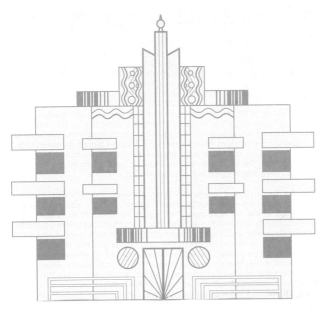

the region, and little is known still about their life and work. Other architects who worked here in the Thirties included Albert Anis, L. Murray Dixon, Roy F. France, Anton Skislewicz, V. H. Nellenbogen, Robert E. Collins, Frank Wyatt Wood, Igor B. Polevitsky, E. L. Robertson and the Kiehnel & Elliott Bureau. Most of the Miami Beach houses date from the late Thirties and early Forties, shortly before America's entry into the Second World War. In an artificially contrived landscape with imported flora and fauna, that was to be symbolised by the flamingo, the endeavour was to present architecture and nature as a tranquil tropical paradise. Today Art Deco stands for the Jazz Age, for the era of Josephine Baker and Marlene Dietrich, but also for the days of the great American roadster.

The term Art Deco derives from an exhibition staged in Paris in 1925, the "Exposition Internationale des Arts Décoratifs et Industriels Modernes". In the United States the term Modern Style was also used as opposed to International Style, the American version of the Bauhaus. In Europe the Paris exhibition in no way marked the launch of a new style that was to embrace every aspect of architecture and daily life as its predecessor, Art Nouveau, had done. But for America, which since the 19th c. had particularly looked to Paris for its art and architecture, this exhibition acted as a catalyst for its buildings and its arts and crafts. The American government sent 108 representatives of the worlds of art and commerce to Paris, as well as delegates from the New York Architectural League, to update themselves on the latest European trends in their fields. There was the widespread feeling in the States that there was little in the way of innovation that they themselves could contribute, but the years that followed saw the development of Art Deco, a style that was to be decorative yet modern. With its penchant for high grade materials, Art Deco was to provide that special touch of class that was needed by big business and the smart hotels. Soon it was setting its stamp on the design of New York's skyscrapers, and, spreading rapidly to America's other big cities, it reached Florida's booming Atlantic coast in the Thirties when the first Art Deco buildings started to go up.

Miami Beach's Art Deco architecture is typically an electrifying application of forms both ancient and modern, with the floral motifs of Viennese art nouveau alongside elements derived from the Aztecs and the Mayas and decorative features from Egypt and Mesopotamia, with a dash of Cubism and Futurism inside and outside. At the same time this unfunctional "modernism" is characterised by the streamlining of its motifs in architecture.

The focus is often on the roof and the entrance as marking the finishing touches of the building. Many are crowned by a pyramidal stepped gable modelled on the ziggurat, the rectangular temple towers erected by the ancient Mesopotamians. Pastel colours predominate. Inside the basic structure is concealed behind costly decorative features so that, for example, murals may be used to make the lobbies appear more impressive but not too clinical.

The Art Deco period spans the years between the two world wars, starting with the ornamental phase. Miami Beach's early Art Deco buildings show an abundance of figurative decoration, often with tropical motifs and serving as reminders of the fact that this is a seaside resort. Later the emphasis is more on aesthetic technology, redolent with the new status symbols of the automobile and the airplane, and even the space rocket. There is increasing use of abstract shapes, horizontal lines, glass, chrome and neon. Typical Miami Beach features include porthole windows, shading "eyebrows" over the large windows, rounded corners and aerial-like finials. Colour and stucco take the place of the marble and bronze found in New York. According to contemporary architect Bernardo Fort-Brescia "Miami Beach's Art Deco is a conversion of the true, big city Art Deco. It is not dominated by bronze and marble, the showy, high class materials of New York's Chrysler Building. The Miami version is deliberately lighter, less pretentious, just colour and stucco, a kind of 'easygoing' Art Deco. We are beside the seaside after all."

Post Second
World War
Architecture

With the end of the Second World War, Florida experienced a sharp upsurge in tourism. Hotels and apartment blocks shot up along the Atlantic Coast, particularly around Miami, Palm Beach and Fort Lauderdale. Large stretches were covered by the kind of highrise developments, packing in the bedspaces, that were subsequently to go up everywhere in places like Spain's Costa del Sol, where beaches were opened up for the holidaymaker. In Miami Beach these complexes threatened to swamp the Art Deco architecture that had been growing up since the Thirties. Besides this host of unlovely "boxes" there were also a number of hotels of architectural interest. These included the Fontainebleau Hilton in Miami Beach, an enormous hotel complex typical of the overbearing architecture of the Sixties.

Miami Beach had the kind of colossal building boom it had seen in the Thirties. In the Seventies and Eighties downtown Miami expanded along the Biscayne Bay shoreline at a breathtaking rate, becoming America's second most important centre for services to big business and high finance, and getting the new skyline to match.

A good example of this is the Centrust Tower, completed in 1987 by America's best known contemporary architect, I. M. Pei, in association with Spillis Candela & Partners. This megastructure dominates Miami's skies by night as well as by day since it has a lighting system designed by Douglas Leigh, known as the lighting king for his work on New York's Empire State Building. The Tower's 387 1000 watt lamps project their light into Miami's night-sky in whatever colour is required, be it green on St Patrick's Day, pink on Valentine's Day, or violet to match Elizabeth Taylor's eyes when she's on a visit – another expression, like many of the Art Deco buildings, of Miami's sense of fun, its passion for glitz and glamour.

Contemporary
architecture

The latest trend has been to lean more towards the traditional, drawing on elements used by the original AmerIndians and features from the Spanish colonial period, as well as traces of the kind of architecture found on Bermuda or in the Bahamas, or the classic Anglo-American monumental style. The rather heavy impact of the enormous highrise buildings of banks, insurance companies, and all the other big business, is thus tempered by these and other post-modernist influences. Some places actually have very handsome modern architecture, and good examples of successful modern highrise can be seen in Miami, Fort Lauderdale and Orlando.

Contemporary
sculpture

Since the Seventies many public places, parks, cultural venues, etc., have increasingly become the location for works of art by contemporary artists, including Claes Oldenbourg, Isamu Noguchi, Nam June Paik, Edward Ruscha, etc., as part of a policy to improve the quality of life and give a greater sense of identity to the community. Roy Lichtenstein's pleasing "Mermaid" in front of the Center for the Performing Arts in Miami Beach quotes the Art Deco in its surroundings. Claes Oldenbourg and his wife Coosje von Bruggen were responsible in the Eighties for the fountain in the hypermodern Metro-Dade Government Center. Entitled "Dropped Bowl with Scattered Slices and Peels", they wanted it to symbolise the multicultural diversity of Miami, which, according to Oldenbourg, is a town engaged in constant development and with a planning system that rests on the lack of planning of its urban development, which does not run according to plan. It is this diversity of cultures and their different forms of artistic expression that have kept artists and architects busy in Florida since the Thirties.

Florida in Quotations

Sir John Hawkins
(1532–95)

The Floridians when they travell, have a kind of herbe dried, who with a cane and an earthen cup in the end, with fire and the dried herbes put together, doe sucke thorow the cane the smoke thereof, which smoke satisfieth their hunger, and therewith they live foure or five days without meat or drinke, and this all the Frenchmen used for this purpose: yet do they holde opinion withall, that it causeth water and fleame to void from their stomacks. The commodities of this land are more than are yet knowen to any man: for besides the land itself, whereof there is more than any king Christian is able to inhabit, it flourisheth the meadow, pasture ground, with woods of Cedar and Cypress, and other sorts, as better can not be in the world. They have for apothecary herbs, trees, roots, and gummes great store. . . . Golde and silver they want not. . . . Of unicornes they have many.
Voyage of Sir John Hawkins, 1565

Baedeker's North
America
(1904)

About Miami and the surroundings:
Miami, with 1680 inhabitants (in 1900) and sub-tropical plants, is the southern terminus of the Florida East Coast Railway and also the most southerly railway station of the United States. It is situated 25°50′ north on the north bank of the Miami River which here flows into Biscayne Bay. The Bay has clear salt water and is protected from the Atlantic Ocean by a row of cliffs (Florida Keys). Its navigable depth is to be increased to 5m. Good angling.

8km south of Miami is Cocoanut Grove (Peacock Inn, $2½–3½) a cocoa-palm thicket with a view over Biscayne Bay

About Palm Beach:
Palm Beach on the narrow strip of land between Lake Worth, 35km long and ¾–1½km wide, and the Atlantic Ocean, is one of the finest winter seaside resorts of the United States. The season (Christmas until April 10th) reaches its zenith in March. In this wonderful area cocoa and other palm trees thrive as well as sub-tropical flowers and bushes; bananas, guava, grapefruit, avocado pears, custard apples, mangoe, plums and fruits of melon trees, etc. all ripen here. From the popular Royal Hotel Poinciana there is an extensive view especially at sunset, and this hotel is connected with the Palm Beach Inn (with a pavilion and swimming pool nearby) by an 800m avenue of palm trees. A long pier offers the opportunity for fishing (tarpon, etc.).
Baedeker's North America 1904, 2nd edition

Henry James
(1843–1916)

Florida does beguile and gratify me – giving me my first and last (evidently) sense of the tropics, or à peu pres, the subtropics, and revealing to me a blandness in nature of which I had no idea.
Letter to Edmund Gosse, February 16th 1905

I am stopping for two or three days at the "oldest city in America" (St Augustine) – two or three being none too much to sit in wonderment at the success with which is has outlived its age.
Letter to Edmund Gosse, February 18th 1905

Roland Hahn
German
geographer

About pensioners' settlements in Florida:
From 1880, when the American Medical Association Journal described the climate of St Petersburg as the heathiest in the world, the influx of rich retired people began. Well aimed advertising campaigns resulted in streams of incomers. So there are excellent retirement settlements for every purse. The most lavish were built like fingers stretching out

into the gulf. Artificial spits of land were formed so that every house could have its own mooring place. Every kind of property can be found including terraces of houses, simple white timber houses and caravan parks. Special facilities such as recreation grounds, parks with concerts, and drug stores with their one-dollar quick blood-pressure checks are also there. These settlements for pensioners are deliberately built so as only to last for 50 years. It is no surprise that 30½% of the inhabitants of Petersburg are over 65 years of age (the average in the USA is 9%). Socialising in the settlements is very variable – according to investigation best in the caravan parks. Between 1965 and 1970 only some 4% of old people moved each year into leisure areas, especially those with expanses of water; to Arizona in particular as well as to Florida. These settlements for pensioners are inhabited almost exclusively by white people. Most of them come from the cities and industrial areas in the north. They live on their social insurance and have the typical life-style of suburbia. Normally they vote Republican and are not very interested in questions of minorities or social programmes.
Roland Hahn, USA, 1981

"It is all quite simple" the agent of "Go Camping" in Miami assured us from whom we were renting a camper for our two weeks coastal round trip in order to be closer to nature and to be with the people in the sunshine of Florida's spring. . . .

Eva Windmöller-Höpker
German author

First we wanted to spend two days in the town of the TV programme "Miami Vice". What a mad place it is! A boom city of bankers and real-estate agents, the economic capital of exiled Cuban and South American mulattos, "New Casablanca" of the Mafia and the cocaine smugglers. In the Calle Ocho, the 8th street in "Little Havana", Salsa-Beat pulsated. Here we ate black beans with rice, rolled over the dam towards the spit of land of Miami Beach. In the hotels by the beach there was false marble, false flowers, false teeth. Flamingo pink is the colour of Miami Beach. Along the south beach, the "Poor Man's Paradise" of old Jewish emigrants, the already forgotten buildings of the 30s relive a swinging Art Deco quarter. And so to cocktails at the chrome hotel bar of the "Carlyle", "Cavalier" or "Cardozo". Near at hand real life – loud, middle-class, proletarian, culturally mixed. How long for?
America, a Picture of a Continent, 1988 (Ed. Peter von Zahn)

Suggested Routes

Grand Circular Tour of Florida

This grand circular tour of Florida (about 1865 miles/3000km), starting in Miami, heads north along the Atlantic coast to Jacksonville, then turns west through the Panhandle and into the western tip of the Sunshine State. At Pensacola it turns back east along the Gulf coast to the Perry area, then southwards, parallel to the Gulf coast, to Pinellas Suncoast, and over the Sunshine Skyway to the Tamiami Trail. This first runs south to Naples and then crosses the southern tip of the Florida peninsula through the Everglades National Park. Back in Miami the tour concludes by taking US Highway 1 (Overseas Highway) down to Key West.

Stage 1   Miami–Palm Beach (US 1, SR A1A; 64 miles/102km):

Miami–Miami Beach–Hollywood–Fort Lauderdale (recommended excursion along Alligator Alley/I–75 west to the Seminole Indian Reservation, or the Miccosukee Indian Reservation)–Pompano Beach–Deerfield Beach–Boca Raton–Delray Beach–Boynton Beach–Lake Worth–Palm Beach–West Palm Beach (recommended excursion west on US 441 to Lion Country Safari in the Loxahatchee National Wildlife Refuge or along Lake Okeechobee).

Stage 2   West Palm Beach–Daytona Beach (US 1, SR A1A; 187 miles/301km):

West Palm Beach–Jupiter–Jensen Beach–Port St Lucie–Fort Pierce–Vero Beach–Melbourne–Cocoa (highly recommended excursion on SR A1A, SR 3, to Cocoa Beach, Merritt Island, Cape Canaveral, Kennedy Space Center)–Titusville (possible excursion west to Orlando, Sea World, Universal Studios, Walt Disney World on SR 50 or the Bee Line Expressway)–New Smyrna Beach (recommended excursion south to the Canaveral National Seashore)–Daytona Beach (recommended excursion south-west on US 92 to DeLand and west on SR 40 to the Ocala National Forest).

Stage 3   Daytona Beach–Jacksonville (SR A1A, US 1; 89 miles/143km):

Daytona Beach–Ormond Beach–Marineland–St Augustine–Jacksonville (recommended excursion east on US 90 to Jacksonville Beach and north-east on A1A to Amelia Island and Fernandina Beach).

Stage 4   Jacksonville–Tallahassee (I–10; 163 miles/262km):

Jacksonville–Osceola National Forest–Lake City (recommended excursion north on US 441 to Okeefenokee National Wildlife Refuge)–Live Oak–Tallahassee (recommended excursion south on SR 61 to Wakulla Springs or south-east on SR 363 to Natural Bridge and south-west on SR 20, SR 375, to Apalachicola National Forest).
      Alternative route (US 17, SR 20, I–75): Jacksonville–St John's River–Palatka–Gainesville–Lake City.

Stage 5   Tallahassee–Pensacola (I–10 or US 90; 191 miles/307km):

Tallahassee–Marianna (recommended excursion north to Florida Caverns)–Chipley (recommended excursion south to Falling Waters)–Ponce de León Springs, De Funiak Springs (north-west of Florida's highest point)–Crest View–Milton–Pensacola (recommended excur-

The "Sunshine Skyways" over Tampa Bay ▶

sion south-west on SR 292 to Gulf Beach, or SR 399 to Gulf Island National Seashore).

Stage 6   Pensacola–Apalachicola (US 98; 182 miles/293km):

Pensacola–Gulf Islands National Seashore (Santa Rosa Island)–Fort Walton Beach–Henderson Beach–Grayton Beach–Panama City–Port St Joe (excursion south-west on CR 30A to St Joseph Peninsula and south on CR 30B to St Vincent Wildlife Refuge) Apalachicola (recommended excursion north on SR 65 to Fort Gadsden).

Stage 7   Apalachicola–Cedar Key (US 98, US 19/98, SR 347; 198 miles/318km):

Apalachicola–Carabelle Beach–San Marcos de Apalache (recommended excursion north on SR 61 to Wakulla Springs and south-east on CR 59 to St Marks National Wildlife Refuge)–Perry–Fanning Springs (then recommended excursion west on CR 320 to Manatee Springs)–Chiefland–Cedar Key (excursion to Cedar Key National Wildlife Refuge).

Stage 8   Cedar Key–St Petersburg/Tampa (SR 24, US 19/98); 147 miles/237km):

Cedar Key–Otter Crossing–Crystal River–Homosassa Springs–Weeki Wachee–Tarpon Springs Pinellas Suncoast–Dunedin–Clearwater–St Petersburg Beach–St Petersburg–Tampa (recommended excursion east on I–4, US 92, SR 60, to Central Florida, Lakeland, Winter Haven and Lake Wales).

Stage 9   St Petersburg–Fort Myers (US 19, I–375, I–75, US 41 Tamiami Trail; 109 miles/176km):

St Petersburg–Sunshine Skyway–Bradenton (recommended excursion east to Gamble Plantation and, on SR 64, to Little Manatee State Recreation Area) — Sarasota (recommended excursion east on SR 72 to Myakka River State Park)–Venice (recommended excursion south on SR 775 to Englewood, Gasparilla Island and Cayo Costa Island)–Warm Mineral Springs–Port Charlotte–Cape Coral–Fort Myers (highly recommended excursion west on SR 867 to Fort Myers Beach, Sanibel & Captiva and north-east on SR 80, SR 29, to Cypress Knee Museum).

Stage 10   Fort Myers–Miami (US 41 Tamiami Trail; 145 miles/234km):

Fort Myers–Bonita Springs (recommended excursion east on CR 846 to Corkscrew Swamp Sanctuary)–Naples–San Marco Island–Collier Seminole State Park–Everglades City (recommended excursion northwest on SR 29 via Copeland to Fakatchee Strand State Preserve)–Cypress National Preserve–Everglades National Park, Miccosukee Indian Village–Miami.

Alternative route (Everglades Alley/Alligator Parkway, I–75): Naples–Fort Lauderdale–Miami.

Stage 11   Miami–Key West–Miami (US 1 Overseas Highway; 310 miles/498km):

Miami–Coral Gables–Coconut Grove Goulds–Homestead–Florida City (recommended excursion south-west on CR 9336 to Everglades National Park to Flamingo)–Key Largo, John Pennekamp Coral Reef–Islamorada–Indian Key (recommended boat trip to Lignumvitae Key)–Long Key–Marathon–Bahia Honda Key–Big Pine Key, Key Deer National Wildlife Refuge–Key West and back.

Short Circular Tour of Florida

The short circular tour of Florida (about 620 miles/1000km) also starts in Miami, and then goes north along the Atlantic coast to Cape Canaveral/Titusville before turning west to Central Florida and over to the Gulf of Mexico at Tampa.

Once on the other side of the Sunshine Skyway, it picks up the Tamiami Trail which runs south parallel to the Gulf coast as far as Naples, crosses the southern tip of the Florida peninsula through the Everglades National Park, and ends up back in Miami.

Miami–Palm Beach (US 1, SR A1A; 64 miles/102km):   Stage 1

Miami–Miami Beach–Hollywood–Fort Lauderdale (recommended excursion on Alligator Alley/I–75 west to Seminole Indian Reservation or Miccosukee Indian Reservation)–Pompano Beach–Deerfield Beach–Boca Raton–Delray Beach–Boynton Beach–Lake Worth–Palm Beach–West Palm Beach (recommended excursion west on US 441 to Lion Country Safari in Loxahatchee National Wildlife Refuge or along Lake Okeechobee).

Palm Beach–Titusville (US 1, SR A1A; 141 miles/227km):   Stage 2

Palm Beach–Jupiter–Jensen Beach–Port St Lucie–Fort Pierce–Vero Beach–Melbourne–Cocoa (recommended excursion east on SR A1A, SR 3, to Cocoa Beach, Merritt Island, Cape Canaveral, Kennedy Space Center)–Titusville (possible excursion east on NASA Parkway to Kennedy Space Center; recommended excursion north on US 1, SR A1A, to Daytona Beach, St Augustine, Jacksonville and Amelia Island).

Titusville–Orlando (SR 50; 45 miles/73km):   Stage 3

Titusville–Orlando (including Sea World, Universal Studios).

Orlando–St Petersburg (US 17/92/441, US 192, US 17/92, US 92; 115   Stage 4
miles/185km):

Orlando–Kissimmee–Walt Disney World–Haines City–Winter Haven (excursion to Cypress Gardens)–Lakeland (possible excursion south on US 17 to Barton)–Plant City–Tampa–St Petersburg (possible excursion to Pinellas Suncoast).

St Petersburg–Naples (US 19, US 41 Tamiami Trail, I–75; 146   Stage 5
miles/235km):

St Petersburg Sunshine Skyway Bradenton Sarasota (recommended excursion east on SR 72 to Myakka River State Park)–Venice (recommended excursion south on SR 775 to Englewood, Gasparilla Island and Cayo Costa Island)–Warm Mineral Springs–Port Charlotte–Cape Coral–Fort Myers (highly recommended excursion west on SR 867 to Fort Myers Beach, Sanibel and Captiva, and north-east on SR 80, SR 29, to Cypress Knee Museum)–Bonita Springs–Naples.
    Recommended excursion east from Bonita Springs on CR 846 to Corkscrew Swamp Sanctuary.

Naples–Miami (US 41 Tamiami Trail; 108 miles/174km):   Stage 6

Naples (recommended excursion south on SR 995 to San Marco Island)–Collier Seminole State Park–Everglades City (recommended excursion north-west on SR 29 via Copeland to Fakatchee Strand State Preserve)–Cypress National Preserve–Everglades National Park, Miccosukee Indian Village–Miami.

Florida by Rail

Passenger travel by rail in Florida is not as important as it used to be. Amtrak intercity services now only run from Chicago, Boston, New York, and Washington down to Jacksonville and Tampa or Miami.

An Amtrak train in transit from New York to Miami

Some counties are trying to make rail travel more attractive with special excursion package deals, etc., and the Tri-Rail service which runs for 67 miles/108km between West Palm Beach and Miami has already proved a success.

Florida from North to South

Anyone wanting to explore Florida from north to south or vice versa can take one of Amtrak's Silver Star or Silver Meteor express trains which do the daily run from Jacksonville via Kissimmee to Tampa (239 miles/385km) or to Miami (419 miles/674km).

Silver Star

The Silver Star service operates daily from Jacksonville to Tampa or Miami. From Jacksonville the line runs along the St John's River down to Palatka, then through north-east Central Florida's lakeland to De Land (bus connection to Daytona Beach), Winter Park, Orlando (bus connection to Walt Disney World) and Kissimmee (bus connection to Walt Disney World) in the middle of Florida, also full of lakes. From here a branch line runs west via Lakeland to the Gulf of Mexico and Tampa (bus connection to St Petersburg and various other destinations on the Pinellas Suncoast, and to Bradenton, Sarasota and Fort Myers).

From Kissimmee to Miami it crosses one of the main citrus-growing areas to Winter Haven (bus connection to Cypress Gardens) then via Sebring and the northern shores of Lake Okeechobee to West Palm Beach, back on the Atlantic coast. The final 65 miles/100km take in such famous beach resorts as Delray Beach, Deerfield Beach (bus connection to Boca Raton), Fort Lauderdale (bus connection to Port Everglades) and Hollywood before terminating in Miami (bus connections to Miami Beach and Key West).

Silver Meteor

The Silver Meteor runs two services out of Jacksonville. The Tampa express covers the same route as the Silver Star (see above). The Miami train takes the line through Central Florida via Waldo (bus connection to Gainesville), Ocala (bus connection to Silver Springs) on the western edge of the limestone scenery of Ocala National Forest, to Wild Wood, traverses Withlacoochee State Forest, touching on Dade City (bus connection to Zephyrhills), before finally reaching Winter Haven (bus connection to the Cypress Gardens) where it continues to Miami on the route already described above.

The Tri-County Commuter Rail Authority operates frequent daily services over a 68 mile/110km stretch of line linking Miami International Airport with West Palm Beach. Out of Miami they run up along the Atlantic coast through famous beach resorts such as Hollywood, Fort Lauderdale, Cypress Creek, Pompano Beach, Deerfield Beach, Boca Raton, Delray Beach, Boynton Beach and Lake Worth as far as West Palm Beach. All these rail stations have speedy bus services to the town centre and beach resorts. The services of local guides are available to Tri-Rail passengers in Fort Lauderdale and Palm Beach.

Tri-Rail

The Seminole Gulf Passenger Service operates excursion trains between Naples, Fort Myers, Punta Gorda, Fort Ogden, and Arcadia, first travelling north to Charlotte Harbor along a scenic section of the Gulf Coast then heading inland up the Peace River Valley.

Seminole Gulf

Cross Florida Bus/Train Service

The Florida peninsula can also be crossed from east to west or vice versa. The Amtrak Passenger Service provides a combined bus and train service which runs daily in both directions, covering the distance between St Petersburg on the Gulf coast and Miami on the Atlantic coast, or across the Panhandle from Jacksonville via Tallahassee to New Orleans (Louisiana).

This service covers the 281 miles/453km in about 6½ hours. The 66 miles/107km section by bus runs from St Petersburg (bus connection to various resorts on the Pinellas Suncoast) via Downtown Tampa (stopover for connection) to the Central Florida resort of Winter Haven (bus connection to Cypress Gardens).

St Petersburg to Miami

  The Winter Haven express train connection to Miami crosses the Florida peninsula via Sebring, passing Lake Okeechobee, to West Palm Beach and then down the Atlantic coast to Miami.

The buses that run daily between Jacksonville and New Orleans via Tallahassee provide a good opportunity to get to know northern Florida and the Panhandle.

Jacksonville/ Tallahassee/ New Orleans

The following bus and rail stations cater for the disabled: Jacksonville, Sanford, Winter Park, Orlando, Lakeland, Tampa, West Palm Beach, Delray Beach, Fort Lauderdale, Hollywood, Miami. The appropriate adaptations are also planned or already under way for the other stations.

Bus and rail stations with facilities for the disabled

Florida from A to Z

Adventureland

See Walt Disney World

Altamonte Springs

See Orlando

Amelia Island, Fernandina Beach   A/B 12

Nassau County
Altitude: 0–23ft/0–7m
Population: 15,000

Amelia Island, which is composed of coral lime, is the most northerly island   ★★Location
in Florida and actually counts as one of the chain of "Golden Isles", which
extend in a line off the coast of the Federal State of Georgia. Until just a few
years ago the island was a well-kept secret among holidaymakers, but the
international tennis tournaments which take place here every year have
now brought Amelia Island worldwide renown.

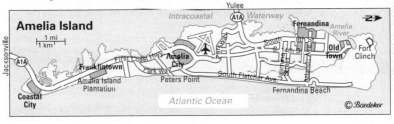

Although a large number of holiday flats and houses have been built during
the last couple of decades, the island has not lost its original character
entirely. Its landscape is characterised by dunes, sandy beaches, as yet not
built on, which stretch for mile upon mile, and dense woodland made up of
evergreen oaks, red maples, cedars, pines, magnolias and palmetto scrub.
The extensive marshland on the lee side of the island is an important
sanctuary for large numbers of sea and other migratory birds.

★Fernandina Beach   A 12

At the northern tip of Amelia Island lies the small but smart seaside resort   Location
of Fernandina Beach (pop. 9000), which has retained much of the charm it
had at the end of the last century.
　Its strategically favourable location at the mouth of St Mary's River has
meant that during the last four hundred years eight different flags have

◀ *The Mediterranean aspect of the Ringling Museum in Sarasota* flown over Fernandina Beach. In 1562 its first European visitor, the Frenchman Jean Ribault arrived. Two years later the settlement of Fort Caroline was established at the mouth of St John's River by some of his countrymen. From 1565 to 1763 the island formed part of the Spanish colonial empire. A Spanish mission station was established but was destroyed by British troops in 1702. The Earl of Egmont owned an extensive indigo plantation on Amelia Island.

During the American War of Independence the island was at times occupied by American troops. From 1783 to 1821 it came under Spanish rule again. When Jefferson's embargo closed American ports to foreign ships in 1807, the small Spanish settlement of Fernandina (named after the Spanish King Ferdinand VII), situated on the north-east tip of the island with a good natural harbour, attained considerable importance as a frontier town. There was a boom in smuggling, and pirates and buccaneers shared out their booty and profits here. In 1812 the "patriots of Amelia Island" overwhelmed the Spanish garrison with the secret approval of the United States and hoisted their own flag, which was replaced the following day by the Stars and Stripes. The Spanish, however, demanded the return of the island and in 1816 completed the construction of Fort San Carlos (today Fort Clinch) on the northern tip.

The year 1817 was the most turbulent in the history of Fernandina. First of all General MacGregor captured the new fort and raised his own private flag. A short time later the pirate Luis Aury gained control of the island and had the Mexican rebels' flag hoisted. In December 1817 American troops finally occupied Amelia Island in order to "put an end to the lawless goings-on on the other side of the border". They administered Amelia Island as "trustees" for the weak Spanish colonial power. In 1821 the United States gained the whole of Florida and in 1847 the extension of Fort Clinch was begun. In the 1850s the site of the town was moved to the terminus of the first railway line belonging to the senator David Yulee. It linked Fernandina to the town of Cedar Key on the other side of the Florida peninsula.

During the Civil War Fort Clinch was held by the Confederates from 1861 to 1862. The years between 1875 and 1900 can be considered the town's Golden Age: the harbour flourished as a result of the export of wood and phosphates, while steamships brought tourists direct from New York to Fernandina. The town's mild winter climate soon became renowned. Ship owners, captains, retired people and wood barons built attractive villas in the Victorian style.

The completion of Flagler's railway line led to the influx of tourists shifting further southwards. Today a National Historic District comprising some 30 blocks of houses is the only reminder of Fernandina's golden period.

At the beginning of the 20th c. people took up hunting at sea. Canning factories which processed oysters, prawns, crabs and shrimps were a major sources of income right up until the Great Depression. Every year at the beginning of May, to commemorate this time, the "Isle of the Eight Flags Shrimp Boat Race Festival" takes place.

In the 1930s the establishment of two large cellulose factories provided new employment and a few years ago the tourist potential of Amelia Island and Fernandina Beach began to be rediscovered.

★Centre Street
Fernandina
Historic District

The centre of Fernandina has managed to retain its late Victorian charm right up to the present day. Most of the best preserved buildings in the 30 blocks of streets which make up the uncrowded town centre date from the 19th c. They reflect the architectural styles which were in vogue in the United States during the period from 1873 to 1900.

A walk along Centre Street is well worthwhile. This leads from the old Shrimp Dock and the Chamber of Commerce (formerly the station for the Yulee railroad which was closed down in the thirties) along Amelia River in an easterly direction. Here, along the old main street, with its preponder-

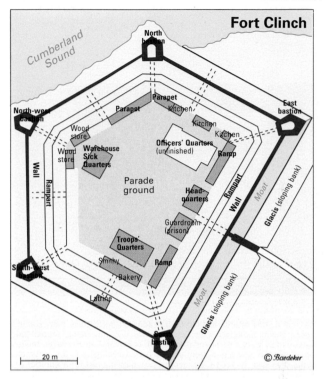

Fort Clinch

North bastion

Cumberland Sound

Parapet

Parapet

Kitchen

Kitchen

Kitchen

North-west bastion

East bastion

Wood store

Wood store

Warehouse

Sick Quarters

Officers' Quarters (unfinished)

Ramp

Wall

Rampart

Parade ground

Head-quarters

Wall

Rampart

Moat

Glacis (sloping bank)

Guardroom (prison)

Troops' Quarters

Smithy

Ramp

Bakery

South-west bastion

Latrine

Moat

Glacis (sloping bank)

Glacis (sloping bank)

South bastion

20 m

© Baedeker

ance of two and three-storeyed brick buildings, the main public buildings and shops are concentrated.

The Palace Saloon built in 1873 (Centre St./2nd St.) with its historic furnishings and brightly-coloured glass windows is the oldest building of its kind in Florida.

The Amelia Island Museum of History (233 South 3rd St.; guided tours Mon.–Sat. 11am and 2pm) offers a wealth of information about Fernandina and its history.

Museum of History

A Historic District Walking Tour enables the visitor to become more familiar with the architecture of the Victorian era in America. Individual houses, often still in private occupation, are visited. The Amelia Island Fernandina Restoration Inc. (102 Centre St.) can supply a brochure in which a circular tour is described, taking in the old centre with its Victorian villas to the north and south of Centre Street. Some of these buildings are occupied today by smart "bed and breakfast inns".

Walking Tour

★Fort Clinch State Park

A 12

At the northern tip of Amelia Island is Fort Clinch State Park (2601 Atlantic Ave.; open daily from 8am to dusk. Fort: open daily 9am–5pm). In 1847 work was begun on this defensive fortification which was intended to make

Location

The exclusive Amelia Island Plantation on the Atlantic

the United State Atlantic coast secure. In addition, the fortress, named after a general who took part in the Seminole War, was intended to protect the estuary of St Mary's River and the harbour of Fernandina. However, building proceeded only intermittently in the period leading up to the outbreak of the Civil War. In 1861 Confederates occupied the fort for a number of months and fitted it out with artillery. Further developments in weapon technology led to the cessation of building in 1867.

The 1082 acre/438ha Fort Clinch State Park was laid out as long ago as 1936. The "Living History" programmes are exceptionally vivid with actors dressed in historical uniforms showing what life might have been like in a small remote garrison during the Civil War period. A museum provides information about this small fortification.

Nature trails lead through a still largely untouched part of the island. Amelia Island and Cumberland Sound are very popular with anglers, and there is an attractive beach on the Atlantic coast suitable for bathing.

Amelia Island Plantation

Holiday area

The exclusive holiday complex known as the Amelia Island Plantation has been growing up among the dunes since 1972. With its golf-courses and sports facilities it ranks among the finest in the United States.

Bathing beach

A beach suitable for bathing stretches for almost 12 miles/20km along the ★ Atlantic coast. Swimmers, surfers and other water-sports enthusiasts will find the very best conditions here. Picnic areas and various other sports and leisure facilities are also popular.

Surroundings

See Jacksonville

Apalachicola

Franklin County
Altitude: 0–20ft/0–6m
Population: 3000

Apalachicola lies 75 miles/120km south-west of Tallahassee on Apalachicola Bay which is separated from the Gulf of Mexico by sandy off-shore islands. This small town was founded in 1822 and initially it made its living from the cotton trade, with large numbers of paddle-steamers plying up and down the Apalachicola River which was used for transporting the bales of cotton. Indeed at times Apalachicola was the most important port on the American Gulf coast after New Orleans and Mobile. By 1838 more than 40 two-storeyed warehouses and trading offices stood along the banks of the river. In 1839 Florida's first railway line was built between Apalachicola and St Joseph. During the American Civil War the harbour was frequently used by blockade breakers and thus was of the utmost importance in providing reinforcements for the Confederates.

The decline of the once-booming town began when new railway lines were opened up to the north. Ports on the east coast, such as Savannah, were now much more easily accessible and Apalachicola became cut off from the lucrative cotton trade. Its harbour was too shallow for ocean-going steamers, and the river did not always have sufficient water for barge traffic to be feasible all the year round. The end of the 19th c. was marked by a cedarwood boom which lasted until the 1920s. After that the little port sank into a slumber from which it has only gradually begun to emerge with the advent of modern tourism. Today Apalachicola lives from tourism and is the centre of Florida's oyster-fishing industry. 90% of the oysters produced in Florida are landed and processed here. When in bad years the oyster populations in Apalachicola Bay are reduced, as a result of too little freshwater reaching the bay because the rivers are affected by drought (for instance in 1988), oysters are transported under refrigeration from Louisiana for processing.

Every year at the beginning of November the Florida Seafood Festival takes place in Apalachicola.

Florida Seafood Festival

Sights

The little town still displays the character of old Florida. There are numerous delightful wooden houses dating back to the 19th c., with verandas typical of the period. Many of these have been lovingly restored during the past few years.

Wooden houses

At the local Chamber of Commerce a leaflet is available with suggestions for a walk round the historical part of Apalachicola.

Of interest is the Gibson Inn (town centre), a hotel dating back to the cedar boom (1909), which was lavishly and faithfully restored during the 1980s. Its fine bar made of dark cedarwood is now used again as the meeting-place of local dignitaries.

Gibson Inn

Raney House (45 Market St.), built in 1838 and an example of the Neo-Classical style of architecture so popular in the southern states, today houses the local Chamber of Commerce (visits possible).

Raney House

Situated on the river bank (Water St./Chestnut St.) is the Cotton Warehouse of 1838, one of a total of 43 such storehouses for cotton.

Cotton Warehouse

Next door is the Sponge Exchange. At the end of the 19th c. sponges gathered by between 80 and 120 local divers used to be sold here.

Sponge Exchange

Apalachicola

Trinity Episcopal Church	Trinity Episcopal Church with its characteristic slaves' gallery (6th St./Broad St./Chestnut Ave.) was rebuilt here in 1837/1838 after being dismantled and brought from New York.
John Gorrie State Museum	The John Gorrie State Museum (6th St./Ave. D; open: Thur.–Mon. 9am–noon and 1–5pm) commemorates the achievements of Dr John Gorrie (1805–55) who in 1851 patented the world's first ice-machine – the forerunner of present-day refrigerators, deep-freezes and air-conditioning systems. It was here that he developed his invention, which came about as a result of his attempts to cool down his yellow fever patients. The contents of the museum include a replica of this first ice-machine.
Marina	In the local marina fishermen and divers can hire boats. There are also opportunities for river trips.
Holiday homes	In common with the rest of the coast of the Gulf of Mexico, the character of the area around Apalachicola has latterly been significantly altered by the construction of apartment blocks and holiday home complexes.

Surroundings

★ St George Island   The shallow waters of Apalachicola are protected by three off-shore sandy barrier islands. St George Island, at 28 miles/45km one of the longest islands along the Gulf coast of Florida, and linked to the mainland by a 4 mile/6½km-long causeway, offers miles of white sandy beaches. Several complexes of holiday apartments are being built here. At the eastern end lies St George Island State Park. Here superb beaches can be reached by crossing the delicate line of dunes along paths made of planks. In 1954 the island was divided down the middle to provide a shipping lane. The 10 mile/16km-long western part, called Little St George Island, which is only

A bird's eye view of the Apalachicola National Forest

accessible by private boats, is, under the name Cape St George State Preserve, a nature conservancy area and retains its unspoilt coastal scenery. Along sections of the beach, which in places is very lonely, magnificent shells can be found. In 1852 the present-day lighthouse was erected some 440yd/400m from the beach. When, however, in 1983, Hurricane Kate moved across this stretch of coastline, it caused enormous shifts of sand to take place. Since that time the lighthouse has stood directly by the beach.

To the west, the neighbouring island of St Vincent, also only accessible by private boat, is a wildlife refuge administered by the National Park Service. Here there are eagles, alligators, deer, sea-turtles and wild turkeys.

★St Vincent Island (National Wildlife Refuge)

Between Apalachicola and Tallahassee extends the Apalachicola National Forest, an enormous practically uninhabited forest area (oaks, cedars, pines, cypresses, etc.) of more than 580,000 acres/234,723ha, with several lakes. The two rivers, Ochlockonee and Sopchoppy (dark-coloured water, deciduous cypresses), are very popular with canoeists. There are also several camping and picnic areas set aside in the forest, as well as a few bathing places.
    Information: USDA Forest Service, 227 N. Bronough St., Suite 4061, Tallahassee, Fl., 32301; tel. 681–7265.

★Apalachicola National Forest

In the western part, on the Apalachicola River and accessible 24 miles/39km to the north on the SR 65, there are only a few earthworks left standing as a reminder of the former Fort Gadsden, as well as displays in the visitors' centre. In 1814 the British erected a fort, which was tolerated by the Spanish on what was their land, and which was used to recruit Indians and fugitive blacks for the war against the USA. The latter took control of the "Negro Fort" after the war and settled here. In 1816 the fort was destroyed by United States troops. The 300 settlers seeking refuge in the fort almost all met their death when in the course of the clashes the magazine blew up. In 1818, during the first Seminole War, Andrew Jackson set up a supply base and garrison, which he named Fort Gadsden, despite strong protests from the Spanish colonial masters. In 1862/1863 the fort was occupied once again, this time by Confederate troops, who controlled the Apalachicola River from here. Malaria, however, forced them to give up this position.

★Fort Gadsden State Historic Site

Continuing westwards along the US 98 it is well worth taking a detour of about 22 miles/35km along the SR 30 to the St Joseph Peninsula and the delightful State Park of the same name, situated at its northern end. This narrow, almost undeveloped peninsula – with to the west the warm water of the Gulf of Mexico, to the east the sheltered St Joseph Bay – is well known for its miles and miles of dazzling white, undisturbed sandy beaches and its sand dunes which in places are as much as 30ft/9m high and which provide protection for a narrow band of pine woods. Large numbers of waterfowl are to be found here. Whole schools of brown pelicans make their way along the water-line at low tide (there is a simple campsite and a few cabins in St Joseph Peninsula State Park).

★St Joseph Peninsula State Park

In the estuarine area of the Apalachicola River a nature conservancy area of close to 247,100 acres/100,000ha has been established. Besides the actual river estuary it comprises marshy woodland, freshwater and saltwater marshes, beaches, coastal lakes and mud-flats with their varied vegetation. Conducted rambles and boat trips can be arranged (tel. 653–8063).

Apalachicola National Estuarine Research Reserve

In the fishing town of Port St Joe an attempt was made in 1838 to draw up a constitution for the new state of Florida, which did not, however, come to fruition until 1845. This event is commemorated by the Constitution Convention State Museum (open: Thur.–Mon. 9am–noon and 1–5pm).

Port St Joe

Big Cypress National Preserve   K/L 12/13

Collier County, Dade County, Monroe County

★Nature reserve

The Big Cypress National Preserve extends over an area midway between Miami and Naples (see entries) in the region of the Everglades. It adjoins the Everglades National Park (see entry) to the north. Vast areas of swamp, grassy marshland areas, savannah-like grasslands, countless large and small tree-islands characterise the landscape. In this environment a wealth of different types of vegetation thrives, including of course cypresses, but also rare orchids, sedges and grasses, various palm-trees as well as palmetto scrub.

The Big Cypress Reserve is furthermore a retreat for a large number of animal species which, in Florida at least, are threatened with extinction. These include the Florida panther, the wood stork, the Everglade kite and the snowy egret.

Development measures

The area has on several occasions in the past been threatened by ambitious development projects. In order, for instance, to open up the Tamiami Trail, thousands upon thousands of old and tall cypress trees were felled in 1928. Even in the 1970s large tracts were drained in order to provide building land. Since then attempts have been made by the state to protect the particularly sensitive ecosystem of Big Cypress by means of tough legislation.

Natural history excursions

Anyone interested in knowing more about the Big Cypress National Preserve should go to one of the visitors' centres situated on the edge of the reserve, from where natural history excursions (guided walks, boat trips) are available. There are also specialist personnel who can give full information about the biological and ecological background to the preserve.

Warning!

Visitors are strongly recommended not to accept the services of certain self-styled private "guides" who tear their way recklessly through the marshland area in their propeller-driven airboats, thereby destroying sensitive biotopes and frightening all kinds of wild animals.

Visitors' centres

Ranger Station Fakahatchee Beach, on the SR 29 north of Everglades City, guided walks by arrangement (tel. 695–4593).

Oasis Ranger Station (open: Thur.–Sun. 9am–4.30pm, guided tours by arrangement; tel. 695–2000) on the Tamiami Trail, Highway 41, about 20 miles/32km east of Everglades City.

Pine Crest Interpretive Center (natural history information centre), situated on the side road running parallel south of the Tamiami Trail (take care! gravel road, danger of sudden flooding) between Monroe Station and Miccosukee Village.

Ochopee

The settlement of Ochopee is at the western access-point to the Tamiami Trail which leads into the nature reserve. Here there are some specially authorised private operators who offer natural history trips on well-established paths.

Florida Trail

To the east of Monroe Station is the finishing-point of one of the stages of the long-distance footpath, the Florida Trail, which runs from Lake Okeechobee (see entry) in the north through a particularly attractive stretch of the Big Cypress Reserve.

Indian Reservations

To the west and north-west of the Big Cypress National Preserve stretch two Indian reservations, the Miccosukee Indian Reserve and the Big Cypress Seminole Indian Reserve, in which several thousand descendants of the original inhabitants of Florida still live.

Epiphytes in the Big Cypress National Preserve ▶

Biscayne National Park · C 15

Location: Dade County; southern part of Biscayne Bay, south of Miami
Founded in 1980 (before that from 1968 a National Monument)

Access

The park cannot be reached by public transport.

The main administrative office of the park is at Convey Point, 9 miles/15km east of Homestead, and can be reached via North Canal Street (SW 328 St.). The Visitor Center on Elliott Key can only be reached by boat.

Information

Biscayne National Park, P.O. Box 1270, Homestead, FL 33090, tel. (305) 247–2400.

★★Nature area

The Biscayne National Park, which extends along the south-eastern coast of Florida, is America's largest marine nature reserve. Just 5% of its area is dry land. The largest part is occupied by Biscayne Bay with its shallow waters, which are warm, amazingly clear and rich in fish, and a chain of 44 tiny islands (the most northerly beginnings of the Florida Keys (see entry)). The Caribbean climatic influence is even here very noticeable.

A special attraction here are the coral reefs which have formed in front of the Keys in the open Atlantic, although for some time they have been threatened by environmental poisoning. Divers are busy here investigating the wrecks of ships which in the past have run aground on the reefs. In 1733 alone 19 Spanish galleons, laden with gold and various other treasures, sank in this area during a hurricane, on their return journey to Europe. The national park represents a veritable paradise for boat-owners, divers, snor-kellers, anglers and ornithologists. The season extends throughout the year, but in the summer months in particular enjoyment can at times be to some extent marred by mosquitoes which keep close to the mangroves, and occasional violent falls of rain and thunderstorms.

Key Biscayne

To the north of the park boundaries lies the popular holiday and excursion island of Key Biscayne with the Bill Baggs Cape Florida State Recreation Area (see Miami). To the south is the John Pennekamp Coral Reef State Park (see Key Largo).

★★Mangrove coast

The mangrove coast on the mainland, which is largely still intact, forms an essential part of the ecosystem of Biscayne Bay. The mangroves are the best protection for the inlying land against the destructive power of hurri-canes. With their tangled roots they keep hold of the finest particles of sediment and thereby filter the water through. They are a playground for the rich fish-life in the bay and they offer the very best conditions for sea-birds and waders. For many years the mangrove thickets were regarded as worthless; until as recently as the 1970s they were cleared and filled in, in order to create marinas, housing developments and holiday villages. Tons of insecticide were sprayed at mosquitoes, whose larvae formed the main source of nourishment for the smaller marine animals. The southern part of Biscayne Bay was largely spared this development. The area was rather isolated and commercially of no great interest. The surprising variety of life in the bay is threatened only by the warm cooling waters of the nearby atomic power station Turkey Point and by the in-troduction of effluents from those parts of the Everglades (see entry) which are built up or used for agricultural purposes. After heavy rainfall the sluice gates are opened as a protection against flooding. Too much freshwater, however, can harm the animals and plants which exist in the brackish water.

Keys

The keys which belong to the National Park are the beginnings of the Upper Keys (the most northerly section of the chain of islands which stretches down beyond the southern tip of Florida as far as Key West) and contain a type of vegetation unique to the United States. The tree-islands in the middle of these keys consist of a mixture of tropical hardwoods and bushes, like those typical of West Indian islands.

A coral reef in Biscayne Bay

In 1513 the Spanish conquistador Ponce de León sailed through Biscayne   History
Bay on his vain quest for the source of eternal youth. Later the earliest
inhabitants of the keys arrived – fishermen or woodcutters seeking mahogany trees for building ships. Settlers then cleared Elliott Key and laid limetta
groves and pineapple plantations. At the beginning of this century divers
from Key West collected sponges here which were much sought after.

Sights

In the park administration building at Convoy Point, 9 miles/15km east of   Convoy Point
Homestead, information is available about the nature reserve and special
events which are organised (open: daily from 8am–dusk).
   The view to the north reveals what is presumably soon likely to be the
highest mountain in Southern Florida, the rubbish mountain of Greater
Miami, christened by the park wardens "Mount Trashmore".

In the Biscayne Aqua Center at the boating harbour (tel. (305) 247–2400)   Biscayne
there are trips available in glass-bottomed boats out to the reefs. Anyone   Aqua Center
wishing to visit the islands and reefs under their own steam can hire a
canoe here, take part in conducted canoe tours or go on a snorkelling or
diving trip (prior reservation advisable). There are half-day excursion trips
to the outlying islands such as Elliott Key (7 miles/11km; visitors' centre,
during the week only open at certain times; ranger station, simple campsite, boating harbour; natural history trail, small beach). During the main
winter season reservation in advance is generally necessary.

The Homestead Bayfront Park (9698 SW 328 St.; tel. (305) 247–1543) does   Homestead
not belong to the National Park. Here there are other facilities available,   Bayfront Park
especially for tourists on boats and sports fishermen.

Boca Grande

See Fort Myers

Boca Raton   J 15

Palm Beach
Altitude: 0–20ft/0–6m
Population: 62,000

Location

The smart health resort of Boca Raton (Span. = "rat's mouth") is situated about halfway between Palm Beach (see entry) and Fort Lauderdale (see entry) on a sheltered Atlantic bay protected by rocks. This seaside resort on the southern edge of Palm Beach County has become a popular destination for winter holidaymakers by virtue of its coastline stretching for almost 6 miles/10km and its pleasant mild climate.

Boca Raton has attained world renown for its top-class tennis and polo tournaments. Tennis stars such as Steffi Graf and Chris Evert live here for part of the year and famous polo-players, including Prince Charles, meet here.

History

In the 17th c. the bay was an anchorage for pirates. Its development into a fashionable seaside resort did not take place until the 1920s when the architect Mizner, already well-known in Palm Beach, bought land here and in 1926 built the Boca Raton Hotel, situated on the beach, which has been the town's emblem right up to the present day. The collapse of the property market in South Florida and the world economic crisis prevented the success of Palm Beach being repeated in Boca Raton. For decades now it has remained a small sleepy resort, distinguished by Addison Mizner's Mediterranean-inspired style of architecture.

Even as late as 1950 the town numbered fewer than 1000 inhabitants. The boom did not come until the 1960s when IBM set up a branch here and Florida Atlantic University (FAU; at present around 10,000 students) was established on the site of a small Second World War air-base.

Boca Raton combines the appeal of a subtropical seaside resort with the cultural and economic advantages of a large town. By means of strict building regulations and numerous public and private improvement initiatives it has still managed to retain much of its old charm.

Holiday Boat Parade

A big event in the annual calendar of the town is the Boca Raton Holiday Boat Parade, which takes place just before Christmas on the Intracoastal Waterway.

Sights

★Boca Raton Hotel

In 1926 the architect Addison Mizner, who in his time enjoyed considerable fame, built the enormous building complex called the "Boca Raton Hotel and Club", which right up to the present day has been the emblem of this Atlantic resort. Inspired by Italian architecture, Mizner built a luxury hotel with a casino and cabaret as well as a lake on which there were Venetian gondolas. For a long time the hotel was the *non plus ultra* of its kind in Florida.

Museum of the Art

In the Museum of the Art at Boca Raton (801 West Palmetto Park Rd.; open: Mon.–Fri. 10am–4pm, Sat., Sun. noon–4pm) there are temporary exhibitions (paintings, sculptures, glasswork, photographs, etc.) by famous artists.

Children's Museum

The Children's Museum is housed in an imposing old building on Crawford Boulevard (No. 498). Here a lot of valuable information is presented in an entertaining way. Young visitors can also experiment for themselves. Opening times can be checked by telephoning (407) 368–6875.

From September to April on the campus of the Florida Atlantic University it is possible to visit a gallery in which interesting art exhibitions are staged. | FAU Art Gallery

From January to April the Royal Palm Polo Club of Boca Raton is the world centre for this exclusive sport. Championship matches with world-class participants take place on Sundays, Wednesdays and Fridays. Information: tel. (407) 994–1876. | Royal Palm Polo Club

Bonita Springs J 12

Lee County
Altitude: 13ft/4m
Population: 14,000

The town of Bonita Springs is situated about halfway between Fort Myers (see entry) and Naples (see entry) on the north-western edge of the Big Cypress Swamp, a wilderness forming part of the vast wetlands of the Everglades (see entry). The Imperial River, which flows through the town, has an exceptionally fine reputation among anglers. | Location

Surroundings

In the Everglades Wonder Gardens (Old US 41; open: daily 9am–5pm), which were inaugurated as long ago as 1936, the visitor can study the many different types of animal life in the Everglades. The extremely rare Florida | Everglades Wonder Gardens

In the cypress swamp

panthers (pumas) occasionally also set foot here, as well as black bears and American crocodiles.

Greyhound Track

The Naples-Fort Myers Greyhound Track is also situated on the old US 41. Dog races are held here several days a week.

Bonita Shores,
Bonita Beach

To the west of Bonita Springs, right on the coast of the Gulf of Mexico, are the two beach and holiday villages of Bonita Shores and Bonita Beach, both of which have a pronounced "family" feel. The mile-long beach offers entertainment to both young and old.

★★Corkscrew
Swamp Sanctuary

About 10 miles/16km east of Bonita Springs stretches a superb nature reserve known as the "Corkscrew Swamp Sanctuary" (access by County Route 846; open: daily 9am–5pm). Its massive deciduous cypresses are up to 500 years old. The reserve is one of the last cypress swamps in Florida to have been preserved in its original state. The enormous grey trees are densely overgrown with ferns, orchids and other epiphytes. The wood storks, which sit brooding in winter high up in the trees, are in danger of becoming extinct. In summer countless orchids are in bloom, accompanied by swarms of mosquitoes. A 2 mile/3km long circular wooden walkway leads from the small visitors' centre through part of the wetland. In the 1950s, when it was planned to clear the whole wilderness of trees and drain it, environmentalists fought vigorously to save it. Donations, coupled with support from the Ford foundation, finally enabled the area to be purchased. Today it is in the hands of the charitable Audubon company.

Boynton Beach   J 15

Palm Beach
Altitude: 0–16ft/0–5m
Population: 47,000

Location

South of Palm Beach (see entry) lies the seaside resort of Boynton Beach, one of the fastest growing settlements along the "Gold Coast". To the west of the town there are citrus plantations and fields of vegetables and flowers grown for cutting.

The settlement, which is named after a major who played a part in the American Civil War, is very popular with deep-sea anglers. Its reputation of being the "Gate to Sailfish Alley" can be explained by its two yachting harbours and its position on Boynton Beach (the Intracoastal Waterway and Lake Worth here connect with the Atlantic and the Gulf Stream, which runs only a few miles out to sea and is rich in fish). The waters of Boynton Beach teem with large numbers of king mackerel which are sought by anglers from all over the world.

Fishing
expeditions

Enthusiastic anglers meet at the Pioneer Canal Park, in the Boat Club Park, at the Sea Mist Marina and at the Intracoastal Bridge, from where they set out on fishing expeditions either out to sea or along the Intracoastal Waterway and in Boynton Inlet.

Surroundings

★Arthur R.
Marshall
Loxahatchee
National Wildlife
Refuge

About 10 miles/16km west of Boynton Beach stretches the nature reserve known as the Arthur R. Marshall Loxahatchee National Wildlife Refuge, which extends over an area of nearly 145,000 acres/58,680ha and includes the north-eastern tip of the Everglades with their distinctive freshwater wetland biotopes. It is possible to take canoe and airboat trips here or go off on naturalist expeditions. In the Visitor Center there is a wealth of information available about the highly sensitive ecosystem of the Everglades.

Bradenton

Manatee County
Altitude: 0–23ft/0–7m
Population: 44,000

Founded in 1878 the town of Bradenton lies close to the coast of the Gulf of Mexico on a promontory between Tampa Bay in the north and Sarasota Bay in the south which is bisected by the Manatee River. The town takes its name from a settler called Braden, whose fortress-like home was in the past a place of refuge for newly-arrived settlers who fled from attacks by the Indian population, which was at that time indigenous in the area. Today Bradenton is a bustling town with a number of commercial enterprises as well as being a base for anglers and holidaymakers who wish to enjoy themselves on the nearby beaches.

Location

Sights

To the north of the town there is a national memorial on Tampa Bay erected to Hernando de Soto (see Famous People) who is supposed to have landed here or nearby at the end of May 1539 with an army of several hundred men. He led the first expedition by Europeans to explore the south-east of the United States as far as the Mississippi.

In the visitors' centre there are weapons from the time of de Soto on display. The centre's "Living History" programme brings visitors direct experience of various aspects of the daily life of the Spanish conquistadores (daily 8am–5.30pm). A trail leads down to the beach and into the mangrove swamps.

★De Soto
National
Memorial

The Gamble Plantation extends to the north-west of the town. For some time now it has been protected as a State Historic Site. In the middle of the 19th c. Robert Gamble, a major with the Confederate forces, ran a sugar-plantation and refinery, occupying an area of 3700 acres/1500ha, which employed some 200 slaves. In 1865 Judah P. Benjamin hid here, when, as minister of the Confederate states, he was fleeing from the Unionists' troops. He finally succeeded in returning to England via Nassau (Bahamas).

The estate-house, which dates from 1844, has been restored in the style of that period and there are conducted tours (Thur.–Mon.). The plantation and visitors' centre are open daily. The various exhibits help to create a picture of the situation in the 19th c.

★Gamble
Plantation

In the eastern part of the town stands Braden Castle, a fortress-style building built by Dr Joseph Braden, which on many occasions was used by the early European settlers as a refuge from attacks by Indians.

Braden Castle

The Manatee Village Historical Park (6th Ave. E. and 15th St. E.) consists of a group of five historical buildings: the old church of 1887, the courthouse of 1860, the old shop "Wiggin's Store" of 1903, the former schoolhouse of 1908 and Stephen's House of 1912. The last-named is a perfect example of a late 19th c./early 20th c. farmhouse which was built in the style characteristic of the Crackers.

Manatee Village

The South Florida Museum (open: Tues.–Sat. 10am–5pm; Sun. noon–6pm) has a large number of exhibits which illustrate the history of the area. These include items representing the civilisation of the Indians as well as relics from the Spanish colonial period. The collection of old medical and dental instruments is of particular interest. There are special displays which deal with the natural history of the area, with special reference to the manatees (sea-cows) which are still frequently to be found in the local waters.

South Florida
Museum, Bishop
Planetarium

Surroundings

★Longboat Key,
Bradenton Beach
Holmes Beach,
Anna Maria Island

To the west of Bradenton and on the far side of Sarasota Bay stretch Longboat Key and Anna Maria Island. In the last few years two beach settlements, Holmes Beach and Bradenton Beach, have been established among the dunes and offer all kinds of facilities for the visitor. Of international renown are the Longboat Key Club, an exclusive golf and tennis club with championship golf courses, and the Colony Beach and Tennis Resort. On Longboat Key it is also possible to go on cycling trips.

Sarasota

See entry

Brooksville   E 11

Hernando
Altitude: 230ft/70m
Population: 8000

Location

The little town of Brooksville lies to the north of Tampa in hilly countryside still used for agriculture and forestry. It is often referred to as the capital of the quarrying and cement industries in the south-east of the United States.

Raid Festival

In the Brooksville Raid Festival several hundred amateur enthusiasts re-enact an episode from the American Civil War: in July 1864 Unionist troops attacked the tiny "peace-loving" town of Brooksville.

Surroundings

★Weeki Wachee
Springs
E 10

About 12 miles/20km west of Brooksville lies one of Florida's most unusual attractions: the Weeki Wachee Springs. Every day as many as 130 million gallons/600 million litres of water gush out of this natural spring basin, which at present has been measured to a depth of 260ft/80m and which is thought to be considerably deeper. A marine diver, who was trying out underwater breathing apparatus here in the late 1940s, recognised the "show potential" of the spring basin and built a viewing room 7ft/2m under the surface of the water, from which underwater acrobatic exercises can be watched. Over the years interest has grown to such an extent that a special chamber which can hold several hundred spectators has been built 16ft/5m under the water and it is now possible to watch fantastically dressed mermaids performing underwater gymnastics four times a day. In the last few years a proper amusement park has been created with a "stroking" zoo, monkey cage, aviary, parrot show, displays of birds of prey, performances of Hans Christian Andersen's play "The Little Mermaid" and wild-water trips on the Weeki Wachee River. On the site there is also a refuge for small and injured pelicans.

Open: daily 9.30am–5.30pm; performances of "The Little Mermaid" four times daily (duration: 30 mins). Information: tel. 1–800–678–9335 (free).

Buccaneer Bay

Not far from the Weeki Wachee Springs another spring basin has been developed for its tourist potential. Here a sandy beach has been created; there are three streams which visitors, using rubber tyres, can ride down, while children can swing through the air like Tarzan or enjoy themselves on an imaginary desert island. Open: April to August daily 10am–5pm.

Withlacoochee
Forest

To the north and east of Brooksville stretches the Withlacoochee Forest. Parts of this forest have already been made a conservation area. Silver Lake, Dade Battlefield and Chinsegut National Wildlife Refuge are of particular interest.

Cape Canaveral, Kennedy Space Center

E/F 14

Brevard County

On the east side of the peninsula of Florida, Cape Canaveral protrudes into the Atlantic – a promontory made up of lagoons, mangroves and marshes, on which the US Air Force's 23 sq.mile/60sq.km rocket testing and starting site is located. Between 1963 and 1973 Cape Canaveral was known as Cape Kennedy in honour of the popular US president who was assassinated in Dallas, Texas.

Location

To the west Cape Canaveral is bounded by Merritt Island, on which the 131 sq.mile/340sq.km Kennedy Space Center with Spaceport USA has been established. This is the starting point for manned space flights.

Merritt Island

To the north of the US space centre are Merritt Island National Wildlife Refuge and Canaveral National Seashore, which together form a 93 sq.mile/240sq.km nature conservancy area, which is made up of lagoons, swamps, marshes and beaches with a rich variety of flora and fauna.

Wildlife Refuge

★★John F. Kennedy Space Center, Spaceport USA

SR 405 (NASA Parkway; turning off US 1); I–95 (Exit 78 or 79).

Access

The NASA (National Aeronautics and Space Administration) installations on the Atlantic coast of Florida are among the most popular sights in the United States. The John F. Kennedy Space Center, the USA "space centre", lies to the east of Titusville (see entry) and extends between the Indian River (see entry) and the sea on Merritt Island and the outlying spits to Cape Canaveral. This rocket testing site, which was established in 1949, was the starting point for the first manned flights into orbit and to the moon, and is where at irregular intervals the American space shuttle takes off and lands. When the US space programme was at its zenith, as many as 25,000 people were employed here.

The launch of a space shuttle can be an overwhelming experience if one is lucky enough to witness it. On launch days the Space Center itself and also the southern part of Cape Canaveral National Seashore are closed to the general public. Thousands of people eager to get a glimpse crowd along the west bank of the Indian River between Titusville and Bennett Causeway or in Jetty Park on Highway A1A in Cape Canaveral or follow the action from boats.

Space shuttle launches

Information about forthcoming lift-offs can be obtained on the following telephone numbers: 1–800–432–2153 (Florida only; no charge); for the rest of the USA: 1–900–321–LIFT OFF (small charge).

The rocket testing site has been here since 1949. In July 1950 a German "V2" was tried out here. The first rockets developed in Alabama by Wernher von Braun and his colleagues for use in space were still being launched from the Cape Canaveral Air Force Station, where as early as 1953 tests on ballistic rockets were carried out. Even the legendary "Polaris" rockets underwent trials here.

History

1958 saw the establishment of NASA (National Aeronautics and Space Administration), the USA civilian air and space travel authority, "for the peaceful use and development of space". Wernher von Braun was the leader of the team which on January 31st 1958 succeeded, with the help of a Jupiter C rocket, in sending the first US satellite, "Explorer 1", in orbit around the earth.

The Cape Canaveral installations were also used for manned space flights ("Mercury" and "Gemini" programmes). On May 5th 1961 Alan Shepard took off here on the first such manned space expedition. With the

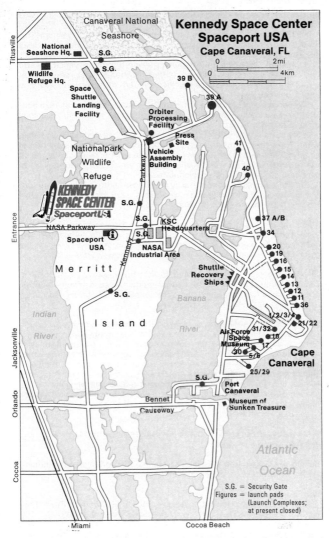

**Kennedy Space Center
Spaceport USA**
Cape Canaveral, FL

S.G. = Security Gate
Figures = launch pads
(Launch Complexes;
at present closed)

beginning of the "Apollo" moon programme, the rocket site, now called the "Kennedy Space Center", was extended on to neighbouring Merritt Island. Unmanned rockets ("Delta", "Atlas Centaur") still, however, continued to take off from Cape Canaveral, sending geostationary weather, environmental and media satellites into space.

The first high point of the Apollo programme was the Apollo 11 mission. On July 20th 1969 Neil Armstrong became the first human being to set foot

◄ *A space shuttle is launched . . .*

on the moon. As part of the Apollo 15 mission a lunar space-ship was deployed for the first time in August 1971.

In 1976 the space travel centre became extended into the "Spaceport" for lift-offs and landings of reusable space-ships, the "Space Shuttle". In May 1979 the space station "Skylab" was put into orbit round the earth.

On January 28th 1986 the American space programme, which hitherto had been so successful, suffered its most serious setback: shortly after lift-off the "Challenger" space shuttle exploded. All seven astronauts on board lost their lives.

Manned space flights were not resumed until the autumn of 1988 after lengthy investigations into the cause of the disaster. "Discovery" then took off on a four-day flight.

In the past few years the US space programme has slowed down somewhat. The decision to refrain from visiting other celestial bodies cannot simply be ascribed to reasons of cost. Instead work is being continued on the construction of an artificial space station which there are no plans to send into orbit in the foreseeable future.

The space flights are monitored by the control centre in Houston, Texas. The Edwards air force base in California is available as an alternative landing place for the space shuttles.

Spaceport USA

There are organised bus tours round part of the enormous site. In the "Spaceport USA" information centre there are various audio-video presentations which outline the present US space programme as well as the technological achievements which owe their success to space travel.

★Rocket Garden

Different types of space-ships and rockets are displayed outdoors, including various carrier rockets, a lunar module, a space shuttle and the prototype of a future space glider. Occasionally a "spaceman" puts in an appearance on the site in his space-suit.

Galaxy Center
★★IMAX Theatre

The development of American space travel is documented in a large exhibition and cinema complex. The impressive holography-video presentations, highly skilful from an instructional point of view, detail the innovations in the fields of medical technology and communications which have come about as a result of space travel. On no account, however, should the half-hour film show in the IMAX Theatre be missed. A gigantic screen, quadrophony with special acoustic effects and fantastic picture sequences enable the spectator to experience the preparations for a space flight and a journey round the earth in the space shuttle. The film is called "The Dream is Alive".

Gallery of Space
Flight

In the Gallery of Space Flight the visitor can see authentic Mercury, Gemini and Apollo space capsules.

Astronauts'
Memorial

Behind the Galaxy Center is the Astronauts' Memorial which commemorates the terrible Challenger disaster of early 1986.

★★Bus tours
(2hrs approx.)

Red Tour:

The Red Tour passes through various areas of the Kennedy Space Center. The first place to be visited is the Industrial Area, the site of the KSC Headquarters. In the old space travel control centre a film presentation and various other exhibits (e.g. particles of lunar soil, the lunar space-ship) enable the visitor to experience the first moon landing.

In the 525ft/160m high Vehicle Assembly Building (VAB), one of the largest buildings in the world, space-ships are assembled. Next door is the Orbiter Processing Facility. In front of this enormous building a "Saturn V" rocket has been set up. Rockets of this type were used between 1967 and 1972 to transport space vehicles of the Apollo programme into space. The moon flights (1969–72) and the Skylab Mission also owed their successes to the starting help provided by the "Saturn V".

Further on, the massive caterpillar tractors can be seen, which are used

The moon-rocket "Saturn V", seen from the rear

to transport the assembled space vehicles on special tracks to the launching pad.

If a lift-off is not actually imminent, the tour also takes in the two launching pads in Complex 39 (Pads A and B), from which the space shuttles are sent into space.

Blue Tour:

The Blue Tour, with its more historical emphasis, goes to Cape Canaveral Air Force Station with the Atlantic Missile Range, where the US space programme was actually started. The lift-off ramps of the Mercury and Gemini rockets, which were launched in the sixties and seventies, can be seen here. In addition the visitor can learn about the various scientific, commercial and military programmes which have occasioned numerous satellites with unmanned rockets to be launched into space.

Spaceport USA, Visitors Center TWRS, Kennedy Space Center, FL 32899.   Information

Daily 9am–sunset, conducted tours from 9.45am.   Opening times

★Canaveral National Seashore & ★Merritt Island National Wildlife Refuge

E 14

The seaside resort of New Smyrna Beach (see entry) is the northern   Nature reserve
gateway to Canaveral National Seashore, a nature reserve of 57,574 acres/23,300ha on the Atlantic coast. This stretch of the Eastern seaboard, despite its close proximity to the NASA Space Station and the lift-off rockets, has to a large extent remained in its original state. Canaveral National Seashore and Merritt Island National Wildlife Refuge, which adjoins it to the south, occupy a substantial part of a barrier island often only a few hundred yards wide with in all 25 miles/40km of untouched

sandy beaches and dunes. Their protection has enabled tree-islands (hammocks) to develop with hardwood trees often centuries old. The Mosquito Lagoon fully justifies its name. A mass of whirring insects, open stretches of water, marshes and swamps are the distinguishing features of this shallow lagoon, which is an ideal breeding ground for various types of marine life (fishes, mussels, shrimps, etc.).

Every year thousands of migratory birds spend the winter on Canaveral National Seashore and on Merritt Island. The many threatened animal species which have found refuge in the two nature reserves include white-headed sea eagles, peregrine falcons, manatees, turtles and various other reptiles. In summer large sea-turtles lay their eggs on the beaches.

Turtle Mound Trail | About 12 miles/20km south of New Smyrna Beach (see entry) on the main road A1A is Apollo Beach, where the visitor can walk along the Turtle Mound Trail (visitors' centre; open: daily 8am–4pm). Between Apollo Beach and Playalinda Beach, which can only be reached from the south (see Titusville), lies Klondike Beach, still undeveloped and largely unspoilt and only accessible on foot. Vehicular access to the beaches is sealed off during space shuttle lift-offs and landings. If walking in the overgrown dunes the visitor should beware of rattlesnakes. When returning from Playalinda Beach the unmade-up Max Hoeck Creek Wildlife Drive parallel to the SR 402 is recommended. The road follows the course of an old railway line through characteristic marshland scenery. Alligators, turtles and large numbers of waterfowl can usually be seen here.

Information | Merritt Island National Wildlife Refuge, P.O. Box 6504, Titusville, FL 32783; tel. 861–0667.

Cape Coral   J 11/12

Lee County. Altitude: 0–10ft/0–3m
Population: 75,000

Location | In terms of area the second largest settlement in Florida, Cape Coral extends along the Caloosahatchee River just where it empties into the Gulf of Mexico, about 19 miles/30km north-west of Fort Myers (see entry). It was only founded in 1958, incorporated in 1970 and today has more than 70,000 inhabitants. Cape Coral is now probably the fastest growing town in the Sunshine State. Several thousand newcomers arrive here each year.

Townscape | Cape Coral has after Jacksonville the largest built-up area in Florida. Since 1958, when the construction boom started, predominantly detached family houses have been built, most with their own yachting berth on one of the countless canals and watercourses which run through the town.

Ecology Park | Of considerable interest is the Ecology Park with its walks, nature trail and look-out tower.

Caloosahatchee River | Recently the Caloosahatchee River has taken over completely the function of a leisure and adventure waterway on which all manner of activities are pursued.

Surroundings

Pine Island | The SR 78 goes across to Pine Island, which lies offshore to the west and is much valued as an anglers' paradise and as an excellent starting point for trips to the neighbouring islands. Several little towns and villages with small motels and apartment blocks are situated on the island: Bokeelia in the north, Pineland, Pine Island Center, Flamingo Bay and St James City in the south.

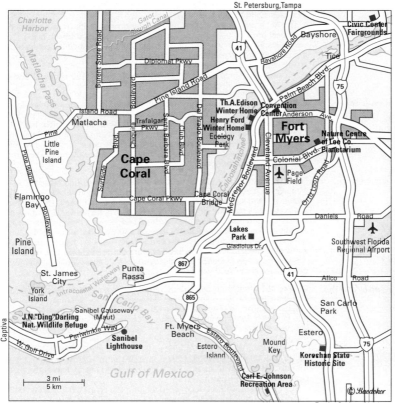

St. Petersburg,Tampa

Bonita Springs,Naples

Since the 1920s the superb climate has made it possible to cultivate tropical fruits such as mangoes, papayas, guavas, lychees. The Sunburst Tropical Fruit Company offers conducted tours through its plantations (daily 9am–5pm).

Tropical fruit growing

The islands of Cayo Costa (Lacosta) and North Captiva, together with certain neighbouring smaller islands at the entrance to Charlotte Harbor, have since 1985 been brought together to form a state park. For long stretches these barrier islands still look exactly as they did 500 years when the first Europeans set eyes on them. Several pre-Columbian mounds (grave and temple mounds made of mussels and oyster-shells) provide evidence of an Indian settlement going back thousands of years.

★★Cayo Costa State Preserve Park

On Cayo Costa it is possible to rent simple huts. Information: tel. 966–3594. On North (Upper) Captiva Island there is a holiday village with a marina which does not form part of the state park.

On Cayo Costa and North Captiva Island there are excellent sandy beaches and dunes along the Gulf coast, which are practically untouched. The sea-turtles which in summer lay their eggs here are in danger of extinction. The mangroves on the land side are one of the largest breeding areas for brown pelicans in Florida. In addition ospreys, white-headed sea-eagles and frigate birds nest here.

The richly varied vegetation on the island reflects its transitional geographical position between the North American and Caribbean areas.

The islands are only accessible by boat. Sometimes shell-collecting trips are offered from the following marinas: Tween Waters Marina, Captiva Island, tel. 472–5161; Pineland Marina, Pine Island, tel. 283–0015.

Information: Cayo Costa State Park, P.O. Box 1150, Boca Grande, FL 33921, tel. 964–0375.

Cabbage Key

Cabbage Key, a small island in Pine Island Sound, is also only accessible by boat. Cabbage Key Inn, which has lately become famous, was built in 1938 on a mussel-shell "mound" belonging to the Caloosa Indians. The inn was the brainchild of the writer Mary Roberts Rinehart and her son. The walls of the inn are plastered all over with signed dollar notes. From the water-tower a fine view can be enjoyed. Nature trails make getting to know the island very straightforward.

Useppa Island

From 1903 to 1939 this island, situated in Pine Island Sound, which is only 1 mile/2km long and ½ mile/1km wide, was the property of B. Collier, a nephew of the streetcar magnate J. M. Roach from Chicago. He founded the exclusive Isaac Walton Tarpon Club for sports fishermen. Members of the club would receive diamond-studded badges with their initials if they caught a tarpon with a weight of at least 150 pounds. In the Collier Inn, which has been restored, there are badges like these on display, including some belonging to presidents and filmstars of the 1920s and 1930s.

Some time ago evidence was discovered of a Calusa Indian settlement dating back some 7000 years.

Charlotte Harbor

In May 1513 Ponce de León discovered the large and sheltered bay of Charlotte Harbor (the name either derives from the Spanish name for "Calusa" or from the English Queen Charlotte) on the west coast of Florida and named it Bahía de Espíritu Santo. A colonial settlement on the mainland was unsuccessful. At the end of the 18th/beginning of the 19th century the pirate Gasparilla had his fortified hiding-place here.

After the Civil War the first American settlers set up their homes along the bay. Since 1921 a road-bridge has spanned the bay at the mouth of the tributary, Peace River. In the 1920s well-to-do sporting fishermen also came here from the north.

Even in 1950, Charlotte County, despite its size (705 sq.miles/1826 sq.km), only numbered 4000 inhabitants. In the 1970s there was an enormous influx of people. Today the municipality has close on 100,000 inhabitants. Fortunately the coastline along here has up to now remained spared the scourge of densely planned apartment blocks.

Gasparilla Island

The bay of Charlotte Harbor is also protected by the long narrow islet known as Gasparilla Island, at which the infamous pirate of the same name stopped on various occasions.

Captiva Island

See Sanibel & Captiva Islands

Cedar Key   D 9/10

Levy County
Altitude: 7ft/2m. Population: 1000

Location

The village of Cedar Key lies on the Way Key on the northern Gulf coast of the Florida peninsula – an area as yet relatively undeveloped from a touristic point of view. It is connected by a causeway road with the mainland, which is some 3 miles/5km away. Cedar Key's existence is largely due to one of the first railway lines which was built, linking the Atlantic with the Gulf coast.

In Cedar Key time seems to have stood still. For some years now artists and writers have been discovering the charm of the islands and its old houses. A quiet stroll can be taken through the streets with their brightly-coloured wooden houses, many of which date back to the second half of the last century.

Hiring a bicycle is an excellent way of getting to know the island. Sports fishermen who are not content with fishing from the pier and lovers of water sports can hire boats. Boat trips through the labyrinth of the "bayous", as the swampy arms of the rivers are known, and excursions to the Cedar Keys, which lie offshore to the west, are also well worth while.

Cedar Key today does not just live from tourism. In the last few years oyster-farming has become a significant commercial activity, and there are also many families which make a living from catching prawns.

Cedar Key is also renowned however for its restaurants specialising in seafood (crabs, shrimps and oysters). A high point in the year is the annual "Seafood Festival" (during the third week-end in October), which attracts thousands of visitors. Another major event is the "Sidewalk Arts Festival" which takes place at the end of April.

Seafood Festival
Sidewalk Arts Festival

The existence of an Indian settlement as early as 500 B.C. has been established. In the 18th/19th c. there were small trading posts on the Cedar Keys. In the middle of the 19th c. during the Seminole Wars an army depot was set up on the neighbouring island of Atsena Otie (Indian name for "cedar island"). After a bad hurricane in 1842 the army left the island. During the 1850s David Levy Yulee, senator of Florida, (after learning of the rich stocks of cedarwood on the Suwannee River) planned his railway line from the Atlantic diagonally across Central Florida to Cedar Key. In 1859 the "City of Atsena Otie" was founded and on Way Key the Florida Railroad Company prepared the opening of the "City of Cedar Key" at its terminus. At the beginning of 1861 the first train from Fernandina Beach reached the terminus on Way Key, while a month later the American Civil War broke out. The new harbour suffered under the sea blockade carried out by the Unionists, but blockade breakers repeatedly managed to get through. Wood and cotton in particular were able to be exported. In the shallow bays salt was obtained for the confederates. At the end of 1861 the railway line was cut off. In 1862 Unionist troops occupied the group of islands, but at the end of hostilities the former inhabitants moved back. In 1866 Senator Yulee, a supporter of secession, was released from prison and his railway started up again. Cedar Key now developed into a port. Sawmills and small wharfs were opened and timber processing, sponge diving and fishing (in particular oyster fishing) flourished. In 1885 Cedar Key on its own numbered 2000 inhabitants while a further 3000 people lived on the surrounding islands. On Atsena Otie, Eberhard Faber Inc. erected a sawmill in 1865. From the raw cedarwood processed here pencils were subsequently produced, which were exported all over the world, including countries in Europe. The rival Eagle Pencil Company was set up in Cedar Key. In 1866 a total of seventeen sawmills were operating on the Cedar Keys. Most of the wood was shipped to the Caribbean and to Mexico.

Mail ships, which plied the route between New Orleans and Key West, regularly called in at Cedar Key. As early as the middle of the 1880s a small road connection was established with the mainland. The port, however, now began to feel the effects of the competition from Henry Plant's new railway to Tampa which benefited from its more favourably located harbour. In 1896 the group of islands was struck once again by a powerful hurricane. Cedar Key's inevitable decline from a commercial port to a fishing village could now no longer be halted. Fabers' factory on Atsena Otie was completely destroyed and the settlement on that island abandoned.

History

By 1900 the population along the present beach had declined and the oyster fishery was likewise in a depressed state. New jobs were again created by the opening of a factory which produced brushes and brooms out of palmetto fibres.

In 1950 this factory was itself closed – developments in plastic production were already well advanced and a tornado had once again inflicted heavy damage. Indeed part of the town burnt down at the same time. In 1929 a National Wildlife Refuge was established on nine of the islands of Cedar Keys. In 1932 the railway was closed, while the two tornados "Agnes" and "Elena" wreaked further havoc in 1972 and 1985 respectively.

Sights

Cedar Key Historical Society Museum, Cedar Key Historic District

The small historical museum (SR 24/2nd St.; open: Mon.–Sat. 11am–4pm, Sun. 1–4pm) displays relics, maps, documents and historic photographs from Cedar Key's heyday. Of special interest are the reports of the visit to Cedar Key by the famous naturalist and wildlife protector, John Muir. The small printed Historical Society guide available in the museum (Historic Old Cedar Key Walking Tour) describes a circular tour through the centre of the town with its charming old houses. These buildings frequently have the verandas and venetian blinds which are so characteristic of the southern states of America.

2nd Street

The main street of Cedar Key is Second (Main) Street and it is here that the Island Hotel is situated. The hotel, which was built in the middle of the 19th c., has a restaurant famous for seafood and fish dishes.

City Dock

City Dock, newly built by the sheltered marina by the last hurricane, has restaurants, small shops with souvenirs and galleries. The pier is shared by fishermen and pelicans.

In Cedar Key

Cedar Key State Museum (Museum Drive, 2 miles/3km from the centre; open: daily except Tues. and Wed. 9am–5pm) is in the western part of the island and has a wealth of information about the history of the island. There is also an interesting collection of shells.

Cedar Key
State Museum

Surroundings

To the west of the town stretches a cluster of more than 100 largely still untouched little islands which now form the nature conservation area known as "Cedar Keys Wildlife Refuge". In this amphibious region, which is only accessible by boat, those interested in natural history can observe an underwater world full of different types of wildlife, as well as a large number of birds which are now very rare elsewhere.

★Cedar Keys
National Wildlife
Refuge

About 15 miles/25km north-west of Cedar Key is the mouth of the Suwannee River. This estuarial area, which is still totally unspoilt, has been designated a nature conservancy area.

★Lower
Suwannee
National Wildlife
Refuge

Those tourists seeking adventure can take a boat out into the labyrinth of tiny waterways (bayous) and islets where they can marvel at the rich birdlife and vast numbers of fish.

See Chiefland

Manatee Springs

Chiefland

D 10

Levy County
Altitude: 36ft/11m
Population: 2000

Situated south-west of Gainesville, the village of Chiefland was founded in 1845 in territory which had long been settled and cultivated by Indians. Today the character of the landscape is determined by the intensive cultivation of melons, maize, groundnuts and tobacco. There are also factories in which the agricultural products are processed.

Location

Every year in Chiefland during the third weekend in June the Watermelon Festival is held in which there is a noisy melon auction and a beauty contest.

Watermelon
Festival

Surroundings

Lying about 37 miles/60km to the north (9 miles/15km west of the US 19/98) in the lower reaches of the Suwannee River is Manatee Springs State Park. In this natural landscape so characteristic of Northern Florida, the crystal-clear water of the Manatee Springs wells up (approx. 650,000 cu.yd/½ million cu.m daily). A short distance from the source the karst spring water empties into the Suwannee River. The spring basin is a popular spot not only for bathers, but for divers and snorkellers as well. A natural history trail leads through a hardwood tree-island (hammock) to an area with large numbers of sinkholes. A wooden walkway enables the visitor to explore a cypress swamp.

★Manatee
Springs State Park

Clearwater

F 10

Pinellas County
Altitude: 0–30ft/0–9m
Population: 100,000

Clearwater

Sunset near Clearwater

Location
The fast-growing town of Clearwater, situated on the Pinellas peninsula between the Gulf coast and Tampa Bay, was founded in the middle of the 19th c. as a holiday destination. In the course of time this capital town of Pinellas County has become a popular place of retirement for large numbers of wealthy people from the northern states of the USA. More recently however many industrial concerns have set up factories here and this has to some extent spoilt the holiday character of the town.

The beach settlement of Clearwater Beach also forms part of the town. It is only separated from the neighbouring settlement of Sand Key by the narrow Clearwater Pass. The 2½ mile/4km-long Garden Memorial Causeway connects the narrow barrier island with the mainland.

Fun'n Sun Festival
The annual "Fun'n Sun Festival" which takes place in March/April is the high point of the winter season, with various sporting tournaments and an entertaining bathtub regatta.

Jazz Festival
Well-known American musicians take part in the Jazz Festival in Coachman Park (to the north of the Memorial Causeway), which is held every year in October.

Kahlua Cup
In the vast Clearwater Marina (yachting harbour on the SR 60) there are boats available for excursions and deep-sea fishing trips. Every year in November the Clearwater Yacht Club organises a regatta for the Kahlua Cup, in which dedicated sailors from all over the world take part.

Baseball Spring Training
Every year in March and April the Philadelphia Phillies baseball team comes to the Jack Russell Stadium (Palmetto St./Stadium Drive) for spring training.

Sights

A whole series of high quality cultural events takes place in the Ruth Eckerd Hall and in the ultra-modern Richard B. Baumgardner Center for the Performing Arts. The theatre belonging to the centre has a capacity of over 2000. The programme of events is completed by concerts given by the local Florida Orchestra and by performances from Florida Opera and Broadway shows.

Ruth Eckerd Hall
Richard B. Baumgardner Center

Clearwater also has the attraction of Boatyard Village (16100 Fairchild Drive), a shopping and entertainments centre which nostalgically recalls the fishing villages of New England as they were at the turn of the century. It is situated in the east of the town on Tampa Bay, not far from the airport. Various restaurants and shops, the Florida Room Pavilion and the Boatyard Stage (live entertainment Mon.–Thur. 10am–7pm, Fri./Sat. 10am–9pm) make it an attractive place to pass the time.

Boatyard Village

Near the airport (Fairchild Drive) can also be found the Military Aviation Museum (restored planes and objects from the time of the Second World War to the present day; open: daily 11am–3pm).

Florida Military Aviation Museum

In the Marine Science Center & Aquarium (249 Windward Passage, on an island in Clearwater Harbor; open: Mon.–Fri. 9am–5pm, Sat. 9am–4pm, Sun. 11am–4pm) research is carried out into marine animals. Attempts are also being made to breed threatened species of sea-turtles and care for sick or injured animals. In an enormous pool it is possible to observe various marine animals (sea-turtles, dolphins and numerous types of fish).

★Marine Science Center & Aquarium

It is well worth while visiting the Florida Gulf Coast Art Center (222 Ponce de León Blvd.) in the district of Belleair, where there are frequent high class art exhibitions.

Florida Gulf Coast Art Center

The Marina of Clearwater

Clermont

Moccasin Lake
Nature Park

Moccasin Lake Nature Park (open: Tues.–Fri. 9am–5pm; Sat., Sun. 10am–6pm) covers 51 acres/21ha. On the Park Trail Lane it is possible to study the flora and fauna which is characteristic of this part of Florida.

The site also demonstrates ideas and possibilities for alternative energy sources.

Surroundings

★Clearwater
Beach

The settlement of Clearwater Beach stretches along an narrow island approximately 4½ miles/7km long, with a beach of white sand which is 100yd to ¼ mile/100m to ½km wide here.

A long fishing pier stretches far out into the sea and from the marina, which is a veritable maze, it is possible to pursue all manner of water sports.

Boat trips

Various boat trips are available from the Clearwater City Marina. It is possible to set off on a pirate cruise in the Gulf of Mexico or spend a pleasant evening on a "dinnerboat".

Ferry Service

The Clearwater Ferry Service at the west end of Drew Street offers trips to Clearwater Beach, Tarpon Springs (see entry) and Caladesi Island.

Heritage Park

Heritage Park, which is well worth a visit (open: Tues.–Sat. 10am–4pm, Sun. 1–4pm) is at Largo, a village to the south of Clearwater. Besides a historical exhibition about the region, several buildings, arranged like an open-air museum, can be visited.

Pinellas Suncoast

See entry

Clermont   E 12

Lake County
Altitude: 112ft/34m
Population: 7000

Clermont, a typical small town in central Florida, was named by its French founder after his home town in France. It is pleasantly situated in gently undulating countryside between Lake Minnehaha and Lake Mineola. During the last few years it has seen a large increase in its population.

The various lakes surrounding the town are connected to one another by small water-channels and constitute an ideal playground for canoeists and anglers.

Sights

★Florida Citrus
Tower

On the US 27, just 1 mile/2km north of the SR 50, stands the Citrus Tower, an observation tower almost 230ft/70m high (open: daily 8am–6pm). The look-out platform offers an excellent view across the hilly countryside with its many lakes and orange groves.

Citrus plantations

In the groves around Clermont there are more than 17 million citrus trees (mainly orange and grapefruit), which occasionally are affected by "northers", as the outbreaks of cold air moving southwards are called. By taking one of the special "Citrus Grove Tram Tours" the visitor can learn much of interest about the cultivation of citrus fruits in Florida. From October to June freshly harvested oranges and grapefruits are prepared for dispatch in the Citrus Packing House. Freshly pressed orange juice, marmelades and various types of confectionery are also available.

House of
Presidents

A visit can also be paid to the nearby waxworks gallery, in which all the presidents of the USA are represented (open: daily 9am–5pm, except May and Sept.).

This winery, about 6 miles/10km north of Clermont, on the US 27, is open to visitors (Mon.–Sat. 10am–6pm; Sun. noon–6pm and by arrangement; tel. 904–394–8627). A small slide show explains the development of viniculture in Florida. The harvesting of the grapes takes place as early as July/August.

Lakeridge Winery & Vineyards

About 6 miles/10km south of Clermont (accessible by the SR 561 and the Lake Nellie Road) lies a delightful park on the southern edge of Lake Louisa. These area is part of the "Green Swamp", an area of wetland which is very important for Florida's water supply. Lake Louisa and the nearby Bear Lake are much frequented by anglers, swimmers and canoeists.

Lake Louisa State Park

Clewiston

See Lake Okeechobee

Cocoa, Cocoa Beach   F 14

Brevard County
Altitude: 0–26ft/0–8m
Population: 30,000

The towns of Cocoa and Cocoa Beach lie on the "Space Coast", as the central section of Florida's Atlantic coast is known. Since the 1960s when NASA started to carry out its space programme, first on Cape Canaveral, then at the Kennedy Space Center on Merritt Island, tourists have come here in ever increasing numbers.

Location

Cocoa was once a sleepy little town on the Indian River and with its offshore islands and 19 mile/30km-long sandy beach was only accessible by boat. It has developed into a lively seaside resort and has become a starting-point for visits to the US space station.

As well as factories connected with the space and high-tech industries, the processing and dispatch of citrus fruit from the Indian River area plays an important part in the town's economy.

Cocoa, today a rapidly growing town, was founded in the 1860s and was initially called Indian River City because of its central position in the important agricultural area along the Indian River.

History

After the Second World War the town enjoyed an enormous boom, partly because of the growth in tourism, partly because of the conversion of the rocket testing site at Cape Canaveral into the US space centre.

Sights

Following the redevelopment of the old town centre at the west end of Hubert Humphrey Bridge, a small but attractive shopping centre has grown up on both sides of King Street. It is well worth taking a stroll through the nostalgic cobbled streets with their old lamps, trees, floral borders, leafy courtyards, narrow passageways and various small boutiques, galleries and craft-shops.

★Olde Cocoa Village

Conducted tours are regularly arranged. Information: tel. 632–1830.

Local theatre groups now give performances in the Cocoa Village Playhouse (300 Brevard Ave.), which, with its attractive façade, was built in 1924 as the "Aladdin Theatre" and has recently been restored. Information: tel. 632–1111.

Cocoa Playhouse

Brevard Museum of History & Natural Science

In the Brevard Museum of History & Natural Science (2201 Michigan Ave.; open: Tues.–Sat. 10am–4pm) the visitor can learn much of interest about the area. Special attention being given to geology, palaeontology, archaeology and local history.

A study trail which starts from the museum takes the visitor through three different mini-ecosystems.

Cocoa Beach

The seaside resort of Cocoa Beach, which used to be widely known for its magical sunsets, is today bounded on the north by the rocket testing site at Cape Canaveral (see entry) and on the south by the installations of the Patrick Air Force Base.

The Pier

The pier (401 Mead Ave.), which extends 820ft/250m into the Atlantic Ocean, offers superb conditions for anglers. Every year angling competitions take place here at Easter and at Labor Day Weekend.

Ron Jon Surf Shop

The Ron Jon Surf Shop in Cocoa Beach (4151 North Atlantic Ave.; open: daily 9am–11pm) is one of the largest specialist shops in Florida for watersports and has become something of an institution. All kinds of things can be bought here, from fashionable T-shirts to surfboards, water-skis and sailing boats.

Port Canaveral

At the harbour at Port Canaveral there are large numbers of crab-cutters and big-game-fishing charter boats which go out into the Atlantic. The harbour is connected to the Banana and Indian Rivers by a lock and the Barge Canal.

Port Canaveral is also an important harbour for cruisers, with the most up-to-date facilities. From here it is possible to set out on trips lasting several days in the direction of the Bahamas and the Caribbean. Many of these leisure-steamers have casinos on board and because of this have a special attraction, as gambling is against the law in Florida. Information available from the harbour master's office (tel. 783–7831) and the cruise companies "Sea Escape" (tel. 1–800–432–0900) and "Premier Cruise Lines" (tel. 1–800–432–2545).

Missile Exhibit

Outside the site of the technical installations of the Air Force Eastern Space & Missile Center and outside the Patrick Air Force Base there are various rockets on display which have gone through trials on the nearby test site.

Surroundings

Observation of rocket launches

Cocoa Beach is an excellent place from which to watch rocket launches. Lift-off times can be ascertained from the Cocoa Beach Area Chamber of Commerce, tel. 459–2200.

St John's River, Lake Poinsett

A short way west of Cocoa, St John's River follows its leisurely course northwards. At Lone Cabbage Fish Camp, 6 miles/10km to the west on the SR 520, trips by propeller-boat on St John's River and Lake Poinsett are available (Air Boats; daily from 10am). The trips pass through cypress swamps and vast stretches of reeds and sawgrass, while alligators, turtles and many species of birds can be observed.

Coconut Grove

See Miami

Coral Gables

See Miami

Crystal River   E 10

Citrus County
Altitude: 0–7ft/0–2m
Population: 4000

The sprawling resort of Crystal River lies on the north-west coast of the   Location
Florida peninsula alongside the river of the same name, which, just a short
distance further on, flows into Kings Bay. There are excellent facilities for
amateur fishermen here, both in the bay with its myriad islands and the
Gulf of Mexico itself.

At the time of the Spanish conquest the area around Crystal River was   History
settled by Timucuan Indians. Several temples and burial mounds are still
preserved today. Later the area was inhabited by Seminole Indians who
retreated here during the Seminole Wars. At the end of the war most of
them were forcibly resettled in Oklahoma.
   During the 1840s white settlers took over the land, which was presented
to them free by the government. Large plantations (mainly sugar-cane)

Pre-Columbian cult site at Crystal River

were established here. In 1884 the cedarwood boom took its grip on Crystal River and a sawmill was built. The rural settlement now numbered 200 inhabitants. In the first years of this century the first hotels were built. Well-to-do people from the northern states started coming here to spend the winter or to enjoy the excellent opportunities for hunting and fishing. In 1920 a large fire destroyed the centre of the village.

By the end of the 1920s Crystal River had begun to be shaken by the approaching ecomonic crisis. Large numbers of properties had to be sold off cheaply or transferred in settlement of tax debts. Then in October 1929 violent rainstorms led to terrible flooding. After the Second World War the population began to rise dramatically and in the last two decades the number of tourists has steadily increased. More and more holiday developments have been built, often with their own marinas.

Sights

★Crystal River State Archaeological Site

From 200 B.C. until the 15th c. Crystal River was an important religious and cultural centre for the Pre-columbian Indians, or "Pre-columbian Mound Builders", as they been called by scientists. Two massive hills, which probably served as shrines and burial mounds, have clearly been identified. By the river there are mounds of empty mussel shells which have been piled up in the course of time. Since excavations began in 1903 it has been established that one of the burial mounds contains more than 450 graves. Stelae, which are scarcely in evidence at all elsewhere in North America, point to contact with the advanced Indian civilisations in Mexico.

The small museum in the visitors' centre provides excellent information about this prodigious archaeological site and its creators' civilisation. There is a path linking the individual mounds.

Open: outdoor sights daily from 8am to dusk; museum Thur.–Mon. 9am–5pm.

Solitude by Crystal River

The main attraction is, however, represented by the karst springs – well in excess of 100 in number – with their gushing crystal-clear water, which feed the Crystal River. In the basins created by these springs excellent diving and snorkelling are possible. Because of their proximity to the Gulf they provide a biosphere for both freshwater and saltwater fish. In particular in autumn and winter they are ideal for watching the inquisitive manatees (sea-cows) which visit the springs because of their constant temperature throughout the year. These animals have, however, recently been considerably endangered by the heavy boat traffic on the river. From October to the end of March therefore, protection zones with speed limits or exclusion zones come into operation.

★Crystal River
Springs

Good bathing is afforded by the sandy Fort Island Gulf Beach, to the west of Crystal River at the end of Kings Bay Road (CR 44), where during the American Civil War an artillery battery was set up.

Fort Island
Gulf Beach

In Crystal River and its surroundings there are four excellent public golf courses (54 holes in all) as well as several private clubs.

Golf courses

Every year in November around Thanksgiving the Manatee Festival Week takes place with large numbers of events, including a canoeing contest held on Kings Bay and a Seafood Festival.

Manatee Festival
Week

About 6 miles/10km from the centre of the town there is a nuclear power station which was brought into operation in 1977. Its cooling waters have a considerable adverse effect on the springs and river flow in the region.

Nuclear power
station

See entry

Homosassa
Springs

Cypress Gardens

See Winter Haven

Dade City   F 11

Pasco County
Altitude: 79ft/24m
Population: 6000

The main town in Pasco County, Dade City lies in hilly country to the north-east of Tampa (see entry) and is the centre of a predominantly agricultural area with broad pastures, horse paddocks, poultry farms and extensive citrus groves. This landscape is spared from becoming monotonous by imposing live-oak trees (*quercus virginiana*) covered with Spanish moss, as well as azaleas.

Location

Sights

The principal place to visit in Dade City is the Pioneer Florida Museum, an open-air museum extending over several acres, which looks back to the days of the early settlers. A small 19th c. church, an old schoolhouse, a dwelling-house dating back to the 1860s and fitted out in the style of the time, an old railway depot with locomotives and wagons as well as various agricultural tools can all be seen.

★Pioneer Florida
Museum

Every year on Labor Day the "Pioneer Florida Day" is held. Then old skilled trades are displayed, "Cracker" meals are served and hilbilly music played.

Festivals

Every year during a weekend in April musicians play on old instruments. Some artists contribute songs dating from the pioneer period.

Surroundings

St Leo Abbey

A few miles south of Dade City the visitor will come to St Leo Abbey, a Benedictine abbey founded in 1889 with a boarding school, which was not finished until 1948. The church, which is built in the Lombard style, is most impressive. Also noteworthy is the large cross of pink marble which was cut in Tennessee.

Dade Battlefield

About 22 miles/35km further north lies Dade Battlefield State Historic Site. Here in 1835 a battle involving huge loss of life took place between Seminole Indians and an army of some 100 whites led by Major Francis Dade. In the tiny museum more information about this event can be obtained.

Dania

See Fort Lauderdale

Daytona Beach   D 13

Volusia County
Altitude: 0–10ft/0–3m
Population: 62,000

Location

A firm beach, constantly busy and stretching for miles, on which it is possible to drive a car, is one of the distinguishing features of Daytona Beach – the other being the world-famous motor-racing circuit. The town is a meeting-place for motor-racing fans from all over the world and motor-cyclists with their shining chrome machines. In addition during the high school spring holidays countless sun-starved students head for Daytona Beach to celebrate the "Spring Break". For decades the long narrow peninsula between the Halifax River and the Atlantic has been lit up by the neon signs of the cheap bars and hotels which line the streets. Since the middle eighties attempts have been made with the help of a costly improvement and redevelopment programme to get away from the image of a down-market holiday destination.

Embry Riddle Aeronautical University

Situated by the airport is the Embry Riddle Aeronautical University, after a similar institution in Arizona the most important aviation and pilot-training centre in the United States.

Every year in April/May an "airshow" is held which attracts countless spectators.

Spring Break

The flocking of students every year in the spring holidays to a beach resort in the south has in the last few decades shifted from Fort Lauderdale (see entry) to Daytona Beach. Today Daytona Beach is the "in" place. It is estimated that from the beginning of March to Easter more than 400,000 young people seeking the sun come here looking for excitement. They crowd into the area between Main Street Pier and the music pavilion at Broadway Park (live music, especially big bands or Dixie music) and hold one large party which lasts for several days. The discos are full to overflowing, as are the amusement parks. With their gleaming convertibles, beach buggies, jeeps, pick-ups and motor-cycles the young men and women ride up and down the beach. Popstars put in an appearance, high-class sporting events take place, as well as all manner of other competitions (e.g. bodybuilding, beauty contests).

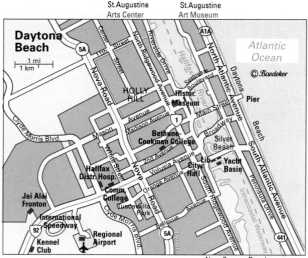

New Smyrna Beach

Of the Timucuan Indian villages shown here on early maps of the region, today the only evidence consists of the "mounds" formed of mussel-shells and stones. British planters from the Caribbean were aware as early as the end of the 18th c. that the ground here was well suited to the cultivation of sugar-cane, indigo and cotton and established the first plantations, which however were all devastated in 1836 by rampaging Seminoles. At the end of the 19th c. the area developed into a favourite playground of the rich by virtue of its mild winters and its attractive scenery.

Sights

To the north of Main Street Pier with its look-out point called "Space Needle" and its tiny chair-lift, and lying just beyond a small amusement park (Forest Amusement Park, Mardi Gras Fun Center), is the newly redesigned Broadwalk Park, which has the function of a broad seaside promenade. A trade-mark of the park is the now rather well-worn Music Pavilion at the north end of the green area. Open-air concerts take place here all through the year. During the "spring break" several tens of thousands of people will sometimes crowd around to listen. Opposite is the towering Ocean Center (1985; centre for conferences and organised events). The nearby recently renovated Peabody Auditorium is the home of the Daytona Beach Symphony Society and the Daytona Beach Civic Ballet.

Main Street Pier, Bandshell, Broadwalk Park, Ocean Center, Peabody Auditorium

The Halifax Historical Society and Museum is housed in the building of the former Merchants Bank (252 S. Beach St.; open: Tues.–Sat. 10am–4pm, in Feb. daily). Exhibits include artefacts from Pre-columbian times, relics from the Spanish colonial era and items representing the early period of motor-racing.

Halifax Historical Society and Museum

South of City Island, which is home to the baseball stadium, municipal library and courthouse, a modern yachting harbour with a small shopping centre was opened at the end of the last decade.

Halifax Harbor, Downtown

As part of the redevelopment of the old town centre, the construction of office buildings, a town hall and court of appeal has been recently carried

Daytona Beach

On Daytona Beach, where cars can drive on the sand

out. Older, and often extemely attractive buildings, such as the historic Kress building, have been rebuilt. New shops have been opened.

★Museum of Arts & Sciences

In Tuscawilla Park to the east of the airport can be found the Museum of Arts & Sciences (1040 Museum Blvd.; open: Tues.–Fri. 9am–4pm, Sat. and Sun. noon–5pm) with an outstanding collection of Cuban folk art (including parts of the art collection of the Cuban dictator Batista). A collection of American art from the 18th, 19th and 20th centuries is also noteworthy.

Of considerable interest are the fossils, skeletons from the Pleistocene period, including the bones of a gigantic sloth, which was found in the nearby Reed Canal Park.

Planetarium

Next to the museum is a planetarium (laser show at weekends).

Educational trails

Various natural history trails start from the museum and take the visitor through one of the few hammocks along the Atlantic coast of central Florida which is still preserved in its original state.

★Daytona International Speedway

Apart from the firm sandy beach, on which cars can be driven, Daytona International Speedway (1801 Volusia Ave./US 92, west of the airport; guided tours outside the racing season: daily 9am–noon and 1–5pm) is the star attraction. The high points in the racing season are the "Speed Weeks" with the "Daytona 500" in February. In March and October big motorcycling races are held. The main grandstand can accommodate 85,000 spectators, while a further 50,000 people crowd into the interior of the "Trioval" with their cars.

Farmer's Market

Every Saturday from 8am until 4pm a farmer's market is held on Daytona Beach City Island.

Ponce de León Inlet Lighthouse

The 164ft/50m high lighthouse on Ponce de León Inlet was built as long ago as 1887 and was operational until 1970. The lighthouse platform affords a good panoramic view.

Daytona lighthouse

Remains of an old sugar-mill

In the former lighthouse keeper's house there is a small museum dealing with the history of seafaring (open: daily 10am–7pm).

To the south of the lighthouse extends the Lighthouse Point Park, an attractive leisure area with a natural history trail running through it. Walkways made of wooden planks lead through the band of dunes to the beach.

Lighthouse Point Park

By the lighthouse there is a small fishing harbour where freshly caught seafood and fish are sold direct from the boats. There are several fish restaurants and deep-sea fishermen can rent boats here.

Fisherman's Wharf

An enjoyable visit can be paid to the Sugar Mill Gardens (open: daily 8.30am–5pm) in Port Orange (southern edge of Daytona) with its remains of a Spanish mission station and a sugar mill which was destroyed in 1836. The dinosaur figures which are dotted around the park seem rather out of place.

Sugar Mill Gardens

A nostalgic red-painted tourist omnibus, called the "Jolly Trolley", runs along the beach (on the A1A).

Jolly Trolley

A paddle-steamer makes trips on the Halifax River, starting from the southwest end of Seabreeze Bridge. In the evening there are "dinner cruises" with Dixieland music. Information: Dixie Queen River Cruises, 841 Ballough Rd., tel. 255–1997 and 1–800–225–9452 (free of charge).

Dixie Queen River Cruises

The local baseball team, which is affiliated with the "Chicago White Sox", plays at City Island Ball Park, tel. 252–0301.

Baseball

Jai Alai, I–95/US 92, opposite the speedway, tel. 255–0222.

Jai Alai

Daytona Beach Kennel Club, by the speedway, races from May to October Mon.–Sat. every evening.

Greyhound racing

Surroundings

★ A1A
Especially attractive from a scenic point of view is a trip along the Highway A1A (First Coast Highway), going directly along the coast northwards through St Augustine to Amelia Island and Fernandina Beach. At Mayport a ferry can be taken across St John's River (106 miles/170km).

DeLand
See entry

Ormond Beach
See entry

Deerfield Beach   J 15

Broward County
Altitude: 0–13ft/0–4m
Population: 47,000

Location
The most northerly coastal resort in Broward County is Deerfield Beach, where a post office was established in 1898 for the first settlers in the region. Until the Second World War the predominant source of income for the people living here was agriculture. During the Prohibition alcohol smugglers used to set off from here on the Hillsboro Canal. It is said that Al Capone wanted to buy Deerfield Island in order to be able to transfer smuggled goods undisturbed.

The coastline in the northern part of Broward County has changed dramatically in the last few years. New industrial sites and business parks have shot up, and by the Atlantic there are rows and rows of holiday homes, hotels and luxury apartments.

Sights

Deerfield Island
The offshore Deerfield Island has been uninhabited up to the present time and can only be reached by boat (Wed. and Sat. organised boat trips). A wooden walkway leads through red, white and black mangroves. The island is a protected area for threatened gopher tortoises and a retreat for various rare animals.

Riverview Restaurant
The now historic "Riverview Restaurant" on the Cove Marina (Intracoastal Waterway) was where the gangster Al Capone (see Famous Personalities) liked to make a stop.

Quiet Waters Country Park, Ski Rixen
Quiet Waters Country Park is very popular because of its five lakes and beaches (6601 N. Powerline Road; open: daily 8am–8pm), but its main attraction is "Ski Rixen", a new type of towrope system which enables water-skiers to ski without a boat. Swimming equipment, water-skis, surf-boards and canoes can be rented.

★ Loxahatchee Wildlife Refuge
Loxahatchee Wildlife Refuge, which lies to the north-west of Deerfield and is almost 148,260 acres/60,000ha in area, is part of the freshwater marsh which forms part of the Everglades. There are several access points to the reserve, which is intended to protect reptiles and numerous rare species of water-bird.

Hillsboro Recreation Area
About 12 miles/20km west of Deerfield Beach is the Hillsboro Recreation Area. Propellor-driven excursion boats leave from the Fishing Lodge. In the winter months in particular, it is possible to observe many different kinds of migratory birds.

The park's administrative office is on the US 441 (between SR 804 and 806). There is additional access further north on the US 98 at "Twenty Mile Bend" (about 19 miles/30km west of Lake Worth).

De Funiak Springs

Walton County
Altitude: 262ft/80m. Population: 6000

The little town of De Funiak Springs, which was founded in 1881, is situated at an important crossroads in the attractive agricultural area in the west known as the "Panhandle". The settlement came into being as a result of land surveyors looking for a suitable route for the Louisville & Nashville Railroad. The settlement, which they founded on the shores of an almost completely circular lake, was named by them after one of their superiors in the railroad company.

Sights

The public library, which is one of the oldest in Florida, is housed in an attractive building dating from 1887.

Public Library

To the south-east of the town is the Ponce de León Springs State Recreation Area, which extends over more than 500 acres/200ha. The central point in this park is a karst spring, which penetrates horizontal layers of chalk and forms a beautiful pool. Here one can bathe, fish or go off walking on well-signed paths. In addition there are organised nature rambles which are led by the park supervisors. Information: Walton County Chamber of Commerce, tel. 892–31 91.

★Ponce de León Springs

DeLand

Volusia County
Altitude: 79ft/24m. Population: 17,000

Just under 25 miles/40km west of Daytona Beach (see entry) lies the little town of DeLand, the administrative seat of Volusia County, which seems completely removed from the hustle and bustle of the coast and the area around Orlando (see entry). It owes its magnificent oak trees to its founder Henry DeLand. This manufacturer from New York had the idea of constructing a modern "Athens in Florida" in the 1870s. From the schoolhouse which was built at the time of the town's foundation developed the private Stetson University, which has close links with the Baptists (about 2300 students; founded in 1886 with the financial support of the manufacturer of Stetson hats).

Location

Sights

At Stetson University (N. Woodland Blvd.; telephone information 734–4121) it is possible, when lectures are taking place, to visit the Gillespie Museum of Minerals (geology and minerals) and the Sampson Gallery of Art.

Stetson University

The DeLand Museum (600 N. Woodland Blvd.; tel. 734–4371) has an ambitious programme of exhibitions featuring internationally known artists. In the Indian section the basketry and ceramics are particularly pleasing.

DeLand Museum of Art

Surroundings

The visitor can travel in leisurely fashion in a houseboat down the nearby St John's River, which is surprisingly rich in fish. Boat rental: Hontoon Landing Marina (2317 River Ridge Rd.; telephone information 734–2007, 1–800–248–2474).

St John's River

★Hontoon Island
State Park

Hontoon Island State Park, situated 8 miles/13km to the south-west in the St John's River area, offers the visitor a glimpse of how Florida originally was – in amongst the increasing number of housing developments which are spreading out along the banks of the river. Cypress swamps, wet savannas and hammocks with evergreen oaks, pines and palms alternate on this island, which can only be reached by boat (ferry from Hontoon Landing, daily 9am until one hour before sunset). A circular path gives access to the island and leads to a 299ft/91m high hill on which there was once a Timucuan temple.

★Blue Springs
State Park

Further upstream, about 2 miles/3km west of the town of Orange City, is the karst spring, known as Blue Springs because of its superb colour (average flow 900 gallons/4095 litres per hour; constant temperature of 72°F/22°C), the waters of which empty into the St John's River only a few hundred yards further on. The spring basin, which is equally popular with both swimmers and divers is from November to March a protection area for manatees. Timucuan Indians lived here for centuries. Now only a few snail and mussel-shell hills provide a reminder of this period. In the middle of the 19th c. the first white settlers came up the St John's River. In 1872 a large wooden house was built on one of the hills piled up by the Indians. Today it once again looks just as it did in pioneering times. There are guided tours (Tues.–Sun. 11am–4pm) which convey how life was in the 19th c. when the settlers' produce from the surrounding area was loaded on to the steam-ships to be taken to Jacksonville. The remains of the landing stage down by the river provide continuing evidence of the heavy use which steamships made of St John's River. Walkways on planks lead through typical ham-mocks to the spring. In winter one can watch the manatees in the clear water of the Blue Springs Run from a small wooden platform. There is a campsite as well as canoe and rowing-boat rental. An attractive two-day canoeing trip goes to Hontoon Island, with an overnight stop at the simple campsite there or, with luck, in one of the six small holiday huts.

Information: Blue Springs State Park, 2100 W. French Ave., Orange City, FL 32763; tel. 775–3663.

De León Springs

About 5 miles/8km north of DeLand is the De León Springs State Recreation Area, a pretty spot which occupies the site of a sugar plantation which was laid out in the 18th c. Here it is possible to bathe in a spring, dive, snorkel, paddle or go for a walk on a nature trail.

★Spring Garden
Ranch

A few miles north of DeLand, on the US 17, Spring Garden Ranch is reached. It is one of the largest stud farms in Florida, in which several hundred horses are kept or reared. The site has various facilities for equine sports, including even a racetrack with a grandstand. Information about events taking place here can be obtained from the DeLand Chamber of Commerce (tel. 734–4331).

Delray Beach

See Palm Beach

Destin   B 3

Walton County
Altitude: 0–39ft/0–12m
Population: 9000

Location

In the middle of the 19th c. Destin was founded as a fishing village on the narrow East Pass at the western tip of the 23 mile/37km-long peninsula which separates off Choctawhatchee Bay. Destin has the potential to develop because of the excellent opportunities it offers for sports fishermen. Unfortunately just recently there have been holiday-home complexes sprouting up everywhere with varying degrees of success.

In the Old Pass Lagoon, which is divided off by the tiny tongue of land called Holiday Isle, fishing boats bob up and down alongside the charter boats belonging to amateur sailors and fishermen.

Every year in October Destin offers the attractions of the Seafood Festival (good fish meals, fishing and sailing competitions) and the large competition prizes of the Deep Sea Fishing Rodeo.

Fishing festivals

Sights

In the Museum of the Sea and the Indians (4801 Beach Highway) much interesting information is provided about the underwater living world and the way of life of North and South American Indians.

Museum of the Sea and the Indians

The interesting Fishing Museum (35 US 98 E.) gives information about the development of fishing in Destin.

Fishing Museum

Surroundings

The freshwater lakes and ponds of Dune Allen Beach at the west end of the SR 30-A attract many amateur anglers. Along Highway 98 development plans are queuing up to be implemented while along this stretch of coast the empty, unspoilt dune landscape is inexorably disappearing. Now tennis courts, golf courses, fitness and beauty studios have begun to form part of the landscape along with massive high-rise complexes with countless holiday apartments right next to the sugar-white sandy beach. The largest and most luxurious holiday development is the relatively sprawling one called Sandestin, which extends between the golf course and Choctawhatchee Bay.

Sandestin

The Grayton Beach Recreational Area (campsite, bathing beach, watersports) lies about 20 miles/32km east of Destin. A natural history trail leads through an area of dunes very characteristic of this section of coastline. Further inland the landscape is defined by low, long-needled fir trees, magnolias, palmetto scrub and the brackish waters of Western Lake. In summer numbers of large sea turtles come here to lay their eggs on the beach.

★ Grayton Beach State Recreational Area

The beach settlement of Grayton Beach is the oldest of its kind in the area In about 1880 a pensioner from New England had his retirement home built here and by the turn of the century a hotel had already been opened. The Louisville & Nashville Railroad Company also advertised a summer halt at Grayton Beach. In the 1920s the little wooden houses, positioned at the end of sandy lanes, so typical of Grayton Beach, began to be built.

Grayton Beach

A detour on the SR 395 leads away from the Gulf coast to Point Washington, one of the old lumberjack settlements established about 100 years ago. The wealth of excellent wood in the region was here turned to profitable use.

★ Eden State Gardens, Point Washington

In the Eden State Gardens (expanses of parkland with old oak trees, camelias and azaleas) stands Wesley House, which was built in 1898 in the plantation style and belonged to the former sawmill owners (conducted tours: Thur.–Mon. 9am, 4pm).

Wesley House

Anyone travelling in a westerly direction on the County Road 30-A along the attractive Gulf coast, will pass through a mixture of older and newer holiday home developments, which belong to the southern part of Walton

South Walton, Emerald Coast

County and are known as the Beaches of South Walton. This section of coastline, which until now has attracted little attention and is still much as it originally was, has, with its white sandy beaches, band of dunes and clear turquoise-blue warm Gulf water, often been called the "Emerald Coast". As early as 3000 years ago Indians startled to settle in the area and from the 15th to the 19th c. Choctaw and Euchee Indians came here every summer to fish. Enormous snail and mussel-shell mounds (Indian middens) still bear witness to their activities.

★Seaside

To the west of Seagrove, the holiday development of Seaside was built in the middle of an area of sand-dunes during the 1980s and subsequently awarded a prestigious prize for architecture. This complex demonstrates that the development of this section of the Gulf coast is possible even today without high-rise buildings and wide roads geared solely to the needs of the motorist. Several hundred pastel-coloured wooden houses in the Victorian style have been built on small plots of land, using as their models similar types of house in Cape May, Nantucket, Charleston, Savannah and Key West. This pedestrian-friendly holiday village, which is practically devoid of cars, is situated by a beautiful beach and has its own almost Mediterranean-style market. The local amphitheatre is well used. Painters and art-dealers have discovered the charm of this unusual new settlement.

Disney World

See Walt Disney World

Dry Tortugas

Location

About 68 miles/110km west of Key West lie the Dry Tortugas, the coral islands and reefs where in 1513 Ponce de León discovered countless sea-turtles laying their eggs.

Access

Charter flights and boat excursions from Key West.

★Fort Jefferson

On the island of Garden Key lies Fort Jefferson which can only be reached by private boat or seaplane (Key West Seaplane Service). In order to protect

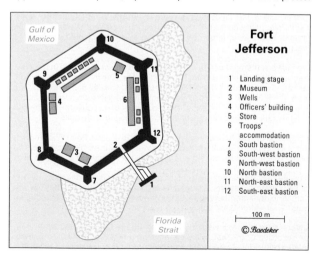

Fort Jefferson

Gulf of Mexico

1 Landing stage
2 Museum
3 Wells
4 Officers' building
5 Store
6 Troops' accommodation
7 South bastion
8 South-west bastion
9 North-west bastion
10 North bastion
11 North-east bastion
12 South-east bastion

100 m

© Baedeker

Florida Strait

shipping transport in the Gulf of Mexico the construction of a fort was begun in 1846. It was soon discovered that the ground did not provide solid enough foundations for the building. The fort was used by the army for many years as a prison (for instance, Dr S. Mudd had to spend two years here because he agreed to set the broken leg of Abraham Lincoln's assassin in 1865). After a devastating hurricane and two yellow-fever epidemics the isolated fort served intermittently as a coal bunker and a radio station for the navy and army, until in 1908 it was designated a "Wildlife Refuge" in order to protect the breeding ground of a species of Caribbean tern, which had almost reached the point of extinction because of egg collectors. In 1935 it became a National Monument.

A large part of the fort can today be visited. As well as a small attractive beach suitable for bathing, there is excellent snorkelling possible in front of the sea walls (equipment supplied by the seaplane company).

Between March and October, the actual breeding island, neighbouring Bush Key, can not be visited. Brown pelicans, cormorants and magnificent frigate-birds with wing-spans of more than 6ft/2m can often be observed. | Bush Key

Dunedin   F 10

Pinellas
Altitude: 0–13ft/0–4m
Population: 35,000

The town of Dunedin, today falling in the catchment area of the vast urban agglomeration of Tampa/St Petersburg, was founded in 1870 as one of the first coastal towns in Florida. At first the settlement was known as Jonesboro after the owner of its single grocery and general store. When two Scottish tradesmen opened a second store in the 1880s, they applied to the the government to be allowed to open a post-office here in Dunedin (Gaelic= place of rest). By so doing, they hoped to gain extra custom. The name "Dunedin" became accepted and soon a wave of Scots people came here to settle. In memory of its Scottish heritage, the town celebrates the "Highland Games" every year in April. | Location

As early as 1830 a French aristocrat had settled in the area and planted the first grapefruit trees in Florida.

Every year in March the "Toronto Blue Jays" baseball team trains in Dunedin (Grant Field, Douglas Ave.). | Baseball Spring Training

Sights

Some of the old houses of Dunedin have been beautifully renovated and their names entered in the national register of monuments. | Historic buildings

In a former station of the "Orange Belt Railroad" of 1889 a small museum of local history has been established (including drawings and relics of Dunedin's Scottish past; open: Tues. and Sat. 10am–noon, Thur. 9.30–11.30am, June to Oct. closed; Information: tel. 733–4151). | Railroad Historical Museum

★Caladesi Island, Honeymoon Island

About 3 miles/5km from Dunedin lie Honeymoon Island and Caladesi Island, two delightful places to visit. Originally there was just one single island but a hurricane in 1921 tore it in two and formed the "Hurricane Pass". | Location

At the beginning of this century an Indian burial ground was uncovered on Caladesi Island. The island remained uninhabited until the end of the | History

105

19th c. when in 1888 it was explored by a Swiss man who was seeking refuge from a storm and who settled there. In the 1960s Caladesi Island became the object of land speculation. There were plans for the construction of holiday homes but finally, however, environmentalists gained the upper hand.

Honeymoon Island State Recreation Area

The holiday area of Honeymoon Island with its beautiful but also much frequented beaches is connected with the mainland by a causeway (Dunedin Causeway Blvd., SR 586; open: daily from 8am; information: tel. 734–4255). It is possible to collect mussels, bathe and fish here. The 500 acre/200ha island is, apart from a small settlement with holiday bungalows, largely preserved in its natural state, with the result that there are good opportunities for observing its nature.

From Honeymoon Island there is a ferry which goes across every hour to Caladesi Island. Seat reservation: tel. 734–5263.

Caladesi Island State Park

The neighbouring 750 acre/300ha large Caladesi Island remains one of the few barrier islands with beautiful sandy beaches bordered by a band of dunes and woodland further inland. Here there are centuries-old live-oak trees, thickly covered with Spanish moss, ferns and other epiphytes. In the east the island turns into a mangrove swamp which is the home of countless waterfowl.

Caladesi Beach

The beach on Caladesi Island is one of the few places in Florida which on summer nights is visited by sea-turtles to lay eggs. The band of dunes, ecologically a very sensitive area, is crossed by wooden walkways which the visitor must at all times keep to. A path about 3 miles/5km long bisects the island and affords an opportunity to observe the natural environment. During the season there are beach rambles led by park rangers.

Ferries

The islands can only be reached by a ferry from Dunedin or Clearwater and Clearwater Beach or by private boat.

Information and reservations

Caladesi State Park, Causeway Blved., Dunedin, FL 33528; tel. (813) 443–5903). It is forbidden to spend the night on the island. A limited number of boats may however moor in the marina for a maximum of one night.

EPCOT Center

See Walt Disney World

Everglades City   K 13

Collier County
Altitude: 0–6ft/0–2m
Population: 1000

Location

The settlement of Everglades City lies south-east of Naples (see entry) on the north-western edge of the Everglades National Park (see entry). From here one can make natural history excursions and boat trips into the Everglades, the Big Cypress National Preserve (see entry) and through the vast network of islands lying to the west which are known as Ten Thousand Islands.

★★National Park Service Boat Tours

At the southern end of the Chokoloskee Causeway (SR 29) the Everglades National Park Service runs the Park Docks and an informative visitors' centre (open: daily 9am–5pm; tel. 695–3311). From here park rangers equipped with an excellent range of knowledge conduct boat trips lasting several hours into the Everglades and the offshore mangroves (departures between 8.30am and 5pm, generally on the hour or by arrangement; tel. 695–2591). During these excursions the visitor learns not only about the original vegetation, but also has the opportunity to observe dolphins in their natural surroundings and numerous bird species which have become very rare elsewhere.

In addition information is given about how the Indians lived here in former times and how they caught their fish.

Surroundings

North-west of Everglades City, beyond the Tamiami Trail (US 41) (see entry) the visitor can take the SR 29 and via Carnestown and Copeland reach the Fakahatchee Strand State Preserve with the Janes Memorial Scenic Drive (only partly asphalted). The nature reserve has arguably the finest scenery in the Everglades area and what amounts to the largest naturally preserved stock of massive old king palms. Although timber used to be felled even here, the habitat is still intact and is a last refuge for the Florida puma, which is threatened with extinction, as well as various other animals which have become rare elsewhere. One can also admire the wide range of orchids which grow here. A small look-out tower at the entrance to the reserve makes it possible to get an

★★Fakahatchee Strand

A pink spoonbill in the Everglades

initial overview of the natural landscape and animal observation points. At the end of the track are the remains of a failed development project, the aim of which was to drain 41sq.miles/106sq.km of swampy landscape by the middle of this century. Enormous damage was done to the delicate ecosystem at that time. A cypress swamp was drained and millions of cubic metres of freshwater – essential for life in the Everglades region – flowed straight into the sea, unused. Some of the plots of land were eventually sold, but in the end the project foundered and the wilderness proved itself to be stronger. Park rangers provide guided tours through the marshland scenery.

Information: Fakahatchee Strand State Preserve, P.O. Box 548, Copeland; tel. 695–4593.

To the south and west of Everglades City stretches the broad amphibious area of Ten Thousand Islands with its primeval labyrinth of mangrove trees. This geographical area of transition between the freshwater of the Everglades and the saltwater of the Gulf of Mexico is the breeding ground for numerous marine inhabitants, as well as being the nesting ground for many sea birds and waders.

★Ten Thousand Islands

Everglades National Park   K–M 13/14

Southern tip of Florida
Area: 2186sq.miles/5661sq.km
Founded in 1947. Since 1982 declared a World Heritage Site by UNESCO.

Access

Plane, railway and bus to Miami, from there 36 miles/58km south-west on the US 1 as far as Homestead/Florida City, then on the SR 9336 to the park entrance on the east side. Although not served by regular bus services, there are organised bus tours (Gray Line, Greyhound/Trailways) and hire-cars.

Limited access from the Tamiami Trail (US 41) at Shark Valley 35 miles/56km west of Miami (tramtours, only during the dry season) and at Everglades City. From here there are no road connections with Flamingo or with the east entrance.

Opening times

The national park is open all the year round. The best time to visit, however, is during the winter months, especially around the end of the dry season (March/April). During the predominantly hot and humid summer months (May to November) some sort of protection from the countless mosquitoes is absolutely essential (available in the park).

Information

The Superintendent, Everglades National Park, P.O. Box 279, Homestead, FL 33030; tel. (305) 247–62 11.

★★Nature reserve

The Everglades National Park is an area of sub-tropical wetland famous for its alligators and countless species of birds. Called appropriately "Pa-hay-okee" (grass river) by the Indians, it is the southern and last remaining part of an area of swamp and marshland which originally covered a third of the Florida peninsula. In the north and east the Everglades have for the most

Mangroves . . .   *. . . and swamp-orchids in the Everglades*

part been turned into fertile agricultural land through drainage schemes. Right up to the boundaries of the National Park, in fact, the land is now being put to agricultural use (notably for the cultivation of winter vegetables for the northern states). Prior to these drainage schemes the Everglades often used to be under water for up to nine months in the year. The special charm of this exotic landscape, which scarcely begins to reveal itself to the hurrying motorist, lies in its unusually rich sub-tropical, partly tropical, unique flora and fauna, as well as its wilderness, which is largely untouched and therefore highly inaccessible. It is necessary to have plenty of time and preferably a boat (boat trips, boat hire in Flamingo City and Everglades City at the western end). It is also very worth while to take part in one of the guided walks through the park. Many visitors are often disappointed during the summer months, because they manage to see relatively few birds or alligators. During the rainy season large areas of the park stand under water, and consequently the animals find a rich diet available to them wherever they go. It is only during the dry winter season that they concentrate on the few places where there is water. Then millions of migratory birds make a stop in the park. Today this unique wilderness with its highly sensitive ecosystem is under severe threat from agricultural development and the incredibly rapid growth in the built-up areas along the east and west coasts. The Everglades form an important store of drinking water.

The reclamation of the wilderness swamps was at first hailed as a major technological feat. Today for many people it represents a complete ecological disaster. For a long time it was believed that making the Everglades into a kind of unapproachable island by designating it a national park under special protection would be sufficient to preserve it. This great natural wetland however lives from water. A stream of freshwater only 6 in./15cm deep, yet 50 miles/80km wide (Shark River Slough), flows very gradually (about 33yd/30m a day) into a scarcely perceptible river-bed through the Everglades, which begins in central Florida in the basin of the Kissimmee River to the north of Lake Okeechobee and finally empties into Florida Bay with an overall drop in altitude of just 15ft/4·6m. The construction of dykes and canals, and the diversion of water for irrigation purposes and to supply the urban area of Miami, today endanger the continued existence of the national park. The reduction in the water reaching the park has also increased the danger of fire in the park. The canals also bring into the park chemicals used in pest control and excess quantities of phosphates and nitrates (in particular from sugar-cane fields and excrement from the intensively farmed grazing areas around Lake Okeechobee), thereby disturbing the ecological balance. By 1995 therefore it is intended that the number of grazing cattle should have been reduced by a third and that the effluents from grazing lands be channelled into special reservoirs, so that no more polluted water can flow into the potentially eutrophic areas of Lake Okeechobee and the Everglades. At the present time agrochemicals are also still penetrating the freshwater table and thus endangering the animal and plant life as well as hastening the process of karst weathering. In the areas near the coast excessive extraction of the ground water has overall had the effect of causing an influx of saltwater (however not just in the Everglades but in the whole of South Florida!).

When the national park was set up in 1947, the Shark River Slough went through its boundary. For the sake of the preservation of the Everglades important areas, the East Everglades, were separated off. In 1989/1990 a law was passed protecting the national park and promoting its extension. By the middle of the 1990s around 17sq.miles/44sq.km of the East Everglades are to be added to the national park with the aim of re-establishing the natural hydrological conditions.

At first glance the landscape of the Everglades – a primeval marshland wilderness with a grassland morass – seems extremely monotonous because it is all more or less on one level. It is fascinating however how differences of altitude of sometimes less than one metre result in divergent

Ecology

Everglades National Park

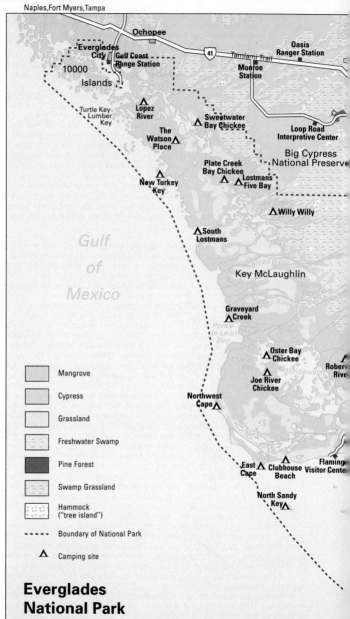

Everglades National Park

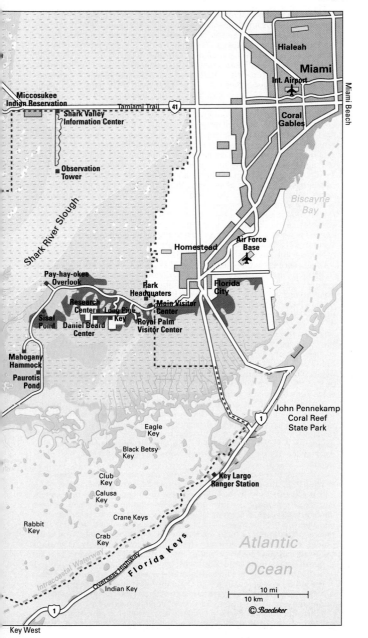

Miami Beach

Miccosukee
Indian Reservation

Tamiami Trail 41

Shark Valley
Information Center

Observation
Tower

Shark River Slough

Pay-hay-okee
Overlook

Research
Center   Long Pine
Key

Sisal
Pond   Daniel Beard
Center

Mahogany
Hammock

Paurotis
Pond

Hialeah

Miami

Int. Airport

Coral
Gables

Biscayne
Bay

Homestead   Air Force
Base

Park
Headquaters

Main Visitor
Center

Royal Palm
Visitor Center

Florida
City

John Pennekamp
Coral Reef
State Park

Eagle
Key

Black Betsy
Key

Club
Key

Calusa
Key

Crane Keys

Rabbit
Key

Crab
Key

Indian Key

Key Largo
Ranger Station

Atlantic

Ocean

Florida Keys

Intracoastal Waterway

Overseas Highway

10 mi
10 km
© Baedeker

Key West

ecosystems. In the shallow waters of Florida Bay there are countless tiny mangrove islands and in the coastal area almost impenetrable mangrove thickets or steppes composed of salt-resistant grasses and other plants, sometimes even succulents ("coastal prairie"). In the interior there is mainly wetland around the broad freshwater affluents or sloughs, with isolated "hammocks" perched on slight eminences (e.g. on former Indian "mounds") with growths of hardwood and tree-islands, which generally protrude just a few inches out of the water, with mahogany trees, evergreen oaks (live-oak), palmetto (palms), strangler figs, and gumbo-limbo trees. Incidentally the last-named are fondly called "tourist trees" by the locals because of their smooth red, often peeling, bark. These hammocks are surrounded by a kind of ditch which protects them well from the grass fires which occasionally flare up during the dry season. In summer the flat areas near the "grass rivers" are covered by several inches of water. In the shallower water rushes up to one yard high predominate, while in the areas of deeper water there is reed-grass (*Cladium Jamaicense*; as much as 11½ft/3·5m long), which can form an inpenetrable barrier and is called "sawgrass" on account of its sharp, toothed edges. At the end of the dry winter season, however, sharp-edged white barrows appear everywhere where the exposed limestone or karst is not hidden under a layer of marl. In the area to the west of the park entrance there are woods of thinly scattered pines (Elliott pines) on chalky, somewhat higher ground. Between the national park and Lake Okeechobee there are extensive cypress swamps (Big Cypress National Preserve) where impermeable layers of marl cover the porous sediments of chalk.

On the access road to the park near Rock Reef Pass, a chalk ridge about 3–7ft/1–2m high, there are sparse cypress woods (Dwarf Cypress Forest; a variety of the leafless cypress) where humus or chalky mud collect in the holes where the chalk has dissolved. In spite of their scanty growth the trees, which in the winter months are completely bare, can grow for more than 100 years.

History

The Seminole Indians were resident in Southern Florida from the middle of the 18th c., but were decimated in the battles between 1835 and 1842, most of the survivors then being moved to Indian territory in Oklahoma. Today only a few families are still living in the nature reserve. There are settlements along the Tamiami Trail and in three reservations in the northern part of the park composed of Seminoles who fled into the impenetrable wilderness before the enforced deportation took place.

It was not until the end of the 19th c. that a start was made on the exploration and reclamation of the swamp areas. The early settlers lived mainly from fishing, hunting herons (their silver feathers were particularly fashionable around the turn of the century) or harvesting tree bark for use in tanning. An additional source of income lay in the sale of mahogany. As early as the 16th c. mahogany trees were being felled by Spanish shipbuilders.

At the beginning of the 20th c. the Everglades started to be cleared. First of all in 1909 the Miami Canal was completed, linking Lake Okeechobee with the Miami River. In the following years an ingenious system of canals and dams was built. In 1926 and 1928 two hurricanes caused serious damage to the area, driving water out of the Everglades into Lake Okeechobee and over the low dykes. Thousands of settlers drowned, which led the federal government to build the Hoover Dyke around the lake. The Everglades were thus cut off from their natural water supply. Droughts occurred, causing fires to get out of control quickly and countless animals to perish. The farmers were soon to discover that in winter their dry ground would burn as easily as tinder. These fires would often spread for miles.

The fertile layer of topsoil would dry to the finest dust and be blown away or, if the rains did start, be washed into the canals. Today it is estimated that during the last 70 years up to 5ft/1·5m of soil has been lost.

If this situation is allowed to continue, the underlying porous limestone will be exposed in numerous places within the next 25 years. In the 1940s people began to make conjectures about the ecological interaction between the various environmental factors and possible effects on the complete ecosystem of Southern Florida and its supplies of ground water.

In 1947, after many years of unsuccessful efforts, the Everglades National Park was set up. As early as the beginning of the century the Audubon company attempted to protect the environment of the area, initially by preserving the stocks of silver herons. Areas were identified where it was forbidden to hunt. 1916 marked the setting-up of the Royal Palm State Park on Paradise Key at the edge of the Taylor Slough. In 1929 an Everglades National Park Commission was formed, but lacked the necessary powers to buy up the land required for a park. In 1934 the American Congress formally approved the setting-up of the national park but again still withheld the appropriate powers to realise the scheme. Not until the end of the Second World War and after a campaign waged by John D. Pennekamp in the "Miami Herald" was it possible to acquire some of the land needed. Many people who owned land in the Everglades made it available for the project. A large share of the credit for preserving the Everglades must also go to Marjorie Stoneman-Douglas, daughter of the founder of the "Miami Herald", in whose honour a visitors' centre is named.

In 1971 Congress finally passed a law ensuring that an adequate supply of water reached the national park and in 1974 another nature conservancy area, the Big Cypress National Preserve (see entry), was set up.

At the present time the park is being extended into the East Everglades. With the help of modern computer techniques, an attempt is being made to control the distribution of water in Southern Florida. Despite this, however, the continued existence of the Everglades remains threatened. In August 1988, when the fields were flooded after heavy falls of rain, the canals were opened. A flood wave of freshwater poured into the saltwater coastal areas and partially destroyed the finely balanced environmental conditions in which marine animals grow and on which the thousands of marsh and sea birds depend. Then, when there was a prolonged period of drought in 1989 and stocks of water became low, to the extent that the inhabitants of the Miami conurbation were facing restrictions, the national park received no water at all for a period of 37 weeks!

The Everglades are a wilderness area. When walking away from the established paths, and when camping and picnicking, it is essential to take certain safety precautions. The poisonous coral snake, the black water moccasin snake, which can grow up to 10ft/3m long, the diamondback snake and a kind of dwarf rattlesnake can all be found here. *Snakes, alligators, poisonous plants and other dangers*

It is necessary to watch out for alligators and also raccoons, which like to beg for food and sift through left-overs. Feeding animals in the park is strictly forbidden.

There are also poisonous plants in the park, for instance the poison ivy (*rhus radicans*) or poisonwood (*metopium toxiferum*), a relation of the stag's horn sumac. Any contact with these plants, especially with their sap, can cause serious illness.

Sights

Information about the national park can be obtained at the visitor center (open: daily 8am–5pm) 11 miles/17km west of Homestead. It is well worth joining the guided walks and canoe trips. During the summer rainy season, however, the programme of outings is somewhat restricted. There is also a film which deals with the special features of this unique nature park. *Visitor center*

After about 2 miles/3km a road branches off leading to the Royal Palm Visitor Center. Here in the Royal Palm Hammock there are a number of tall king palms. The Anhinga Trail, which is well worth following even in summer, branches off at the visitors' centre. But it is in the dry season, *Royal Palm Visitor Center, ★Anhinga Trail, Gumbo Limbo Trail*

A dolphin not in captivity . . .   *. . . and an osprey at its nest*

especially, that this wooden walkway, which is just ½ mile/1km long and leads into the Taylor Slough (a very slow-flowing freshwater stream), offers the visitor the best opportunities to observe the animals. With a little luck and patience one can see alligators, turtles, herons or anhingas, a type of bird with a snake-like neck related to the cormorant which can spear fish under water with its long beak. After a catch the bird sits for a long time almost motionless with its wings outstretched, drying its feathers.

The Gumbo Limbo Trail, which is also ½ mile/1km long, leads in the opposite direction. Here it is possible to see one of the characteristic tree-islands, a hardwood "hammock", with its densely growing evergreen oaks, as well as king palms. gumbo limbo trees and wild coffee, closely overgrown with epiphytes, ferns and orchids.

Long Pine Key

The next turn-off leads after 6 miles/10km to Long Pine Key Camp Ground on the shores of a small lake. Here the visitor can experience a quite different type of scenery. Various paths lead through an airy pine forest, the undergrowth of which is extraordinarily varied. More than 200 different types of plants can be found here, including some 30 which hitherto have only been found in the Everglades.

★Pa-ha-okee
Overlook Trail

After another 6 miles/10km there is a short walk of about 400 yards which leads to a small observation platform affording a good view across the Pa-ha-okee (=grass river). Information boards explain about the cycle of rain, drought and fire which led to the formation of the Everglades. Of interest on the approach road are the characteristic pond cypresses, standing well apart from one another, which are bare during the winter and give the impression of being dead.

★Mahogany
Hammock Trail

7 miles/11km further on, a wooden walkway leads from the car park through another tree-island. Here there are massive old mahogany trees growing among the thickets, including the oldest one in the USA. Of special interest are the colourful little liguus tree-snails.

On the edge of the hammock can be found the rare paurotis palm, which does not flourish anywhere else in the USA.

11 miles/18km further on, a wooden walkway just under ½ mile/1km long leads through the mangroves along the bank of West Lake (a saltwater lake). The visitor is here in a transitional area between the interior of the park and the coast. By close inspection it is possible to distinguish the various types of mangrove: red, black and white mangroves as well as buttonwood. The red mangrove with its bent roots protruding above surface level is the most widespread.

West Lake Trail

Flamingo, the only tourist centre in the park, is situated on Florida Bay. It has a natural history exhibition, restaurant (generally closed in summer), campsite, petrol station, marina and boat and canoe rental. Flamingo Lodge offers simple accommodation. The rare pink spoonbill, often confused with the flamingo, can occasionally be seen.

Flamingo

Flamingo itself was originally a small fishing village. Before the national park was set up, its few inhabitants attempted to earn a living from charcoal burning, farming (vegetables and sweet potatoes were sold to Key West), making sugar-cane syrup and collecting heron feathers. Because of this the majestic silver heron and the pink spoonbill came very close to extinction. During Prohibition alcohol was also illicitly distilled here.

When the national park was set up in 1947 some of these illegal distilleries were discovered in remote areas.

At the harbour in Flamingo houseboats can be rented providing a peaceful way of exploring the hinterland. Excursion boats also depart from Flamingo several times a day on tours through the mangroves (restricted service in summer). Park supervisors explain the natural history of the area. In the evening a Sunset Cruise enables one to experience nightfall in Florida Bay, while in winter there are conducted tours through the wilderness.

A canoe trip on the 3 mile/5km-long Buttonwood Canal to Coot Bay is well worth doing at any time of the year. The visitor will come across

One of the last crocodiles in the Everglades

A board-walk in Shark Valley

alligators and large numbers of birds. Occasionally one of the very rare American crocodiles can be seen.

A popular canoe trip is one taking in Buttonwood Canal, Coot Bay and Mud Lake and going as far as Bear Lake (12 miles/19km; about 6 hours; in summer not recommended because of mosquitoes). In good weather canoe trips are also possible on the shallow waters of Florida Bay. Almost one third of the park area falls within Florida Bay, a maze of tiny islands and promontories to the west of the keys. Large parts of the bay as well as most of the islands are closed to visitors to protect colonies of breeding birds as well as the endangered American crocodile.

Snake Bight (good for bird-watching at low tide) or Bradley Key are also favourite places to visit. Anyone taking part in the canoe trip to Cape Sable will need to make an overnight stop here, though a stay on the shell covered beach can be made unbearable during the rainy season by the swarms of mosquitoes and sandflies.

The 100 mile/160km-long Wilderness Waterway from Flamingo to Everglades City will not appeal to all visitors, involving as it does a week's travel by canoe (special permit essential). At certain points along the route there are "chickees" or wooden platforms, which have chemical toilets and where a small tent can be pitched for the night. This canoe trip offers a unique experience of the natural world. Here among the mangroves, vast numbers of fish, turtles, water birds of different types and inquisitive manatees can be seen.

Closer acquaintance with this primordial landscape can be made by taking one of the trails in the Flamingo area, for instance Christian Point Trail (4 miles/6km), Snake Bight Trail (4 miles/6km), Rowdy Bend Trail (5 miles/8km), as well as the longer Coastal Prairie Trail (13 miles/21km), which was once used by cotton-pickers and fishermen. Some of these trails pass through scenery which one would not expect to find in the Everglades. In the "Coastal Prairie" with its highly porous limestone subsoil there are agaves, yucca plants and even cacti. Snake Bight Trail, which passes through a tropical tree-island, ends with a wooden walkway which is ideal for bird watching.

Bear Lake Trail, 2 miles/3km long, begins at the end of the unmade-up Bear Lake Road, which runs parallel to Buttonwood Canal and leads through a dense hardwood tree-island and mangrove thickets to Bear Lake.

Bear Lake Trail

One section of Shark Valley is accessible, but only from the Tamiami Trail (US 41; approx. 30 miles/48km west of Miami). If the path is not under water it is possible to make a 15 mile/24km round trip and gain an impression of the interior of the Everglades and observe some of the animals characteristic of this part of Shark River Slough, such as alligators, turtles, otters, racoons, deer, wood storks and a wealth of waterfowl (guided tours). The area is also popular for walking and cycling trips (cycle rental available; information: tel. 305–221–8455). The 66ft/20m high observation tower at the vertex of the path offers an excellent view of Shark River Slough and the "Saw Grass Prairie". Display boards give information about various aspects of the ecosystem. The area has been made accessible by a number of short paths. The Bobcat Hammock Trail (about ½ mile/1km, wooden walkway) and the Heron View Trail, which runs parallel to East Loop Road and has a bird-watching platform, are not just of interest to ornithologists.

Shark Valley

See entry

Miccosukee Indian Village

See entry

Everglades City

Fernandina Beach

See Amelia Island

Florida Bay   L/M 13/14

Monroe County

Florida Bay extends like a continuation of the Gulf of Mexico between the southern tip of the mainland peninsula of Florida and the chain of islands called the Florida Keys (see entry). The shallow bay, which is interspersed by numerous coral and mangrove islands, forms part of the enormous nature conservancy area known as Everglades National Park (see entry) and is the breeding ground for a rich variety of underwater life as well as being the natural habitat of countless sea and wading birds.

Location

Florida Caverns

See Marianna

Florida Keys   L/M 12–15

Island chain lying off the southern tip of the Florida peninsula.
Monroe County

About 31 miles/50km to the south of Miami a narrow promontory of land leads to the Florida Keys (Span. cayo=reef), a chain of coral islands of varying sizes 120 miles/180km long extending between the Atlantic Ocean and the Gulf of Mexico. Until the devastating hurricane of 1935 there was a

Location and ★★area of outstanding natural beauty

117

Flying over the Keys

railway line linking the islands all the way to Key West, where ships connected with Havana in Cuba. Today the daringly designed "Overseas Highway" (US 1) crosses 42 bridges and numerous artificial causeways on its way to the southernmost point of the United States. Since 1980 the islands of Sands Key, Elliot Key, Cotton Key and Old Rhodes Key, which lie off the shores of Biscayne Bay, have formed part of the Biscayne National Underwater Park.

Key Largo	6 miles/10km; Key Largo (pop. 11,000) is the main town on the largest island of the Florida Keys (30 miles/48km long).
★John Pennekamp Coral Reef, Marine Sanctuary	East of Key Largo stretches the John Pennekamp Coral Reef State Park (22 miles by 6 miles/35km by 10km approx.) and the Key Largo National Marine Sanctuary, the only living coral reef on the USA mainland, which can be visited in glass-bottomed boats. The rich variety of underwater life and the various shipwrecks are an attraction for large numbers of snorkellers and divers. A visitor center with an interesting aquarium is to be found at Mile Marker (MM) 102·6; beaches, rental of canoes, sailing boats, diving and snorkelling equipment. Key Largo's newest attraction is in the Koblick Marine Center of the Marine Resources Development Foundation, "Jules Undersea Lodge", the first submarine hotel in the world (MM 103·5).
Christ of the Deep	At Dry Rock Reef there is a statue of Christ standing several metres under the water.
Rock Harbor, Tavernier, Plantation Key	From Key Largo the road leads on through Rock Harbor and Tavernier (9 miles/14km, pop. 2500; the actual descendants of fishermen and "shipwreckers", who migrated here from the Bahamas, known as "Conchs", still live here and cultivate principally coconuts, pineapples, Key limes and tomatoes; and then on to Plantation Key (pop. 3000). In the 19th c. this island was just a single pineapple plantation.

10 miles/16km; Islamorada (pop. 2000), a 12 mile/19km-long settlement lying across seven islands, which proudly lays claim to being the "Sportsfishing Capital of the World". There are excellent facilities for deep-sea fishing (charter boats), diving and snorkelling.

A free trolley-bus service runs between MM 103 and MM 80.

Islamorada

This underwater archaeological preserve is signed from Islamorada. Its focal point is the wreck of a silver carrying ship which sank in 1733.

San Pedro Archaeological Preserve

On Windley Key (MM 84·5), in a lagoon created by coral quarrying undertaken to build the railway, lies the Theatre of the Sea, inaugurated in 1946. The most important attractions are the sea-lions and dolphin shows, a trip on the "bottomless" boat through the dolphin lagoon and the "Dolphin Encounter", one of four places on the Keys where it is possible to swim with dolphins (advance booking essential; 9.30am–4pm displays and guided tours).

Windley Key
★Theatre of the Sea

A visit is also recommended to Indian Key State Historic Site, a presently uninhabited island, 964 acres/390ha in size, situated ½ mile/1km before reaching Lower Matecumbe Key, on which Captain J. Housman settled in 1930. The original settlement, which prospered and was for some time the administrative capital of Dade County, was destroyed by an Indian attack in 1840.

Lignumvitae Key State Botanical Site, on the bay side, is named after the tropical hardwood which is widespread on the island, but which is predominantly to be found in the Caribbean and South America. The site boasts a unique plant life which is only to be found on the Keys. A nature trail goes round the tiny island. In Matheson House, built out of coral in 1919, the way of life which existed on the Keys during the 1930s has been recreated. At MM 78·5 (Indian Key Fill) the Park Service boat departs on trips to the islands: 8.30am to Indian Key, 1.30pm to Lignumvitae Key (daily except Tues. and Wed.). Mosquito protection is strongly advised.

★Lignumvitae Key

10 miles/16km: Long Key with Long Key State Park, MM 68·5 (long sandy beach with picturesque Austral pines, beautifully situated campsite, nature trail and canoe trips available).

The road continues over the new Long Key Viaduct, at 3½ miles/5·5km the second longest bridge in the Keys, which spans picturesque Conch Key with its white beach houses and jetties and Duck Key with its exclusive hotel and expensive holiday homes.

Long Key

10 miles/16km: Grassy Key with the Dolphin Research Center, formerly known as "Flipper's Sea School" (MM 59), a private non-profit-making research centre for dolphins and other marine mammals. The television series "Flipper" was filmed here in the 1950s. The dolphins live in a natural bay divided by low fences and are able at any time to take a "holiday" by swimming off into the ocean. Generally, however, they return of their own volition after just a few days. There are learning programmes and by prior arrangement "Swimming with the Dolphins".

Grassy Key,
★Dolphin Research Center

Further on are Crawl Key and Fat Deer Key with the residential areas of Key Colony and Cocoplum Beach.

9 miles/14km: Marathon on Vaca Key, centre of the Middle Keys, is with a population of 10,000 approx. the second largest town on the Keys. A fishing village grew up here as early as the 1820s. Around the turn of the century farmers settled here from the Bahamas. In 1908, when the railway line was being built there was a large camp on Knight Bay for over 5000 building workers, and until the completion of the railway there was a regular ferry connection between here and Key West. The town also owes its name to the railway workers. Marathon experienced another boom during the Second World War, when the water conduit linking the marine base on Key

Marathon

West with the mainland was laid. In 1960, however, Hurricane Donna inflicted immense destruction. Today, with its marinas, the town enjoys an excellent reputation worldwide for sports fishing.

Crane Point
Hammock

This nature preservation area occupies 130 acres/52ha and operates as an "interactive museum", in which various species threatened with extinction can be observed.

Pigeon Key

A delightful detour can be made to Pigeon Key (5 miles/8km) with its attractive old wooden houses in the shadow of coco-palms and pines. It can only be reached from Marathon over the old Seven Miles Bridge, a partly restored old bridge which has been proudly dubbed the "longest fishing pier in the world". Until 1987 the University of Miami had a marine research centre on the island.

★Seven Miles
Bridge

The new Seven Miles Bridge, completed in 1982, leads to Bahia Honda, which counts as the beginning of the Lower Keys.

★Bahia Honda

13 miles/21km: Bahia Honda State Recreational Area (MM 37) with its unspoilt white sandy beach which is ideal for swimming, snorkelling and wind-surfing. Nature trails take the visitor through the characteristic keys landscape.

Big Pine Key,
★Key Deer Refuge

6 miles/10km: Big Pine Key, at over 10sq.miles/26sq.km the largest island in the Lower Keys, possesses in its National Key Deer Refuge a wonderful preservation area for the timid miniature deer of the Keys. The numbers of these animals, which stand only some 2ft/60cm high, were decimated to just a few hundred, and their survival is constantly under threat from the heavy motor traffic and the increasing urbanisation of the island. There are guided canoe tours and walks available. At Blue Hole, a small freshwater lake, birds, turtles and alligators and other animals can all be seen.

In the marina of Marathon

Big Pine Key, in particular Ramrod Key (MM 27·5) and Summerland Key, are starting-points for sailing, snorkelling and diving excursions to the offshore Loe Key National Marine Sanctuary (coral reef and wreck of the frigate H.M.S. "Loe" which was sunk in 1744).

Next comes Cudjoe Key, symbolised since 1980 by "Fat Albert", a massive   Cudjoe Key
white torpedo-like balloon which is equipped with a special radar system which enables it to survey the lower airspace. It is used not only for military purposes, but also is intended to help in the struggle against drug smuggling. The road leads on over Sugarloaf Key (with several marinas) and Boca Chica (naval air base) to Stock Island and thence to Key West.

30 miles/48km; see entry   Key West

Florida Trail   B–M 7–14

The Florida Trail is a properly marked long distance footpath crossing the   Long distance
Sunshine State. Three decades ago members of the Florida Trail Associ-   footpath
ation began to plot and mark the route of this path. Up to the present several stretches of the trail and a circular path around Lake Okeechobee (complete length: about 460 miles/740km) as well as about 500 miles/ 800km of marked connecting paths have been completed.
   The Florida Trail will eventually be 1250 miles/2000km long and link Gulf Island National Seashore at Pensacola with the Big Cypress National Preserve between Naples and Miami. The path goes through largely untouched countryside, at the present time beginning with a marked trail through Blackwater River State Forest. Then from the Apalachicola National Forest the trail leads through St Mark's National Wildlife Refuge to the Suwannee River and then through Osceola Forest and Ocala National Forest to central Florida. Several detours take in interesting wildlife areas. Some stretches of the path are well suited to walks lasting a single day. The trail should however only be attempted by experienced walkers, who can spend the night in the simple campsites or in the open air on the hunting preserves.
   Information and tours: Florida Trail Association, P.O. Box 13708, Gainesville, FL 32604; tel. (904) 378–8823, 1–800–343–1882 (only within Florida).

Fort Lauderdale   K 15

Broward County
Altitude: 0–10ft/0–3m
Population: 153,000

Broward Boulevard and Andrews Avenue form a kind of system of co-   Layout of the
ordinates. It is from here that all the street numbering begins and as in   town
Miami and other American towns the streets are given the additional lettering NW, NE, SW and SE, depending on the quadrant in which they fall, with avenues, ways, roads and terraces running in a north–south direction and streets, places, drives and courts from east to west.

The town of Fort Lauderdale, administrative seat of Broward County,   Location
proudly calls itself the "Venice of America". More than 165 miles/265km of artificial waterways, navigable by boats and almost all lined with palms, cut across the town and link up the exclusive residential areas or "finger islands" with their tropical gardens and private jetties. The sheltered yachting harbour on the Intracoastal Waterway is one of the largest in the USA. More than 30,000 yachts are registered in Broward County alone. In addition there are more than 10,000 tourist boats which come here during the main winter season. Most visitors to Fort Lauderdale come because of the

6 mile/10km long beautiful sandy beach. The highway A1A (here: Seabreeze/Atlantic Blvd.) runs for the most part along the beach, while the hotel and apartment buildings only begin on the other side of the beach promenade. In the last few years Fort Lauderdale has increasingly developed into a modern commercial and industrial centre, its downtown area characterised by imposing office towers made of steel and glass. Previously shipbuilding was of considerable importance, while today to an increasing extent the companies are those of high-tech industries. However, the town has still been able to retain some of its former sophistication. Greater Fort Lauderdale today comprises 28 independent municipal districts. 70% of the approximately 1·3 million inhabitants of the conurbation were not however born here.

History

A small fort built in 1837 and named after its commander W. Lauderdale, formed the nucleus of the little settlement which started to develop in the 1880s along New River. The father of present-day Fort Lauderdale is Frank Stranahan from Ohio, who set up a trading station here in 1893, which the Seminoles made use of to sell their skins and furs. In 1896 Flagler extended his Florida East Coast Railway, taking it through the tiny settlement on New River to Miami. In 1906 drainage ditches started to be made in order to divert water from the Everglades and in 1911 Fort Lauderdale was incorporated as a settlement.

West Palm Beach

Hugh Taylor Birch State Park

In 1912 the North New River Canal to Lake Okeechobee was completed. With this a link was created with Fort Myers and the Gulf coast. In the 1920s in common with other places Broward County was gripped by the land boom.

Hollywood by the Sea was built, which by 1926 already had 20,000 inhabitants (4000 more than neighbouring Fort Lauderdale!). Hollywood was planned and developed as a completely new town by J. W. Young, a businessman from Indianopolis, who had already previously earned and lost a fortune in the Californian land boom. The ground plan of the town which he devised is, with its series of circles designed to slow down through-traffic, still recognisable today. The economic crisis of the 1930s had just as disastrous an effect on Young's fortunes as it did on those of Charlie Rodes, the other planner who had a lasting impact on the town's appearance. It was he who, using Venice as a model, created the series of parallel canals and artificial islands. In the 1930s the first college students came to Fort Lauderdale and after the Second World War the town enjoyed a colossal boom as a tourist destination.

The town became famous at a stroke at the end of the 1950s when it acquired the status of a holiday resort for college students as a result of Connie Francis and the film "Where the Boys are". *Spring Break*

Fort Lauderdale was suddenly an "in" place. Since then thousands of young people have flocked there every year for the "spring break" in order to enjoy themselves to the full. More recently, however, Fort Lauderdale has not been so busy, the high-school and college students electing to frequent other places, such as Daytona Beach.

Sights

As long ago as the 1960s efforts have made to breathe new life into the old town centre on New River. Between the river and Broward Boulevard *Downtown*

View over Fort Lauderdale

several high-rise office blocks have been built in recent years, including the ultra-modern Federal Building.

Riverwalk
An attractive 2 mile/3km-long promenade has been laid out along New River. It connects the newly built Broward Center for the Performing Arts (201 SW 5th Ave.) with the Au Rene Theater (2700 seats) and links the Community Hall (350 seats) with the Discovery Center and Stranahan House in the old town centre as well as with Las Olas Boulevard.

Historic Area
In the old town centre some buildings dating back to the turn of the century have been restored and in the district known as "Himmarshee Village" (200–500 SW 2nd St.) the studios and galleries of various artists can be found.

★Museum of Discovery and Science
Museum opened in autumn 1992 (401 SW 2nd St.). Its aim is mainly to initiate younger visitors into the world of science and technology, art and history with hands-on exhibits, a five-storey high six-channel sound IMAX cinema and special programmes of exhibits and events. Open: Mon.–Sat. 10am–5pm, Sun. noon–5pm.

King Cromartie House
King Cromartie House (229 SW 2nd Ave.), one of the oldest buildings in the town, was built on New River in 1907 by E. M. King, one of the largest builders in the region. Mementoes of the pioneer period and special exhibitions can be seen.

Schoolhouse
To the north of New River Inn stands a reconstruction of the town's first schoolhouse, built in 1899.

Historical Museum
The town's historical museum (219 SW 2nd Ave.) deals mainly with the period 1870 to 1930.

★Stranahan House
The settler Frank Stranahan, who ran a trading station and ferry here, built this house (now a museum) in 1901. Today it stands directly alongside the Henry Kinney Tunnel of the US 1 (1 Stranahan Place/Las Olas Blvd.; open: Wed., Sat. 10am–3.30pm, Fri. 10am–3.30pm and 5.30–8pm; closed in July and August).

★Las Olas Boulevard
Running between the Museum of Art and the Atlantic Ocean is Las Olas Boulevard, the attractively laid-out main shopping street of Fort Lauderdale. A sophisticated image is created by the evocative gas lamps, smart expensive boutiques, galleries, antique shops and restaurants. Every year in the middle of March the Las Olas Art Festival takes place here, in which artists from other regions of the USA participate.

Broward County Main Library
Broward County Main Library (100 S Andrews Ave.), with its highly original atrium, was built in the middle of the Central Business District during the 1980s.

★Museum of Art
The Museum of Art (1 E Las Olas Blvd.; open: Tues. 11am–9pm, Wed.–Sat. 10am–5pm, Sun. noon–5pm) was also built in the 1980s with the help of private donations. As well as Pre-columbian, Oceanic and West African art there is an important collection of paintings, sculptures and prints by various representatives of surrealism and abstract expressionism. These also include works by the widely known "Copra" group of artists, which was formed in 1948 by the Danish artist Asger Jorn.

The Strip
The section of Atlantic Boulevard between Las Olas Boulevard and Sunrise Boulevard is generally known as "The Strip". Here there are many hotels, restaurants, night-clubs and discothèques, some of the bars boasting live entertainment every evening.

Bonnet House
The gentleman's residence, Bonnet House (900 N Birch Rd.; open: Tues, Thur. and Sun. May–Nov. by arrangement; tel. 563–5393), which takes its

name from a type of lily to be found in the nearby Everglades, is situated right by the Atlantic in the middle of a large garden. The estate once belonged to the painter Frederick Bartlett. His studio and some of his works can be viewed.

America's craving for places where it can worship its outstanding sportsmen is embodied in the International Swimming Hall of Fame (501 Seabreeze Blvd.; open: daily 9am–5pm). Here there are mementoes of swimming stars from over 100 countries on display, including Johnny Weissmuller (later to become famous for portraying Tarzan on films) and Mark Spitz. Top-class events take place all the year round in the swimming stadium.

International Swimming Hall of Fame

Just offshore from the beach at Fort Lauderdale stretch three coral reefs where divers can explore shipwrecks. The USS "Lauderdale", which had been taken out of service, was sunk here in the summer of 1991 between Port Everglades and Hillsboro Inlet. It is hoped to create artificial coral reefs with these wrecks.

★ Coral reefs

In the marine animal park Ocean World (1701 SE 17th St. Causeway; open: daily 10am–6pm) trained dolphins, sea-lions and parrots can be seen, as well as a special underwater show. There is a pool where dolphins can be fed and stroked and another where sharks can be fed by hand.

★ Ocean World

Among the popular places to visit are Flamingo Groves (a park rich in colours with a flamingo colony), Butterfly World (brightly-coloured butterflies of every type) and Coconut Creek with its coconut palms.

Flamingo Groves, Butterfly World, Coconut Creek

Port Everglades

The harbour of Port Everglades is one of the deepest sea harbours between Norfolk and New Orleans. In 1989 the modern container terminal with its

Colour on the beach of Fort Lauderdale

railway link was opened. This, the second most important cruise harbour (over 2 million passengers every year), is also the departure point for boat trips to the Bahamas and the Caribbean.

Cruises

Day cruises can be taken on MV "SeaEscape" (daily except Sat.; casino; free telephone information 1–800–327–7400). This type of excursion is also offered by ships of the "Discovery Cruise Line" (tel. 1–800–937–4477).

Navy

Ships of the US Marines often dock here, from submarines to aircraft carriers. Visits are possible from time to time.
Information: Navy Hotline, tel. 523–3404, ext. 626.

Sea Life Viewing Area

In the Sea Life Viewing Area (Eisenhower Blvd./SE 26th St.) the visitor can feed manatees, turtles and fish. Indigenous sea-cows and large numbers of tropical fish live in the warm water, which comes from a power station's cooling process, especially during the winter months.

Convention Center

At the north end of the harbour is the ultra-modern Greater Fort Lauderdale/Broward County Convention Center (1950 Eisenhower Blvd./SE 17th St.), which was completed in 1991. This complex also includes hotels and a large shopping centre. The fountain in front of the convention centre is decorated by a 36ft/11m-high and 151ft/46m-long fish sculpture, which was fashioned by the American sculptor Kent Ullberg out of bronze.

Hugh Taylor Birch State Recreation Area

This recreational area was named after a nature-loving colonist who came here in 1893. Situated on the A1A and East Sunrise Boulevard, it has a fine bathing beach. It is possible to find examples of the original plant life of the area hereabouts. Natural history tours are organised and canoes and cycles are available for rental.

North Beach Park

A few years ago North Beach Park (3501 N Ocean Dr., Hollywood) was opened to the public.

★John U. Lloyd Beach State Recreational Area

On a still undeveloped stretch of coastline at the southern entrance to Port Everglades is the John U. Lloyd Beach State Recreational Area (6503 N Ocean Dr.). This wide 2 mile/3km-long sandy beach is one of the finest along the Atlantic coast and generally gets very busy from early morning onwards.
　　Wooden walkways lead through dunes and mangrove swamps. In the winter months there are nature walks led by guides with specialist knowledge, while at this time manatees make for the warmer waters of Whiskey Creek. Sea turtles also come here to lay their eggs on land.

Dania

Location

To the south of Fort Lauderdale and the airport lies the town of Dania (pop. 13,000), which was founded in 1896 by Danish settlers who grew tomatoes here. In 1904 Dania became the first incorporated settlement in Broward County and attempts were then made to annex Fort Lauderdale, which at that time had not yet been incorporated. Today Dania is primarily a popular winter resort with a wide sandy beach.

Main Street

Dania's Main Street is famous, numerous antique dealers having set up here in business.

Fishing Pier

Dania's Fishing Pier (100 W Dania Beach Blvd.) is almost always full of anglers. Many of the shops, which specialise in fishermen's requirements, are open 24 hours a day.

Sea Fair

In the "Sea Fair" entertainment and shopping centre, on the edge of the John U. Lloyd State Park, there are a number of ice-cream parlours and smart boutiques. Other attractions include live music, sports performances and other events. Canoes and jet-skis can also be rented here and even a round-trip on a helicopter can be booked. Trips along the Intracoastal Waterway on the "Sea Rocket" (140 passenger seats), which resembles a racing boat, are very popular.

Fort Myers
J 12

Lee County
Altitude: 0–16ft/0–5m
Population: 54,000

The town of Fort Myers, on the broad bay formed by the estuary of the Caloosahatchee River between Naples (see entry) and Sarasota (see entry) is the commercial and administrative centre of Lee County.

Location

Fort Myers achieved fame when Thomas Alva Edison established his winter residence here. The main attractions are his house, now preserved as a museum, his laboratory and the attractive subtropical garden, and

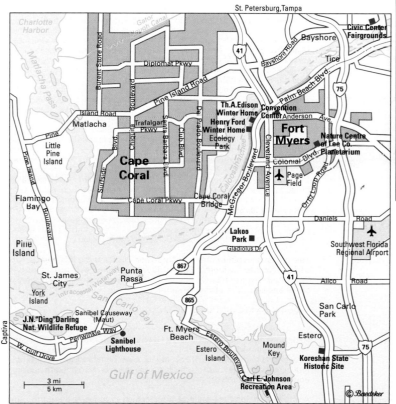

every year his birthday in February is celebrated with a spectacular light show.

There are more boats registered per head of the population here in Fort Myers than anywhere else in the United States and there are more than three dozen marinas and yachting harbours.

The Lee Island Coast is the name given to 50 miles/80km of white sandy beaches, notably on the outlying barrier islands with their almost Caribbean atmosphere. Over the last few years there has been a massive building boom here which has increasingly affected sections of coastline which until now have been largely untouched by any development.

The beaches, both on the mainland and on the offshore islands of Sanibel and Captiva, which in places are unbelievably beautiful, are home to more than 400 different types of mussel.

Those with a spirit of adventure can cross the Florida peninsula by boat on the Caloosahatchee River and the Okeechobee Waterway.

History

A wealth of archaeological finds in the Fort Myers area and on the offshore islands testifies to a settlement history stretching back some 7000 years. At the time of the Spanish conquest of Florida there was a highly developed centre of the Calusa Indian civilisation here, but even as early as the 17th/18th c. they began to be wiped out as a result of imported diseases and armed fighting with the Spanish. It is thought that the largest settlement of this tribe was on Pine Island. A fortified site, known as a "mound", serves as a reminder of this period. Starting from the place which today is called Pineland, the Indians dug an artificial canal across the island to Matlacha. Many mounds were levelled by the first white settlers who saw them as welcome ready-made material for road-building. Fort Myers itself grew out of the old Fort Harvie which was set up here during the Seminole War of 1841/42. Between 1850 and 1858 the fort was occupied once again and named after a Lieutenant A. C. Myers. Fort Myers was also important in the American Civil War, its garrisoned troops being engaged in catching wild cattle or attacking Confederate depots in order to supply Unionist ships patrolling in the Gulf off Sanibel Island.

In 1866 the first civilian settled in the newly abandoned fort. Ten years later the first post office was set up. Theatre, school, church, banks and the first shops were all concentrated in First Street, as well as the Keystone Hotel where the inventor Thomas Edison stayed on his first visit to Fort Myers in 1885.

The railway link, coupled with an increasing stream of tourists, also occasioned by the fame of Edison, who had established his winter residence here, created the conditions for a development boom in this small town during the 1920s. In the thirties North Fort Myers was established on the other side of the river. The region registered its largest period of growth, however, in the seventies and eighties as new housing and holiday developments were built in Cape Coral and other places.

Shopping

The largest shopping centre in south-west Florida is the Edison Mall (US 41/Colonial Blvd.), with more than 150 retail shops and 18 restaurants. At Royal Palm Square (1400 Colonial Blvd.) there are another four dozen or so shops and bars in an attractive setting.

Sights

Downtown

At the local Chamber of Commerce (1365 Hendry St., tel. 334–1133; open: Mon.–Fri. 9am–4.30pm) a leaflet is available which sets out a circular walk through the historic centre of Fort Myers. Even here there has been extensive renovation work during the last few years. It is well worth walking down First Street, the old main street of the town.

Burroughs Home

A good example of the style of architecture in vogue at the turn of the century is provided by Burroughs Home (2505 First Street; conducted tours

Edison's winter residence

by arrangement, tel. 332–1229), which has just recently been substantially renovated.

The Palm Alley of Fort Myers is famous. For a distance of 15½ miles/25km, king palms imported from Cuba line the length of McGregor Boulevard which leads to the Gulf coast. They were planted in 1900 at the instigation of Thomas Edison who wanted to make the road going past his estate more attractive.

★Palm Alley

The most important place to visit in Fort Myers is Seminole Lodge, the estate of Thomas Alva Edison (2350 McGregor Blvd.; open: Mon.–Sat. 9am–4pm, Sun. 12.30–4pm). On a boat trip down the Caloosahatchee River during the 1880s, the American inventor Thomas Alva Edison saw Fort Myers for the first time. Impressed by the abundance of bamboos growing along the river, he decided to build his new winter residence here. At that time he was experimenting with bamboo fibres, which he was using as filaments in his new electric lights. He had, moreover, been advised by his doctors to spend the winters in a warmer climate. In 1886 he had a holiday home built by the Caloosahatchee River where in the end he was to spend 46 winters. The various sections of the building, which were prepared out of pinewood in the state of Maine, using Edison's own designs, were brought to the Gulf coast by ship. Edison's holiday home is thus one of America's first prefabricated houses.

★Thomas Alva Edison Winter Home

In front of the entrance to the house there is an Indian banyan tree with long branching roots. This was given to Edison in 1925 by his friend, the rubber and tyre manufacturer, Harvey Firestone, who often stayed in Fort Myers himself. Edison was very interested in plants, not just those which were a source of fibres but also indigenous latex-bearing plants, the juices of which were suited to rubber production. Together with Henry Ford and Harvey Firestone he founded the Edison Botanical Research Company in 1920.

World's first electric light bulb

The swimming-pool which Edison installed in his garden was one of the first of its kind in the American South.

The main house and the visitors' house are still fitted out as they were during the inventor's lifetime. They are lit by electric light bulbs which Edison produced in 1912.

Seminole Lodge was for a long time only accessible by boat from the Caloosahatchee River. Edison's guests were therefore often compelled to pay quite long visits.

In his workroom and laboratory Edison devised and developed a large number of epoch-making technical innovations. His inventions led him to acquire well over 1000 patents. There is a small museum which deals with the high points of his illustrious career.

★Henry Ford
Winter Home

Since 1990 it has also been possible to visit the neighbouring winter residence of the automobile manufacturer Henry Ford, known as "Mangoes". Ford, who was the first person to produce cars in series, acquired the residence in 1916 and used to spend the winter months here close to his friend Thomas A. Edison, until the latter's death in 1931. In 1945 he sold Mangoes and in 1988 the house came into the possession of the town of Fort Myers. Today the villa is set out again just as it was in Henry Ford's lifetime.

Historical
Museum

The Fort Myers Historical Museum (2300 Peck Street; open: Mon.–Fri. 9am–4.30pm, Sun. 1–5pm) is situated in the buildings of the old Peck Street Station, which ceased being used in 1971 but has subsequently been restored. Of particular interest is the section devoted to the culture of the Calusa Indians, a historical model of the town, and "Esperanza", a private Pullman railway wagon built in 1930.

Nature Center
and Planetarium
of Lee County

On Ortiz Avenue, not far from the motorway I-75, is the site of the Nature Center and Planetarium of Lee County. Information about various different biotopes (e.g. pinewoods and cypress swamps) is presented here. The free-flight aviary and a planetarium (laser show on Fri./Sat. evenings) are also enjoyable to visit.

Boat trips

Everglades Jungle Cruises, Fort Myers Yacht Basin (tel. 334–7474), offer various excursions. During the winter high season there are trips down the Caloosahatchee River from Fort Myers Yacht Basin on the "Fort Myers Princess" (Information: tel. 275–9716). There are also sailing trips lasting several hours out into the Gulf of Mexico which leave from the Gulf Star Marina at Fort Myers Beach.

Fort Myers Beach, Estero Island

Location

Fort Myers Beach is a seaside resort, situated on the narrow 7 mile/11km long Estero Island, especially popular with families with children. The sandy beach falls away very gradually. All types of water-sports can be enjoyed here and in the marina there are large numbers of charter boats available for sailing and deep-sea fishing. In winter the shallow waters of Estero Bay are the mooring-place for a large fishing fleet. There is a promenade with small shops and restaurants.

Shrimp Festival

The local "Shrimp Festival" takes place every year in the first half of March.

History

In 1566 the Spanish conqueror Pedro Menéndez de Avila had a small fort built here, but the first Anglo-American settler, Robert Gilbert, did not come to this sandy island until 1898.

★Carl E. Johnson
Recreation Area

On the southern end of the island lies the Carl E. Johnson Recreation Area with the small island of Lovers Key. A tram tour leads through the man-

Estero Island

grove thicket and over a wooden bridge spanning Oyster Bay to the island itself, which has a superb tree-lined sandy beach which only really gets busy at weekends.

Surroundings

About 12 miles/20km to the east at Alva (19050 SR 80 E) one of Florida's new wine-growing estates can be visited. There is wine-tasting (white and rosé wines), a tram tour through the vineyard and a nature trail.

Eden Vineyards

About 16 miles/25km to the south on the Estero River, the Koreshan State Historic Site, an unusual pioneer settlement, is reached (South US 41/ Corkscrew Rd., Estero; open: daily 9am–4pm). It was here around the turn of the century that a religious sect sought to realise its vision of the perfect town. Koreshanity, one of America's strangest sects, was founded by the dominant personality of Dr Cyrus Read Teed of Chicago at the end of the 19th c. After a "vision", he changed his name to Koresh (i.e. Cyrus in Hebrew) and brought his followers – mainly town-dwellers and intellectuals – to Florida, in order to lead a pure and genuine life in the wilderness by the Estero River. The followers of Koreshanity lived a life of celibacy in communes and there were no individual possessions. Teed was convinced that his new sect would develop into one of the world's great religions. He therefore planned a city for 10 million inhabitants which, with its broad avenues, would extend for more than 100 miles/160km. However, when Teed died in 1908, his sect expired with him.

Koreshan State Historic Site

The River Nature Trail along the Estero River is very attractive. The river, which is rich in fish, is also a popular canoeing route (canoe rental available nearby). There is a campsite and also a camp-fire programme organised by the park rangers.

Estero River Nature Trail

131

St Lucie County
Altitude: 0–26ft/0–8m
Population: 37,000

Location

The town of Fort Pierce is the administrative and commercial centre of the predominantly rural St Lucie County. It is situated on the section of coast between Palm Beach and Cape Canaveral (see entries), known as "Treasure Coast", which is still relatively uncrowded. The hinterland is characterised by large expanses of grazing land, fields of vegetables and citrus plantations.

The town itself lies on the west bank of the Indian River (see entry), which is here spanned by two bridges leading to the offshore island. North and South Hutchinson Island are separated by the narrow Fort Pierce Inlet. Both islands have excellent sandy coral beaches. In previous centuries many ships were dashed to pieces on the outlying coral reefs.

History

The area around Fort Pierce was a settlement area of the Tequesta Indians in pre-Columbian times. From 1838 to 1842, during the Seminole Wars, there was a fort here. In the course of time, a settlement grew up here but it was not incorporated until 1901.

Since the 1970s Fort Pierce has been affected by the general drift in population to Southern Florida.

Sights

St Lucie County
Historical Museum

The local museum at the eastern end of South Bridge gives an introductory look at the history of settlements in the area. The Seminoles are given as much coverage as the Spanish era (which includes treasures from the Spanish galleons which came to grief along the coast). Gardner House (414 Seaway Drive; open: Tues.–Sat. 10am–4pm, Sun. noon–4pm) has been restored and is fitted out in the turn-of-the-century style.

★Fort Pierce Inlet
State Recreation
Area

The Fort Pierce Inlet State Recreation Area is 340 acres/138ha in size and lies at the south end of North Hutchinson Island between the Atlantic and Indian River (about 4 miles/6km east of the A1A). It includes a popular beach at Fort Pierce Inlet (small quay, nature trail through characteristic coastal woods), the very attractive Pepper Beach as well as the mangrove-covered Jack Island. In winter many different types of sea and wading birds can be observed.

UDT-Seal
(Frogman)
Museum

The UDT-Seal (Frogman) Museum (3300 North A1A; open: Tues.–Sat. 10am–4pm, Sun. noon–4pm) in North Hutchinson Island Pepper Park gives information about the submarine combat units of the US Marines and their training.

"Urca de Lima"
Underwater
Archaeological
Preserve

In the summer of 1715 a convoy of Spanish merchant ships making the crossing from Cuba to Europe ran into a hurricane just off the Florida coast. The "Urca de Lima", richly laden with vanilla, cocoa and other tropical goods, ran aground off Pepper Beach. Since the 1920s divers have made efforts to explore the wreck. So far only a dozen cannon and a few anchors have been recovered. The ship evidently had no precious metals on board.

The Savannas

The recreation area known as the Savannas (1400 E Midway Rd.), which is more than 500 acres/202ha in size, is particularly attractive to children, having a "stroking" zoo, a botanic garden and a small lake. There is also a campsite.

Fort Walton Beach   B 3

Okaloosa County
Altitude: 0–26ft/0–8m. Population: 22,000

The family resort of Fort Walton Beach is situated on the north-western Gulf   Location
coast, at the west end of Choctawhatchee Bay, which is 29 miles/47km long
and as much as 8 miles/13km wide. This, the largest settlement on the coast
between Pensacola and Panama (see entries), is also an important garrison
of the US armed forces. Eglin Air Force Base, which lies inland from Fort
Walton Beach, is, with its 30,000 employees, one of the largest US military
bases.

The existence of many shopping centres with branches of the large
American department stores, as well as several high-ranking educational
establishments, emphasises the importance of the town as a centre for a
large surrounding area.

A small industrial park, which was built at Fort Walton Beach in the 1980s,
has been welcomed in the locality.

The original Indian inhabitants had been living in this coastal region for the   History
best part of 10,000 years. About 500 years ago Indians adhering to the
Mississippi culture erected hills known as "mounds" for their ritualistic
needs. During the American Civil War the few white settlers of Santa Rosa
and Walton County formed the "Walton Guards" who guarded the eastern
entrance to Pensacola and the Santa Rosa Sound. Some of them came back
to the coast at the end of the war. One of these first settlers was J. T. Brooks.
The settlement which originally began life as Brooks Landing became in
the course of time Fort Walton Beach.

By the end of the 1930s Eglin Air Force Base had been established here
and right up to the present day it has been one of the decisive economic and
development factors in the life of the region.

A desolate stretch of the beaches of Fort Walton

Sights

★Indian Temple
Mound Museum

It is well worth visiting the Indian Temple Mound Museum (139 Miracle Strip Parkway/Highway 98; open: Mon.–Sat. 9am–4pm June–Aug.; Mon.–Fri. 11am–4pm, Sat. 9am–4pm rest of year). On an artificially erected hill, an Indian shrine has been faithfully reproduced. The nearby museum explains about the different Indian civilisations as well as the development of the region during the colonial period.

Air Force
Armament
Museum

Anyone interested in military aircraft and weapons should visit the Air Force Armament Museum (open: daily 9.30am–4.30pm) at the main entrance to Eglin Air Force Base.

Gulfarium

Situated right by the sea, the "Gulfarium" (on Okaloosa Island; US 98) is a marine zoo (open: all the year round 9am–dusk; dolphin displays daily 10am, noon, 2pm and 4pm).

Santa Rosa Island,
★★Gulf Island
National Seashore

Lying offshore from Fort Walton Beach is the narrow coral island of Santa Rosa, which extends about 50 miles/80km westwards as far as Pensacola (see entry). The eastern tip of the island is known as "Okaloosa Island". Large areas of its deserted sandy beaches and band of dunes, with their characteristic flora of marram grass, magnolias and palmetto scrub, form a nature conservancy area known as Gulf Island National Seashore.

Gulf coast

The drive along the Gulf coast passes through much attractive scenery. The route follows Highway US 98 as far as Destin (see entry) and then continues along the Florida State Road 30-A to Panama City Beach (see entry).

Gainesville

C 11

Alachua County
Altitude: 187ft/57m
Population: 85,000

Location

The university town of Gainesville is situated in the north of Central Florida and is the administrative capital of the predominantly rural Alachua County. The town is famous as the seat of the University of Florida, which was founded in 1853 and is the oldest and, with more than 30,000 students, also the biggest high school in the "Sunshine State". Its superb sports and training facilities as well as its mild climate all the year round mean that it attracts athletes from all over the world. The appearance of the town is characterised by its many lakes and green spaces.

History

The present settlement was founded in 1854. The name goes back to General Edmund Gaines, who led the American troops in the Second Seminole War (1835–42). Before that, however, there existed a small Indian settlement in this area. In the 1820s American settlers occupied the land, which the Seminoles had been forced to evacuate after the Treaty of Moultrie Creek (commemorative sign in Westside Park, NW 34th St./NW 8th Ave.). During the Second Seminole War the American settlers built a small fort. Some of them also formed the "Spring Crove Guards", who carried out defensive patrols in the surrounding area.

Sights

Northeast Historic
District, Thomas
Center

Protected by a preservation order, the Northeast Historic District (63 blocks of houses with almost 300 at least partially restored buildings) provides eloquent testimony of the diversity of building styles which were prized between 1880 and 1930. Only the bell-tower remains of the old courthouse of 1886, however (E University Ave./NE 1st St.) In the Neo-Classical Thomas

Center (306 NE 6th Ave.; open: Mon.–Fri. 9am–5pm, Sun. 1–4pm) there are temporary exhibitions and various other events. The former post office today houses the Hippodrome State Theatre (25 SE 2nd Place).

The Florida Museum of Natural History, on the historic campus of the University of Florida in the west of the town, is well worth a visit (Museum Rd./Newell Drive; open: Tues.–Sat. 10am–5pm, Sun. 1–4pm). This museum has one of the best natural history exhibitions in the United States. The habitats typical of Florida (fossil sites, savanna, mangrove thicket, deciduous hammock, cave) can all be seen on diorama. The anthropological-ethnographical section of the museum with its reconstructions of a Maya temple and an Indian village are also of great interest.

Some of the university buildings date from the last century and are built in the historicist style. Visitors to the campus need a visitor's pass, which is obtainable at the main entrance (Tigert Hall, SW 13th St./SW 2nd Ave.).

★Florida Museum of Natural History, University of Florida

The Fred Bear Museum (Fred Bear Drive/Archer Rd.; open: Wed.–Sun. 10am–6pm) on the west edge of the town displays the collections (hunting trophies, history of archery since the Stone Age) of the enthusiastic archer, Fred Bear, who supported big-game hunting with bow and arrow all over the world as well as the setting-up and maintenance of national parks.

Fred Bear Museum

To the north of Archer Road there are some botanical gardens, 62 acres/25ha in size, on the shores of Lake Kanapaha (4625 SW 63rd Blvd.; open: Wed., Sat. and Sun. 9am–dusk, Mon.–Tues. and Fri. 9am–5pm). Of special note are the various types of bamboo growing there.

The name "Kanapaha" comes from the language of the Timucuan Indians and means palmetto-leaf or hut. Within the site of the botanical gardens the visitor will find numerous traces of Indian civilisation.

Kanapaha Botanical Gardens

Nature lovers will enjoy visiting Bivens Arm Nature Park (3650 S Main Street; swampland, oak-tree-islands) on the edge of the town.

Bivens Arm Nature Park

At Morningside Nature Center (3540 E University Ave.; open: daily from 8am, visitors' centre Wed.–Sun. 9am–5pm) the visitor can walk for mile after mile along tracks and wooden paths and experience the characteristic habitat of the northern areas of Central Florida. The model farm which forms part of the centre shows how small farmers managed to scrape a living here in the 19th c.

Morningside Nature Center

Surroundings

An interesting excursion can be made leaving Gainesville on the US 441 in a southerly direction. At the very edge of the town a 28 sq.mile/73 sq.km nature conservancy area begins, with swampy grassland and high wetland grasses, interspersed with the odd hardwood hammock. Paynes Prairie, a large flat basin, owes its formation to the dissolving of the limestone outcrops and constant subsidence in the area. In the 17th c. one of the largest estates of Spanish Florida existed here. In 1871 the basin was completely flooded when the drainage channels from the Alachua Sink were blocked. Paddle-steamers travelled around on the newly-formed lake. In 1891 the drainage system was suddenly freed again and for days on end the paddle-steamers lay on dry land. Today's grassland area is named after the Seminole Captain Payne, who was killed here by American soldiers in 1812. His comrades-in-arms carried out various attacks from here during the Second Seminole War. American troops pushed their way into what was still Spanish territory in order to punish the Seminoles for supplying food to the beleaguered town of St Augustine and giving refuge to slaves fleeing from the plantations in Georgia and Alabama. Paynes Prairie is an old Indian settlement area. Ceramic finds can be dated back to about 10,000 B.C.

★Paynes Prairie State Preserve

Today, Paynes Prairie, with its many ponds and three lakes, provides a habitat for large numbers of water-birds, alligators and snakes. In addition countless migratory birds, including cranes, spend the winter here. Shortly before Micanopy we leave the US 441 and, going along Park Drive, after a total of 10 miles/16km, we reach the visitors' centre with its small museum (open: 9am–5pm). From the observation tower there is a good view across the preserve. Park rangers regularly offer guided nature tours. Lake Wauberg, with its small campsite, is good for bathing.

Micanopy

The village of Micanopy 10 miles/16km further south is a perfect example of a typical Florida settlement. The main street with its junk and souvenir shops embodies American small-town life from the last century. When Hernando de Soto came through this region on his ill-fated expedition in 1539, there was a Timucuan Indian village here. The first white settlement was founded in 1821 and called Walton. The present name refers back to the leader of the Seminoles, who actively sought an agreement with the white man.

Cross Creek,
★Marjorie Kinnan
Rawlings State
Historic Site

About 15 miles/24km to the south, in Cross Creek, stands the house in which the famous American authoress and Pulitzer prizewinner Marjorie Kinnan Rawlings (1896–1953) lived from 1928 to 1941. In this typical cracker-house with its small farm, orange and pecan trees, she wrote her famous books, including "The Yearling" and "Cross Creek", in which she depicted with great sympathy the life of whites and blacks in Florida during the 1930s.

The wooden cracker-house with its typical veranda is today preserved in its original state. Since the filming of "Cross Creek" in 1983 there have been large numbers of visitors to the estate (open: Thur.–Mon. 10–11.30am, 1–4.30pm; half-hourly guided tours; Access from Micanopy on SR 346/SR 325).

In the Devil's Millhopper State Geological Site

An extremely interesting place to visit about 4 miles/6½km north-west of Gainesville is the Devil's Millhopper State Geological Site. This is a doline which was formed when the roof of a river cavern collapsed. It is thought that this happened in two stages. The doline is now about 118ft/36m deep and at its upper edge has a diameter of some 499ft/152m. In the doline, which is significantly cooler in summer, the plant life is of special interest and is not dissimilar to that of the ravines of the Appalachians, which begin some 370 miles/595km further north. From the layers of stone which have been uncovered here, geologists have been able to draw important conclusions about the past 20 million years of the earth's history. A wooden stairway leads the visitor down to the bottom of the cool lush green doline. In the visitors' centre excellent explanations are provided of the geological and natural history of the site.

★Devil's Millhopper State Geological Site

Not far from Devil's Millhopper is the San Felasco Hammock Wildlife Reserve, a nature conservancy area which is famous not only for its remarkable flora and fauna, but also for traces of pre-historic settlements in the area.

San Felasco Hammock

Gulf Islands National Seashore

B 2–5

Location: coastal zone on the Gulf of Mexico between the Mississippi Delta and Fort Walton Beach. Area: 211sq.miles/546sq.km.

The nature reserve known as Gulf Islands National Seashore takes in, besides individual areas on the mainland of north-west Florida (the "panhandle"), large parts of the long series of offshore islands and promontories which extend for over 150 miles/240km from West Ship Island (near the Mississippi Delta) as far as the east end of Santa Rosa Island near Fort

★★Nature reserve

On guard by the beach   On the coral reef

Walton Beach (see entry). The Florida section of this seashore includes parts of Perdido Key to the west of Pensacola (see entry), the Naval Live Oaks Reservation east of Gulf Breeze and the fortifications on the site of Pensacola Naval Air Station as well as a large part of Santa Rosa Island (Fort Pickens Area, Santa Rosa Day Use Area and Okaloosa Area).

The reserve is administered by the National Park Service, which also runs a visitors' centre. There are recreational facilities available on the fantastically beautiful fine-sand beaches. The remains of fortifications dating back to the first half of the 19th c. (see Pensacola) can be seen. It is not uncommon to see Americans, equipped with folding chair and cool-box, casting their fishing-line into the gentle surf (in saltwater no permit is needed for fishing). Nature trails enable the visitor to learn about the natural environment on these barrier islands. In Fort Barrancas (Pensacola Naval Air Station) there are conducted tours.

Dunes

These flat sandy barrier islands, which protect the mainland from storms, are subject to constant changes and climatic shifts (especially in a westerly direction), according to the state of the wind and current. Strong winds and hurricanes can quite easily cause partial flooding of an island and separate off parts of it. In 1979 Hurricane Frederic shifted a whole row of dunes on Santa Rosa Island. Along the Gulf of Mexico there is a band of dunes partially overgrown with marram grass. Behind these, protected from the salt spray, low trees and palmetto scrub are able to grow. Where the dunes are less recently formed there can be a sequence of small oak-trees, magnolias and pine-trees, bordered by freshwater and saltwater marshes. Herons and ospreys, various water-birds, alligators, turtles and snakes find a rich source of food here.

Perdido Key

At the eastern end of Perdido Key, which is a protected area (accessible from Pensacola on the SR 292), Johnson Beach is a popular place to bathe. Divers can explore the remains of Fort McRae, which sank into the sea off the eastern tip.

For the last few years those areas which do not form part of the nature reserve have been developed for tourism.

Big Lagoon State Recreation Area

A visit to the Gulf Island National Seashore can be completed by visiting the imaginatively developed Big Lagoon State Recreation Area on the mainland opposite (access from the SR 292A/SR 293). Various nature trails take the visitor through typical coastal scenery. From an observation tower on East Beach there is a view across to Big Lagoon and Perdido Key on the other side of the Intracoastal Waterway.

Santa Rosa Day Use Facility

Between Pensacola Beach and Navarra Beach the SR 399 stretches for miles through the dunes of Gulf Island National Seashore. The Santa Rosa Day Use Facility beach is recommended for bathing (information centre; sanitary block).

Other sights

Anyone going to Gulf Island National Seashore should not fail to visit the following places: Fort Barrancas, Pensacola Naval Air Station, Fort Pickens and Naval Live Oaks (all to be found under the entry for Pensacola), as well as Okaloosa (see Fort Walton Beach).

Pensacola

See entry

Hollywood   K 15

Broward County
Altitude: 0–13ft/0–4m
Population: 125,000

Location

The satellite town of Hollywood, sometimes also called Atlantic City of the South, is located between Miami (see entry) and Fort Lauderdale (see

Hollywood "by air"

entry). It was founded by J. Young, who had the Hollywood Beach Hotel built here during the 1930s. Recently this popular seaside resort has greatly altered in appearance. Many of the old hotels along the 4 miles/6km-long, palm tree-covered beach promenade have been replaced by large apartment blocks with souvenir shops, cafés and restaurants.

Sights

The shop-lined coastal road Ocean Walk leads to J. Young's Hollywood Beach Hotel (101 N. Ocean Drive).

Ocean Walk

Souvenirs, textiles and food made by the Indians themselves can be bought in the Seminole Indian Village (3551 SR7/Sterling Road; open: Mon.–Sat. 10am–4pm). Traditional craft techniques can also be seen here, as well as alligator and poisonous snake displays. There is also a small zoo with native animals. A bingo hall operated by the Indians (Seminole Indian Bingo, 4150 N. SR7; open: daily from noon) is situated on the other side of the road. As gambling is banned in Florida many visitors, mainly elderly tourists, come here to try their luck on Indian soil.

★Seminole Indian Village

Those not satisfied by the beaches of the Gold Coast can seek enjoyment in the Atlantis Six Flags (Water Kingdom; 2700 Stirling Road), an adventure pool with a number of slides and a wave machine.

Six Flags Atlantis

The Topeekeegee Yugnee Recreation Area (Indian = meeting place, usually called T–Y for short; 3300 N. Park Road, north of Sheridan Street) is popular with local residents. It offers a freshwater lake, water slides in the Falling Waters Swimming Lagoon, boat and canoe rental, sailing and wind surfing.

Topeekeegee Yugnee Regional Park

Surroundings of Hollywood

Hallandale
Hallandale (population 38,000) lies in the Miami catchment area. It was founded at the end of the 19th c. by Swedish immigrants and is named after their leader. Despite numerous multi-storey apartment blocks, Hallandale still retains its old, small town character. It is particularly popular with well-to-do American pensioners and tourists.

Fashion Row
A particular attraction is Discount Fashion Row (also known as Schmatta Row; Hallandale Beach Blvd./Dixie Highway), where fashion clothes, shoes and jewellery are sold very cheaply.

Hollywood
Greyhound
Dog Track
Greyhound racing takes place from Christmas until about the end of April on the track at the Hollywood Kennel Club (831 N. Federal Highway/Pembroke Road).

Gulfstream Park
Gulfstream Park extends along Hallandale Beach Boulevard. It contains the famous racecourse where the Florida Derby is held once a year. Racing takes place here almost daily from the middle of January until April.

Davie
Davie (population 36,000) lies to the west of Hallandale. It developed after 1906 with the draining of the Everglades. Many of its first settlers were employed beforehand on the building of the Panama Canal and consequently named their new hometown *Zona*. Later the settlement was named after the region's most important landowner and cattle breeder. The spirit of the Wild West pioneers still lives on in the town.

★Flamingo
Gardens
Flamingo Gardens (3750 Flamingo Road; open: daily 9am–5pm) attract many visitors. All that is symbolic of Florida can be found here; flamingoes, alligators, a lush, exotic plant world with marvellous orchids, Everglade swamps and orange trees. The hardwood tree island Pine Island Ridge Hammock is covered with evergreen oaks (live oaks), thought to be about 2000 years old, and other tall trees. Seminole artefacts are on exhibition in the Everglades Museum. This also has a transport museum attached to it containing vehicles typical of Florida, such as the airboat and the swamp buggy as well as some oldtimer vehicles.

Olde Florida
Folk Festival
A yearly highlight in the Flamingo Gardens calendar of events is the Olde Florida Folk Festival held in the middle of September. Anglo-American and Spanish-Mexican folklore occupies much of the gardens, with old crafts also on display. Indian traditions can also be seen.

Davie Arena
Davie Arena (Orange Drive/64th Ave.) is well-known for its weekly rodeos. Once a month the Five Star Pro Davie Rodeo is held here, featuring professionals from throughout North America. Concerts, circus performances and sports events also take place here.

★Everglades
Holiday Park
The Everglades Holiday Park (US 27/Griffin Road; open: daily 9am–5pm) offers airboat tours, during which much can be learnt about this unique natural landscape. Alligator shows are presented in an Indian village. Boat rental; accompanied fishing trips.

Homestead

See Miami

Homosassa Springs   E 10

Citrus County
Altitude: 10ft/3m
Population: 7000

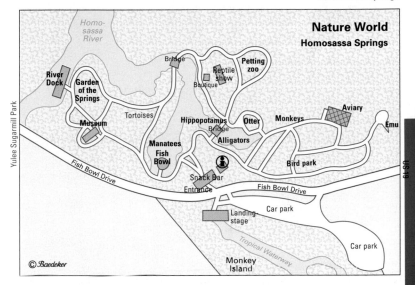

Homosassa Springs and Old Homosassa, which have grown together into the present sprawling residential and holiday resort along Homosassa River on Florida's north-west coast, are famous owing to the Homosassa Springs Wildlife Park. David L. Yulee, who built the first stretch of railway on the Florida peninsula, owned an extensive sugar plantation on Homosassa River. He was the first white settler in this area. After the American Civil War the region recovered slowly, its few inhabitants being predominantly self-sufficient or living by fishing. The nearest central town was then Cedar Key, some 62 miles/100km further north. During the 1880s Homosassa gained a railway connection, which simplified the transportation of wood and fish to Tampa. At the turn of the century this coastal area with its rivers rich in fish was discovered by a number of millionaires from America's north coast. Homosassa Springs was intended to become the centre of the development, with an elegant hotel complete with its own railway station built close to the source of the Homosassa River during the 1920s. Most of its prosperous guests travelled here in their own luxurious Pullman coaches, which were then parked in sidings at the hotel. After the Depression Homosassa went into hibernation until the 1960s, when the hotel was demolished to make way for a supermarket.

Location

Sights in the area

Since it opened in 1962, Homosassa Springs Wildlife Park (Fish Bowl Drive, 1 mile/2km west of the US 19; open: daily 9am–5.30pm, last entry 4pm) has become one of the main attractions on Florida's north-west coast. Shoals of fish and manatees can be observed in their natural habitat through large windows. Used as a fish pond, the pool can be freely entered from the sea via the Homosassa River.

★★Homosassa State Springs Wildlife Park

Up to 5½ million gallons/23 million litres pour from the powerful karst source of the Homosassa River in one hour. Throughout the year the water temperature remains at about 72°F/22°C. Particularly in winter, when the water in the nearby gulf has cooled, thousands of fresh and saltwater fish and some manatees seek out the relatively warm spring water.

141

At the "Blue Pool" of Homosassa

The clear, 56ft/17m-deep pool, the source of the Homosassa River, which flows into the Gulf of Mexico after 9 miles/14km, was already renowned for its rich fishing before the Second World War. Wooden footbridges were built, enabling visitors to watch the fish in the crystal clear water. In 1962 Homosassa Springs was developed into a centre of tourism. As well as the Fish Bowl, pools containing alligators and American crocodiles, a zoo (whose exhibits include tortoises, otters, monkeys, varieties of birds of prey, flamingos, turkeys and emus), a hands-on zoo and a snake display all combine to attract visitors. In addition, injured or orphaned manatees are nursed back to health at Homosassa Springs. Some years ago a hippopotamus called Lucifer made numerous appearances in front of film and television cameras. There is also a small natural history museum here.

Excursion boats depart from the dock daily until 4pm to penetrate the adventurous-looking landscape of forests and rivers.

★Yulee Sugar Mill Estate Historic Site

The remains of David Yulee's sugar plantation located on the edge of Old Homosassa, about 2½ miles/4km west of the US 19/98 on the SR 490, can be visited. Along with the prestigious manor house it was totally destroyed during the American Civil War by Union troops. The sugar boiling house was restored in 1851. Guided tours can be undertaken, with special notices explaining the sugar production process that used to be carried out here.

Chassahowitzka National Wildlife Refuge

Chassahowitzka National Wildlife Refuge, a 296,520 acre/120,000ha nature reserve reachable only by boat, extends to the south-west of Homosassa between the mouth of the Homosassa River and the Chassahowitzka River. The extremely sensitive ecosystem provides a refuge for countless waterfowl. Access to the many small islands is not allowed. Flat bays, a tangle of river inlets and mangrove and coastal swamps enrich the scenery. As well as numerous species of birds, alligators, racoons, deer, wild turkeys, red lynxes and otters can be observed here.

The administration building is located on US 19 about 4 miles/6km south of Homosassa Springs; tel. (904) 628 2201.

See Brooksville

Weeki Wachee Springs

See entry

Crystal River

Indian River   D–H 13–15

Indian River, actually a flat lagoon with an average depth of 3ft/1m located behind offshore, narrow sandy islands, extends for a distance of about 124 miles/200km parallel to Florida's Atlantic coastline, approximately from New Smyrna Beach to St Lucie Inlet at Stuart. It forms part of the Intracoastal Waterway (see entry). Particularly in the south, between Sebastian and Vero Beach, the lagoon is very flat and forms a labyrinth of swampy islands, on which many species of waterfowl find sanctuary and nesting places. Many migratory birds also alight here.

A channel for water-craft has been dredged and marked. The calm waters of the lagoon prove ideal for all water sports. Indian River reaches its widest point (6 miles/9km) in the north at Merritt Island. It is joined to Mosquito Lagoon (see Cape Canaveral, Canaveral National Seashore) by a narrow channel. Boats reach the sea via five narrow passages (St Lucie Inlet, Ft. Pierce Inlet, Sebastian Inlet, Barge Canal/Port Canaveral, Mosquito Lagoon). Several bridges (mainly drawbridges) span the waterway, which can lead to considerable queues when many boats are trying to reach the beaches on the offshore islands. The brackish water behind the sandy islands is home to a rich variety of fauna. Scientists have established that 310 species of birds and 700 species of fish live here. About three dozen species of animals, whose existence is endangered elsewhere, can be seen here.

From March until October several hundred manatees stay in Indian River and its tributaries. They can mainly be seen in Eau Gallie River, in Crane Creek and in Turkey Creek.

Manatees (seacows)

Manatees (seacows), gregarious relatives of the elephant, grow to a length of approximately 10ft/3m and live in brackish water. They eat up to 110lb/50kg of sea grass or riverbank plants a day. The heavy boat traffic using Florida's waters has endangered their continued existence. Almost all the older animals bear the scars of injuries sustained through unpleasant encounters with boat propellers.

During the last few decades large citrus fruit plantations have been developed in the hinterland of Indian River. The pink-fleshed grapefruit grown here taste especially good. The local oranges also win praise as being particularly sweet and juicy.

Citrus fruits

Intracoastal Waterway   B–M 2–15

The Intracoastal Waterway is an important American inland waterway, which greatly enhances Florida's tourist trade in private boats. Excursion boats also use sections of it.

Course

The waterway makes extensive use of the calm lagoons and areas of brackish water lying behind the spits and sandy islands of the Atlantic/Gulf coastline. Channels close to the coast link shipping channels and individual bays and rivers, making it possible to travel out from New York to Key West or via the Okeechobee Waterway to the Gulf coast and along as far as Brownsville on the Texan–Mexican border. Not all sections of the waterway are generally navigable for cargo ships.

Within Florida the marked Intracoastal Waterway follows a completely sheltered course along the Atlantic coast from Jacksonville in the north southwards to Miami (348 miles/560km). As far as Ft. Pierce the shipping channel is barely 13ft/4m deep, from there to Miami only 8ft/2.5m deep. Leaving Miami the route for larger vessels follows the open Atlantic side of the Key (152 miles/245km). Only boats with a depth of less than 5ft/1.5m can navigate the extremely attractive route on the shallow Gulf side (171 miles/275km).

The West Coast Intracoastal Waterway between Ft. Myers and Anclote Key at Tarpon Springs (162 miles/260km) has been open since 1967. From here to St Mark's Lighthouse (east of Apalachicola), however, the last part of the marked channel has been missing until now. The scarcely 13ft/4m deep, marked shipping channel leading to Pensacola only begins again at Caravelle.

Also of interest to tourists is the Okeechobee Waterway which joins the Atlantic to the Gulf of Mexico. Beginning at St Lucie Inlet at Stuart it continues via Lake Okeechobee and the Caloosahatchee River to Ft. Myers (134 miles/216km, four locks). Smaller boats can be sailed from Lake Okeechobee via the Kissimmee Waterway, which links various lakes in central Florida to Kissimmee, the gateway to central Florida's tourist attractions.

Smaller boats can also navigate St John's River for 141 miles/227km between Mayport/Jacksonville and Sanford, as well as Apalachee River from Apalachicola to the Jim Woodruff Lock on the dammed Chattahoochee River (107 miles/172km). From here it is possible to "sail" via Flint River to Bainbridge (Georgia) and via Chattahoochee River to Columbia (Alabama).

Islamorada

See Florida Keys

Jacksonville   B 12

Duval County
Altitude: 0–23ft/0–7m
Population: 690,000

Location

The town of Jacksonville, located in the extreme north-east of Florida, was originally a port, an industrial area and a military base. After a period of stagnation "Jax" has developed again into an important trade and financial centre. With an area of more than 772sq.miles/2000sq.km the town is the largest in the USA and, as regards population, the largest in Florida.

During the 1980s Jacksonville developed completely new precincts. A number of skyscrapers were erected along St John's River and some banks and insurance companies have located their headquarters here.

Within the south-east of the USA Jacksonville's port has become the most important centre of trade with the Caribbean and South America. The opening of a branch of the world-famous Mayo Clinic here in 1986, held to be the new centre of medicine for the whole of the south-east of the USA, has increased the town's prestige.

Some important seats of learning are situated in Jacksonville including the University of North Florida, Jacksonville University and the Edward Waters College.

The navy continues to be one of the town's largest employers. More than 50,000 people work for the armed forces at the Naval Air Station, at Cecil Field and at Mayport Naval Station. In addition there are more than 16,000 pensioners.

Jacksonville is also enjoying increasing popularity as a congress town, brought about by the construction of a new congress centre and several large hotels.

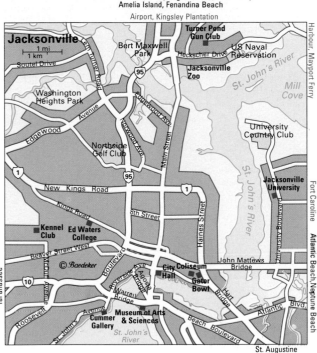

Little Talbot State Park, Huguenot Memorial Park,
Amelia Island, Fenandina Beach

Airport, Kingsley Plantation

Jacksonville

In pre-Columbian times a settlement of Timucuan Indians lived here on a ford of St John's River. During the short British rule of Florida in the second half of the 18th c. the first trunk road, the so-called King's Road (today part of US Highway 1), was laid from St Augustine to Savannah (Georgia). With the help of a ferry the obstacle then posed by St John's River at the town now known as Jacksonville was overcome. Small settlements grew up on both sides of the river crossing. At the beginning of the 19th c. the first American settlers came to the area. The town of Jacksonville, named after the American general and Florida's first governor, was founded in 1822. In 1854, however, the young settlement was almost completely destroyed by fire and in 1857 an epidemic of yellow fever decimated the population. Jacksonville was badly affected during the American Civil War. Present-day defence installations continue to act as reminders of those troubled times.

History

St John's River subsequently gained increasing importance as an artery and an axis for opening up the hinterland. River boats carried more settlers and supplies inland. Jacksonville, with its sheltered harbour only 17 miles/28km from the sea, developed into a main handling centre of cotton, timber and cattle.

During the winter months after the Civil War increasing numbers of affluent Americans from the north-east of the USA moved to Florida. Elegant hotels and shops opened in Jacksonville, and excursion steamers operated on the river. By 1884 the surrounding beaches could be reached by train. Tourist hotels were built in Mayport and on Fort George Island. Jacksonville's

"JAX" (Jacksonville), seen from the air

By St John's River

boom in tourism was, however, to collapse suddenly, when Henry Flagler's railway line reached St Augustine in 1888.

In the same year a serious epidemic of yellow fever raged again. Catastrophic frosts at the close of the 19th c. brought about the end of citrus fruit cultivation in north-west Florida. During the Spanish-American war for Cuba a military camp was built at Jacksonville.

On 3rd May 1901 a large part of the town was once more destroyed by fire. The rapid rebuilding came under the overall control of the New York architect Henry J. Klutho. The public buildings, churches and villas built by him continue to characterise the townscape and form the heart of the restored Riverside, Avondale and Springfield districts. His ten-storey Bisbee Building was Jacksonville's first skyscraper.

The film industry began to blossom in Jacksonville before the First World War. Motor racing, which was becoming increasingly popular at nearby Atlantic Beach, also stimulated Jacksonville's growth.

During the First World War shipbuilding boomed. Thousands of soldiers passed through Jacksonville's training camp.

The Depression in the 1920s and 1930s affected Jacksonville particularly badly. Many thousands were unemployed. A new economic boom did not occur until the outbreak of the Second World War. Work was carried on day and night at the dockyards. The military training camp in the south-west of the town was developed into an enormous US Naval Air Station.

In the years after the war, particularly in the 1960s, Jacksonville experienced a new crisis, only ended in the 1980s by a clever development policy, since when a flourishing centre of trade and service has grown out of a foul-smelling industrial town. Jacksonville has even been able to tackle industries on the prevention of air pollution and to impose fines.

Sights

The centre of Jacksonville experienced a very difficult redevelopment phase some years ago. Glittering new skyscrapers rose up on the north bank of St John's River, along with offices, theatres, shops and various large businesses.

Three different-coloured bridges link North Bank with South Bank: Acosta Bridge (a toll bridge) is orange, Main Street Bridge (a drawbridge) is blue and Hart Bridge is green.

Downtown

Jacksonville Landing is an open-air meeting place on North Bank west of Main Street Bridge. Officially opened in 1987, it faces on to St John's River and is an attempt at creating a modern architectural structure which is both a market place, a festival ground and a "glutton's alley" (constructional concept of the Festival Market Place).

★Jacksonville Landing

South Bank, where Riverwalk was completed in 1985, can be reached by water taxi across St John's River. This attractive centre complete with hotels and restaurants, around which various events take place, has been built on former industrial and dock land. A wooden promenade (approximately 1 mile/2km long) leads from Schoolboard Building to Acosta Bridge. Street artists, traders and musicians and a marvellous view of central Jacksonville's silhouette have rapidly turned Riverwalk into a popular meeting place.

★Riverwalk

Friendship Park is particularly busy at midday with employees from the surrounding offices. A fountain, whose jet reaches a height of 118ft/36m, stands in the centre of the park and is illuminated at night.

Friendship Park

South Bank is dominated by Gulf Life Tower, a modern complex of high-rise buildings completed in 1967.

Gulf Life Tower

Jacksonville

★Museum of Science & History

The recently-extended Museum of Science & History (1025 Gulf Live Drive/ South Main St.; open: Mon.–Fri. 10am–5pm, Sat. 10am–6pm, Sun. 1–6pm) is located close to the fountain. The museum offers both children and adults an insight into the world of science and technology. Physics demonstrations can be observed in the Science Theater and the Planetarium, and there are natural history exhibitions, exhibitions dealing with Florida's history and Indian culture as well as a series of temporary exhibitions. Main attractions are the "Dinosaurs Alive" show with life-size replicas of various dinosaurs and "The Living World" show (marine aquarium, an aviary of song-birds, living insects, amphibians and reptiles).

Independent Life Building

Completed in 1975, the 37-storey Independent Life Building (1 Independent Drive) on North Bank remained for many years north Florida's tallest building. Tours: Mon.–Fri. 10am and 2pm; marvellous view from the 33rd floor.

American Heritage Life Tower

Next to the Independent Life Building stands the shining façade of the new American Heritage Life Tower. This insurance "palace" has 23 floors and is characterised by red granite and blue-tinted windows.

Barnett Bank Tower

Designed by the architect Helmut Jahn, a German now living in Chicago, the 40-storey Barnett Bank Tower on Bay Street has a Post-Modern appearance. This administrative centre is at present Florida's second tallest building.

Southern Bell

The massive high-rise insurance building which accommodates the Southern Bell telephone company (301 Bay St.) stands two blocks further to the west. It was built in 1983.

Civic Auditorium

Among the concerts that take place in the Civic Auditorium (300 Water St.; tel. 633 2900) are those given by the famous Jacksonville Symphony Orchestra.

Prime Osborn Convention Center, former Union Station

In no time at all the Skyway Express whisks passengers from the town centre (200 W. Bay St.) to the Convention Center, completed in 1986. Union Station (1000 W. Water St.), built in 1919 by the New York architect K. M. Murchison, has been integrated into the Convention Center. The huge former station concourse is vaulted by a 75ft/23m-high cupola. In its heyday 142 trains and more than 30,000 travellers passed through the station in one day, but in 1974 Amtrak transferred its station to the north-west of the town. However, in 1982 a new use was found for the protected building.

Today the restored concourse with its marble floor, to which a modern wing has been added, is used as a lobby. A new purpose was even found for the old ticket counters.

Florida Theatre Performing Arts Center

The Florida Theatre Performing Arts Center (128 E. Forsyth St.), built in 1926/ 27 as a picture palace, has taken on a new life and now stages all manner of cultural events. Painted terracota figures and ornamental bands decorate the façade of the brick building. The lavishly-furnished auditorium with its huge balcony is once again able to accommodate almost 2000 visitors.

★Cummer Gallery of Art

The recently-renovated, private Cummer Art Gallery (829 Riverside Ave.; open: Tues.–Fri. 10am–4pm, Sat. 12–5pm, Sun. 2–5pm), south-west of Fuller Warren Bridge, has gained a good reputation as an art museum. The Cummer family's private collection forms the basis of the museum. The works on display encompass both Greek antiquity as much as 20th c. art. The 700-piece collection of old Meissen porcelain is worth viewing, as is that of Eastern Asian art.

Jacksonville Art Museum

Jacksonville Art Museum (4160 Boulevard Center Drive; open: Tues.–Fri. 10am–4pm (also Thur. 4–10pm), Sat., Sun. 1–5pm) lies about 1 mile/2km south-east of the town centre. It exhibits pre-Columbian art, an unusual collection of Chinese and Japanese porcelain, and contemporary art. Periodic exhibitions.

Every autumn the Florida National Jacksonville Jazz Festival takes place in the Florida National Pavilion (1410 E Adams St.), attracting more than 50,000 visitors to the enormous covered stage in Metropolitan Park on the eastern edge of the town centre. Until a few years ago the park was a wasteland, cut through by a wide urban motorway.

Metropolitan Park, Florida National Pavilion

In 1887 several suburbs were incorporated, including Springfield, a settlement on the northern border of the town centre. Many buildings designed by well-known architects were erected between 1900 and 1920, and several hundred of these are already listed under a preservation order. A small shopping centre has been built in North Main Street.

Springfield Historic District

Riverside (1900–32) and neighbouring Avondale (1920–40), south-west of Fuller Warren Bridge, form another well-kept, old villa quarter. Until the Second World War it was Jacksonville's most prestigious residential area. Riverside Avenue, St John's Avenue and Park Street are nowadays prestigious addresses for practices and offices.

★Avondale/ Riverside Historic District

The Palm Beach-based architect Addison Mizner combined both the Byzantine and the Romanesque style in the impressive Riverside Baptist Church, built in 1925. The quarter's charm is provided by a number of art galleries, the River City Playhouse, antique shops and boutiques. Many more small shops and restaurants, as well as tree-lined, cobbled streets and small gardens can be found in Five Points Village in Riverside and in Avondale Shopping Village.

The San Marco quarter on the south bank still retains its unique charm. Many of the part Art Deco villas built at the beginning of the 20th c., some of which stand right on the water's edge, have been attractively renovated. San Marco Square, with its fine restaurants and shops, forms the centre of the quarter. Jacksonville Theatre (2032 San Marco Blvd.) is the town's oldest building and employs a full-time company.

San Marco

Jacksonville University was founded in 1934 and has 2500 students. Its campus extends along the east bank of St John's River. Among its important buildings are an oceanography centre, the Historic Society Library (of importance for the study of the region's history), the Alexander Brest Museum (which includes exhibits from pre-Columbian times, European pottery, porcelain and glass and ivory carvings from the Far East) and the home of the German-born composer Fritz Delius (1862–1934) which is now open to the public.

Jacksonville University

The modern zoo (8605 Zoo Blvd.; open: daily 9am–5pm) is situated in the north of the city on Trout River. Several hundred species of animals can be viewed here. A wooden footbridge crosses natural-looking swampland. Visitors can ride on elephants and take a nostalgic steam train ride. Excursion boats to the zoo depart the town centre hourly.

Zoological Park

America's largest brewery located its ultra-modern production plant in the north of the town (111 Busch Drive) in 1967. Its yearly output measures approximately eight million hectolitres and serves the whole of the south of the USA. Tours: Oct.–mid May Mon.–Sat. 9am–4pm, June–Sept. 10am–5pm; tasting.

★Anheuser-Busch Brewery

The suspension bridge which spans St John's River at Dames Point was completed in 1989. The bridge measures more than 2 miles/3km and accommodates the six lanes of the I–295. It joins the northern industrial areas to the residential areas south of the river. The mid-section of the bridge hangs on thick steel cables from two 473ft/144m tall pylons.

Dames Point Bridge

Surroundings

★ Fort Caroline
National Memorial

A wooden fort has been reconstructed on the banks of St John's River about 10 miles/16km east of the town centre. French Huguenots attempted to form a settlement in this area in the 16th c. The first clashes between France and Spain for supremacy in the North American continent occurred in 1565.

The history of the first settlement and the 16th c. political situation is explained in the Fort Caroline National Monument (12713 Ft. Caroline Road; open: daily 9am–5pm).

In 1564 René de Laudonnière founded a settlement here with about 300 followers, after Jean Ribaut had been shipwrecked two years earlier. The small settlement could not be self-sufficient as practically no one understood anything about farming – most of the new settlers were sailors and soldiers. With the help of the resident Timucuan Indians a small triangular fort was built. However, serious problems arose when some of the garrison wanted to go treasure-hunting. When mutineers attacked Spanish ships and a village on Cuba the Spanish became aware of these French intruders in Florida, to which they had laid claim but had not yet settled. With the deterioration of supplies during the winter Laudonnière authorised an attack on a village of hitherto well-meaning Indians. During their retreat, however, the French were ambushed and lost everything. Disappointed and near to starvation, they were on the point of returning to their homeland when Ribaut arrived in the summer of 1565 with provisions and reinforcements. At the same time the Spanish general Menéndez reached the coast of Florida with orders to drive the intruders out. After his first attempt at taking Fort Caroline failed, Menéndez founded St Augustine (see entry) about 31 miles/50km further south. Ribaut now made the fateful decision to attack the Spanish there. His ships encountered a hurricane and, after their capture at Fort Matanzas, most of the ships' survivors were put to death by the Spanish as heretics. Meanwhile Menéndez attacked Fort Caroline by land. Only a few of the surprised French could escape by ship. In 1568 some Frenchmen returned and, with the help of Indians, managed to destroy the Spanish strongholds which had since been built. A number of the troops were able, however, to flee to St Augustine. Florida remained in Spanish ownership.

Mayport

Mayport, one of the USA's oldest fishing villages, lies some 8 miles/13km further east. Charter boats depart here on deep sea fishing trips. Many crab boats tie up in the harbour.

Mayport Naval
Station

Mayport Naval Station is one of the largest naval bases on the American east coast. Aircraft carriers and units of the sixth US fleet are stationed here. Weekend guided tours (information: tel. 264 5226).

Fort George
Island,
★ Kingsley
Plantation
National
Historic Site

Ferries take visitors from Mayport to St George Island, located in the mouth of St John's River. By the 16th c. the Spanish had already established a small mission here but it was not until 1730, when British troops penetrated Florida, that the island gained its present name. The governor of Georgia had a small fort built here. During the last years of Spanish colonialism three Americans won land rights here and laid out plantations, including Kingsley Plantation, named after one of its later owners. It is one of the few remaining examples of this economic system in the south-east of the USA. Don Juan McQueen House was built in 1791, Kingsley Mansion dates from 1817. Cotton and sugar cane was grown on the plantation, and Florida's first orange groves were planted here. Remains of the earlier slaves' quarters can be seen near to the entrance. Open: daily 9am–5pm, guided tours: Thur.–Mon. 9.30am, 11am, 1.30pm and 3pm.

Buccaneer Trail

Buccaneer Trail, part of the A1A, starts at Fort George Island and follows the north Atlantic coast northwards. This approximately 16 miles/25km-long

Jacksonville beach

stretch as far as Fernandina Beach offers the most delightful landscape along Florida's east coast. Lonely beaches still extend for miles here.

Just 19miles/30km north-east of Jacksonville the A1A leads to the 2471 acre/1000ha Little Talbot Island State Park, situated on an almost original coral island complete with white beach. The marshland on the leeward side of the island offers refuge to hundreds of thousands of migratory birds, sea birds and waders. The landscape is characterised by dunes and pine woods. In summer turtles lay their eggs on the 5 miles/8km-long beach. Parking information; tel. 251 3231.

★Little Talbot Island State Park

A number of seaside resorts are strung together like pearls along an approximately 19 miles/30km-long white-sanded beach south of the St John's River estuary. These resorts profit from Jacksonville's regained economic strength and are prized by many wealthy inhabitants of the nearby city.

Atlantic Beach, Neptune Beach, Jacksonville Beach

The resort of Jacksonville Beach (population 20,000) lies 14 miles/23km east of the town centre and is strongly influenced by tourism. In 1988 an extensive renovation project was undertaken here. Particularly attractive are "The Seawalk", a promenade which extends along the Atlantic and which has a music pavilion where concerts and other events are staged, and "Seawalk Plaza", with small shops, restaurants and bars.

Jacksonville Beach

New owner-occupied flats adjoin the northern end of Jacksonville Beach. They have been built in the style of the Casa Marina, a prestigious beach villa dating from 1925.

Jacksonville Pier (36th Ave. South), popular with anglers and strollers, is 1201ft/366m-long and illuminated at night. The beach attracts many windsurfers.

Pier

Jensen Beach

★Seminole Beach, Kathryn Abbey Hannah Park — Seminole Beach with Kathryn Abbey Hannah Park is the most beautiful section of beach near to Jacksonville. It extends from south of Mayport Naval Station to 3 miles/5km north of Atlantic Boulevard and offers a campsite, a freshwater lake and nature trails through typical coastal woodland planted with perennial oaks and palms. The beach is supervised during the peak holiday period.

Sawgrass — The professional golfers' Tournament Players Association is based in Sawgrass. The town has recently developed into a Mecca for golfers and boasts eight excellent golf courses complete with their own exclusive hotels.

Amelia Island — See entry

Okefenokee Swamp — See entry

Ponte Vedra — See entry

Jensen Beach   G/H 15

Martin County. Altitude: 0–53ft/0–16m. Population: 10,000

Location — Jensen Beach was founded in 1871 and is named after a Danish sailor who was probably its first inhabitant. The town was formerly known for its pineapples but now tourism dominates.

Pineapple Festival — The Pineapple Festival, featuring a street market, a pineapple parade and beauty contests, takes place annually at the end of November.

★Hutchinson Island — Jensen Beach Causeway offers good fishing and leads to the offshore, narrow Hutchinson Island with its excellent bathing beach. Swimming, surfing or simply the natural surroundings can be enjoyed here.
   Colossal turtles come to lay their eggs on the beach during the summer and the restrictions then brought into force are observed by environmentally-aware tourists.

St Lucie River, Indian River — Fishing trips can be undertaken from Jensen Beach to St Lucie River and Indian River.

Juno Beach

See Palm Beach

Jupiter   H 15

Palm Beach County. Altitude: 0–10ft/0–3m. Population: 25,000

Location — Jupiter is the oldest settlement in Palm Beach County and was composed originally of a fort built in 1838, i.e. during the Second Seminolian War. The lighthouse, a red brick building begun in 1853 and around which a small settlement grew up, is the town's emblem. Its name is supposed to date back to the Jobe Indians, although a misinterpretation linked the name with the Roman god Jupiter. During Prohibition, Jupiter Inlet was a harbour and anchorage for smugglers but now it is a quiet, well-tended bathing resort.

Loxahatchee Historical Society Museum — Loxahatchee Historical Museum maintains an interesting small museum (805 US 1 North; open: Tues.–Fri. 10am–4pm, Sat., Sun. 1–4pm) in Burt Reynolds Park. On display are Seminolian cultural items, salvage from shipwrecks and exhibits from the age of railway construction.

The lighthouse standing on the cliffs above Jupiter Inlet is one of the oldest of its type along the American east coast. It is now under the jurisdiction of the US coastguard. The tower houses a local history exhibition.

Lighthouse

At the end of the 19th c. an early settler built a small house on an Indian mound, which is now open to the public as a museum. The furnishings date from its early days.

Dubois House

Jonathan Dickinson State Park (16450 S.E. Federal Highway, Hobe Sound) covers an area of 4942 acres/2000ha and lies about 6 miles/10km north of Jupiter. It owes its name to a Quaker who was shipwrecked here at the end of the 17th c. and was saved by Indians.

★Jonathan Dickinson State Park

The national park surrounds the lower reaches of the Loxahatchee River (mangrove and cypress swamps, areas of dunes) and is a protected home to countless species of animals. The park has several paths, including the River Trail along the side of Loxahatchee River, and Kitching Creek Trail, an observation platform and cycle and riding trails. Canoe rental. Open: daily 8am–dusk. The number of visitors is regulated during winter.

Loxahatchee River

About 5 miles/8km further north is an area of beach and saltwater marshes barely 2sq.miles/5sq.km in size. Left in its original state, it is kept as a game preserve mainly intended to offer protection from hunters and tourists to the turtles who come ashore here. Informative trails are marked and much of interest about this biological system can be learned in the Nature Center (open: daily).

Hobe Sound

Tours of the Intracoastal Waterway by paddle-steamer or catamaran depart from Jupiter Harbor.

Boat excursions

Kennedy Space Center

See Cape Canaveral

Key Biscayne

See Biscayne National Park. See Miami

Key Largo

See Florida Keys

Key West

M 12

Monroe County. Altitude: 0–7ft/0–2m. Population: 25,000

Key West (from the Spanish *cayo huesco* = Bone Island) is located on a coral island at the south-west tip of the Florida Keys (see entry) and is the most southerly point of continental USA. The island lies only 90 miles/145km from Cuba and used to be a notorious pirates' lair. In 1822 it became a naval base intended to protect seafaring. It remains a navy base today and also has a diving school.

★★Location

In 1845 Key West was an important harbour and prospering town. Its inhabitants, migrants from the Bahamas, lived very well by exploiting the many ships which ran aground here. By about 1870 Key West had become

History

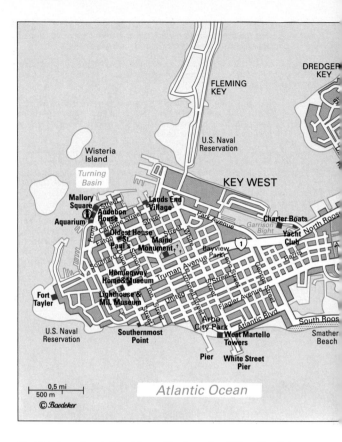

Florida's largest and richest town. The imposing 19th c. Conch houses continue to bear witness to the affluence of the "shipwreckers" and the trading captains.

Cigar production, brought to the island by exiled Cubans, became the main industry for a time until its transfer to Tampa. The real development of tourism as an important part of the economy began at the turn of the century, in particular after Flagler's railway reached Key West in 1912 to connect with ferries to Havana. The multinational origins of Key West's population and their happy lifestyle, reminiscent of the Caribbean, soon attracted artists and authors to the island. Ernest Hemingway, Tennessee Williams and, for a time, John Dos Passos lived here during the 1930s and 1940s. In 1934 the town went bankrupt and in 1935 a violent hurricane destroyed the railway line.

Sights

Centre of tourism

Nowadays Key West is considered to be one of the most tolerant towns in the USA. Its Caribbean charm draws 2.5 million visitors a year. Despite the hustle and bustle of tourism, however, Key West remains a popular haunt of artists, writers and people who have rejected established society.

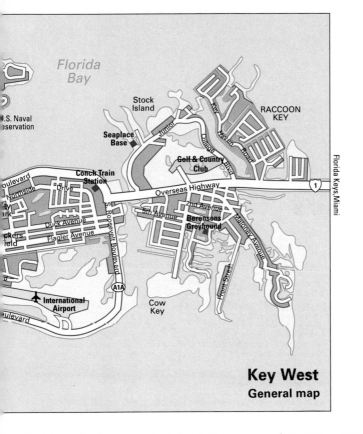

Key West
General map

The town only begins to come alive in the late afternoon; every evening the sunset is celebrated in the cheerful, funfair-like atmosphere of Mallory Square.

★Mallory Square

Situated at the south-west end of the island, Old Town, with its numerous brightly-painted, wooden 19th c. houses, is Key West's main attraction. This closely-built, historic quarter with its lovingly restored Conch houses (Conch is the name given to inhabitants of Key West who were born in the Florida Keys or in the Bahamas) occupies about a quarter of the island.

★Old Town

Duval Street, which links the Gulf of Mexico to the Atlantic, and its delightful side-streets are lined with boutiques, art galleries, pavement cafés, restaurants and bars.

Duval Street

The Pelican Path tour, featured in one of the brochures available from the Chamber of Commerce (402 Wall St.), leads walkers past 49 of the town's historically-interesting buildings.

Pelican Path

Key West Aquarium (1 Whitehead St; open: daily 10am–6pm; guided tours) is a notable attraction. Exhibits worth seeing include the large pool

Key West Aquarium

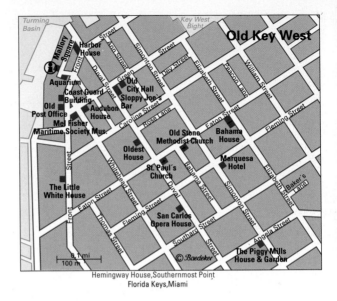

Hemingway House,Southernmost Point
Florida Keys,Miami

inhabited by giant turtles, barracudas and Florida lobsters, as well as the shark pond.

Mel Fisher's Treasure Exhibit

Spanish gold jewellery, silver coins and other valuables are on display at Mel Fisher's Treasure Exhibit (200 Greene St./Front St.; open: daily 10am–6pm; film presentations). Mel Fisher recently recovered the exhibits from the Spanish silver ships "Atocha" and "Santa Margarita" which sank off the Marquesas during a hurricane in 1622. There are also exhibitions of underwater archaeology.

★Audubon House & Gardens

Audubon House (205 Whitehead/Greene St.; open: daily 9.30am–5pm) is a typical Conch house. Audubon, the famous painter of animals and plants, stayed here in 1832. The house has now become a museum, with 18th/ 19th c. furniture and some of his original works. Some of the original drawings of native birds by Audubon have been filmed. A large number of species of tropical plants can be admired in the magnificent garden.

Captain Tony's Saloon

Between 1933 and 1937 the present Captain Tony's Saloon (Greene St.) was Sloppy Joe's Bar, where Hemingway would sit on the stool reserved for him and decide how to spend his day. The ceiling and the walls are now plastered with visitors' cards.

★Sloppy Joe's Bar

The new Sloppy Joe's Bar (201 Duval St.; open: daily 9am–4am) is located around the corner in busy Duval Street. Photographs and mementoes of Hemingway decorate the walls.

Curry Mansion

Curry Mansion (511 Caroline St.), a 25-room villa, was built in the Victorian style at the end of the 19th c. and belonged at that time to one of Florida's richest men. It is worth viewing the exhibition of antiques (particularly the Tiffany glass). The building is now an elegant inn.

Turtle Kraals Land's End Village

Turtle Kraals and Land's End Village are situated at the other end of Greene Street. Earlier settlers kept giant turtles, a main source of food, in captivity here on the jetties in the bay. Giant turtles, nowadays under protection, can

Key West: A pub with a "big name"

still be seen here. There are several restaurants specialising in seafood in Land's End Village, and fishing boats bob up and down in Key West Blight.

Wrecker's Museum (Oldest House, 322 Duval St.; open: daily 10am–4pm) is a typical wooden house and was built in 1829. It documents the lifestyle of its earlier owner, one of the successful wreckers and trading captains.

★Wrecker's Museum

Fort Zachary Taylor State Historic Site (open: daily 8am–dusk, guided tours; daily 2pm) lies at the south-west end of the island and can be reached via Southard Street. This brick-built fortress was constructed with great difficulty between 1845 and 1866 as part of the American sea defence system. It played an important role during the Civil War as a Union base against blockade runners. The fort was modernised again during the Spanish-American War. Since 1947 it has served as a naval base. Cannon and a large number of weapons from the time of the Civil War can now be seen in this historic building. The collection of old photographs is of interest. A popular beach is nearby.

Fort Zachary Taylor State Historic Site

Key West's chief attraction is the Ernest Hemingway Home & Museum (907 Whitehead St.; open: daily 9am–5pm). This delightful house was built in 1851 in the Spanish Colonial style and was acquired by Hemingway in 1931. Until 1961 a great deal of his work was written here. During the course of a guided tour original furnishings and pieces of memorabilia can be seen. Countless descendants of Hemingway's cats romp in the lush, tropical garden.

★Ernest Hemingway Home & Museum

The lighthouse (938 Whitehead St.) was built in 1847 and offers a marvellous panoramic view. Today it is a museum.

Lighthouse Museum

At the end of Whitehead Street a huge concrete buoy marks the southernmost point of continental USA. Cuba lies only 89 miles/144km from here – closer than Miami.

★Southernmost Point

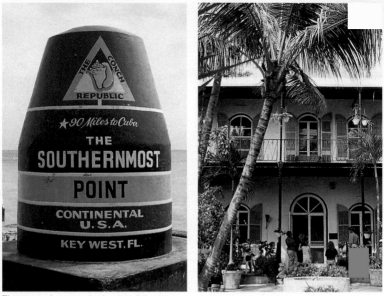

The most photographed point of Key West   Ernest Hemingway's house

| East Martello Tower & Art Gallery | Work on the East Martello Tower (3501 S. Roosevelt Blvd., close to the airport; open: daily 9.30am–3pm) began in 1862, i.e. during the Civil War. However, this brick fortress, intended to support Ft. Taylor on the Atlantic side, was never completed. A small museum (memorabilia about the Keys) and an art gallery are now housed here. |

Periodic exhibitions on a variety of themes are also staged here.

Circular trips

| Old Town Trolley | Old Town Trolley, one of the little trams reminiscent of San Francisco's Street Cars, carries its passengers past all of the island's most interesting places. It departs Mallory Square throughout the day from 8.55am to 4.30pm. A round trip lasts 90 minutes. |

| Conch Tour Trains | Conch Tour Trains leave from Mallory Square Depot and 3850 N. Roosevelt Street (length of trip is one and a half hours). Much information about the old Key West, Indians, pirates, shipwreckers and the time of Hemingway is imparted during the tour. |

Bathing beaches

Good bathing beaches can be found at the end of Duval Street, on the southern side of Roosevelt Boulevard and between White Street and Reynolds Street. In addition, boats can be taken across to some small islands with their sandy beaches.

| Capt'n's Corner | Excursions in a glass-bottomed boat, diving courses, diving and snorkel trips to the coral reef as well as an evening Sunset Cruise with musical accompaniment can be booked at Capt'n's Corner at the north end of Duval Street. |

Boat trips from Key West

Glass-bottomed boat trips into the world of the wonderful and still almost undamaged coral reefs that surround Key West can be taken from the northern end of Duval Street. Timetable and prices: tel. 296–6293.

★★Coral reefs

It is worth taking a boat trip from Key West to the western-lying, mangrove-covered Marquesas Keys, which form the centre of the far-reaching Key West National Wildlife Refuge (protecting, among others, terns, various species of heron and various types of coral).

★Marquesas Keys

Kissimmee   F 12

Osceola
Altitude: 0–66ft/0–20m. Population: 30,000

The little town of Kissimmee in central Florida is located only 19 miles/30km south of Orlando (see entry) and is conveniently situated on the US 192 and Interstate 4. Today it forms the gateway to Walt Disney World, an entertainment and leisure centre which has completely changed this previously remote and rural region during the last two decades.

Location

Tranquil, pastoral Florida with its countless lakes, streams and cypress swamps, and its narrow country roads lined by towering varieties of oak, on whose branches garlands of Spanish moss swing in the wind, can still be found, however, away from the main roads.

The first white settlers came to the Kissimmee area in 1878. A little later a Philadelphian businessman acquired about 4 million acres/1.6 million ha of land here at a bargain price and had an enormous sugar-cane plantation, including one of America's first sugar factories, constructed on it. In 1883 present-day Kissimmee was founded on part of the plantation, which, in the same year, also gained a railway link to St John's River. Four years later Kissimmee became the administrative seat of the newly-founded Osceola County. At that time the region had just 815 inhabitants.

History

After the cutting of subsidies for home-grown sugar, large-scale sugar-cane production was abandoned and was replaced by cattle rearing. The growing of citrus fruits and vegetables was also forced here, and two cigar factories also set up business.

When Walt Disney's entertainment empire came to central Florida the quiet of Kissimmee was seized by tourism. Hotels and motels, shopping centres and restaurants, a number of dinner-theatres and various entertainment establishments are strung together along US 192, the Irlo Bronson Memorial Highway which leads to Disney World.

Sights

The old Main Street and Broadway Boulevard have been smartened up again during the past few years and numerous small shops now enliven the scene. It is worth seeing Osceola Courthouse (built in 1889), Makinson's Hardware Store (1895) and the Arcade Theater (1925). The Monument of Statues (small pyramids) stands in Monument Street in Lake Front Park and deserves attention. The various building stones used come from all 50 of the American states.

Town centre

Old Town Shopping Center (5770 W. Irlo Bronson Memorial Highway; open: daily 10am–10pm) is built in the style typical of the turn of the century. In addition to the countless small shops and bars, the centre houses the "Big Eli" big wheel dating from 1928, a merry-go-round of little horses constructed in 1909 and the Little Darlin's Rock 'n' Roll Palace (1950s Rock 'n' Roll shows every evening) – all nostalgic attractions.

Old Town Shopping Center, Little Darlin's Rock 'n' Roll Center

Kissimmee

Kissimmee Livestock Market, Silver Spurs Rodeo

Despite the vast numbers of tourists who are attracted here by Walt Disney, Kissimmee remains Florida's centre of cattle-rearing. Large-scale cattle auctions take place here every Wednesday morning, once a year in February there is a grand agricultural show and twice a year the Silver Spurs Rodeo is held. This rodeo is supposed to have been initiated by Milt Hinkle, a man who knew the Wild West hero Wyatt Earp, the Mexican bandit Pancho Villa and the Apache leader Geronimo personally and who accompanied the later American president Teddy Roosevelt on his journey to South America.

Alligatorland

About 1500 alligators are kept in the Alligatorland Safari Zoo (4580 W. Irlo Bronson Highway, US 192; open: daily 8.30am–dusk). The undisputed star is Big Boy, a reptile weighing approximately 1488lb/675kg.

Flying Tigers Warbird Air Museum

Exhibits in the Flying Tigers Warbird Air Museum (231 N. Hoagland Blvd.; open: Mon.–Sat. 9am–6pm, Sun. 9–5pm) include a Consolidator B–4J Liberator, a restored fighter plane from the Second World War, as well as two B–25 Mitchells, a TBM Avenger and a F4U Corsair.

Gatorland Zoo

The open mouth of an enormous alligator marks the entrance to Gatorland Zoo (14501 S. Orange Blossom Trail, US 17–92/441: open: daily 8am–dusk) situated between Kissimmee and Orlando (see entry). The zoo was set up shortly after the Second World War by Owen Godwin under the name of Snake Village and Alligator Farm and was intended to afford inhabitants of the state and tourists a closer view of Florida's animal world. Nowadays, as well as a number of zoo animals collected from all around the world, about 5000 alligators and crocodiles live in the 35 acre/14ha site. These animals are reared here commercially.

Various types of snake can be observed in an open enclosure in a quasi-natural environment.

The watery playground of Water Mania

Originally founded as a research institute for the extraction of snake venom, the Reptile World Serpentarium (5705 E. Irlo Bronson Memorial Highway; open: Tues.–Sun. 9am–5.30pm, closed Sept.) now offers a safe view of poisonous snakes from around the world. Extraction of venom takes place daily at 11am, 2pm and 5pm.

Reptile World Serpentarium

Alligators and tortoises are also kept here.

Tupperware, the producer of synthetic kitchenware, is based in Kissimmee. Exhibition and museum (US 17–92/441; guided tours Mon.–Fri. 9am–4pm).

Tupperware Exhibit and Museum

A visit to the "House of the Future" (4800 W. Irlo Bronson Memorial Highway, US 192/SR 535; open: daily 10am–9pm) will show how architects and technicians envisage life in the 20th c. This energy-saving house is completely run by computer.

★Xanadu

The Elvis Presley Museum (5570 W. Irlo Bronson Memorial Highway; open: daily 10am–10pm) commemorates the legendary rock'n'roll singer.

Elvis Presley Museum

Families with children would do well to visit the 38 acre/15ha Water Mania (6073 W. Irlo Bronson Memorial Highway) which has a wave pool, various enormous water-slides and a small beach area.

Water Mania

Lake Tohopekaliga (29sq.miles/75sq.km) is Florida's fourth largest lake and lies to the south of Kissimmee. Its abundance of perch make it very popular with anglers.

Lake Tohopekaliga

St Cloud (population 10,000) is situated south-east of Kissimmee. It evolved from a winter camp for injured Civil War veterans which began life in 1920.

St Cloud

A few miles to the south-east of the town, the lands of Green Meadows Farm extend along Poinciana Boulevard. Here visitors can experience an American version of "life on the farm". There is a hands-on zoo and riding opportunities for children.

Green Meadows Farm

Arabian Nights (6225 W. Irlo Bronson Memorial Highway, E. Highway 192/I–4) includes riding games, chariot racing, dressage, Lipizzaner quadrilles, quarterhorses doing square dancing.

Dinner-Theater

Fort Liberty Wild West Dinner Show & Trading Post (5260 US 192, east of the I–4) – replica Wild West fort, various shows.

Medieval Times Dinner & Tournament (4510 W. Highway, 6 miles/10km east of the I–4); medieval open-air museum, replica of a fort; knights' banquet; old handiwork, torture chamber.

See entry

Orlando

See entry

Walt Disney World

Lake City

B 10

Columbia County
Altitude: 197ft/60m
Population: 10,000

The small town of Lake City lies on an important crossroads a few miles south of the border with Georgia. For many mid-Western holiday-makers it is a base for their journey to the south of Florida. In addition a number of

Location

Henderson House in Lake City

pensioners from the north have settled here. The economy of Lake City and its surroundings is based on forestry, tobacco-growing (large auctions every July/August) and cattle-rearing. The discovery of extensive phosphate deposits around Suwannee River has brought further economic growth. A number of firms dealing in the construction of prefabricated buildings and mobile homes have also based themselves here.

History

Lake City developed from a Seminolian village. An Indian headman from this village apparently took part in the Dade Massacre of 1835, which caused the onset of the Second Seminolian War. At the end of hostilities a small number of whites came to live here. The settlement was first called Alligator and only later gained its present name.

Sights

Downtown

Some of the typically Victorian wooden houses (e.g. T. G. Henderson House, 207 S. Marion St.) as well as quite a number of shops along Main Street have been restored during the past few years.

Florida Sports Hall of Fame

Since 1989 Lake City has been the home of the Florida Sports Hall of Fame (I–75/US 90), presenting popular sports and sportsmen from the Sunshine State.

Surroundings

Olustee Battlefield State Historic Site

In February 1864 about 5500 Union soldiers and about 5200 Confederates opposed each other at Ocean Pond, approximately 15 miles/24km east of Lake City. It was the most important battle to take place in Florida during the American Civil War. The Confederates were victorious and thus secured the provision of supplies for the southern states. The Battle of Olustee (named after the hamlet situated 2½ miles/4km to the south) is documented in the small museum and along a short path around the battlefield. Every February the battle is re-enacted during the Olustee Battle Festival and Re-enactment.

Osceola National Forest, established in 1931, lies to the north-west of Lake City. 246sq.miles/638sq.km in size, it is the smallest of Florida's national forests. Extensive pinewood forests, countless lakes, ponds and pools as well as cypress swamps characterise the landscape. To the north forest gradually gives way to the Okefenokee swampland. As a limited amount of industry is allowed in the national forests – as opposed to the national parks – a dispute has recently arisen over the preservation of this huge wilderness in Florida's north-east. The controversy was stirred up when it was suggested that open-cast mining of phosphate deposits could begin.

★ Osceola
National Forest

A charming recreational area has arisen at Ocean Pond, the national forest's largest lake. Remotely located on the northern bank is the Ocean Pond Campground, from where daring nature-lovers can penetrate the hinterland via the almost permanently damp Osceola Trail.

Ocean Pond

Big Gum Swamp Wilderness, with its extensive cypress swamps, lies north of the SR 250.

Big Gum Swamp
Wilderness

Osceola National Forest contains 38½ miles/62km of the Florida Trail from White Springs at Suwannee River to the Olustee Battlefield.

Florida Trail

A visit to Ichetucknee Springs State Park (SR 47 and 238/US 27), about 12 miles/20km south-west, can prove charming. Several powerful karst springs feed Ichetucknee River which flows into the Santa Fe River. For conservation reasons a maximum of 3000 visitors are allowed here a day.
　Traces of Indian settlements have been discovered at the springs. The Spanish who penetrated the New World temporarily maintained a missionary station here.
　Phosphate has been mined here since the beginning of the 20th c., to which evenly terraced and re-afforested areas bear witness.

★ Ichetucknee
Springs State
Park

River Tubing, the slow navigation of the crystal-clear, temperate karst waters using old car tyres or air-beds is a particular attraction.

River Tubing

The Stephen Foster State Folk Culture Center has been built on the banks of the Suwannee River at White Springs, just 12 miles/20km to the north-west. It commemorates Stephen Foster (1826–64), the composer of American folk songs. His songs "Old Folks at Home" and "Oh, Susanna!" have become world famous. The 200ft/61m tall tower (carillon) and the folklore exhibition are of note. The high spot of the many folkloristic events that take place during the year is the Florida Folk Festival on Memorial Day weekend.

Stephen Foster
State Folk
Culture Center

The old Springhouse, a wooden galleried building standing in water, is somewhat remote. Health cure treatments were carried out here at the beginning of the century. The Indians of the region had already prized the sulphurous springs, viewing them as holy places.

Springhouse

Lakeland

F 11/12

Polk County
Altitude: 220ft/67m. Population: 72,000

Lakeland, a town of great variety, is located in southern Central Florida and lies at the heart of a cultural landscape characterised by enormous citrus

Location

plantations. Fruit processing and packing are consequently its most important branches of industry along with phosphate mining and the fertiliser industry.

Within the town and its surroundings there are thirteen lakes, some large, some small, all of which offer anglers and lovers of water-sports excellent opportunities to indulge in their pastimes.

Sights

Lake
Hollingsworth,
Florida Southern
College

Florida Southern College, founded in 1885, is to be found near Lake Hollingsworth, an attractive lake south-west of the town centre. A number of its buildings, constructed from 1938 onwards and including the Anne Pfeifer Chapel (1941), were designed by the famous architect Frank Lloyd Wright. They form the largest remaining example of the work of the master builder L. Spivey. The principal of the college at that time asked his friend Wright to design the "first real American" university campus including the landscape and local building materials.

Orange Cup
Regatta

Every April, Lake Hollingsworth plays host to the Orange Cup Regatta for high-speed motorboats.

★Polk Museum
of Art

Polk Museum of Art (800 E. Palmetto St.; open: Tues. to Sat. 10am–4pm, Sun. noon–4pm, closed Aug.) displays mainly temporary exhibitions in addition to a small collection of pre-Columbian art and European 18th c. and 19th c. pottery. Every May the museum stages the two-day Mayfaire-by-the-Lake-Festival (street musicians, various market stalls, artists and artisans exhibiting their work).

Sun & Fun
Fly-in

In April aviation enthusiasts from all over the world assemble at the town's airport for the Sun & Fun Fly-in. The sky above Lakeland is then filled with air acrobats.

Lake Okeechobee   H/J 13/14

South Florida
Area of water: approximately 734sq.miles/1900sq.km

Natural area

Lake Okeechobee is the largest freshwater lake in the United States of America south of the Great Lakes. At the same time it forms the core of a powerful freshwater river, which pours out of Orlando, situated about 99 miles/160km further north, down into the Everglades.

The name Okeechobee originates from the language of the Seminolian Indians and means large water.

1928 hurricane

In 1928 approximately 2400 people died at Lake Okeechobee when a mighty hurricane swept across southern Florida. The waters of the flat lake were first forced northwards, and later – after a change in the wind direction – southwards into the Everglades. This led to devastating flooding which caused immeasurable damage, mainly to the farming industry.

Hoover Ring Dyke

So that such a catastrophe would never happen again, work began in 1929 on the Hoover Ring Dyke. It was completed in 1971.
At certain places motorists can drive up on to the crown of the dyke and enjoy a view across the lake. However, a scenic tour of the lake is hardly worth undertaking.

Water
reservoir

Parallel to this a cleverly-conceived system of canals and sluices not only regulates the water-level in the lake but also enables the use of the lake to provide drinking water to the fast-growing densely-populated towns along the Atlantic coast. It has also afforded the opportunity to meet the booming agricultural need for water.

It has sadly had to be learnt over the past few years that Lake Okeechobee and its surroundings react extremely sensitively to environmental interference of any sort. Hydraulic engineering processes have greatly affected the natural surroundings here and have severely disturbed the ground water flows in the Okeechobee area. The heavy use of herbicides and pesticides through both agriculture and the building industry in the catchment area of Lake Okeechobee and its basin have caused considerable damage to the quality of both surface water and ground water close to the surface. It has also threatened or destroyed the habitats not only of wild plants and animals (especially fish and birds) which thrive here but also the extensive flora and fauna of the Everglades. Ecologists and hydraulic engineering technicians are now working feverishly to organise the water industry in the Lake Okeechobee region to be as environmentally-friendly as possible.

Sensitive ecosystem

Lake Okeechobee is a paradise for anglers, who mostly fish for perch, catfish and bream here. Around the lake there are several fishing camps and marinas with ramps for boats. A stretch of canal passes through the lake linking the St Lucie Canal, coming from the Atlantic coast in the east (see Stuart), to the Caloosahatche River, which flows into the Gulf of Mexico at Ft. Myers (see entry). Using this route it is thus possible to cross the Florida peninsula by houseboat from east to west (or vice versa).

Recreation and leisure area

During the winter many campers crowd this area and large settlements of caravans spring up. The beaches of the Gold Coast, Miami and the attractions of central Florida can all be reached in a relatively short time from here.

Surroundings

The small country town of Okeechobee (30ft/9m above sea-level, population 5000) lies at the northern point of the lake. It is the administrative

Okeechobee

Lake Okeechobee, the largest freshwater lake in Florida

centre of the county of the same name as well as the centre of a relatively sparsely populated area heavily influenced by agriculture, in particular by cattle-rearing and milk production and, increasingly, the cultivation of citrus fruits and vegetables.

History

During the Christmas period of 1837 a decisive battle in the Second Semi-nolian War took place here. About 800 white soldiers and volunteers took part, led by Zachary Taylor, who was later elected to the post of 12th president of the United States partly on account of his service in Florida. A plaque by the side of the US 441, about 6miles/10km south-east of Okeechobee, commemorates this event.

Settlement

White people first settled at Lake Okeechobee towards the end of the 19th c. They chose the point where the Kissimmee River enters the lake (today Okee-Tanti State Park). At first really rough customs predominated. Cowboys, fishermen and woodcutters from the region spent their free time here.

Okeechobee gained its present character when it became connected to Flagler's railway line. It was expected that the town, because of its con-venient location, would develop into a Chicago of the South, and suitable public buildings were built accordingly.

Brighton Indian Reservation

Brighton Indian Reservation is situated a few miles west of Okeechobee. With an area of 58sq.miles/150sq.km it is the second largest Seminolian reservation. The Indians run a few camp sites, and during the winter they can be seen by the side of the through roads (US 78, CR 721) selling fruit or home-made souvenirs.

Belle Glade

Belle Glade (population 17,000) lies on the south-east bank of the lake. It has an interesting local history museum (including exhibitions dealing with the culture of the Calusa and the Seminolian Indians as well as sugar-cane production).

Many vegetables are grown to the north and the west of Belle Glade, whose permanently mild climate allows three harvests a year.

Clewiston

Enormous fields of sugar-cane fill the land around both Clewiston and Belle Glade. The large sugar-cane factories can process up to 20,000 tons a day.

Cypress Knee Museum

The Cypress Knee Museum, in which strangely-twisted aerial roots of swamp cypresses are exhibited, can be found to the west of the lake at Palmdale on the US 27. With a little imagination the most diverse figures can be recognised. It is worth taking a short walk (½ mile/1km) across a wooden footbridge through a wooded island and a cypress swamp.

Lake Wales F/G 12

Polk County
Altitude: 148ft/45m. Population: 10,000

Location

Located in Central Florida Lake Wales is surrounded by citrus groves, small pine forests, hills, which seem to extend as far as the eye can see, pastures and a large number of lakes, very popular with anglers. Some small indus-trial concerns, predominantly the cultivation and processing of citrus fruits, shape the economic life of the small town.

Lake Wales Mardi Gras; Black Hill Passion Plays

The Lake Wales Mardi Gras, a type of carnival with a procession and a fancy dress ball, an art exhibition and various musical presentations, takes place every year in February/March. The passion plays, staged in the amphi-theatre (2 miles/3km south of the town on the US 27 A; tel. 813/676 1495) enjoy nationwide importance.

Fall Fest & Pioneer Days

At the end of October/beginning of November the town celebrates its past for two days with a procession, exhibitions and displays of old craft techniques.

Sights

The Dutch-born philanthropist, publisher and author Edward Bok had a bell tower with a chime of 57 bells built on the highest point of the Florida peninsula, the 295ft/90m high Iron Mountain. It can be reached via Burns Avenue CR 17 A and is open daily from 8am until 5pm. The largest bell weighs about 11 tons. The tower and the carillon were officially inaugurated in 1929 by the then president Calvin Coolidge. The "Singing Tower" is built of red and grey Georgia marble and of Coquina limestone brought from St Augustine on the Atlantic coast. It is now surrounded by a charming small park where all kinds of bright flowers bloom including azaleas (flowering time Dec.–Apr.), magnolias, camellias (flowering time Nov.–Mar.) and gardenias, so typical of the south of the United States. The garden also contains lush green bracken, various bushes, palms, live oaks and pine trees.

It is worth viewing the richly-decorated façade of the tower. The frieze around the tower depicts Florida's animal world. Samuel Yelin's bronze door is decorated with scenes from the story of the Creation.

★Bok Tower
Gardens

A short peal of bells is rung every half an hour, a long one daily at 3pm. There are occasional special performances (including moonlit concerts and bank holiday events).

Carillon

In the Old Cracker House (open: daily 9am–5pm), a house typical of Florida during the time of the pioneers, much of interest can be learnt about the building of the tower and park and also about their founder.

Old Cracker
House

Near to Bok Tower is a trail which leads through the Pine Ridge Nature Reserve with its typical plant and animal life.

★Pine Ridge
Trail

The former Seaboard Coastline railway station, dating from 1928, now houses the Lake Wales Museum & Cultural Center (325 S Scenic Highway US 27A; tel. 813/676 5443; open: Mon. to Fri. 9am 5pm, Sat. 10am–4pm). It documents the development of the citrus plantation and cattle industries and the production of turpentine.

The Depot –
Lake Wales
Museum &
Cultural Center

Surroundings

It is worth making a detour to the 4942 acre/2000ha State Park at Lake Kissimmee (open: daily 7am–dusk), about 16 miles/25km east of Lake Wales and reached via the SR 60, Boy Scout Road and Camp Mack Road. Visits are particularly rewarding at the weekend when park employees enact the lives of Florida's 19th c. cowboys and cattle breeders.

A large part of the park is occupied by the Osceola Plain between Lake Kissimmee, Rosalie and Tiger, with hammocks, cypress swamps, open pine woods, swamps and a rich animal life. Birds, including the white-headed sea eagle, nest here. Lynxes and a number of Florida panthers, which have become extinct in other places, prowl through the more remote reaches of the park. Nature lovers set off from the small camp site on birdwatching excursions (viewing platform at Lake Kissimmee).

★Lake Kissimmee
State Park,
Kissimmee
Cow Camp

Babson Park Audubon Center (open: Tues. to Sat. 10am–5pm), a few miles south of Lake Wales, is also worth visiting. It houses an exhibition devoted to the region's wildlife and also has a trail along which local natural history is explained.

Babson Park

Lake Worth

J 15

Palm Beach
Altitude: 20ft/6m. Population: 30,000

Location	The town of Lake Worth, named after an American general who distinguished himself in the campaigns against the Seminolians and the Mexicans, lies to the south of Palm Beach (see entry). The first settlers came during the 1870s to the southern end of a narrow island and the mainland opposite. A little later a ferry service between Jacksonville and Fort Worth was instigated and a hotel was built.
Land boom	During the 1890s boom in land most of the settlers sold their plots to a Chicago firm of estate agents, who began planning a new settlement on Lake Worth's west bank. At first progress was slow and by 1912 there were only 308 permanent inhabitants. Today Lake Worth is an attractive American holiday resort and very forward-thinking – travel on the town's buses is free.

Sights

Lake Worth Pier	Lake Worth Pier, to be found at the end of Lake Avenue, projects almost 985ft/300m into the sea. It is popular with anglers.
Beach	The beautiful beach has a swimming pool, restaurant and golf course.
Lake Worth Museum	Lake Worth Museum (414 Lake Ave.; open: Mon. to Fri. 10am–4pm) deals mainly with local history and is housed in a City Hall building.

Surroundings

Polo fields	The world famous polo fields Gulfstream Polo Field and Palm Beach Polo Field are located 8 miles/13km and 12 miles/20km respectively from Lake Worth. From April to December high-ranking tournaments of this exclusive sport are held here. Now and again Prince Charles, the heir to the British throne, can be seen here.

Leesburg   E 11/12

Lake County
Altitude: 82ft/25m. Population: 15,000

Location	Leesburg, a small town lying in the lake-filled heart of Florida, is a marvellous starting point for tourists who want to become acquainted with Florida by houseboat. More than 1300 standing inshore waters can be reconnoitred within the immediate vicinity. Leesburg is also the economic centre of a region heavily influenced by agriculture. One of the world's largest cold-storage depots for citrus fruit concentrates was built here a few years ago.

Sights

Venetian Gardens	The Venetian Gardens, more than 74 acres/30ha in size, are situated a few miles to the east of the town and are well worth a visit. They offer the opportunity to swim, to sail or simply to relax.
★Lake Griffin	North-east of the town lies Lake Griffin, on whose foreshore a leisure and recreation zone has been demarcated. The area is known for its Floating Island. This is a swamp vegetation island which drifts leisurely on the water and the swamp. Trails and a camping area have been established.

Live Oak   B 5

Suwannee County
Altitude: 102ft/31m. Population: 7000

Live Oak was founded in 1863 during the building of the railway and is located approximately half way between Tallahassee (see entry) and Jacksonville (see entry) in the north of Florida. It forms the centre of the "Old South's" Suwannee Valley Region. During the 19th c. paddle-steamers operated on the Suwannee River, which forms the district's border for about 99 miles/160km and which has become well-known through Stephen Foster's song "Old Folks at Home". For a long time the river was the most important means of transport for the region's sugar, cotton and tobacco plantations. In later years timber was also transported across the river.

Location

Suwannee County remains a predominantly rural area chiefly producing tobacco, as well as cotton, sugar-cane, corn and peanuts. Live Oak is home to Florida's largest and oldest tobacco market, where auctions are held every July/August.

Economy

The old town centre was redeveloped as part of the Main Street Development Program. The former goods depot now houses the small Suwannee County Museum which is concerned mostly with local history.

Town centre

Suwannee River begins its course in the Okefenokee swamps of southern Georgia and flows powerfully through the north of Florida. It is popular with both canoeists and anglers. The countless crystal-clear springs near Live Oak tempt many to go snorkelling and diving.

Suwannee River

Most popular with divers are the Branford Springs, 25 miles/40km south of Branford (US 129/US 27 West), the Peacock Slough with 20 different springs and flooded sink-holes further upriver near the SR 51 south of Luraville, or Troy Springs, 6 miles/10km north-west of Branford, with an approximately 82ft/25m deep source pool.

Branford Springs, Luraville, Troy Springs

Suwannee River State Park lies about 14 miles/22km west of the US 90 at the point where the Withlacoochee flows into the Suwannee River. It consists of a typical piece of Florida's original river landscape.

★Suwannee River State Park

South of the confluence the remains of Confederate graves can be found. These men were killed during the Civil War while defending the railway bridge across the Suwannee River, thus protecting the important supply line to the southern states. The ferry investor and a sawmill had had the small settlement of Columbus established here before the Civil War but all that remains of it today is a cemetery in the pine wood, and the old post road (reachable via the Sand Hill Trail). Of particular scenic charm is the Suwannee River Trail which leads along the river's high bank.

Longboat Key

See Bradenton. See Sarasota

Marco Island   K 12

Collier
Altitude: 0–53ft/0–16m. Population: 10,000

Marco Island is the most northerly of the Ten Thousand Islands, a labyrinth of larger and smaller mangrove islands lying off the Everglades. Archaeological excavations have uncovered valuable finds and point to a 500-year Indian settlement here. In 1922 Barron G. Collier acquired the largest part of Marco Island in order to construct a new deep water and oil harbour. It was thought that a large amount of petroleum would be discovered here.

Location

Since the 1960s Marco Island has experienced a constant growth in tourism. Beautiful beaches and the most marvellous fishing grounds tempt

Marco Island

Marco Island Crescent Beach

increasing numbers of visitors. The 6 mile/10km-long and 4 mile/6km-wide island, about 19 miles/30km south of Naples (see entry), is now connected to the mainland by two bridges (US 41/SR 92 or 951).

Sights

Old Marco Village | Old Marco Village, at the northern end of the island, is very attractive. A number of old buildings and some exquisite shops and restaurants help to brighten up the scene.

Port of Marco | The Port of Marco harbour has a nostalgic shopping centre. Royal Palm Drive is very charming.

★Beach | Fashionable hotels and apartment blocks line the attractive, wide sandy beach which extends for 4 miles/6km.

Interior of the island | The interior of the island is crossed by many canals. Many of the villas have their own landing stages and swimming pools, with protection from mosquitoes.

Goodland | The former fishing village of Goodland with the Coon Key Pass Marina (604 E. Palm Ave.) is situated to the south-east of the island. It is mainly used by fishermen and deep-sea anglers.

★Tigertail Beach & Park | Tigertail Beach & Park (Hernando Drive), on the north-west side of the island, is one of south-west Florida's most beautiful public beaches.

Marco Island Trolley | A great deal about the island and its past can be learnt during a tour on the ethnic Marco Island Trolley, sadly only in service during the winter season. An embankment built by Calusa Indians from shells can also be seen during the trip.

Surroundings

If time allows, an excursion on the "Island Princess" through the extremely impressive and still very unspoilt seascape of the Ten Thousand Islands should not be missed. Information – Marco Island Chamber of Commerce; tel. 394 3101.

★Ten Thousand Island Nature Cruises

Collier-Seminole State Park lies in a transitional zone and encompasses both areas of swampland (Big Cypress Swamp), hardwood hammocks with a number of royal palms, and the almost inpenetrable mangrove thickets of the coastal area. Nearly two-thirds of its 10sq.miles/26sq.km remain an undeveloped wilderness. A number of nature trails and a 13 mile/21km canoe trail can be used to explore the nature reserve.

★Collier-Seminole State Park

The canoe tour, in particular, demands some experience of coping in the wild and should only be undertaken during the winter because of mosquitoes. Be careful – it is all to easy to get lost in the tangle of mangrove islands.

More specific information about the condition of the ecosystem and about fish and plants can be obtained in the visitors' centre. The Indian presence in this area is also explained here. Information – Collier-Seminole State Park Ranger Station, Marco, FL; tel. 394 3397.

Marianna   A 5

Jackson County
Altitude: 118ft/36m
Population: 7000

Founded in 1829, the small country town of Marianna is dissected by the Chipola River. It lies on the border with both Georgia and Alabama and is the administrative seat of predominantly-agricultural Jackson County (peanuts, soya beans, corn). Various buildings dating from the time of the American Civil War bear witness to the "Old South".

Location

Sights

Chipola River, which flows through Marianna, offers very good opportunities for canoe tours.

Chipola River

Merritts Mill Pond is to be found east of Marianna. It is fed its blue-shimmering water from an underwater cave in the Blue Springs region.

Merritts Mill Pond

It is worth paying a visit to the Florida Caverns, about 3 miles/5km north of Marianna. These dripstone caves were discovered by the Spanish in 1693. It is thought that this system of caves was a place of refuge used by the Indians, who also hid here in 1818 from Andrew Jackson (see Famous People). Only a small section of the caves, which were formed chiefly by the Chipola River, are accessible. Within the caves enormous stalactites and stalacmites greet the eye. The high water-level necessitates the wearing of a diving suit to pass along the passages which connect many siphons and individual halls. Guided tours take place daily from 9am to 5pm. Nature trail. Visitors' centre. Information; tel. 482 95 98.

★Florida Caverns State Park

By following County Road 276 in a south-westerly direction for approximately 15 miles/25km out of the town a geomorphological phenomenon typical of Florida can be viewed – a "sink-hole", over the edge of which a natural waterfall (Florida's only large waterfall) tumbles approximately 98ft/30m into the lush greenery below. The water then disappears again into an underground system of caves. An informative trail leads to the first oil well discovered in Florida, which is, however, not very productive.

★Falling Waters State Recreation Area

Marineland

Lake Seminole,
Three Rivers
State
Recreation Park

A trip to Lake Seminole (US 90/SR 271), 25 miles/40km east of Marianna, takes the traveller through a landscape still largely undisturbed by tourism. This artificial lake, situated on the border with Georgia and Alabama, covers an area of 58sq.miles/150sq.km and is surrounded by forest. Together with the Three Rivers State Recreation Area it offers plenty of excellent opportunities for anglers and water-sports lovers. The remains of dead trees around the banks of the lake, some of which appear quite eerie, bear witness to the extensive areas of swamp and forest which covered the flat valleys here before the successful completion of the Jim Woodruff Dam (sluice, generation of energy) in 1957. Before the dam was built, the water-level in both the Chattahoochee River and the Flint River was usually not sufficiently deep for boats to be able to negotiate them. Today it is once again possible to travel along the Apalachicola River and via the artificial lake to the town of Columbus, situated approximately 93miles/150km further to the north in Georgia.

Marineland

See St Augustine

Melbourne   F 14

Brevard County
Altitude: 0–23ft/0–7m
Population: 60,000

Location

Melbourne, lying in a sheltered position on the "Space Coast" (Florida's mid-Atlantic section, named after the nearby US space centre), developed rapidly during the 1980s. Its proximity to Cape Canaveral (see entry) has led numerous electronics companies to base themselves here.

The beautiful and particularly long beaches and dunes, planted with marram grass and palmetto and seagrape brushwood, have been decisive in the positive development in tourism.

Sights

Brevard Art
Center & Museum

Brevard Art Center & Museum (1463 Highland Ave.; open: Tues.–Sun. 1–4pm) has a series of exhibitions by both local and internationally-known artists.

Brevard
Zoological Park

Melbourne's small zoo (3880 W. New Haven Ave., US 192; open: daily 9am–5.30pm) is aimed predominantly at younger visitors.

Florida
Institute of
Technology (FIT)

Florida Institute of Technology (7000 students) was founded in 1958.

The campus contains an attractive botanical garden.

Fishing Piers

Both the Eau Gallie Fishing Pier (at the west end of the Eau Gallie Causeway) and the Melbourne Beach Fishing Pier (at the west end of Ocean Avenue) afford the opportunity to fish in Indian River from firm ground. Boats can be chartered from various marinas.

Surroundings

Recreation parks

Wickham Park, with its two lakes and its leisure facilities, lies to the west of Melbourne.

Long Point Park offers a camp site and fishing opportunities. It is located near to Sebastian Inlet, north of Melbourne.

A number of residential and holiday resorts bearing fine-sounding names are ranged along the offshore, narrow barrier island: Satellite Beach (10,000 inhabitants; a series of high-rise complexes which developed rapidly on the edge of the beach), Indian Harbour Beach (population 8000; a charming development immediately on the water's edge), Indiatlantic (population 4000; an attractive village with the especially beautiful, sandy Paradise Beach) and Melbourne Beach (4000 inhabitants; a quiet beach resort). The beautiful beaches of Spessard Holland Park lie to the south.

Beach
settlements

Since 1971 a 98ft/30m long dragon, built of 20 tons of concrete and steel, has surveyed boat traffic on Indian River and Banana River from the southern tip of Merritt Island (north of the Eau Gallie Causeway). The lindworm is the work of the sculptor Lewis Vandercar from Tampa, who added four small dragons in 1982. According to an Indian legend a dragon arose from the floods of Indian River and chased away a group of mainland Indians who wanted to attack the village on the island.

★Merritt Island
Dragon

Miami

K/L 15

Dade County
Altitude: 0–26ft/0–8m
Population: city centre 386,000 (metropolitan area two million)

The city of Miami lies on the south-east side of the Florida peninsula. It is separated from the Atlantic Ocean by the Biscayne Bay lagoon and by Miami Beach with its sprinkling of impressive hotels and apartments.

Location

The proximity of the tropics and the warm Gulf Stream make the climate in a dry winter pariculary mild (January's average temperature is 66°F/19°C); in contrast the summer is very damp and warm (August's average temperature is 82°F/28°C). During summer and autumn Miami is occasionally at risk from tropical hurricanes which can reach speeds of up to 118mph/190kph.

Climate

The favourable climatic conditions in winter have accounted for the boom in tourism in the Miami area, which welcomes more than seven million visitors a year. Miami is home to the world's most important passenger harbour (approximately three million passengers yearly) and about 22 million passengers pass through its important international airport each year. The importance of its holiday and business trade is demonstrated by the presence of more than 600 large hotels and motels, several thousand restaurants and cafés and four dozen foreign consulates. Until the end of the 1970s Miami lived predominantly by tourism and by the retired people who moved here from the north. Following a change in banking regulations and the subsequent influx of capital from Latin America and Saudi Arabia the metropolis of the "Sunshine State" developed into an internationally important seat of banking and finance, to which more than 170 financial institutions have moved. The tertiary sector (trade and the service industries) occupies a prominent position in the economic life of the city. Manufacturing occupies only third place as an employer – Miami is traditionally an important site of the aviation, space and food industries. Other important branches of the economy include an up-and-coming film industry and some famous biomedical research centres.

Economy

At the turn of the century Miami had a population of fewer than 5000; today it forms the centre of a metropolitan area encompassing 27 municipalities and inhabited by about two million people. Of these, approximately 250,000 are coloured, originating mainly from the Caribbean (in particular from Haiti, which had suffered a situation bordering on civil war), and almost 400,000 are Spanish-speaking Latinos from Cuba and Central America. More recently, they have been joined by several thousand migrants from South America, predominantly from Brazil.

Population

In 1513 the Spaniard Ponce de Léon reconnoitred Biscayne Bay for the first time and in 1567 the Spanish Jesuit mission station Tequesta was established within the region of present-day Miami as a base for the silver fleet setting out for Europe.

After the Spanish withdrawal in 1821, R. Fitzpatrick became the first American to settle here. With the help of slaves he laid out cotton plantations and planted tropical fruits in this humid, mosquito-infested area. Fort Dallas was established in 1836 during the Seminolian wars. In 1871 William Brickell built a post and trading station at the mouth of Miami River (*Mayami* means great water in Indian). Five years later a northern Yankee lady named Julia Tuttle acquired a large piece of land north of Miami River. It is thanks to her that Henry M. Flagler extended his East Coast railroad to Miami in 1895/6 and opened the Royal Palm Hotel at its provisional terminus. At that time Miami had barely 5000 inhabitants. The Spanish-American War of 1898 brought the young town rich gains. In 1912 a strong wooden bridge was built across to the offshore island of Miami Beach. The population grew continually and by 1925 85,000 people were living here. A hurricane which raced across the flourishing town in 1926 dealt it a powerful economic setback. The economic crisis of the following years also left its mark.

During the Second World War many thousands of wounded servicemen were sent to Miami for treatment and to recover, a large number of them choosing to settle here. After the Second World War a building boom on a hitherto unknown scale began which continues to this day. Cuba's Castro-led revolution caused many of the islanders to turn their backs on their homeland and to migrate to Miami. These Cuban refugees were to have a considerable share in the ensuing development of the Miami region.

In the early 1980s another wave of thousands of Cubans flooded into the Miami area. Countless refugees from Haiti also fled here by boat; today most of them eke out an existence as underdogs.

During the last ten days of August 1992 Hurricane Andrew swept across the Miami region causing serious damage, particularly in the southern suburbs. The whirlwind claimed at least 24 victims, while more than 200,000 people were made homeless.

Sights

Buses, with exteriors reminiscent of the old trams, depart from Bayside Marketplace on the harbour promenade several times a day. In the course of a one-and-a-half-hour tour they pass by all of Miami's and Miami Beach's historically-important buildings.

Bayfront

The southern section of palm tree-decorated Biscayne Boulevard, bordered to the east by Bayfront Park and to the south by Miami River, forms Miami's main artery. The west side of the boulevard is lined by some magnificent high-rise buildings, including the 456ft/139m-tall One Biscayne Tower, completed in 1972, and, behind that, the First Federal Building (509ft/155m).

Bayfront Park, which extends to the east of Biscayne Boulevard, was completely redesigned some time ago. Pepper Fountain, electronically-controlled, provides an attractive detail. The park contains an amphitheatre, where all types of musical productions are staged, and a tower for laser shows.

There are also three important memorials within the park: the Torch of Friendship, symbolising the diverse connections which link the city of

◀ *Downtown Miami at night*

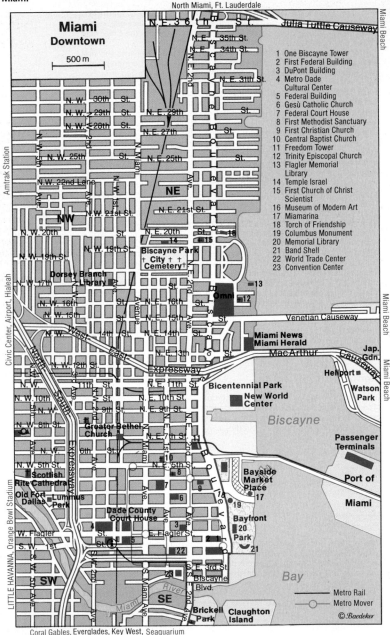

Miami

Miami Downtown

500 m

1 One Biscayne Tower
2 First Federal Building
3 DuPont Building
4 Metro Dade Cultural Center
5 Federal Building
6 Gesù Catholic Church
7 Federal Court House
8 First Methodist Sanctuary
9 First Christian Church
10 Central Baptist Church
11 Freedom Tower
12 Trinity Episcopal Church
13 Flagler Memorial Library
14 Temple Israel
15 First Church of Christ Scientist
16 Museum of Modern Art
17 Miamarina
18 Torch of Friendship
19 Columbus Monument
20 Memorial Library
21 Band Shell
22 World Trade Center
23 Convention Center

North Miami, Ft. Lauderdale

Julia Tuttle Causeway

N. E. 36th St.

N. E. 35th St.
N. E. 34th St.
N. E. 31st St.

Miami Beach

N. W. 30th St.
N. W. 29th St.
N. W. 28th St.

N. E. 29th St.
N. E. 27th St.

N. W. 25th St.
N. E. 25th St.

N. W. 22nd Lane
N. E. 21st St.

NE

N. W. 21st St.
NW

N. W. 20th

N. E. 20th St.
N. W. 19th St.
N. W. 19th St.

Temple Israel 14

First Church of Christ Scientist 15
16

N. W. 17th

Dorsey Branch Library

Biscayne Park City Cemetery

N. W. 16th
N. E. 16th St.

13

N. W. 15th
N. E. 15th St.

Omni 12

Amtrak Station

Venetian Causeway

Miami Beach

N. W. 14th St.
East
West

N. E. 14th St.
N. E. 13th St.

Miami News
Miami Herald

Jap. Gdn.

Civic Center, Airport, Hialeah

Expressway

MacArthur Causeway

Heliport

N. W. 12th St.
N. E. 11th St.
N. W. 11th St.

Bicentennial Park

New World Center

Watson Park

Miami Beach

N. W. 10th St.
N. E. 10th St.

North

N. W. 9th St.
N. E. 9th St.

N. W. 8th St.

Biscayne

N. W.
N. E. 7th St.

Greater Bethel Church

West

Passenger Terminals

N. W. 6th St.

Miami

N. E. 5th St.

Port of

N. W. 5th St.

Scottish Rite Cathedral

8

Bayside Market Place

Miami

Old Fort Dallas

7

9

17

Lummus Park

6

19

Dade County Court House

3

Bayfront 20 Park

LITTLE HAVANNA, Orange Bowl Stadium

E. Flagler St.
W. Flagler St.
S. W. 1st St.

5

2

21

22

S. E. 3rd St.

23

Biscayne Blvd.

SW

S. W. 2nd

SE

Miami River

Bay

Brickell Park

Claughton Island

Coral Gables, Everglades, Key West, Seaquarium

—— Metro Rail
◯ Metro Mover

©Baedeker

176

Miami to the countries of middle and south America, the World War II Memorial, commemorating the dead of the Second World War, and the Challenge Memorial, which honours the crew of the Orbiter who died in 1986.

Bayfront Park is bordered by Bayside Market Place and the modern yacht harbour Miamarina (formerly Pier 5 of the seaport; 208 moorings; boat excursions, deep-sea angling, made famous by the television series "Miami Vice" as the mooring place of Sonny Krockett's houseboat). Attractive shops, elegant restaurants and the Pier 5 Market (souvenirs, arts and crafts, street music with a Caribbean/Mid-American flavour) leave a lasting impression. Two bridges lead from the market to the Bayfront Park Amphitheater, opened to the public in 1988.

★Bayside Market Place, Miamarina

A particular attraction of the yacht harbour is H.M.S. "Bounty" (open: daily Mon.–Thur. 10am–6pm, Fri./Sat. 10am–10pm, Sun. noon–8pm; entry fee), a replica of an 18th c. three-master used in the 1962 film "Mutiny on the Bounty" starring Marlon Brando.

H.M.S. "Bounty"

The New World Center/Bicentennial Park, north of Bayfront Park, replaced old parts of the harbour as part of an ultra-modern redevelopment scheme carried out in the city.

New World Center/ Bicentennial Park

A prominent building along Bayfront Boulevard is Freedom Tower built in the wedding-cake style. This construction, dating from the early years of the city, is one of the oldest skyscrapers in the south of the USA and was for a long time the publishing base of the "Miami Herald".

Freedom Tower

Downtown

Busy Flagler Street is presently experiencing a revival. It leads westwards from Biscayne Boulevard and passes first by the Guzman Cultural Center (1926; formerly the Olympia Theater, renovated in 1972), then by Dade County Court House (1926) and on to the ultra-modern Federal Building (Government Center). It continues past the attractive, Mediterranean-style Metro Dade Cultural Center with the Center of Fine Arts (periodic exhibitions), the Main Library and the Historical Museum of Southern Florida (early Indian tribes, pirates, pioneers, 3-D films about Miami; open: Mon.–Sat. 10am–5pm, Thur. until 9pm, Sun. noon–5pm).

Flagler Street

The Centrust Bank Tower, a skyscraper with 52 floors and brightly illuminated at night, was completed in 1987 and has become a new symbol of Downtown Miami. This tower-shaped, high-rise building was designed by I. M. Pei, America's most famous contemporary architect, in partnership with Spillis Candela & Partners. The megastructure's multi-coloured lighting system, which also makes it visible from afar at night, was devised by Douglas Leigh. Several hundred 1000-watt lamps bathe the tower in Irish green on St Patrick's Day, for example, and in the red of love on St Valentine's Day.

★Centrust Bank Tower

The 55 storeys of the ultra-modern South East Financial Center make it even taller than the Centrust Tower.

South East Financial Center

Other notable buildings in the city centre include the DuPont Building, the Catholic Gesu Church and the Federal Court House.

Other buildings

Lummus Park lies further to the west, on the other side of the north–south city motorway. It contains the buildings of Fort Dallas (originally used to accommodate slaves working on the first plantation established here), which was constructed in 1836 at the mouth of Miami River and which was transferred here after a fire, and Wagner House (a typical pioneer's house dating from the mid 19th c.).

Lummus Park, Fort Dallas

Little Havana

★Calle Ocho
(8th Street,
Tamiami Trail)

From Bayfront Park (Brickell Ave.), 8th Street extends westwards across Miami River. Excluding its high-rise centre, the street is known as "Calle Ocho" and later leads into the Tamiami Trail (see entry) which crosses the Everglades.

"Little Havana"

The quarter of the city situated on the western edge of Downtown Miami and dissected by 8th Street is called "Little Havana", with the street itself known as "Calle Ocho". The names are derived from the large number of Latinos, mainly Cubans in exile, who live here. The bright shops, small markets and friendly cafés and restaurants within the area lying between SW 12th Avenue and SW 27th Avenue create a particularly relaxed atmosphere. Spanish is the colloquial language of "Little Havana". To maintain the Cuban character of 8th Street, its historical buildings are now protected.

Domino Park

Older Cuban exiles meet in attractive Domino Park (SW 15th Ave.) for a traditional game of dominoes.

Orange Bowl

Orange Bowl (football), a particular attraction of the quarter, has become famous as the venue for a music festival.

Dade County
Auditorium

Countless music lovers and friends of the performing arts are drawn to Dade County Auditorium (2901 W. Flagler St.; 2500 seats) in the west of the city.

Avenue of the
Americas

To the north of Bayside Marketplace, the Avenue of the Americas is a highway on stilts, which swings above Biscayne Bay and leads to the Port of Miami.

Port of Miami

Location

The Port of Miami, located on Dodge Island and Lummus Island (both artificially created), is presently the world's most important sea passage terminal. More than a dozen cruise ships can berth here at any one time and every year approximately three million cruise passengers are catered for, the majority of whom sail to the Bahamas or the Caribbean islands.

At present the port is being extended to the east. Facilities to berth large freight ships have already been created.

MacArthur Causeway – Julia Tuttle Causeway

MacArthur
Causeway

The western bridgehead of MacArthur Causeway, presently under construction, is situated north of Bicentennial Park. It leads to Miami Beach.

Miami Herald

The Miami Herald/Miami News Building stands immediately on the bridgehead.

Watson Park

Crossing the "highway on stilts", travellers immediately reach pretty Watson Park with the Japanese Garden (pagoda, tea house, waterfall), and a Tivoli-like pleasure garden.
   Helicopter tours can be undertaken from the heliport here, and trips to the Bahamas by seaplane also depart from here.

Venetian
Causeway

About 985ft/300m further to the north, Venetian Causeway crosses Biscayne Bay to Miami Beach and links the man-made Venetian Islands.

Omni
International

The Omni International Miami towers up to a height of 295ft/90m above the northern bridgehead of Venetian Causeway. Completed in 1977 the complex has a very plain exterior. It contains a 556-room hotel, several shopping levels, eight restaurants, six cinemas and a number of other facilities including a historic carousel.

Cuban, American and international artwork is exhibited in the Bacardi Art Gallery, located even further to the north.

Bacardi Art Gallery

Little Hai'ti

The city's "Little Hai'ti" quarter has evolved in North East Miami. About 70,000 of the almost 200,000 Haitians who have settled in the Miami region live here. Most arrived by boat as destitute refugees from the Hispaniola islands. The predominantly dark-skinned people live in an area encompassing 200 blocks and have already opened more than 400 small shops.

Location

The Caribbean Marketplace (5927 NE 2nd Ave.) is particularly colourful. Tropical fruit can be bought here, as well as Caribbean craftwork and naïve Haitian paintings.

★Caribbean Marketplace

North West

The ultra-modern Civic Center and the Metropolitan Medical Center, a very famous clinic in the USA, are situated in the north west of the city.

Civic Center, Medical Center

The large Miami Stadium (which stages baseball, among other sports) can be found further to the north.

Miami Stadium

Miami River – Brickell Avenue

Biscayne Avenue ends at Miami River. During the 1980s a very impressive example of high rise architecture was built on the northern bank of the river. Neat apartment complexes have been constructed on the opposite bank and on neighbouring Claughton Island.

Miami River

The bridge across the estuary of Miami River links the busy city centre to the prosperous residential areas between Biscayne Bay and Brickell Avenue.

Miami Bridge

Brickell Avenue, originally built as a residential road ("Millionaires' Street") for wealthy, old-established families, is lined by modern administrative high-rise buildings and condominiums. It has become famous as the "Wall Street" of Miami. More than 100 financial institutions, all of which operate worldwide, maintain extremely prestigious and highly-profitable branches here.

★Brickell Avenue

Brickell Park, south of Miami Bridge, is very attractive and well-tended.

Brickell Park

Brickell House (no. 501), built in 1871, is noteworthy.

Brickell House

Rickenbacker Causeway (toll) leads from the southern end of Brickell Avenue across flat Biscayne Bay to Virginia Key, covered with mangroves, and on to the island of Key Biscayne.

Rickenbacker Causeway

Virginia Key – Key Biscayne

Miami's Marine Stadium is situated on the eastern bridgehead of Rickenbacker Causeway. Water sports events, pop concerts and firework displays are staged here.

Miami's Marine Stadium

Miami

NOAA

The American meteorological service maintains one of its most important branches nearby: the weather conditions above Florida and almost the entire Caribbean area are observed from the research centre of the National Oceanic & Atmospheric Administration (NOAA). This allows the population of the Sunshine State to be warned in time of threatening whirlwinds.

★Seaquarium

It is worth visiting the Miami Seaquarium (open: daily 9am–6pm, last entry 4.30pm), southern Florida's largest tropical seawater aquarium and home to many different marine creatures, at the southern tip of Virginia Key. Its special attractions include the Golden Aquadome, the killer whale Lolita, the dolphin Flipper, made famous by television, an artificial coral reef and an underwater viewing station (including sharks).

Marine Laboratory

Nearby is Miami University's Marine Laboratory (oceanographic research centre).

Virginia Beach

This beautiful bathing beach is located on Virginia Key's east coast.

★Key Biscayne

Bear Cut Bridge (toll) leads finally to the island of Key Biscayne, known above all to those interested in golf and tennis as a venue for important tournaments. There are a number of important sports facilities (including the International Tennis Center and the Crandon Park Marina) on Key Biscayne, as well as several resorts.

Bill Baggs Park

Bill Baggs Cape Florida State Park, with its magnificent sandy beach, is to be found at the southern end of the island. A very interesting exhibition dealing with the Seminolian wars is displayed in the little keeper's room in the lighthouse (1825).

★Coconut Grove

Location

The present-day suburb of Coconut Grove is 20 years older than Miami. It was founded in about 1840 by the dark-skinned migrants from the Bahamas called *Conchs*. Intellectuals from New England immediately appeared and had trim winter homes built for themselves here. A number of artists followed and lent the area their own character.

Coquina little houses

Simple little half-timbered houses, stronger buildings constructed from local Coquina limestone and magnificent villas built in the Mediterranean style standing amid densely overgrown tropical gardens give atmosphere to the settlement.

★Villa Vizcaya (Dade County Art Museum)

The beautiful Villa Vizcaya (3251 S. Miami Ave.; open: daily 9.30am–4.30pm) lies a short distance south of Rickenbacker Causeway and is set in a classical garden with artistic fountains. The villa was built between 1912 and 1916 in the style of the Italian Renaissance as a winter home for the wealthy harvester manufacturer James Deering.

The collection of French, Spanish and Italian art, the various pieces of furniture, the carpets and sculptures, and the collection of old Baedekers exhibited in the opulently-furnished rooms of the mansion, now the Dade County Art Museum, are noteworthy.

Ermità de la Caridad

The Ermità de la Caridad (3609 S. Miami Ave.) is located further south. This sacred building, almost 99ft/30m high, has been built facing Cuba and is visited mainly by the faithful among the Cuban exiles.

Museum of Science & Planetarium

The Museum of Science & Planetarium (3280 S. Miami Ave.) is situated further to the south-west. It offers a scientific exhibition, an observatory and a space show. Open: (museum) daily 10am–6pm; (observatory) Thurs.–Sun. 8–10pm.

Villa Vizcaya: Italianate Renaissance in Florida

Miami City Hall, the Dinner Key complex with auditorium (mainly musical presentations) and the Marina (370 moorings for yachts, the world's largest boat exhibition in October) are other notable groups of buildings.

Other buildings

Main Highway, with its street cafés, speciality shops and boutiques, is a main artery, especially in the area around Grand Avenue which leads into the original Black Grove artists' quarter.

Main Highway

Coconut Grove Playhouse (3500 Main Highway; theatre built in 1926) and Barnacle House (3485 Main Highway, built by Commodore Munroe in 1891) are of note.

Playhouse

Mayfair Shopping Center in Mary Street has for years been one of the most exclusive shopping centres in the western hemisphere.

★Mayfair Shopping Center

Standing opposite is Cocowalk, opened in 1991, a tempting shopping and leisure centre. Its many boutiques, cafés, restaurants and its two small theatres offer a diversion.

★Cocowalk

The genteel lagoon settlement of Cable Estate, composed of luxurious villas standing in magnificent gardens complete with their own yacht moorings, lies to the south of Coconut Grove.

Cable Estate

Coral Gables

The suburb of Coral Gables (population 47,000) lies to the south-west of the city centre. This residential area, no longer as distinguished as before, was built in 1926 by George Merrick in the Mediterranean style, according to plans drawn up by his father. It enjoys extensive parkland and sports

Location

grounds, including the Biltmore Golf Course, the Granada Golf Course and the Riviera Golf Course.

City Hall	Coral Gable City Hall, built in the Spanish Renaissance style, stands at the northern end of LeJeune Road.
★Miracle Mile	Miracle Mile begins at City Hall. It is Coral Gables' well-known main shopping street, which has recently been successfully revived after a period of stagnation.
Colonnade Building	The Colonnade Building, built and used by Merrick, is an architectural eye-catcher. It has a rotunda, a variety of ornamentation and a Spanish tiled roof and today forms part of the Colonnade Hotel.
Coral Gables House	Both the exterior and the interior of Coral Gables House (907 Coral Way) have been restored in the 1920s style and are worth seeing. George Merrick spent his youth here.
DeSoto Plaza	The fountain in nearby DeSoto Plaza was built in the 1920s by D. Fink and is delightful.
★Venetian Pool	Venetian Pool, a very attractive open-air swimming pool built into an abandoned coral limestone quarry, is located to the south-west of the town hall.
Coral Way	The area around Coral Way is typically residential. It is worth viewing Coral Gables House (907 Coral Way), George Merrick's family home built between 1898 and 1907.
★Biltmore Hotel	The former Biltmore Hotel (architect: George Merrick) was opened in 1926 and is now once more an architectural *pièce de résistance*.
	During the Second World War it was transformed into a hospital and it stood empty from 1968 until 1986, when it was allowed to go to rack and ruin. In the past few years, however, it has been lavishly restored. A decision on its further use has not yet been made.
University of Miami	The more than 247 acre/100ha campus of the University of Miami (founded in 1926, 14,000 students) extends along the foreshore of the Coral Gables Waterway.
Lowe Art Museum	The Lowe Art Museum (open: Tues.–Sat. 10am–5pm; Sun. noon–5pm) belongs to the university and exhibits examples of the artwork of the Pueblo and the Navajo Indians. American painting, the Kress collection of old masters and Renaissance and Baroque art can also be admired here.

South Miami

★Parrot Jungle and Gardens	Parrot Jungle, a densely-overgrown, tropical region home to parrots, marabons, cockatoos and flamingos, lies near Matheson Hammock Park in South Miami. Daily displays take place in the "Parrot Bowl". There is also a flamingo lake and a parrot circus (open: daily 9.30am–6pm).
Sausage Tree	The unique "Sausage Tree" (*Kigelia Pinnata*) with its sausage-like fruits can be seen a little to the south.
Fairchild Tropical Gardens	Fairchild Tropical Gardens (10901 Old Cutler Road), a botanical garden with tropical vegetation (including many unusual varieties of palm), lies approximately 1 mile/2km south of Parrot Jungle.
Matheson Hammock Park	Matheson Hammock Park, situated nearby, is the oldest park in the Miami region created for the purpose of relaxation. It has mangrove forests and a beautiful bathing beach.

Metro Zoo (open: daily 9.30am–5.30pm), one of the largest zoos in the USA, is to be found in South Miami. It was only opened in 1982 and was designed along the most modern scientific lines. More than 100 species of animals live here in enclosures akin to their natural environment. Main attractions are the Bengali tigers, koala bears and an enormous aviary with more than 300 different birds.

★Metro Zoo

Hialeah

The suburb of Hialeah (from the Indian meaning "beautiful river") extends to the south of the city centre. It was begun in 1921 and today accommodates about 140,000 inhabitants. Hialeah Park, with its racecourse, lake, colony of flamingos, numerous other unusual birds, aquarium and exhibition of coaches, is very impressive.

Location

Opa Locka

Opa Locka (north of Hialeah) is a classic example of a 1920s settlement and was conceived by the architect in the Moorish style. The streets are laid out in a crescent shape and named after characters in the 1001 Arabian Nights fairy story. It is worth viewing City Hall and the Heart Building/Opa Locka Hotel with its cupolas and minarets. The Arabian Nights Festival is held here in May.

1001 Arabian Nights

North Miami

North Miami is a suburb located about 9 miles/14km from the city centre. It is worth visiting the Miami Wax Museum (13899 N. Biscayne Blvd.) with its 40 dioramas dealing with the history of Florida ("From the Stone Age to the Space Age").

Miami Wax Museum

The suburb of North Miami Beach lies a few miles further to the north. Its main attraction is the Cloisters of the Monastery of St Bernhard (Ancient Spanish Monastery), a monastery built in 1141 in Segovia in Spain which the publisher William Randolph Hearst (1863–1951) had transported to America.

The Cloisters

Florida International University is situated in the Sweetwater suburb. The work of the university is chiefly centered on the problems of the Caribbean area.

Florida International University

Miami Beach   K 15

A total of five causeways and bridges lead from Miami across Biscayne Bay, which reaches a width of up to 2½ miles/4km, to a fairly narrow spit of land almost 10 miles/16km in length. Here, where mosquito-infested mangrove swamps flourished until the turn of the century, a beach settlement has evolved. In the course of a few decades it has grown into the largest relaxation, pleasure and seaside resort in the USA.

Location

Until 1912, the area now called Miami Beach remained a sandy island in Biscayne Bay waiting to be discovered. John Collins, the founder of the settlement, and Carl Fisher, a millionaire who had already built the motor-racing circuit at Indianapolis, vigorously supported the development of the young beach resort.

History

The construction boom of the 1920s and the 1930s was only checked by the devastating hurricane of 1926, the worldwide economic crisis in 1929 and

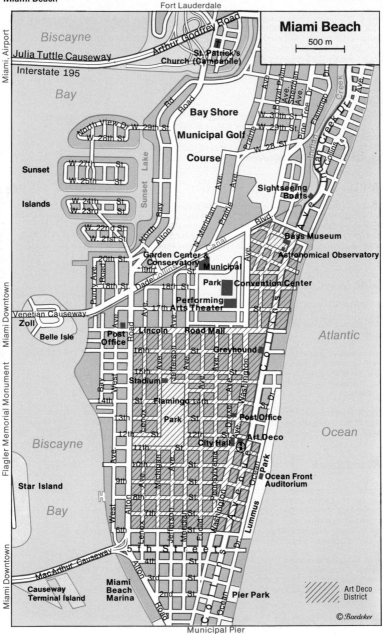

Miami Beach

Miami Beach

500 m

Fort Lauderdale

Biscayne

Julia Tuttle Causeway

Interstate 195

Bay

Miami, Airport

Arthur Godfrey Road

St. Patrick's
Church (Campanile)

Bay Shore

Municipal Golf

Course

Sunset

North View Dr. W. 29th St.
W. 28th St.
W. 27th St.
W. 25th St.

Islands

W. 24th St.
W. 23rd St.
W. 22nd St.
W. 21st St.

Sunset Lake

W. 30th St.
W. 29th St.
W. 28 St.

Sightseeing
Boats

20th St.
19th St.
18th St.
18th St.
17th St.

Garden Center &
Conservatory

Municipal

Park

Convention Center

Performing
Arts Theater

Bass Museum

Astronomical Observatory

Venetian Causeway

Miami Downtown

Zoll

Belle Isle

Lincoln

Road Mall

Post
Office

16th St.

15th St.

Stadium

14th St.

13th St.

Flamingo

Park

12th St.

City Hall

11th St.

10th St.

9th St.

Star Island

8th St.

7th St.

6th St.

Biscayne

Bay

Flagler Memorial Monument

Miami Downtown

MacArthur Causeway

Causeway
Terminal Island

Miami
Beach
Marina

Miami Beach Marina

5th Street

4th St.
3rd St.
2nd St.

Pier Park

Greyhound

Post Office

Art Deco

Ocean Front
Auditorium

Lummus Park

Atlantic

Ocean

Art Deco
District

© Baedeker

Municipal Pier

Bird's eye view of Miami Beach (setting for "Miami Vice")

the travel restrictions imposed during the Second World War. The Art Deco style of building (see Introduction, Art and Architecture) flourished during the 1920s, 1930s and 1940s. Numerous famous architects designed buildings which at first appeared eclectic, but which later were reminiscent of the building styles of the Aztecs and the Mayas, the Babylonians and the Egyptians and of the Israelites. This was combined with elements of the mechanical age including the streamlined shapes of the then still revolutionary new means of travel (the car, the aeroplane and the rocket).

After the end of the Second World War Miami experienced a renewed upswing. Even criminals, including drug chiefs and gun-runners, felt drawn here. By the beginning of the 1980s the resort had begun to suffer greatly from the influx of refugees from the Caribbean (predominantly from Cuba and Haiti), which led to an enormous increase in the crime rate.

Within the past few years Miami has tried to clean itself up and, in particular, to make itself attractive to European visitors.

★★Art Deco District

More detailed information about the history of Art Deco can be found in Art and Architecture (see Introduction). Stimuli for a trip to the Art Deco District will be found in the Art Deco District Welcome Center (661 1201 Washington Ave.; tel. 672 2014). The Art Deco Weekend takes place in the district in the middle of January.

The Art Deco District, which has been placed under a preservation order, is located between 5th Street in the south and Indian Creek in the north, and between Ocean Drive/Collins Avenue and Lenox Avenue. The district contains several hundred buildings, most of which were constructed in the 1930s and have recently been lovingly restored. This now historical quarter of the city, notorious in the 1960s as "the old people's home of America", has experienced an astonishing revival in the past few years. Many of the

Expansion

Art Deco on Ocean Drive

old hotels and apartments are being used once again for their original purpose. Cafés and restaurants, brightened by coloured neon lighting, are particularly inviting.

★Ocean Drive

Beautiful Art Deco buildings line Ocean Drive. Many of the façades are known through commercials and scenes from feature films. Particularly attractive are Beacon (732 Ocean Drive; 1936; architect Henry Hohauser), the tower-crowned corner house Waldorf Towers (860 Ocean Drive; 1937; architect Albert Anis), Breakwater (940 Ocean Drive; 1939; architect Anton Skislewicz), Cardozo (1300 Ocean Drive; 1939; architect Henry Hohauser), with its bar which is very busy by both day and night, and Cavalier (1320 Ocean Drive; 1936; architect Roy F. France).

Ocean Drive is adjoined by a wide and very firm sandy beach which is popular throughout the year.

★Collins Avenue

Collins Avenue, often called The Strip, is the main artery of Miami Beach and is also flanked by very appealing Art Deco buildings. Particularly noteworthy are Tiffany (801 Collins Ave.; 1939; architect L. Murray Dixon), Franklin (860 Collins Ave.; 1934; architect V. H. Nellenbogen), Fairmont (1000 Collins Ave.; 1939; architect L. Murray Dixon), with its famous café-terrace, Essex House (1001 Collins Ave.; 1938; one of Henry Hohauser's most interesting constructions built in the style of the "Nautical Moderne"), the former Hoffman's Cafeteria (1450 Collins Ave.; 1939; architect Henry Hohauser), which later became the Club Ovo and the China Club, Haddon Hall (1500 Collins Ave.; 1941; architect L. Murray Dixon), the high-rise St. Moritz (1565 Collins Ave.; 1939; architect Roy F. France), the apartment house Surfcomber (1717 Collins Ave.; 1948; architects' office MacKay and Gibbs) and Greystone (1926 Collins Ave.; 1939; architect Henry Hohauser).

Three of the largest Art Deco hotels – the National, the Delano and the Ritz Plaza – were built in Collins Avenue in the 1940s. Their streamlined and structural details are deliberately reminiscent of 20th c. revolutionary means of transport; i.e. of rockets, submarines and aeroplanes.

Washington Avenue, along which are ranged a number of notable Art Deco buildings, is Miami Beach's main shopping street. The George Washington Hotel (534 Washington Ave.; 1924; architect William P. Brown) was one of the first beach hotels in Miami Beach. Also of interest are the Hotel Taft (1044 Washington Ave.; 1936; architect Henry Hohauser) and the Kenmore (1050 Washington Ave.; 1936; architect Anton Skislewicz), the Main Post Office (1300 Washington Ave.; 1939; architect Howard L. Cheney) in the "Deco Federal Style" with a decorated rotunda, and the Old City Hall (1130 Washington Ave.; 1927; architect Martin Luther Hampton).

Washington
Avenue

In earlier years artists set up home around Spanish-looking Española Way. Later it declined into a red-light district but its earlier charms have recently been rediscovered. The rich decoration of the 1925 façades has recently been restored by Polonia Restauration. The striking building at the entrance to Española Way is the Cameo Theater (1938; architect Robert Collins).

★Española Way

Striking buildings along Euclid Avenue are The Denis (no. 841; 1938; architect Arnold Southwell), The Enjoie (no. 928; 1935/36; architects Albert Anis and Henry J. Maloney) and The Siesta (no. 1110; 1936; architect Edward A. Nolan).

Euclid Avenue

Palm Gardens (no. 760), a complex built in the Mediterranean style, was constructed in 1923 to the design of H. H. Mundy.

Meridian
Avenue

Remarkable Art Deco buildings in 21st Street are the former, luxury Plymouth Hotel (no. 226; 1940; architect Anton Skislewicz) and the neighbouring Adam's Hotel (1938; architect L. Murray Dixon). Completed in 1939, Governor (no. 435) is one of Henry Hohauser's masterpieces. Nearby is the Tyler Apartment Hotel (no. 430; 1937; architect L. Murray Dixon). Also of note is Abbey (no. 300; 1940; architect Albert Anis). The clubhouse of the Municipal Golf Course stands on the corner of Washington and 21st Streets. This recently-restored building was designed in 1916 by August Geiger.

★21st Street

The Bass Museum of Arts (2121 Park Ave.; open: Tues.–Sat. 10am–5pm, Sun. 1–5pm) was designed by Russell T. Pancoast and built in 1930.
    The coral building, reminiscent of the architecture of the Mayas, is decorated with reliefs by Gustav Bohland.

★Bass Museum
of Art

The museum exhibits paintings by old and new masters, including Albrecht Dürer, Peter Paul Rubens ("The Holy Family") and some of the Impressionists.

Collections

The particular characteristics of the Collins Park Hotel (designed by Henry Hohauser and built in 1939) are its contrasting wings and its soaring columns.

Collins Park
Hotel

Other sights

Lincoln Road Mall extends not far to the north of Española Way. It is a pedestrianised shopping street which, by the 1950s, had already become known as the "Fifth Avenue of the South".

Lincoln Road
Mall

Numerous art galleries, art schools, boutiques and friendly cafés have become established along Lincoln Road (between Lenox Ave. and Pennsylvania Ave.).

Lincoln Road
Arts District

Conceived by R. A. Benjamin in 1934, the Colony Theatre (1040 Lincoln Road) is a prime example of Art Deco in Miami Beach. After extensive

★Colony Theatre

renovation work it was reopened with great pomp in 1976 and is now one of the focal points of the city's cultural life.

Lincoln Theatre

Lincoln Theatre, a classic Art Deco functional building designed by Robert E. Collins and built in 1935/36, is now home to the renowned New World Symphony.

★Municipal Park

Municipal Park occupies a very central position. Its attractions include the modern City Hall with the Red Sea Road sculpture, Miami Beach Garden Center & Conservatory (rare tropical plants, flower exhibitions) and the enormous Convention Center, which was considerably enlarged in 1988 and which has already been the venue of some important congresses.

Holocaust Memorial

Located behind the Convention Center, the monumental Holocaust Memorial commemorates the violent deaths of some six million Jews before and during the Second World War.

★Theater of the Performing Arts

Close by is the Theater of the Performing Arts (3000 seats), since named after the famous comedian Jackie F. Gleason. Many Broadway productions and classical plays are staged here.

★Mermaid

Roy Lichtenstein's sculpture entitled Mermaid stands on the forecourt of the theatre. It was inspired by the shapes and colours of local Art Deco.

Walk of the Stars

Since the mid 1980s a number of important stage stars have left their footprints and their signatures on the neighbouring Walk of the Stars.

★Fontainebleau Hilton ("Big Blue")

Completed in the 1960s the giant Fontainebleau Hilton hotel (with more than 1200 rooms and suites) dominates the northern side of Collins Avenue (no. 4441). A variety of health care facilities, an artificial grotto complete with waterfall, tropical lagoon and swimming pool – where Gert Fröbe played the villain in the James Bond film "Goldfinger" – and an attractive beach bar all help make life more pleasant. At the southern entrance to the hotel complex a wall-painting by Richard Haas depicts what can be found behind the high wall.

Beachfront Promenade

A wooden promenade follows the edge of the beach for some miles between 21st Street and 46th Street. Joggers and walkers will be encountered here from early in the morning until late at night.

Indian Creek

Indian Creek, often used as a backdrop for dramatic film chases both in water and on land, separates the narrow spit of northern Miami Beach, lined with hotels and apartment blocks, from the exclusive residential area along Alton Road.

Haulover Beach Park

Haulover Beach Park lies in the north of Miami Beach. It contains several recreational facilities, an area of beach and a yacht harbour.

International Yacht Harbor

An ultra-modern yacht harbour has recently been constructed on the eastern bridgehead of MacArthur Causeway. It offers several hundred moorings, charter boats, deep sea angling and diving trips, and the opportunity to go to sea in a glass-bottomed boat.

South Pointe Park Beach

Popular South Pointe Park Beach, with its bathing beach, angling pier, promenade and picnic areas, extends along the southern end of Collins Avenue.

Penrod's Beach Club

Penrod's Beach Club is located not far to the north at the beginning of Beach Drive. Its exceptional food and drinks and its discothèque, which remains open until 5am, has made it currently in vogue, particularly with young people.

The man-made islands of Star Island, Palm Island and Hibiscus Island lie between MacArthur Causeway and Venetian Causeway. Many illustrious characters, such as Al Capone, Liz Taylor, Don Johnson and Madonna, have lived here.

Star Island, Palm Island, Hibiscus Island

On a small island to the north of Star Island stands an obelisk dedicated to the memory of Henry Morrison Flagler (see Famous People). At the suggestion of Julia Tuttle he used his Florida East Coast Railway to turn Miami into a centre of tourism.

Flagler Memorial

Surroundings of Miami and Miami Beach

L 15

Densely-populated Miami has recently expanded ever further to the south. Travellers driving in a southerly direction from Miami on Highway US 1 pass through the suburbs of South Miami, Kendall, Rockdale, Perrine, Goulds, Princeton, Leisure City and, finally, Homestead. This area was severely affected by Hurricane Andrew in 1992. The whirlwind created a trail of disaster straight through the south of Dade County. Countless homes fell victim to the destruction and tens of thousands of people were made homeless.

South Dade

Snake venom is extracted in the Serpentarium (12655 S. Dixie Highway). Tours by arrangement.

Serpentarium

Weeks Air Museum (14710 SW 128th St.; open: daily 10am–5pm) is located at Tamiami Airport. Aircraft used in both the First and the Second World War are displayed here, including a B 17 ("Flying Fortress") and a P 51 Mustang.

Weeks Air Museum

See South Miami.

Metro Zoo

Oldtimer trains can be seen at the Gold Coast Railroad Museum (12450 Coral Reef Drive, reached via SW 152 St.; open: Mon–Fri. 10am–3pm, Sat., Sun. 10am–5pm). Exhibits include a Pullman wagon used by US Presidents Roosevelt, Truman, Eisenhower and Reagan. Trains in the museum are put into service at the weekends and during the school holidays.

Gold Coast Railroad Museum

It is well worth paying a visit to Monkey Jungle (14805 SW 216th Street; open: daily 9.30am–6pm), located about 3 miles/5km east of Goulds. The monkeys roam freely in a jungle-like reserve, which visitors can observe from caged catwalks.

Monkey Jungle

The town of Homestead (10ft/3m above sea-level, population 27,000) is the centre of an intensively farmed area (including vegetables and avocado plantations) and an important US Air Force military base in the south-east of Florida.
   Excursions are available from Homestead to the Florida Keys (see entry) and to Biscayne National Park (see entry) which lies 9 miles/14km away and which offers snorkelling, diving trips and tours in glass-bottomed boats.
   A journey south-eastwards via Card Sound Road (tollbridge) to John Pennekamp Coral Reef (see Florida Keys) proves very attractive.

Homestead

Coral Castle (28655 S. Dixie Highway; open: daily 9am–6pm) is a very imposing structure. It was built by a Latvian immigrant between 1920 and 1940 from coral limestone.

Coral Castle

There is even an artificial ice-rink in tropical Florida. Those wishing to practise here should give advance notice (tel. 223 70 60).

Ice Castle

Chekika, a leisure area where it is possible to swim, fish and camp, lies about 11 miles/18km north-west of Homestead. Its vegetation likens it very much to the Caribbean.

Chekika

★Redland Fruit & Spice Park	Redland Fruit and Spice Park (Redland Road; open: daiy 10am–5pm) lies a few miles to the north of Homestead. More than 500 types of tropical fruits, vegetables and spices can be studied here, including 100 different citrus fruits and four dozen varieties of banana. Fruit stall and fruit juice bar.
Orchid Jungle	Orchid Jungle (26715 SW 157th Ave.; open: daily 8.30am–5.30pm), a small botanical garden with marvellous orchids, is to be found nearby.
Florida City	The little town of Florida City lies in the south of Dade County and is the most southerly suburb of the Miami Metropolitan Area. It is a very good starting point for excursions to the Everglades National Park (Flamingo 46 miles/74km – see entry).
Florida Pioneer Museum	Indian artefacts and furnishings from the early 20th c. are displayed in the Florida Pioneer Museum (826 N Krome Ave.; open: Oct.–May daily 10am–5pm).
Farmers Market, Agro Tours	The Farmers Market (300 N Krome Ave.) is held daily. Educational trips (Dec.–Mar. Mon.–Fri. twice daily) leave here for the intensively-used horticultural area of South Dade County. As well as four dozen types of vegetable, the following fruits are grown here: avocados, lemons, limes, oranges, lychees, mangoes, papayas, cumquats, grapefruit and tangerines.
Florida Keys	See entry.

Miccosukee Indian Village   K 14

Dade County. Altitude: 10ft/3km
Population: approximately 5000 (the entire reserve)

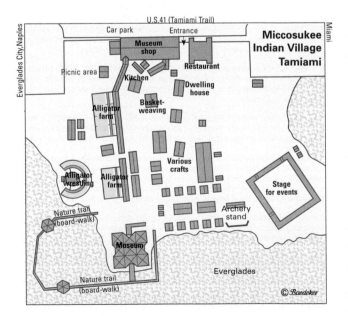

Through the Everglades by air-boat

Alligator wrestling

The Miccosukee Indians, who can be classed ethnically with the Semi-nolians, live on a reservation on the Tamiami Trail (see entry) in the Everglades (see entry). These Indians have kept themselves to themselves for a long time and have shied away from any contact with white people.

More recently, the younger descendants of these native Indians in particular have reorientated themselves and many of them go to school or to work in Miami (see entry). Others accompany tourists on expeditions into the Everglades or sell home-made souvenirs.

Lying approximately half-way between Miami (see entry) and Everglades City, one of the Indian villages has blossomed into a tourist attraction. The building style of Indian *Chekees* can be studied in a kind of open air museum here. These open huts, raised on stilts, were constructed by the Indians for centuries on the hammocks and higher regions of the Everglades, and it was on their platforms that they played out their lives. Indian women show visitors the materials used for clothes and demonstrate how they were made. Indian men can be observed carving wood and explain how materials are chosen for their very manoeuvrable canoes. The production of attractive rag dolls and beadwork can also be seen.

★Indian Village

    Much of interest about the history of the Miccosukee Indians and their life-style can be learnt in a small museum.

A number of strong Indians understand the public appeal of wrestling with alligators. In undertaking this they rely on experience gained over the centuries in hunting for these creatures.

Gator
Wrestling

    Occasionally, spectators are allowed to hold small alligators and can thus feel the suppleness of these lizards.

From the other side of the road natives accompany their guests on airboat tours of the part of the Everglades which belongs to the reservation. A

Airboat Tours

191

number of Indian families are also visited. Such trips are forbidden in the actual national park.

Information   Miccosukee Indian Village, P.O. Box 440021, Miami FL Yr144; tel. (305) 223 83 80.

Open   Daily 9am–5pm.

Naples   K 12

Collier County
Altitude: 0–10ft/0–3m. Population: 20,000

The town of Naples, the administrative seat of Collier County, lies on the southern Gulf coast and remained until recently a very quiet seaside resort, mainly visited by wealthy pensioners.
  A combination of its marvellous beaches and its successful local industry has led Naples to develop increasingly into an active and stylish resort and a centre of intensely developing urbanisation.

History and
Economy

In 1877 Hamilton Disston, a wealthy Philadelphian businessman, acquired a strip of land on the south-west Gulf coast. He planned to join in with the general land speculation of the time and to develop a genteel seaside resort here, but little enthusiasm was shown for this. Ten years later rich citizens from Kentucky became interested in Naples and founded the Naples Town Improvement Company. The first winter residences and housing schemes grew up and the town went from strength to strength economically.
  The town's name was derived from a number of Neopolitan fishermen who settled here.

The 1920s saw the real development of Naples into a seaside resort. In 1926 the railway came here and two years later the Tamiami Trail became the

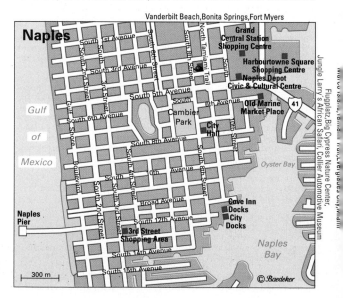

first country road to reach Naples. During the Second World War Naples Airfield was established as a training field for bomber pilots. After the war the influx of a permanent population began. Ironically enough, the destruction caused to a large part of the town in 1960 by Hurricane Donna, which was preceded by an almost 13ft/4m high tidal wave, turned out to be a blessing in disguise. Naples became known throughout the whole of North America. Reconstruction work began very cautiously and earlier building errors were avoided. The money paid out by the insurance companies involved created a powerful economic upswing in the region. Between 1970 and 1985 the population of the Naples area more than doubled. Today the region boasts almost 100 well-equipped hotels, motels and resorts. Artists, authors and musicians, as well as outdoor and angling enthusiasts, have spent the winter in Naples for many years. An above average number of leading white-collar workers and self-employed people have chosen to retire to the town. In addition, several new industrial parks have evolved, in which mainly hi-tech firms and service industries have settled. The land around Naples, Collier County, has long been one of Florida's most important agricultural regions (cattle raising, the cultivation of vegetables, melons, pineapples and cut flowers, mainly gladioli).

Sights

The old town has been able to retain much of its southern, almost Caribbean charm. It is characterised by elegant shopping streets (3rd St., 5th Ave.), two-storeyed, lovingly-restored, pastel-coloured 1920s houses with wrought-iron balconies, cobbled courtyards and well-tended streets shadowed by palms or flowering tropical trees.

★Olde Naples

A leaflet detailing a tour of Olde Naples is available from the Collier County Historical Society, which is located in historical Palm Cottage (137 12th Ave. South), built in 1895.

Anglers on Naples Pier

A stern-wheel boat in the harbour

Naples

Former Railway Station	The passenger train service to Naples stopped in 1970. The former railway buildings on 5th Street South and on 10th Street now house the Naples Depot & Civic Center as well as the Grand Central Station Shopping Center.
★★Pier	One of Naple's attractions is its wooden pier (end of 12th Ave. South) which extends for more than 985ft/300m into the sea and which is shared amicably by anglers, brown pelicans and sun-worshippers. Built in 1888/89 it was initially of great importance for the transport of freight and the first winter holiday-makers. Destroyed by Hurricane Donna in 1960, this symbol of Naples' beach has, however, been reconstructed.
★Old Marine Market Place at Tin City	Located on Gordon River Bridge, Old Tin City (1200 Fifth Ave. South/US 41), the old fishing harbour with the boatyards of the Neopolitan fishermen, has been restored and transformed into a small shopping centre. A number of street cafés and restaurants prove tempting. Deep sea angling excursion boats depart from here.
Dockside Boardwalk	Dockside Boardwalk (1100 6th Ave. South), another small centre with shops and restaurants, lies nearby. It represents a part of old Florida.
★Naples Nature Center	The conservation organisation The Conservancy Inc. maintains a conservation centre on a 13½ acre/5½ha site in the municipal area of Naples (1450 Merrihue Drive/14th Ave. N; open: daily Jan.–Mar. Mon.–Sat. 9.30am–4.30pm, Sun. 1–5pm, otherwise shorter opening times; tel. 262 03 04). It contains a natural history exhibition, a care centre for sick and injured wild animals, and various informative trails. It is worth taking a boat trip on mangrove-lined Gordon River (mid Sep.–Mar.). The organisation also maintains the Briggs Nature Center (see Surroundings), located near the access road to Marco Island.
Collier County Museum	A visit to the Collier County Museum (3301 Tamiami Trail East/Airport Road; open: Mon.–Fri. 9am–5pm, Sat. 10am–4pm) can prove of interest. Situated 2 miles/3km to the south-east on the other side of Naples Bay, the museum presents the history of the region from its settlement by Indian natives to the present. Typical Seminolian Chickees and the cross section of an Indian fortification can be studied in the open-air exhibition ground.
Collier Automotive Museum	Opened in 1988, the Collier Automotive Museum is situated in the industrial area north of the airport (2500 S. Horseshoe Drive; open: Wed.–Sun. 10am–6pm). More than 70 vintage vehicles (in working order) and classical sports and racing cars are on show, including America's largest collection of Porsches.
Coastland Center	The Coastland Center (US 41/Golden Gate Parkway; open: Tues.–Sat. 10am–1pm, Sun. 1–5pm May–Nov.; daily 10am–5pm rest of year) is Naples' largest air-conditioned shopping centre. Branches of large department stores and about 100 other shops can be found here.

Surroundings

Jungle Larry's Zoological Park at Caribbean Gardens	Jungle Larry's Zoological Park (1590 Goodlette Road/SR 851; open: daily 9.30am–5.30pm), a zoological and botanical garden with many African animals living in tropical surroundings, lies about 2½ miles/4km north of the town. Animal displays, hands-on zoo, tram tours.
Port Royal	The settlement of Port Royal, standing on the promontory in the south of Naples Bay, is Naples' most exclusive residential area. Mangrove-lined streets and waterways wind through Port Royal, which was developed in the 1960s by an estate agent from Chicago.
★Everglades Parkway	Everglades Parkway (I–75, toll), better known as Alligator Alley (Gator Parkway), leads from Naples straight through the northern Everglades

eastwards to the Atlantic coast. Using this parkway, Fort Lauderdale and the Miami area (see entries) can be reached within two hours.

Briggs Nature Center is situated in the Rookery Bay National Estuarine Research Reserve. It is The Conservancy Inc.'s second largest research and information centre in this region. The centre is reached via a turning some 3 miles/5km along Shell Island Road and provides information about the extremely sensitive ecological area here at the entrance to the Everglades in the Gulf of Mexico. Boat trips, guided natural history walks. A boardwalk leads through the higher areas. Information is available from the Rookery Bay Reserve Manager, 10 Shell Island Road; tel. 775 88 45. ★Briggs Nature Center

★Beaches

The Naples catchment area contains more than 37 miles/60km of excellent sandy beaches where it is still possible to find quiet spots even in the high season. Imposing apartment buildings and holiday complexes are concentrated on a number of beach areas, mainly in the north of this vast town (Moorings, Park Shore, Pelican Bay). Clam Pass Beach, between Naples and Vanderbilt Beach (Sea Gate Drive), is considered to be a particularly beautiful beach (tram tour through mangroves, wilderness preserve, palms).

The historic Ritz Carlton Hotel (280 Vanderbilt Beach Road) stands on the edge of the beach. Its appearance, its luxury and its traditions are reminiscent of the old grand hotels. Located to its north, the Wiggins Pass State Recreation Area (Gulfshore Blvd North/111th Ave.) is very popular and, particularly in winter weekends, overcrowded. Here wooden walkways cross the sensitive area of dunes to the beach.

In the early summer, visitors, accompanied by park attendants, can watch giant turtles laying their eggs on the beach in the darkness.

Luxury accommodation at Vanderbilt Beach

Further to the south the beaches of Park Shore Beach (Park Shore Drive, backed by large apartment complexes) adjoin the Venetian Bay villas built in a Mediterranean style and the attractive shopping centre The Village and, on the other side of Doctor's Pass, Lowdermilk Park (Banyan Blvd.; public transport).

Many of the older residential areas (e.g. Port Royal) are intersected by canals. Most of the luxurious villas have their own landing stages. Deep sea anglers and sailors can moor their boats in one of the 30 or more yacht harbours and marinas.

In addition, Naples can boast Florida's most exclusive and most beautiful golf courses.

New Smyrna Beach   D 13

Volusia County
Altitude: 0–10ft/0–3m
Population: 17,000

Location
The town of New Smyrna Beach lies barely 12 miles/20km south of Daytona Beach (see entry), protected behind a barrier island on the west side of the Intracoastal Waterway (see entry). Its 8 miles/13km-long white, but fairly firm, beach borders the Atlantic and attracts many visitors who, thanks to the nearby Gulf Stream, can swim here throughout the year. In the last few decades New Smyrna Beach has developed from a sleepy fishing village into a tranquil, unaffected holiday resort. Numerous holiday homes and apartment complexes have been built along the beach. Many surfers come here when the waves are particularly strong.

History
The discovery of Indian "mounds" (made from seashells) supports the view that there was a settlement here in pre-Columbian times. The "Turtle Mound" on the barrier island is the highest elevation in the surrounding area. Wooden steps lead to the summit of this hill made of seashells. Ponce de León is supposed to have found refuge here in Mosquito Lagoon in 1513 when he got caught in a bad storm off Cape Canaveral and before he was driven back on to the ship by hostile Indians.

Settlement
The first Anglo-American settlers arrived here in 1767. Led by the Scottish doctor Dr Turnbull, several hundred new settlers came here predominantly from Greece, Italy and the Mediterranean island of Minorca to cultivate cotton, indigo and sugar-cane. Turnbull named the new colony New Smyrna after the birthplace of his Greek wife. By 1777, however, the colony had been abandoned because of organisational difficulties, leaving the foundations of buildings and well-shafts. The network of canals laid out by the colonists is still in use today.

The ruins of a sugar mill are all that remain of the next, equally fruitless attempt at forming a settlement here some 50 years later.

Sights

Smyrna Dunes Park
At Ponce de León Inlet, at the northern tip of the offshore peninsula, boardwalks lead across the sand dunes and through densely overgrown areas. Signs give information about the flora. There is a small observation tower. Beach.

★New Smyrna Sugar Mill
The protected ruins of a large sugar mill, which was for a few years the centre of an extensive sugar plantation, lie about 2 miles/3km west of the town, north of the SR 44. In 1830 two New York businessmen acquired land for a sugar plantation on the border of the settlement of that time. One of

ten large concerns on Florida's east coast was then built. Sugar production
flourished during the 1930s. Sugar was exported via St Augustine, Jacksonville or Savannah/Georgia. Molasses, a by-product, was transported to
the Caribbean for the production of rum.

After the Federal army's failed attempts to resettle all Seminolians into
the area west of the Mississippi, incensed Indians attacked New Smyrna in
1835, carried off cattle and slaves and set fire to the whole plantation. The
Second Seminolian War had begun.

Today the remains of the sugar mill can be visited (open: daily
10am–5pm; natural history trail).

Highway A1A leads to Apollo Beach, approximately 12 miles/20km further
to the south, and to the Turtlemouth Trail (visitors' centre; open: daily
8am–4.30pm). The undeveloped central part (Klondike Beach) between
Apollo Beach and Playalinda Beach, accessible from Titusville (see entry),
can only be reached on foot. Access to the beaches is forbidden during the
lift-off and landing of space shuttles. Beware of rattlesnakes if walking in
the overgrown areas of dunes. Max Hoeck Creek Wildlife Drive, an unmade
road which runs parallel to the SR 402, is recommended for the return
journey from Playalinda Beach. The route follows an old railway line
through typical marshland where alligators, tortoises and many waterfowl
can be seen.

Black Point Wildlife Drive on Merritt Island leads through pinewood
forests and marshland. Various species of sea birds and waders can be
observed, particularly in the winter.

Information is available from the Merritt Island National Wildlife Refuge,
P.O. Box 6504, Titusville, FL 32780; tel. 861–0667.

★Apollo Beach

New Smyrna Beach is the northern gateway to Canaveral National Seashore (see Cape Canaveral), a 56,833 acre/23,000ha nature reserve on the
Atlantic coast. A part of the east coast very close to the NASA space centre
has been retained in its original form. Canaveral National Seashore and the
Merritt Island National Wildlife Refuge, on its southern border, include a
large part of a barrier island only a few hundred yards wide in places and
with about 25 miles/40km of unspoilt sandy beaches.

★★Canaveral
National
Seashore

Ocala

D 11

Marion County
Altitude: 49ft/15m
Population: 43,000

The little town of Ocala lies in the north of central Florida, in the middle of
numerous lakes and watercourses, and overgrown forests. Ocala is the
administrative seat of predominantly-agricultural Marion County and the
economic centre of the wide band of surrounding countryside. Crackers,
descendants of the first pioneers who first made their living from turpentine extraction and cattle rearing and who later became increasingly involved with the cultivation of citrus fruits, still live here. Since the 1960s the
rearing of saddle-horses and racehorses has been very important.

The region around Ocala is today one of the areas with the greatest
growth in population. During the 1980s the average increase amounted to
6.5% per annum.

Many modern hotels and motels have sprung up in and around Ocala
owing to its location on important major roads and its relative proximity to
the large tourist attractions in central Florida.

Location

Spanish records tell of a dense Indian settlement in the area around the
present-day town of Ocala. The name of the settlement was probably
derived from a village of Timucuan Indians. Timucuan graves were discovered during the 1960s on an island in Lake Weir, about 15½ miles/25km
further south.

History

In 1827/28 the military base Fort King was built here. During the Semi-nolian Wars warlike clashes with Indians led by Osceola (see Famous People) occurred in the region around the fort. In the surrounding area plantations were laid out by owners, mainly from South Carolina. People and freight were transported across Silver River and Oklawaha River. Oranges were soon also grown and for a long time Marion County was the most southerly area where this fruit was cultivated. The region was badly affected by frost in the winter of 1894/95 and again at the beginning of the 1980s. Crops and trees were killed by frost and many of the older citrus planters gave up.

Sights

Brick City

The small country town of Ocala still retains much of its provincial atmosphere. Many of the brick houses built after 1883's devastating fire remain standing around Ocala Square in the town centre. They are now under a preservation order. Various restaurants, street cafés, shops and boutiques enliven the scene.

Ocala Square

During renovation work the pavements were recobbled and the square gained a small pavilion, a fountain and lighting reminiscent of the turn of the century.

Ocala Historic District

A wealthy residential area lying to the east of the town centre (East Fort King Ave., SE 8th St., SE 3rd St., SE 13th St.), Ocala Historic District has numerous wooden houses of varying styles, built in the Victorian manner. Many of them are still used as family homes, while others are occupied by offices, shops, restaurants and an art gallery.

★Appleton Museum of Art

The Appleton Museum of Art (4333 E. Silver Springs Blvd., SR 40; open: Tues.– Sat. 10am–4.30pm (also Thur. 4.30–8pm), Sun. 1–5pm) was opened in 1987. It contains the collections of the industrialist Arthur I. Appleton from Chicago, including art objects dating from five millenniums (including Greek and Roman antiquity, Indian advanced civilisations, West African dance masks and gar-ments, and 18th and 19th c. European pieces of art and furniture).

Surroundings of Ocala

★Horse rearing

The rich pastureland on the relatively dry chalky soil around Ocala, the hard spring water, large amounts of flat land, favourable climatic conditions – basic requirements also seen in the traditional Blue Grass region in Ken-tucky – and the increase in riding for pleasure have caused the rearing of thoroughbred horses to flourish. Since the 1950s a number of stud farms have been established, which have already produced many winners.

Auctions

The horse auctions held during the well-known Ocala Week in October in the Southeastern Livestock Pavilion and in the Ocala Breeders Sales Com-plex attract custom from all over the world. Arab thoroughbreds are magni-ficently bridled for the Arabian Extravaganza held every spring.

Classic Mile

Top-class competitions are held on the new Classic Mile Horse Race Track west of Ocala. Information can be obtained from the Florida Thorough-bred Breeders' Association, 4727 NW 80th Ave., Ocala FL 32678; tel. (904) 629 21 60 or (904) 629 35 26.

Don Garlits' Museum of Drag Racing

It is worth paying a visit to Don Garlits' Museum of Drag Racing (13700 SW 16th Ave.; open: daily 9am–5.30pm) in the suburb of Belleview, 6 miles/10km to the south on the I-75. "Big Daddy" Don Garlits is America's best-known drag racer. With his "Swamp Rats" he was the first to set the record speed of more than 249mph/400kph and he won more than 120 national titles.

★Silver Springs

Silver Springs, one of the region's chief attractions (open: daily 9am–4pm), lies approximately 1 mile/2km east of Ocala on the SR 40 (Silver Springs Blvd.). This strongly-flowing spring, whose waters are at a constant temperature of approximately 73°F/23°C, was already attracting numerous visitors at the time when paddle-steamers navigated Silver River. With a force of 812cu.ft/23cu.m per second it is one of the world's most powerful artesian wells.

Location

Glass-bottomed boats, from which the river's exotic underwater life can be observed, operate on Silver River, which is fed by seventeen springs. A visit is also paid to the place where diving scenes for the James Bond film "Never Say Never Again" and for other films were shot.

In the course of a Jungle Cruise a variety of zoo animals can be seen on the river bank. A hands-on zoo and alligator and snake demonstrations (Reptile Institute) complete the entertainment.

Jungle Cruise

The Antique & Classic Car Collection has been on show since 1990.

Oldtimer Exhibition

Water-babies should visit the adjoining Silver Springs Wild Waters, an adventure pool with a wave machine and several small waterchutes (open: daily 10am–7pm Jun.–Sept.; 10am–5pm rest of year).

Wild Waters

Excursion to Orange Lake

A charming excursion can be made along the SR 475 northwards from Ocala to Orange Lake.

The town of Reddick, located about 12 miles/20km to the north on the SR 475, is the centre of thoroughbred horse rearing in Florida. The countryside here is characterised by gently rolling hills, miles of fences enclosing permanently green pastureland interrupted only by large or small islands of massive oaks and pine trees (a number of which are hundreds of years old), and farmhouses, some very picturesque.

Reddick

The small village of MacIntosh (population 500) is reached after a further 6 miles/10km and lies next to Orange River.

MacIntosh

Orange Lake, approximately 19sq.miles/50sq.km in size, is known to amateur anglers primarily for its perch. Here visitors will find a piece of Florida from the turn of the century. Imposing oaks, draped with Spanish moss, flank the streets, which are lined with renovated houses.

Orange Lake

A drive around Orange Lake leads to Cross Creek (see Gainesville), where the home of the authoress Marjorie Kinnan Rawlings can be found.

The US 301 is reached at Island Grove. Follow this road for 19 miles/30km to return to Ocala.

Dunnellon, a village with a population of 2000, lies 25 miles/40km to the west at the point where Rainbow River flows into Withlacoochee River. It evolved at the end of the 19th c. at the time of the phosphate boom.

Dunnellon

The Boomtime Days in April relive the bad old days. In the summer "river-tubing" (in which participants try to navigate part of Rainbow River or Withlacoochee River upstream in old car tyres) enjoys great popularity.

★Ocala National Forest

K 11/12

Ocala National Forest, designated a nature reserve in 1908, extends for 514sq.miles/1331sq.km east of Ocala. It constitutes a part of Florida's typical wooded landscape, now almost unique. The more elevated western and central section is characterised by extensive Sand Pine forests, growing on very dry, sandy soil, which tower island-like out of the dense

Natural Area

scrubland (known as the Big Scrub). Deciduous cypresses dominate the depressions. A number of hammocks (islands of hardwood trees), containing magnolias, oaks, laurels and some palms (*Sabal Palmetto*), relieve the landscape.

The national forest is a retreat for a variety of species of endangered creatures. White-headed sea eagles, black bears, countless alligators and, occasionally, a Florida puma can be encountered here. The Ocala National Forest does not hold the status of an official national park, consequently distant parts of it, which are located outside of the designated Wilderness Areas, are worked by the timber industry.

The countless lakes and slowly meandering rivers fed by crystal clear springs within the national forest have made it a popular holiday area and a paradise for campers, anglers and outdoor enthusiasts. A drive along the SR 19 through the national forest proves particularly delightful. Information is available from the ranger's office, about 12 miles/20km east of Silver Springs on the SR 40.

Juniper Springs, Alexander Springs, Salt Springs

The three most powerful karst springs, Juniper Springs on the SR 40, Alexander Springs near to DeLand (see entry) and Salt Springs on the SR 19, are well-equipped with camp sites, trails, changing cubicles and canoe rental. Canoe trips on the sluggish Oklawaha River, where paddle-steamers, once so important for the development of central Florida, used to operate (canoe rental in Fort McCoy), and from Juniper Springs to Lake George and St John's River are popular.

Okeechobee

See Lake Okeechobee

Okefenokee Swamp (National Wildlife Refuge)   B 10/11

★Natural area

Nature-lovers should make an excursion to Okefenokee Swamp, more than 772sq.miles/2000sq.km in size, lying to the north-west of Jacksonville (see entry). It extends from Osceola Forest (see entry) in the north for 40 miles/60km further north to the state of Georgia. The "land of shaking earth", as this native home of the Choctaw Indians was once called, is as important to Florida's ground water streams as the Everglades in the south are to the "Sunshine State". A tangle of lakes and watercourses, cypress swamps, marshy grassland and "swimming" islands (they shake when walked on, but can nevertheless bear the weight of whole forests and Indian villages) feed Suwannee River, which flows into the Gulf of Mexico after more than 249 miles/400km, and St Mary's River, which flows into the Atlantic 50 miles/80km further to the east, as well as countless karst springs.

The Okefenokee National Wildlife Refuge encompasses about 90% of the swampland and offers refuge to numerous endangered species of wild animals such as black bears, various wildcats, red deer and countless birds. Approximately 10,000 alligators are estimated to be at present in Okefenokee Swamp.

Information

Okefenokee National Wildlife Refuge Office, P.O. Box 338, Folkston, GA 31537; tel (912) 496 33 31; open: Mon.–Fri. 7am–3.30pm.

Orlando   E 12/13

Orange County
Altitude: 105ft/32m
Population: 164,000 (metropolitan area approximately one million)

Twilight over Orlando

The city of Orlando lies in the west of central Florida at the crossroads of several important highways, which lead in all directions from here. Orlando is also the centre of one of the world's most popular tourist areas (about ten million visitors a year). Both the opening of Walt Disney's second pleasure park in 1971 and the attractions of Sea World and the Universal Studios have contributed to this popularity. The US space centre in Orlando can be quickly and easily reached.

The attractiveness of the city is reflected in the large growth of its population. At present an average of 600 people settle in Orlando and the surrounding area each week. Unemployment figures are significantly lower than the national average.

The building of the giant pleasure park, still under construction, has brought numerous investors into the area, who have developed enormous hotels, countless motels, whole residential areas and commercial enterprises, mainly in the south-west. Swamp and scrubland, orange groves and forests have had to yield to new leisure parks, pools, shopping centres and filling stations.

At present the Orlando area offers approximately 70,000 hotel and motel beds, more than 2000 restaurants, 44 golf courses and numerous large and small attractions. The region enjoys almost constantly warm weather.

Location

The first white American settlers – volunteers, who had fought against the Seminolians – came to this area in the 1830s. In 1837 the young settlement was still called Jernigan, but in 1857 its name was changed to Orlando. Various adventurous exploits surround the origin of this name.

For a long time Orlando was a dreamy little town inhabited by Crackers, who ran small farms, and was surrounded by large cotton plantations. Having belonged for a long time to "Mosquito County", which extends from St Augustine as far as Key West, Orlando became the administrative seat of Orange County in 1857.

History

Orlando

The American Civil War brought an end to cotton growing. During the 1870s cattle raising was the first line of employment.

Orlando experienced an upswing in its economy in the 1870s, caused by the recent arrival of the railway in nearby Sanford. Orlando's warm climate and its flourishing orange groves soon became famous in the cooler regions of the American north-east.

During the 1920s the Orlando area was gripped by land speculation. By the 1950s the long-distance economic effects of the rocket launches taking place at Cape Canaveral (see entry) had made an impact. When the rumour went around in the mid 1960s that Disney was to build an even larger pleasure park at Orlando than the one at Anaheim in California, the economic upsurge in the Orlando area went from strength to strength. In 1983 the new international airport was opened and remains one of the world's most modern.

Today Orlando is Florida's fourth largest city and the centre of one of the USA's most economically-important regions.

Sights

Orlando's large places of interest are widespread. If time is of the essence visitors would do best to hire a car or join an organised sightseeing tour.

Downtown – Church Street

★Church Street Station

In the city centre the area around the old silver-domed station, forgotten for decades, was renovated. Orlando's leisure and shopping complex Church Street Station (129 W. Church St., between Garland Ave., South and Pine St.; open: daily 11am–2am), with a variety of shops and bars, was created in two restored blocks of houses. Particular attractions for visitors are Rosie O'Grady's Good Time Emporium (music and entertainment in the style of the 1920s and 1930s), Apple Annie's Courtyard (blue grass and folk music), Cheyenne Saloon & Opera House (country and western music), Phineas Phogg's Balloon Works (hot-air balloon decor, discothèque) and The Orchid Garden Ballroom & Desert Café (crystal palace in the style of the turn of the century, rock 'n' roll music).

Old Duke

The "Old Duke", a series 060 steam-engine built in Ohio in 1912 for transcontinental travel, is a special attraction. It appears in the 1960s film "Wings of Eagles", starring John Wayne and Henry Fonda, parts of which were shot in Pensacola.

Carriage Drives

Romantic carriage drives around Lake Eola are popular. They depart from Church Street Station every evening.

Church Street Exchange

The Church Street Exchange shopping centre (open: daily 11am–11pm) was opened in 1988. About five dozen boutiques, fast-food restaurants and amusement arcades are located on three floors.

Church Street Marketplace

For some years fashion boutiques and other shops have set themselves up in old, renovated buildings very close to Church Street. Church Street Marketplace is still very new.

Lake Eola

Lake Eola and the surrounding areas of well-tended parkland, situated on Rosalind Street and Robinson Street, are very attractive. At night the fountains are illuminated. Open air concerts often take place here.

Loch Haven Park

Follow Orange Avenue (leading to Winter Park) for 3 miles/5km further north to reach Loch Haven Park. Divided in two by Princeton Street, this extensive park is bordered to the east by Mills Avenue (US 17/92). It contains three museums and the Civic Theater of Central Florida (1010 Princeton St.; Broadway and children's programmes, musicals).

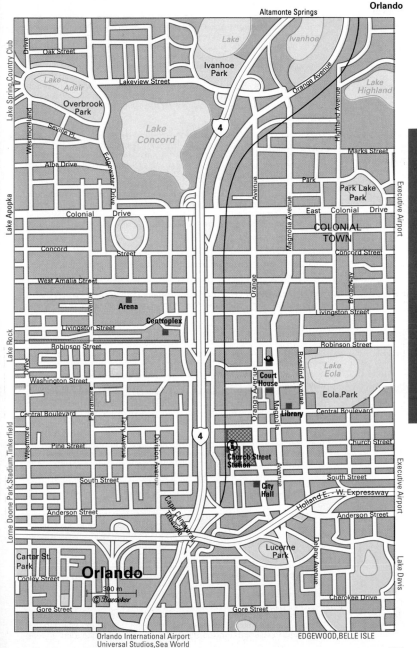

Orlando

Altamonte Springs

Lake Spring,Country Club

Oak Street

Lake Adair

Overbrook Park

Sevilla Pl.

Westmoreland

Alba Drive

Edgewater Drive

Lakeview Street

Lake Concord

Lake Ivanhoe

Ivanhoe Park

Ivanhoe

Orange Avenue

Lake Highland

4

Highland Avenue

Marks Street

Avenue

Park

Park Lake Park

Magnolia Avenue

Lake Apopka

Colonial   Drive

Concord

Street

West Amalia Street

Avenue

Arena

Centroplex

Livingston Street

Lake Rock

Robinson Street

Drive

Washington Street

Paramore

Central Boulevard

Westmore

Lorne Doone Park,Stadium,Tinkerfield

Pine Street

Gary Avenue

Division Avenue

Orange

East   Colonial   Drive

COLONIAL TOWN

Concord Street

Broadway

Livingston Street

Robinson Street

Lake Eola

Court House

Orange Avenue

Rosalind Avenue

Library

Magnolia

Eola.Park

Central Boulevard

Church Street

4

Church Street Station

City Hall

Avenue

South Street

South Street

Executive Airport

Holland E. - W. Expressway

Anderson Street

Cape Canaveral Tidewater

Anderson Street

Delany Avenue

Executive Airport

Lake Davis

Carter St. Park

Conley Street

Orlando

300 m

© Baedeker

Gore Street

Lucerne Park

Gore Street

Cherokee Drive

Orlando International Airport
Universal Studios,Sea World

EDGEWOOD,BELLE ISLE

203

Orlando

★Museum of Art   The Orlando Museum of Art (2416 N. Mills Ave.; open: Tues.–Sat. 9am–5pm, Sun. noon–5pm) enjoys widespread fame for its excellent collection of pre-Columbian art. It displays a series of exhibitions of American and African art from the 19th c. and the 20th c., as well as touring exhibitions with exhibits on loan from international museums.

Orange County Historical Museum   The Orange County Historical Museum (812 E. Rollins St.; open: Mon.–Sat. 9am–5pm, Sun. noon–5pm) is devoted to central Florida's past. A lovingly-furnished kitchen dating from pioneering days and an 1820s fire station are very attractive.

Orlando Science Museum, John Young Planetarium   The Orlando Science Center and John Young Planetarium (810 E. Rollins St.; open: Mon.–Thur. and Sat. 9am–5pm, Fri. 9am–9pm, Sun. noon–5pm) explain the links between science and natural history. Visitors can carry out a number of experiments themselves. The planetarium offers an insight into the history of the universe.

Harry P. Leu Botanical Gardens   A few minutes more by car to the south-east leads to a charming botanical garden (1730 N. Forest Ave.; open: daily 9am–5pm), in the centre of which stands the restored Leu House (open: Tues.–Sat. 10am–3.30pm, Sun. and Mon. 1–3.30pm), a typical farmhouse to be found in Florida at the turn of the century.

Turkey Lake   The shores of Turkey Lake is a popular recreation area, offering a camp site, a hands-on zoo, a conservation centre and various paths for both walkers and cyclists.

Mystery Fun House   A visit to the Mystery Fun House (5767 Major Blvd.) can prove very amusing. Distorting mirrors, mazes, laser games, etc. provide plenty of variety.

International Drive   E 12

Location   International Drive has been built during the past two decades a few miles south-west of the city centre. Approximately 4 miles/6km long and generously-planned, it provides a fast way to reach Orlando's mega pleasure parks. Branches of almost all of the USA's important hotel chains and far in excess of 100 restaurants have been established here. In addition there are some administrative multi-storey buildings and a modern office complex, complete with both a congress and an exhibition centre.

★Wet 'n' Wild   Wet 'n' Wild (6200 International Drive; open: spring daily 10am–6pm, summer daily 9am–9pm, autumn daily 10am–5pm; information; tel. 351 32 00, 1 800 992 WILD) is a large leisure pool offering various attractions such as wavepools, a water playground for children and breathtaking waterchutes (including Stuka, a steep, 250ft/76m-long chute where freefall is almost achieved, Black Hole, a 30-second plunge on a small raft in complete darkness, and the Raging Rapids, wild water rafting in inflated tyres).

Elvis Presley Museum   Approximately 350 pieces of memorabilia connected to the rock 'n' roll idol can be viewed in the Elvis Presley Museum (7200 International Drive; open: daily 9am–10pm). The collection includes various personal effects, a guitar and clothes worn by Presley when performing.

Fun 'n' Wheels   The pleasure park Fun 'n' Wheels (6739 Sand Laxe Road/International Drive: open: in the high season daily 10am–midnight, otherwise Mon.–Fri. 4–11pm, weekends 10am–midnight) provides go-kart lovers with four different tracks. There are also motor scooters and a big wheel.

Mercado Mediterranean Village   The Mercado Mediterranean Village (8445 International Drive; open: daily 10am–10pm) is an attractive shopping centre containing about 60 different shops and restaurants (including the Royal Orleans Restaurant offering cajun music and Creole food), as well as a tourist information office. The Mercado Mediterranean Village represents an attempt to emulate the atmosphere and style of a Spanish village. Children love Mugsy Macaw, a colourful parrot, who is content to mix with shoppers.

The Mardi Gras Dinner Theater attracts guests in the evening. A typical Southern States dinner is accompanied by an approximately two-hour long show including elements of Caribbean and South American carnivals, and New Orleans jazz.

Mardi Gras
Dinner Theater

The Dinner Theater King Henry's Feast (8984 International Drive), a few hundred yards further on, deserves a visit. Every evening a 16th c. banquet, with knights, travelling entertainers and musicians, takes place here. Table manners also reflect the customs of that time!

King Henry's
Feast

Universal Studios

E 12

Universal Studios (I–4, exit 30 B; 1000 Universal Studios Plaza; open: daily 9am–7pm, extended hours during peak season; information; tel. 363 80 00) were opened in 1990 and are the most recent of Orlando's large attractions. The film industry was already installed in the "largest film and television studios outside of Hollywood" in October 1988.

Location

During a tour of the extensive site with its various studios much is learned about the production of television and cinema films and advertisements. Visitors can also be present at the recording of television shows. For outdoor shoots, mock streets have been constructed based on those to be found in New York City, in the Chicago of the 1920s and in San Francisco (Fisherman's Wharf), where actors play out well-known scenes from "Ghostbusters", "The Blues Brothers", old gangster movies and more

Tours

"Miami Vice" in action

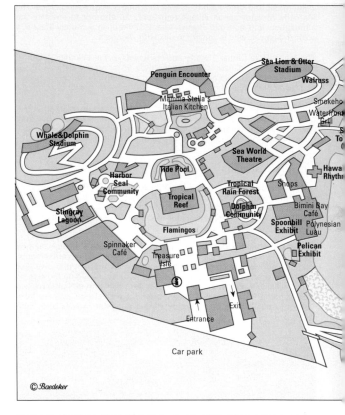

© Baedeker

recent productions. More than three dozen outdoor film sets have been built, including the famous house from the Hitchcock thriller "Psycho" and the legendary "Hard Rock Café".

★ Kongfrontation

Nerves will come under particular strain on a trip on a replica of a New York elevated railway, during which King Kong is suddenly unleashed. At the end of the ride, which gives the sensation of plummeting into the depths, passengers can begin to recover.

E.T.

A journey can be undertaken with E.T., the extraterrestrial fantasy creature, to his home planet.

Back to the Future

Doc Brown accompanies interested visitors on a trip in the time machine "Back to the Future".

★ Earthquake

A tube train journey below San Francisco takes the breath away, when the earth suddenly shakes and floods of water pour into the underground shaft. Bridges disintegrate and a filling station explodes. Be prepared to leave this part of the Universal Studios drenched in perspiration.

Nickelodeon

Children have most fun in the Nickelodeon Studio, where the popular television show is made using members of the public.

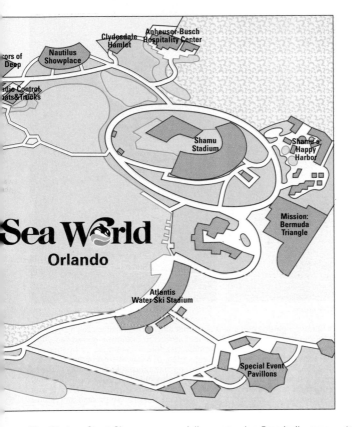

The Western Stunt Shows are especially spectacular. Daredevil young people dressed as cowboys work with talented experts in pyrotechnics to demonstrate how dangerous scenes for westerns are produced.

Shots ring out, cowboys fight and fall from roofs and balconies. Fronts of houses collapse. Despite all this, the participants emerge unscathed.

★Western Stunt Shows

Criminals are chased along an artificial waterway just as in "Miami Vice" – powerboats roar, a small plane crashes, a freighter explodes and the harbourmaster's office is blown up.

This crazy stunt show can be witnessed in the afternoons and evenings.

★Powerboat Chases

★★Sea World

E 12

The Sea World of Florida (7007 Sea World Drive; open: summer daily 8.30am–9pm, otherwise daily 9am–7pm; information; tel. 351 36 00 or free-phone in Florida 1 800 432 11 78) lies a bare 12 miles/20km south-west of Orlando's city centre and south of the "Beeline Expressway" (SR 528). This aqua-zoo, one of the largest of its type, contains a number of aquariums, an artificial tropical coral reef with thousands of fish, shark and sting-ray pools, dolphinariums, otter, seal, walrus and penguin enclosures,

Location

Dolphins as draught animals   *"Shamu", a killer whale on dry land*

a flamingo garden and countless other attractions. Visitors see a colourful programme of events, with the real attraction being the shows featuring trained dolphins and killer whales. In addition, waterski acrobatics are demonstrated and there is a great variety of musical entertainment. Since 1989 Sea World of Florida has belonged to the Busch Entertainment Corporation, as have the other Sea World parks in California, Ohio and Texas. This corporation, which is owned by a large brewery, also maintains Busch Gardens/Dark Continent, a zoo and leisure park in Tampa (see entry), and Cypress Gardens at Winter Haven (see entry).

Sky Tower

Sky Tower offers an overview of Sea World's several dozen hectares of grounds.

Polar Animals

Penguins and polar birds can be observed in an artificial Arctic under a sub-tropical sun.

Shark Pool

Intimidating sharks circumnavigate a 131ft/40m-long pool. Their movements can be watched from an underwater acrylic glass tube. Two different multi-media programmes give information about sharks and their position in the marine ecosystem.

Sting-rays

Before visiting the beach anyone holidaying in Florida really should study at close hand the sting-rays in Orlando's Sea World, thus hopefully sparing themselves an unpleasant encounter with one of these very well-camouflaged sea creatures.

★★Dolphin
Stadium,
★★Shamu
Stadium

Demonstrations by trained sea mammals in the dolphin and the whale stadiums are very impressive. In one stadium different types of dolphin show off their tricks in the company of white Beluga whales, while in the other arena presentations featuring killer whales (*orcinus orca*), native to all the seas of the world, can be seen. Stars of the shows are Shamu (the first killer whale born in captivity, who now weighs more than three tons) and Namu, born in July 1989. During the show much can be learned about these very sociable relatives of the dolphins. Killer whales are often feared because of their size and their teeth!

Many of the legends of the north-west coast American Indians surround these toothed whales who eat fish or sea mammals. Some individual Indian clans (e.g. the Killer Whale Clan of the Tlingit Indians in Alaska) worship the whale because of its strength and speed.

Shows in the otter stadium are also very entertaining. Comical otters and clapping, splashing sea lions and walruses demonstrate their skills.

Otters, sea lions and walruses

A magnificent waterski show featuring some very difficult acrobatics can be watched from the stands of the Atlantis Theatre.

Atlantis Theatre

It is also worth paying a visit to the Sea World Theatre, where animal training is explained to visitors in an informative way.

Sea World Theatre

During an approximately two-hour long Animal Lovers Tour (not included in the entrance fee, best booked as far in advance as possible!) visitors can take a look backstage at Sea World and are taken in to the research and animal-rearing centres.

Animal Lovers Tour

In the summer a day at Sea World ends with a Magic Night Show (light entertainment) and a firework display.

Magic Night Show

Book in good time for a seat at a Polynesian Luau (a lavish banquet accompanied by a South Seas show) in the Hawaiian Village.

Hawaiian Village, Polynesian Luau

Surroundings of Orlando

Orlando is bordered in the north by Winter Park (founded 1882, population 23,000), which developed at the turn of the century as a winter holiday resort and is now an affluent college town (Rollins College at Lake Virginia, founded 1885) with many prestigious villas.
  Its main street is Park Avenue has many small boutiques, art galleries and antique shops, some of which are very exclusive.
  Boat trips (312 E. Morse Blvd.; departures daily 10am–4.30pm), during which a number of the beautiful villas along the waterside can be admired, are popular.

★Winter Park

A visit to the Charles Hosmer Morse Museum of American Art (133 E. Welbourne Ave.; open: Tues.–Sat. 9.30am–4pm, Sun. noon–4pm), opened in 1942, can also be recommended as it houses what is without doubt the most important collection of works by the artist and artisan Louis Comfort Tiffany (1848–1933). This glassware, which is at present enjoying renewed popularity, is among the most original Art Nouveau pieces. Numerous paintings, glass windows, lamps and pieces of jewellery have come from the former Tiffany house on Long Island. Others represented in the exhibition include the French glass engraver Emile Gallé, the American artist and author John LaFarge and the architect Frank Lloyd Wright, all of whom gained importance during the Art Nouveau period.

Morse Museum

Every weekend (Fri.–Sun. 8am–5pm) a lively flea market is held about 12 miles/20km north of Orlando (Highway 17/92, direction Sanford), which is attended by representatives of numerous commercial and private dealers. Entertainment is provided by country and western music, bingo and the Fun World pleasure park.

Flea World

Altamonte Springs (89ft/27m above sea-level, population 35,000), a highly-regarded residential suburb of Orlando, lies approximately 8 miles/13km north of the city.

Altamonte Springs

Ormond Beach

★Wekiwa Springs
State Park

Travel just 5 miles/8km further north-west to reach another popular destination for excursions, Wekiwa Springs State Park (1800 Wekiwa Circle; tel.
887 31 40) near the small village of Apopka. In the south-east section of the
park there is a mighty spring feeding a crystal-clear pool, which is very
tempting to swimmers. Nature lovers can encounter a variety of scenery.
The waters of Rock Spring Run and Wekiwa River are recommended for
canoe trips.

Sanford

The town of Sanford (population 23,000) lies near to Lake Monroe approximately 20 miles/32km north of Orlando, on the route to Daytona Beach.
Founded in 1837, this former trading post is now the centre of a large citrus
fruit and vegetable growing area and the terminus for motor rail trains
coming from the north-east of the USA. St John's River is navigable to this
point. Of interest to tourists are the Central Florida Zoological Park (Zoo;
US 17/92; open: daily 9am–5pm) and paddle-steamer trips (from Monroe
Harbour, SR 42; information; tel. 321 50 91) on St John's River. During the
last century this sort of paddle-steamer brought pioneers to central Florida.
   A 3500 year-old cypress tree stands in Big Tree Park (General Hutchison
Parkway, Longwood; open: Mon.–Fri. from 7am, Sat./Sun. from 9am). The
138ft/42m-tall tree is one of the oldest trees still intact in the USA.

Fort Christmas

By following the SR 50 eastwards towards Titusville for about 25
miles/40km drivers reach the town of Christmas with its reconstructed fort
dating from the time of the Seminolian Wars. Fort Christmas (1300 Fort
Christmas Road; open: Tues.–Sat. 10am–5pm, Sun. 1–5pm) was built
during the Christmas period of 1837, thus during the Second Seminolian
War. Documents, historical maps, weapons and other everyday objects
belonging to the first settlers and pictures of the Seminolian leader
bear witness to the not-so-distant past when the land was taken over by
whites. Many visitors send postcards from the small post office of
Christmas/Florida.

Disney World

See Walt Disney World.

Ormond Beach   D 13

Volusia County
Altitude: 0–23ft/0–7m
Population: 30,000

Location

Ormond Beach, a seaside resort only a few miles north of Daytona, was
known far afield at the turn of the century as a millionaires' colony. Those
without winter villas at fashionable Palm Beach enjoyed the peace and
favourable climate here on the Halifax River.
   The town's name dates back to an English planter who acquired a large
piece of land here from the Spanish in 1804. However, the Second Seminolian War brought a temporary halt to the early plantation industry in
Florida's central Atlantic coastal area. In 1873 a tuberculosis sanatorium
was built on the west bank of Halifax River. By the time that Flagler's East
Coast Railway had reached the town and the Ormond Hotel (complete with
golf course) had been completed in 1887, Ormond Beach was a fashionable
health resort where the rich of that time (Vanderbilt, Astor, Gould, Rockefeller, etc.) wintered.

Sights

Beach

The firm, 23 miles/37km-long beach, which reaches a width of up to
492ft/150m, was the scene of the first great motor races. By 1902 a speed
record of 56½mph/91kph had been achieved.

Halifax River

Halifax River, part of the Intracoastal Waterway, flows through the centre of
the holiday resort, separating the long off-shore peninsula with its beaches
(many hotels and apartments) from the town centre on the mainland.

From 1914 to 1937, when he died aged 97, John D. Rockefeller spent winters in his villa here (25 Riverside Drive; open: Mon.–Fri. 10am–3pm, Sat. 10am–noon), built in the style of the turn of the century and called The Casements after its unusually-shaped windows. Today Hungarian popular artwork, Italian ceramics and memorabilia from the American Boy Scout movement are displayed in the large villa with its octagonal atrium. Periodic exhibitions by local artists are also staged here.

The Casements

The Birthplace of Speed Museum (160 E. Granada Blvd.; open: Mon.–Sat. 11am–5pm), housed in the nearby former police and fire station, documents the beginnings of motor racing on Ormond Beach and the development of the motor industry. A replica of the "Stanley Steamer", which reached a speed of 127mph/204kph in 1906, should not be missed.

Birthplace of Speed Museum

Tomoko State Park (Old Dixie Highway, SR 201), about 4 miles/6km further north, is another popular venue for an outing. A Timucuan Indian village once stood here where the Tomoka River flows into the Halifax River. When Florida came into British possession in 1763 a plantation was developed here, growing indigo, sugar-cane and rice. Since then the natural vegetation of the old fields has taken over again. A visitors' centre provides information about the area and local natural history. Nature trail, boat excursions on the Tomoka River, camp site.
Information; Tomoka State Park, 2099 N. Beach St., Ormond Beach, FL 32074; tel. 677 39 31.

Tomoko State Park

The ruins of a large plantation (Old Dixie Highway to Old Kings Road/CR 2001), destroyed by the Seminolians in 1836, lies between Ormond Beach and Bunnell at Bulow Creek. In 1821 Major Ch. W. Bulow acquired almost 4942 acres/2000ha of wilderness here with a view to establishing a plantation. Until its destruction in 1836, cotton, sugar-cane and indigo were cultivated here. Only the foundations of the old manor house at Bulow Creek can now be seen. A short footpath leads past the former slave quarters to the ruined sugar mill.
The history of the plantation and its economic system is presented in the Interpretive Center. Information; Bulow Plantation State Historic Site, P.O. Box 655, Bunnell, FL 32010; tel. 439 22 19; open; daily 9am–5pm. Canoe tours of the Tomoka River (16 miles/26km) and of Bulow Creek (13 miles/21km).

★Bulow Plantation State Historic Site

Ormond-by-the-Sea, a town with approximately 10,000 inhabitants (most of whom are pensioners), adjoins Ormond Beach to the north. Halifax River, mainly calm here, provides a paradise for windsurfers and water-skiers. A number of yacht harbours and marinas on Halifax River between Flagler Beach and Ponce de León offer perfect conditions for water sports. Boats and canoes can be rented at a number of places.

Ormond-by-the-Sea

The Flagler State Recreation Area extends for approximately 11 miles/18km north of Ormond Beach along the Atlantic. It has a sandy beach, ramps for boats, a tent site and short circular pathways.

Flagler Beach State Recreation Area

Overseas Highway

See Florida Keys

Palatka
C 12

Putnam County
Altitude: 23ft/7m
Population: 11,000

Location   The old settlement of Palatka (Indian meaning = river crossing), once
            inhabited by Indians, lies on a bend of the St John's River which flows
            northwards from here. After the American Civil War, when it became
            fashionable to winter in Florida, many rich Americans from the North-East
            travelled here via Jacksonville on the new East Coast railway and by
            paddle-steamer. However, Palatka's economic boom only lasted for a short
            time, and, with the further development of Florida, the town sank back into
            obscurity.

            Today the small town forms the centre of an agricultural region, more
            recently touched by industrialisation. Dozens of marinas and camps for
            anglers attract tourists with specialist hobbies.

Sights

★Bronson-   The three-storeyed Bronson-Mulholland Mansion (100 Mulholland Park;
Mulholland   open: Tues., Thur. and Sat. 10am–5pm) is a very beautiful example of the
Mansion   Antebellum architecture of the Southern States. The house was built for a
               judge in the middle of the last century.

Azalea Festival   The yearly Azalea festival is held here on the second weekend in March.

★Ravine Gardens   The Ravine Gardens are located barely 1 mile/2km south-east of the town
                  and are worth visiting (open: daily 8am–dusk). Countless thousands of
                  azaleas bloom here in the spring, with many other plants in flower through-
                  out the rest of the year. The entrance to the gardens is flanked by the Court
                  of States building, with a 66ft/20m-tall obelisk, and the Civic Center.
                     The three pieces of land called "ravines" are wild and romantic, and
                  crossed by paths.

Lake Ocklawaha   Approximately 12 miles/20km further south-west Lake Ocklawaha has
                  been dammed to ensure that the Cross Florida Barge Canal receives suffi-
                  cient water. Good angling opportunities, boat excursions.

Palm Beach West Palm Beach   H/J 15

            Palm Beach County
            Altitude: 0–16ft/0–5m
            Population: Palm Beach 10,000, West Palm Beach 68,000

Palm Beach   The seaside resort of Palm Beach, with its elitist reputation, lies on the
                "Gold Coast", some 74 miles/120km north of Miami (see entry). This play-
                ground of the wealthy has developed over the last hundred years on a long
                sandy island. Members of the jet set meet here, mainly at Christmas or
                Easter, on the very long, wide beach, at polo or on one of the excellent golf
                courses or tennis courts. Elegant Worth Avenue (Rodeo Drive) and the
                many luxury hotels and gourmet restaurants are also very busy at those
                times.
                   Internationally-famous hotels, rich in tradition, (e.g. The Breakers) adjoin
                the beach. Many rich families from the worlds of economics, politics,
                culture and society own holiday homes here on Ocean Boulevard, as do the
                Kennedys, Estée Lauder and Burt Reynolds. The Professional Golfer's
                Association (PGA) is based in Palm Beach Garden.

West Palm   The town of West Palm Beach, located on the mainland, was originally a
Beach   residential area for the very large numbers of staff employed in the beach
                hotels and their families. As time passed the resort developed into a centre
                of tourism, even for those of modest means, and its residential population
                also increased rapidly.

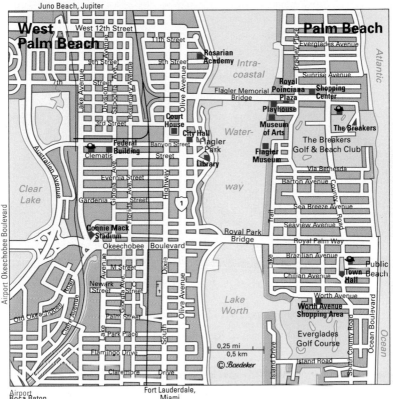

West Palm Beach is now the administrative and economic seat of the region. Electronics firms have set up in business here and financial and tax advisers have moved here in pursuit of wealthy clients, who spend their winter and spring holidays or their retirement in the town.

Almost every month approximately 2000 newcomers can be counted in the Palm Beach area who, for some time, have been predominantly in the age group from 20 to 40.

Despite recent radical alterations to the skyline of the twin-town during the last two decades and the recent boom in new hotels and apartments, well-tended villas continue to characterise the townscape. Most of them date from the 1920s and the 1930s and have been built in the Spanish-Mediterranean style, considered modern at that time. They are painted gleaming white.

Skyline

Palm Beach owes its name or more precisely its beautiful palms to a Spanish ship which ran aground here in 1878, laden with wine and 20,000 coconuts. The handful of settlers living on this rather inhospitable coast planted the coconuts, from which a palm grove is said to have grown. The

History

Flagler's "Whitehall"

Gulf Stream flows only a bare 1 mile/2km–3 miles/5km from the coast. The fine sandy beach, dotted with palm trees, and the deep-blue, gradually turning to turquoise, warm water of the Atlantic, with its long swell, have attracted visitors from all social classes for the last 100 years.

Flagler

Henry Morrison Flagler (see Introduction, Famous People), who, together with John D. Rockefeller, founded the Standard Oil Company (earlier called ESSO, now known as Exxon), was, together with the architect Addison Mizner, the man who shaped Palm Beach. After 1874 he spent his winters in warm Florida, although at first in St Augustine. At the beginning of the 1890s he discovered the charming, palm-decorated island of Palm Beach, which at that time could only be reached by a difficult boat journey to Jupiter, from where the owner of a small guest house collected his guests in a carriage. In 1894 Flagler extended his Florida East Coast Railroad as far as Lake Worth and had the legendary Royal Poinciana hotel built. Subsequently many of America's most prominent citizens stayed here. An incomparable land and building boom began almost overnight. In 1895 Flagler gave the go-ahead to the building of the somewhat less formal Palm Beach Inn, immediately adjoining the Atlantic, for younger clients. The hotel was extended several times and then renamed The Breakers in 1901 because of its position. Its guests included the Rockefellers, the Astors and the Morgans as well as the newspaper magnate W. R. Hearst and US President Harding. The hotel burnt down in 1925 but was reconstructed in its present form a short time later. At the beginning of the 20th c. Addison Mizner was a sought-after architect who principally built luxury villas on Long Island near New York. He came to Palm Beach in 1918 and created his Spanish-Mediterranean style, which is now considered typical of Palm Beach. The Everglades Club (1918) and The Cloisters Inn (1925; now called the Boca Raton Hotel & Club) are the most famous of his creations.

Sights in Palm Beach

Worth Avenue, the city's main shopping street, has achieved world-wide fame. The elegant shopping centre The Esplanade (150 Worth Ave.) also tempts visitors to browse among its exclusive shops and galleries. Names such as Cartier, Yves St-Laurent and Van Cleef & Arpels are to be found here, as are Sotheby's, Saks Fifth Avenue and Gucci. Well-maintained Worth Avenue possesses a unique atmosphere. Most of the buildings have been retained in Mizner's Mediterranean style. Here and there *vias* lead into small courtyards, filled with plants.

★Worth Avenue, The Esplanade

In 1901 Flagler, the railway magnate, had a palatial 73-room villa called Whitehall built on the bank of Lake Worth. He then made a present of it to his third wife. Until his death in 1913 Flagler wintered here with his family. During the 1920s the villa was sold, developed into a luxury hotel and extended. The house was turned into a museum in 1959/60 and the hotel torn down. Address; Morrison Flagler Museum, 1 Whitehall Way, Coconut Row; open: Tues.–Sat. 10am–5pm, Sun. noon–5pm; last tour 3.30pm.

★Henry Morrison Flagler Museum

Flagler's own private railway carriage (1886), which he used on his first visit to Key West in 1912, stands in the grounds.

Today "The Breakers" hotel is a symbol of Palm Beach. Built in 1926 immediately adjoining the beach, it was designed by the architect Leonard Schulze (who also designed the Waldorf Astoria Hotel in New York) and is now a protected building. The Breakers has retained its magnificent grand hotel elegance.

★The Breakers

The Hibel Museum of Art (150 Royal Poinciana Plaza; open: Tues.-Sat. 10am–5pm, Sun. 1–5pm; Nov–May concerts every second Sun. at 3pm) was built in 1977. It exhibits works by the artist Edna Hibel (born 1907), who made a name for herself as a painter of porcelain (particularly for Rosenthal).

Hibel Museum of Art

"The Breakers", a luxury hotel and protected monument

Society of the Four Arts	Palm Beach's active cultural life revolves around the buildings of the Society of the Four Arts, founded in 1936. Here on the Four Arts Plaza are an art gallery with a sculpture garden, a library and a theatre.
Bethesda-by-the-Sea	The Bethesda-by-the-Sea church (Barton Ave./South County Road) was constructed in 1925 in the neo-Gothic style.
Bicycle Trail	An almost 13 miles/20km-long, well-signed bicycle trail begins at Four Arts Plaza and first takes cyclists through areas of villas to Lake Worth Inlet. The Kennedy family home stands on the corner of Queens Lane/N. Ocean Drive. The trail returns along Ocean Drive and past The Breakers hotel and its golf course. The eye-catching villa on the corner of Ocean Drive/Barton Avenue belongs to Estée Lauder, the cosmetics queen. Further to the south is the castle-like villa Mar A Lago (118 rooms, built in 1923 by Marjorie Merriweather Post), which was bought for a good price by the much-talked-about financier Donald Trump in 1985.
	Bicycle rental; Palm Beach Bicycle Trail Shop, 105 N. County Road/ Sunrise Avenue; tel. 659 45 83.

Sights in West Palm Beach   H/J 15

Raymond F. Kravis Center for the Performing Arts	The Raymond F. Kravis Center for the Performing Arts (701 Okeechobee Blvd.; tel 833 83 00), completed in 1992, stands at the centre of the old heart of West Palm Beach. It comprises a large theatre and a concert hall, where the Philharmonic Orchestra of Florida and the Palm Beach Symphony sometimes perform.
★Norton Gallery of Art	The Norton Gallery of Art (1451 S. Olive Ave./US 1; open: Tues.–Sat. 10am–5pm, Sun. 1–5pm) is prized as one of the USA's best regional museums. Of note are the collections of French Impressionist pantings, 20th c. American art and Chinese art. Sculpture garden.
The Armory Art Center	A series of exhibitions by contemporary artists from Florida can be viewed in the former National Guard arsenal (1703 S. Lake Ave.; open: Tues.–Sun. 9am–5pm).
Union Congregational Church	In Georgia Avenue stands the Union Congregational Church (no. 2727); inside can be seen some very beautiful stained glass of German origin.
South Florida Science Museum, Planetarium & Aquarium	The South Florida Science Museum (including a planetarium with a giant telescope), the Native Plant Center and the South Florida Aquarium (4801 Dreher Trail N; open: daily 10am–5pm, Fri. also 5–10pm; laser show Fri. 9pm and 11pm) stand in Dreher Park.
Dreher Park Zoo	The small Dreher Park Zoo (1301 Summit Blvd.; open: daily 9am–5pm) is home to both native animals (including the rare Florida panther) and exotic animals. Hands-on zoo.

Surroundings of Palm Beach and West Palm Beach

★Lion Country Safari	Lion Country Safari (Southern Blvd./West SR 80; entry daily: 9.30am–5.30pm), a safari and leisure park, is situated about 17 miles/27km west of the city. Drive (keep windows and doors closed!) through the grounds, where a variety of wild animals, including lions, can wander at will. The Safari Village contains a hands-on zoo, an aviary and a dinosaur and reptile park.
Singer Island	The narrow Singer Island peninsula extends north of Lake Worth Inlet. The sewing machine industrialist, Singer, wanted to develop a large holiday complex here in the 1920s, but the construction of a magnificent hotel,

designed by Addison Mizner, was halted by a hurricane in 1926 and the grand plans to open up the area could not be continued with. Today Singer Island possesses its own charm. The bathing beach is considered one of the finest in the region. Street cafés and small boutiques enliven the scene.

See entry

Boynton Beach

Delray Beach, a large town with 43,000 inhabitants, lies about 12 miles/20km to the south and is famous above all for its wide, white sandy beaches. Until recently predominantly a residential town, an increasing number of hi-tech companies have started up here. The Historical Society maintains a small museum detailing local history in a restored Victorian holiday house (5 N.E. 1st Street; open: Tues.–Fri. 10am–3pm).

Delray Beach

The Morikami Museum and its beautiful Japanese Garden (4000 Morikami Park Road; open: Tues.–Sun. 10am–5pm) can be found about 3 miles/5km west of Delray Beach. Japanese settlers, including George Sukeji (1886–1976), on whose pineapple and vegetable fields the museum has been built, established a flourishing Japanese community here. Japanese tea ceremonies, a bonsai collection of plants native to Florida, nature trail. End Feb.; Hatsume Fair (Japanese arts and crafts), mid Aug.; Bon Festival (Japanese summer festival).

★The Morikami Museum and Japanese Garden

See entry

Boca Raton

Palm Beach Shores (population 1000), a peaceful village of villas situated a few kilometres to the north, has a marvellous bathing beach. A number of high-rise hotels and apartment blocks have recently been built here, as have marinas on the Intracoastal Waterway.

Palm Beach Shores

The John D. MacArthur Beach State Park (about 2 miles/3km north of Palm Beach Shores on the SR A1A; open: daily from 8am) occupies the narrow part of the peninsula. There is a beautiful bathing beach, as well as dunes, a lagoon and sign-posted nature trails. The visitors' centre (open: Tues.–Sun. 9am–5pm) offers information about the ecology of the area.

John D. MacArthur Beach State Park

Palm Beach's modern port began operating in 1990 on the mainland opposite. Cruises to the Bahamas and the Caribbean depart from here. Information; tel. 1 800 841 7447 (no charge).

Port of Palm Beach

In 1888 the small seaside resort of Juno Beach (population 2000), with its fantastic beach, became the terminus of the first railway line in this region and, from 1889 to 1899, the administrative centre of Dade County. When Flagler built his Florida East Coast Railroad in 1893 he tried to buy up the existing railway line. As terms could not be agreed, Flagler by-passed Juno Beach, which subsequently sank into obscurity.

Juno Beach

The Marine Life Center in Loggerhead Park (1200 US 1; open: daily 10am–3pm) is a marine research and conservation centre. It provides information about turtles, dolphins, whales and a variety of species of fish, as well as crabs, mussels, tortoises and snakes. During the summer period, when turtles lay their eggs, evening walks are held (Turtle Walks; 9pm–midnight).
The park also has a beautiful bathing beach (supervised), a nature trail, cycle paths and play areas.

★Marine Life Center, Loggerhead County Park

Panama City   B 5

Bay County
Altitude: 0–30ft/0–9m
Population: 40,000

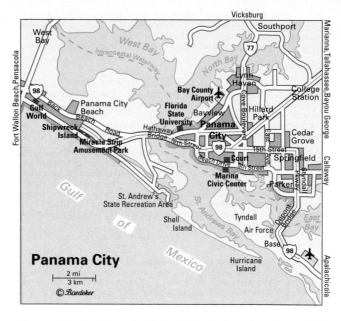

Panama City

2 mi
3 km

© Baedeker

| Location | Panama City, a thriving port and industrial centre, lies at the eastern end of "Miracle Strip". This northern strip along the Gulf of Mexico is about 100 miles/160km long and extends as far as Pensacola (see entry). The "Strip" boasts a number of beaches of fine, white sand. |

Location

Panama City, a thriving port and industrial centre, lies at the eastern end of "Miracle Strip". This northern strip along the Gulf of Mexico is about 100 miles/160km long and extends as far as Pensacola (see entry). The "Strip" boasts a number of beaches of fine, white sand.

Free trade zone

Panama City is Florida's largest free trade zone. Its major employers include a large paper and cellulose mill as well as the Tyndall Air Force Base and the Naval Coastal Systems Center.

Miracle Mile

"Miracle Mile" has seen the development of the almost self-contained tourist centre known as Panama City Beach, offering plenty of entertainment, pubs, pleasure parks, amusement arcades and shopping centres.

Intracoastal Waterway

Sailing enthusiasts can take the sheltered Intracoastal Waterway to either Apalachicola in the east or to Pensacola in the west.

History

In 1765 English immigrants founded the settlement known as St Andrews (now a part of Panama City) in a protected bay.

It was in the early 1900s when the first chalets were built along the magnificent beaches and the place began to develop as a tourist and holiday centre. Better roads and the construction of a bridge helped to make Panama City one of the most popular summer resorts in the southeast of the USA. For a long time it was perhaps somewhat disparagingly called "Baja Georgia" or "Redneck River".

Today its many hotels and condominiums as well as the numerous small motels are filled in the summer months with package tourists from the northern states of the USA and from Canada. In Bay Point and Edgewater will be found some spacious and luxurious holiday villas. There are also several golf-courses and marinas which serve as a base for those who enjoy deep-sea fishing and diving.

Panama City: Miracle Strip

Sights

Hathaway Bridge across North Bay links the port of Panama City with the long, flat beaches along the Gulf of Mexico, where the tourist infrastructure is mainly geared to package holidaymakers with children. This is the start of the most scenic and charming stretch of Highway 98. Alternatively, County Road 30-A also runs along the coast. Near Panama City Beach and Laguna Beach, Highway 98, known as Miracle Strip Parkway, is studded with motels and apartment-blocks, restaurants, fast-food bars and souvenir shops, as well as some lavishly equipped mini-golf courses. County Pier and City Pier are very popular with anglers and sun-worshippers.

Panama City Beach, Laguna Beach

With some 30 attractions and rides the Miracle Strip Amusement Park at 12001 West Highway 98 is the largest amusement park in North Florida. Nearby lies Shipwreck Island Water Park, a combination of an amusement park and fun-pool.

Amusement Parks

Opposite is the Visitor Information Center. From an elevated viewing-terrace there is a beautiful view of the Gulf Coast.

Info Center

The "Gulf World" aqua show near the 1640ft/500m-long City Pier at 15412 West Highway 98-A gives performances by dolphins, sea-lions, parrots and divers. Other attractions include various aquaria, a colony of penguins and a dolphin-pool.

Gulf World

The Museum of Man in the Sea at 17314 Hutchinson Rd. portrays the history of diving, concentrating on technical developments in diving apparatus. It also shows films by the pioneer of underwater filming, Jacques Cousteau.

Museum of Man in the Sea

A visit to Shell Island will be found worthwhile. This uninhabited island, some 7½ miles/12km in length, has a fresh-water lake and some isolated

★Shell Island

dunes screening St Andrews Bay, where there are some pleasant spots for bathing, or the visitor can collect shells or go for a stroll along the beach.

Excursion boats	Boats to the island ply from Bay Point, Anderson Marina, St Andrews State Park and Treasure Island Marina.
★St Andrews State Park	State Park, at the eastern tip of the Panama City Beach peninsula, a favourite holiday spot for locals, has some beautiful bathing beaches and a camp-site. In summer cycles and boats can be hired. Paths with information boards will help to familiarise the visitor with the local fauna, and animals such as alligators and waterfowl can be observed.
Junior Museum of Bay County	The Junior Museum of Bay County at 1731 Jenks Ave., Panama City provides a brief introduction to various scientific phenomena, as well as describing the culture of the native Indians. There are also nature-trails and an open-air museum.

Surroundings

Boat excursions	A glass-bottomed boat leaves from Treasure Island. Passengers can observe the submarine life in the shallow waters near the coast. From Holiday Lodge Marina there are trips round the bay and also to watch the dolphins.
Ebro Greyhound Track	During the summer season greyhound races are held at the Ebro Greyhound Track off the SR 79/90 east of Panama City.

Pensacola   B 2

Escambia County
Altitude: 0–13ft/0–4m
Population: 60,000

Location

Pensacola, a port and economic and industrial centre at the western tip of the Florida "panhandle", is the second oldest town in the state and can look back on more than four hundred years of history.

In recent years a large number of historically important buildings have been lovingly restored. Examples of this are some on Seville Square with balconies and wrought-ironwork reminiscent of the Spanish Colonial period, while the magnificent villas in the North Hill Preservation District, most of which were built after the American Civil War, still exude something of the charm of the Old South.

Natural harbour

Deep and sheltered, Pensacola Bay is Flor-

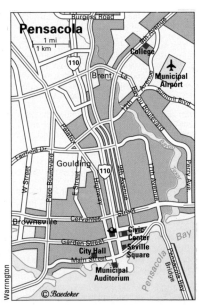

ida's largest and best natural harbour, the advantages of which were appreciated centuries ago by Spanish, French and British fleets and later by both Confederate and Unionist forces. The flag flying over the town has changed thirteen times in its history. Since 1914 Pensacola has been the US Naval Aviation Station.

Major industries include wood-working and paper, chemicals and food.

Industry

Pensacola is very proud of the little University of West Florida, which was founded in 1963 and now has 6000 students.

University of West Florida

A short distance from the town centre the visitor will find some beautiful beaches – Santa Rosa Island, "Miracle Strip", Gulf Breeze, Pensacola Beach, Navarre Beach, Perdido Key – where a number of holiday complexes have been built since the 1960s. Fortunately many of the sand-dunes on Santa Rosa have been preserved as part of the Gulf Island National Seashore (see entry).

Tourism

The eastern part of the 50 mile/80km-long island off Navarre Beach belongs to the Eglin Air Force Base (see Fort Walton Beach) and is closed to the public.

Eglin Air Force Base

In 1559, six years before St Augustine (see entry) was founded, Don Tristan de Luna landed with 500 soldiers and some 1000 colonists near the present Naval Aviation Station. Attempts to erect dwellings were thwarted by a hurricane, however, and it was the early 18th c. before the fort known as "San Carlos de Austria" was built and a permanent township established. During the Franco-Spanish War Pensacola was the scene of much fighting and changed hands several times. After the town had been destroyed by the French the Spaniards built a new settlement which was easier to defend on Santa Rosa Island, but this also fell victim to a hurricane in 1752.

History

The historic town centre around Seville Square dates back to a small fortified Spanish settlement of 1752. Pensacola was ceded to Britain at the end of the Seven Years' War. In the two centuries which followed the British developed the old Spanish outpost into a base of some importance, with a catchment area extending far into Alabama and the Mississipi region. At that time the timber trade and export of furs played an important role.

Spanish occupation

In 1781 the Spaniards returned to Pensacola, and under the 1783 Treaty of Paris the whole of Florida was returned to Spain. Pensacola became an asylum for escaping slaves and for Indians driven out by the whites, as well as being a pirates' lair.

In 1814 and 1818 Andrew Jackson repeatedly occupied Pensacola. In 1821 Florida was formally handed over to the United States; during the next thirty years Pensacola became an American naval base and Fort Pickens, Fort McRae and Fort Barrancas were built. During the American Civil War Fort Pickens, held by Union troops, played an important part in blockading the Gulf Coast which was held by the Confederates.

The end of the Civil War saw the beginning of the boom years in the lumber trade. The long trunks of the local yellow pine were very much sought after. The harbour was extended, Pensacola was given a railway and its population grew rapidly. As a result of over-felling of trees in Western Florida this boom came to an end by the turn of the century, and people then concentrated on fishing. However, over-fishing meant this industry was short-lived too.

The Pensacola region can thank the US Navy for its more recent development; in 1914 the navy built its Aeronautical Station here, which led to expansion of the town, the arrival of new industries and increased employment. Finally, in 1931 the first bridges across Pensacola Bay were completed, making it possible for people to drive to the beaches on Santa Rosa Island.

As described above, Pensacola has had a varied history. In all five different flags have flown over the town at various times, resulting in its becoming

Fiesta of the Five Flags

known as the "City of the Five Flags". Early in May every year the "Fiesta of the Five Flags" is celebrated in the town centre; the highlight of this celebration is an enactment of the landing of the town's first founder, Don Tristan de Luna, on the white sands of Pensacola Beach and his being greeted by the Indian chief Mayoki.

Sights

Seville Square

Park-like Seville Square, with its ancient oaks, has been tastefully restored in recent years. Some of the houses date from the first half of the 19th c. Most were built shortly after the American Civil War. Some function as museums, art galleries and antique shops.

★Historic Pensacola Village

Historic Pensacola Village is in the area formed by Zaragoza Street and Tarragona Street and is open Mon.–Sat. 10am–4.30pm, Sun. 1–4.30pm. It comprises a group of prettily renovated old buildings which reflect life during the Spanish, French and British colonial periods as well as at the end of the last century. Dorr House, at 311 Adams St., Seville Square, was built in 1871 during the timber boom. Lavalle House, at 205 East Church St., in the Creole style, dates from 1810, making it one of the town's oldest houses. Opposite, in the Hispanic Building (once a storehouse) at 203 Zaragoza St., will be found the West Florida Museum of History. In the Plaza Ferdinand VII the former City Hall, built in 1907, now houses the Wentworth Jr. Florida State Museum. The old State Prison, built in 1906 in the Spanish style at 407 South Jefferson St., is now the Pensacola Museum, with art exhibitions and collections by local artists. In the Museum of Transportation and Commerce, in the building at the corner of Zaragoza Street and Tarragona Street dating from 1898–1903, the visitor can gain an insight into the region's economic history and developments in modes of transport; the exhibits include an ancient printing press and old trams.

Across the way, at 210 Zaragoza St., stands Jubilee Panton Cottage, built in 1808 and now housing exhibitions on the history and social position of negroes in Florida. Old Christ Church, at Zaragoza St./Adams St., dates from 1830, making it the oldest church in West Florida; it now contains the Pensacola Historical Museum.

At the corner of Barrack Street and Main Street stands the attractive Victorian L and N Marine Terminal, built in 1903, the harbour terminal of the Louisville and Nashville Railroad Company.

Palafox Pier

In the south of the town Palafox Street ends at the popular Palafox Pier. At the corner of Palafox Street and Cedar Street stands the old 1888 McKenzie-Oerting Co. building; fishermen and seamen obtained their equipment and provisions from this firm of ships chandlers from 1869 right up to 1971. Fishing cutters tied up here until 1966.

★Palafox Historic Business District

Since 1979, whenever the old business premises along Palafox Street have been restored great care has been taken to replace the old wrought-iron balconies in their original form. Palafox Square, between Garden Street and Government Street is now the heart of the old town centre which has regained its popularity. In 1981 the Saenger Theatre at 118 South Palafox St. was re-opened; when it was first officially opened in 1925 it was Florida's largest theatre and has welcomed players from many other states and countries.

★North Hill Preservation District

North Hill Preservation District, embracing Palafox Street, LaRua Street, Reus Street and Blount Street, to the north-west of the old town centre, is an area of superb villas most of which have been preserved in their original state. Most of these houses, standing in the shade of giant oaks, were built between 1870 and 1930.

In Fort George Park, at the corner of Palafox Street and LaRua Street, many remains of British fortifications dating from the 1770s have been unearthed.

In the small premises of the J. W. Renfroe Pecan Company at 2400 West Fairfield Drive visitors can watch pecan nuts being packed, especially during the autumn harvest period.

J. W. Renfroe Pecan Company

Constructed in 1912, the buildings of the old L & N Railroad Station at Gregory Street and Alcaniz Street were allowed to fall into disrepair for a number of years after it closed down in 1971. Now, however, it forms part of a hotel complex.

L & N Railroad

Surroundings

South-west of the town centre, at the end of Navy Boulevard, lies the Naval Air Station (NAS), where American navy pilots are trained. Sherman Field is the home of the famous "Blue Angels" squadron, which takes part in spectacular air displays twice a year. Visitors may just be fortunate enough to see the aircraft-carrier "USS Lexington" berthed in the harbour.

Naval Air Station

Within the grounds of the NAS will be found the National Museum of Naval Aviation (open: daily 9am–5pm), which provides an insight into the history of the American fleet air arm. More than 100 aircraft are on display, including old biplanes and seaplanes as well as modern jet machines. Also of interest is the command capsule of the "Skylab" space laboratory, in which a marine crew circled the earth for 28 days.

★National Museum of Naval Aviation

Still standing in the grounds of the NAS are an 1858 lighthouse and the Batteria de San Antonio, built by the Spaniards in 1797 to defend the harbour. Above stands Fort Barrancas, built by US troops between 1834 and 1844. There were Spanish and British fortifications here back in the 17th and 18th c.

Batteria de San Antonio, Fort Barrancas

Access to the suburb of Gulf Breeze is by way of Pensacola Bay Bridge which was constructed in the 1970s; the older bridge built in 1956 now serves as a pier for anglers.
About 10 miles/16km further east on the US 98 at 5801 Gulf Breeze Parkway lies The Zoo, the "panhandle's" only zoological and botanical garden. The US 98 Highway leads east from Gulf Breeze through an area with large forests of oak trees (*quercus virginiana*) which forms part of Gulf Island National Seashore (see entry). Nature-paths lead through the largely unspoiled forest.

Gulf Breeze, The Zoo, Naval Oaks

The beach resort of Pensacola Beach lies on the barrier reef which stretches for almost 50 miles/80km as far as Fort Walton Beach (see entry). The shining white sands were only opened up to tourists during the last twenty years or so.

Pensacola Beach

Large areas of Santa Rosa Island form part of Gulf Island National Seashore (see entry), a national park which stretches for almost 150 miles/240km along the Gulf Coast from Panama City Beach to the mouth of the Mississipi. The fine sand was swept down into the Gulf of Mexico from the foot of the Appalachians many thousands of years ago. Marram grass grows in profusion on the dunes.

Santa Rosa Island

At the western end of Santa Rosa Island lies Fort Pickens, built between 1829 and 1834 as part of a chain of fortifications which included Fort McRee (1835–39) at the eastern end of Perdido Key and Fort Barrancas on the mainland, and which were built to defend the entrance to Pensacola harbour. The ruins of the brick-built Fort Pickens are open to visitors. From 1886 to 1889 the Apache chief Geronimo and seventeen of his braves were incarcerated here.

Fort Pickens

Round Trip taking in Pensacola–Santa Rosa Island–Milton–Pensacola

After crossing Pensacola Bay Bridge the first stop is at Pensacola Beach. From here there is a 15 mile/25km drive along the SR 399 through the

★Route

223

Pensacola: ruins of Fort Pickens

charming dunes of Santa Rosa Island to Navarre Beach, a small holiday resort with a few hotels. After crossing Santa Rosa Sound follow the SR 87 north through the wooded Eglin Air Force Base until it meets the US 90 Highway some 20 miles/33km further on.

Some 5 miles/8km west lies the township of Milton. It has a population of 7000, comes under the administration of Santa Rosa County, is home to the local chemical industry and boasts a number of prettily-restored buildings from the Civil War period. The Imogen Theatre (1913) houses a small municipal museum. The wooden St Mary's Episcopal Church, built in 1878, is still in its original condition.

A trading post was established here on Blackwater River back in 1825. Later Milton became a centre for timber, turpentine and cotton, which is still grown in Santa Rosa County.

Blackwater River State Forest

North-east of Milton the Blackwater River State Forest in the Western Highlands reaches as far as Alabama where it becomes the Conecuh National Forest. This largely undeveloped hilly region of long-needled pine trees is home to the red lynx, otter, red deer and wild turkey. The Florida Trail for walkers, which is still being added to, begins in the Blackwater River State Forest. In spring and autumn a walk can be enjoyed along the 21 miles/34km-long Andrew Jackson Red Ground Trail, which follows an old trading trail. Leisure facilities have been installed in the southern part of the forest. In spite of their dark colour, caused by tannin seeping in from the deciduous cypress trees, the Coldwater, Blackwater and Juniper Rivers which flow through the forests are excellent for canoe trips; canoes can be rented and a transport service is provided by firms in Milton. The white sandbanks and sandy river banks form a marked contrast to the dark-coloured water.

The route returns to Pensacola along the I–10 by way of Bagdad, where the typical 19th c. wooden houses and small post office, which was used again between 1913 and 1986, are worth studying.

Taylor County
Altitude: 43ft/13m
Population: 9000

The little township of Perry proudly calls itself "Tree capital of the South"; it is the county town of Taylor County, a relatively thinly-populated and mainly wooded region in the north-west of the Florida peninsula, and is about 50 miles/80km south-east of Tallahassee (see entry). One of its main employers is the paper mill owned by Proctor and Gamble, which employs about 1000 people.

In early October each year the Florida Forest Festival is held here, with what is claimed to be the largest free "fish fry" in the world.

In the course of their expeditions the first Spanish conquerors passed through the extensive pine-forests near Perry. A few simple fortifications were built here during the wars against the Seminole Indians. The first settlement was founded here in 1857 and was called "Rose Head". In 1879 it was given its present name in honour of Governor Perry. At that time Taylor County could boast a mere 2000 inhabitants. By the end of the 19th c. the region's timber wealth was realised, particularly in connection with ship-building. Trees yielding turpentine oil were widely grown.   History

In 1902–03 the first railroad line from Live Oak reached Perry. A further line was added in 1906, and in 1907 it was linked by a branch line to the Atlantic Coast Railroad, making Perry a proper rail junction. Beef cattle from inland were loaded here and the first saw-mills were built.

In 1910 Hampton Springs Hotel, with its own railroad station, was built near a sulphurous spring outside the town; it prospered until the Depression, after which it declined and was finally destroyed by fire in 1954.

At the end of the 1930s the once rich forests became largely denuded of trees, and because it took a long time to re-stock them the saw-mills had to close. It was 1951 before the timber industry reasserted itself here in the shape of a paper mill using wood pulp.

In the post-war years, until the Interstate road network was built, Perry was an important stopping-place for tourists travelling to Southern Florida.

Sights

Forest State Capital Museum was opened in 1973. Situated at 204 Forest Park Drive, it can be reached on the US 19/27A/98 Highways, and is open Thur.–Mon. 9am–noon and 1–5pm. It provides a good insight into the history of the lumber industry, which is still the third most important branch of Florida's economy. This modern museum, built mainly of wood, gives detailed information about the forest and Florida's 314 different species of trees and types of wood, with the emphasis on various aspects of forestry and the timber business as well as turpentine production in the old days. The exhibits are completed by a very natural-looking small cypress swamp and a hardwood hammock.   ★Forest Capital State Museum

Near the museum will be found "Cracker Homestead", a typical home of the first farming settlers, thousands of which were built early this century in the pine-forests of North Florida. It is a simple log-cabin with the typical veranda and a kitchen built on, the whole surrounded by a wooden palisade.   ★Cracker Homestead

The term "cracker", used to describe the first people to settle in Florida, is derived from the crack of the whip with which the pioneers drove their cattle and teams of oxen. The "Cracker Homestead", a reconstruction of a log-cabin as used by a pioneering family in 1863, shows how the white settlers lived right up to the early 20th c.

225

Surroundings

Keaton Beach, Steinhatchee

The traveller can make a detour off County Road 361 southwards to the popular excursion spot Keaton Beach on this largely unspoiled area of the Gulf Coast and then on to Steinhatchee, a small fishing village at the mouth of the river of the same name where many come to fish for sport. Steinhatchee grew up in the 1870s when the first settlers made rafts from the trunks of cedar trees and then rowed along the coast to Cedar Key (see entry).

Pinellas Suncoast   F/G 10

Pinellas County

Location and ★★topography

"Pinellas Suncoast" is the name given to a 28 mile/45km-long section of the coast of the Gulf of Mexico north of Tampa Bay with the eight holiday resorts of Pinellas County situated by the sea and also on the offshore chain of islands. The best-known are St Petersburg (see entry) and St Petersburg Beach, followed by Tarpon Springs, Dunedin and Clearwater Beach in the north, Indian Rocks Beach/Redington Beach and Madeira Beach on Sand Key as well as Treasure Island. There were nearly four million visitors here in 1991.

Miles of beaches covered in almost snow-white sand and the warm, crystal-blue waters of the Gulf of Mexico with its gentle surf make this section of the coast an ideal holiday spot for water sports enthusiasts. The season lasts the whole year, and statistics claim that the sun shines on 361 days in the year. Even in winter the temperatures are nearly always above 61°F/16°C.

Sailing, wind-surfing and parascending are popular as are deep-sea fishing, diving and water-skiing. Golfing and tennis enthusists will also get their money's worth. Families with children will appreciate the flat and as yet uncrowded beaches as well as the relative proximity of the tourist attractions of Central Florida (see Tampa, Orlando, Kissimmee).

Tarpon Springs   F 10

Location

The Greek heritage and atmosphere of Tarpon Springs (pop. 16,000), a seaside resort in the north of Pinellas County, make it one of the most unusual places on this coast. Waterways meander through the town and small shops, delicatessens, restaurants and bars almost make the visitor feel he or she is actually in Greece itself.

Sponge-diving

Tarpon Springs is today still the town of the sponge-diver, even though sponges are no longer "harvested" off the Gulf Coast of Florida, being in fact brought here from the sponge reefs off the coast of Central America. In the early 19th c. people began to collect sponges thrown up on the beach at Key West and to clean them and sell them. Some sailed out to the reefs to pull sponges off with hooks and rods and large sponge reefs were subsequently found off Tarpon Springs.

History

The first settlers arrived in Tarpon Springs in 1876. The town was founded in 1882. Around the turn of the century the first Greek sponge-divers came to Tarpon Springs, bringing their skills and equipment with them. By 1905 there were 1500 Greeks living here, with their own boat and house designs, dress, food and customs. In 1939 the Greek sponge-diving fleet comprised more than 200 boats. Although today the synthetic version can be produced much more cheaply, there is still a heavy demand for natural sponges.

Pinellas Suncoast: St Pete Beach, Treasure Island ▶

Events

A Greek Wine Festival is held every March. In May Sponge Docks form the backcloth to a Fishermen's Festival, when culinary delights of Greek fish cuisine are on offer.

Sights

Dodecanes
Boulevard

A stroll along Dodecanes Boulevard, on the southern bank of the Anclote River, with its moorings for crab-fishermen and sponge-divers ("Sponge Docks") can be a true delight. Sponges of all kinds and various price levels can be purchased.

Spongerama

Near the harbour once used by the sponge-divers Spongerama (510 Dodecanes Blvd; open: daily 10am–5pm) provides an insight into the development of the sponge-diving industry and the situation of the Greek immigrants.

St Nicholas Greek
Orthodox Church

The Greek Orthodox Church of St Nicholas, built in 1943 at 30 North Pinellas Ave./Orange St., is an adaptation of the Hagia Sophia in Istanbul. The church is furbished with valuable icons, beautiful stained-glass windows and Greek marble.

It is here that the Feast of the Epiphany is celebrated on January 6th with magnificent ceremony and in accordance with orthodox rites. Congregations of up to 40,000 assemble. In the course of the celebrations the boats are blessed and young boys dive for a golden crucifix.

Indian Rocks Beach   G 10

Location

The beach resort known as Indian Rocks Beach, a 9 mile/15km stretch of shore between Tom Stuart Causeway (also called "Madeira Beach Causeway") actually consists of seven independent communities lying in a row along Gulf Boulevard – Redington Beach, North Redington Beach, Redington Shores, Indian Shores, Indian Rocks Beach, Bellair Shores and Bellair Beach.

Redington Beach has remained completely as it was, while the other places have recently been extended into very luxurious holiday complexes.

★Suncoast
Seabird
Sanctuary

Founded in 1971 by the zoologist R. T. Heath Jr., Suncoast Seabird Sanctuary situated at 18328 Gulf Blvd, Indian Shores (open: from 9am daily) runs a large treatment centre for injured wild birds. In large enclosures and aviaries visitors can see brown pelicans, cormorants, herons, ducks and other sea-birds, as well as eagles, owls and many song-birds.

Tiki Gardens

Tiki Gardens, at 19601 Gulf Blvd./196th Ave. North Indian Shores (open: daily 10am–8pm), is a small leisure park with a South Sea atmosphere. The Polynesian Adventure Trail leads through a delightful park with reproductions of Polynesian temples and deities. Colourful tropical plants, peacocks and parrots bring the scenery to life.

★Hamlin's
Landing,
"Starlite Princess"

Hamlin's Landing, at 401 Second St. East, Indian Rocks Beach, is a complex of buildings in the style of the Victorian epoch covering an area of some 15 acres/6ha by the Intracoastal Waterway. Wooden wharves and balconies, colourful shops and friendly fish-stalls, together with the hotel all contribute to the atmosphere of nostalgia.

Also very reminiscent of days gone by is the paddle-steamer "Starlite Princess" which offers excursions and cruises with evening meal on the Intracoastal Waterway.

Madeira Beach   G 10

Location

The resort of Madeira Beach (pop. 5000) in the south of Sand Key, linked to the mainland only ½ mile/1km away by the Tom Stuart Causeway, is a favourite spot with anglers.

On mild summer nights giant turtles, threatened with extinction, come up onto the 2½ mile/4km-long beach and sand dunes to lay their eggs.

Giant turtles

St John's Pass, a narrow passage between Sand Key and its neighbour Treasure Island, first appeared in 1848 when a devastating hurricane drastically altered the Gulf coastline.

St John's Pass

John's Pass Village (12901 Gulf Blvd. East), a fishing port and boat harbour in the style of the end of the last century, has grown up close to St John's Pass. The wooden buildings house small shops, galleries and fish-stalls. Every year in October/November the "Seafood Festival" is held here, with fireworks and all kinds of events.

★John's Pass Village

At several of the marinas along the Intracoastal Waterway boats can be chartered, although it is cheaper to join excursions on one of the "party boats" which can carry about 50 anglers.

Fishing trips

Treasure Island   G 10

This island in the south of the "Suncoast", some 4 miles/6km long and at the most 1½ miles/2·5km wide, separated from St Petersburg Beach by the "Blind Pass" and now connected to the mainland by a bridge, has a population of about 7000 and can boast a particularly wide beach. Many of the villas on the Intracoastal Waterway have their own boat moorings here. The first hotel here was built in 1915; the wood used in its construction was conveyed by ship from Cedar Key.

Location

In years gone by pirates used to hide on Treasure Island, and during the pioneering period it was rumoured that valuable treasure was buried there. To date all attempts to find it have proved fruitless. In memory of those wild times "Pirate Days" are acted out on July 4th every year.

Pirate Days

St John's Pass Village

Gulf cruises	From the north end of the island (St John's Pass, 129th Ave./Gulf Blvd.) pleasure ships with a casino leave on excursions into the Gulf of Mexico. For information tel. 1–800–852–PLAY.
Clearwater	See entry
Dunedin	See entry
St Petersburg Tampa	See entry

Pompano Beach   J/K 15

Broward County
Altitude: 0–10ft/0–3m. Population: 73,000

Location	Just a few miles north of Fort Lauderdale (see entry) lies Pompano Beach, a popular seaside resort built on drained swampland – hence the numerous canals – on the Atlantic Intracoastal Waterway. Hotels, motels and other holiday complexes are dotted along the lengthy beach like a string of pearls.
History	Pompano was founded in 1884, but it did not develop into a holiday resort until the 1920s, following the completion of the Dixie Highway which opened up the Atlantic Coast. W. Kester, an enterprising businessman, built holiday homes along the beach for visitors from the north of the United States seeking sunshine holidays.
Seafood Festival	An important event in the annual calendar is the Pompano Beach Seafood Festival and Fishing Rodeo held in May.

Sights

Fisherman's Wharf	Many visitors are attracted to "Fisherman"s Wharf", a 360yd/330m-long pier on Pompano Beach Boulevard which was rebuilt a few years ago.
Hillsboro Inlet	The town continues to expand westwards, but in the north Ocean Boulevard (SR A1A) crosses the busy Hillsboro Inlet. Deep-sea fishing trips leave from Fish City Marina. On the opposite side an extremely powerfully lit lighthouse, built in 1906, illuminates the harbour entrance.
Fern Forest Nature Center	In the Fern Forest Nature Center (201 Lyon Road South; open: daily from 8.30am) some 250 acres/100ha of original countryside – the Cypress Creek floodplain – have been preserved. Here visitors can study over thirty different species of fern, rare trees and countless tropical plants in the course of a half-hour walk along the Cypress Creek Broadwalk or a one-hour walk to Prairie Overlook.
	Guided tours: Sat., public holidays at 2pm. Small natural history museum.
Pompano Park Harness Raceway	Horse races are held from November to early April at the Pompano Trotting Course (Powerline Road/Atlantic Blvd.). There are free guided tours of the stables.
Farmers Market	Hammondville Road is the scene of the world's largest market for winter vegetables. Interested visitors can watch the proceedings.
Goodyear Blimp Visitor Center	From November to May airships advertising the Goodyear tyre firm can be seen flying over Pompano Beach, and these can be studied more closely at their airfield at 1500 North East 5th Ave. There is a small exhibition on the history of airship travel.

In 1984 the good ship "Lowrance" was sent to the bottom near the coast off Atlantic Boulevard. The wreck has since been invaded by reef-forming organisms and is now the largest artificial reef off the east coast of Florida. Many divers go down to inspect it.

Lowrance Artificial Reef

West of Pompano Beach lies Coconut Creek (pop. 20,000), a residential complex of mainly apartments and town houses. In Tradewinds Park (3600 West Sample Road; open: daily 8am–5.30pm) a visit to "Butterfly World" will be found rewarding. Here an attempt is being made to save many species of butterflies which are threatened with extinction. Other attractions in Tradewinds Park are a picturesque windmill, a small museum, a zoo where the animals can be stroked, various nature-paths and a botanical garden. At the weekends canoes can be hired and there are pony rides and treks available.

Coconut Creek, Tradewinds Park, ★Butterfly World

Ponte Vedra Beach   B/C 12/13

St John's County
Altitude: 0–10ft/0–3m

The narrow promontory of Ponte Vedra with its famous beach reaches from Jacksonville to St Augustine (see entries). The chief town of Ponte Vedra Beach was known locally before the First World War as Mineral City, because important minerals used in weapon production were mined here. Today it is a popular residential district for well-to-do retired people and high-earners from Jacksonville (see entry). The old mines are now disguised with lakes and lagoons which add to the region's charm.

Location

Near South Ponte Vedra Beach is where Ponce de León (see Famous People) landed and named the newly discovered land "La Florida". At the time he thought he had discovered a large new island. For six long months he sailed the coasts of Florida seeking the legendary Bimini and ended up at Charlotte Harbor (see Punta Gorda) on the Gulf Coast. He finally returned to Puerto Rico without having found treasure.

South Ponte Vedra Beach

Punta Gorda   H 11

Charlotte County
Altitude: 0–69ft/0–21m. Population: 12,000

The little town of Punta Gorda lies where Peace River enters Charlotte Harbor. As well as being heavily dependent on cattle-raising the capital of Charlotte County is also a centre of the fishing industry. For some years now the population of Punta Gorda has been increasing rapidly; new residential estates have been added and the building industry is flourishing.

Location

In 1513 Ponce de León (see Famous People) arrived in Charlotte Harbor and probably came ashore here. In 1521 a further Spanish expedition reached Punta Gorda. Spanish missionaries spread the Gospel here in the 16th and 17th c. In the 18th and 19th c. the beaches around Charlotte Harbor became a favourite pirates' lair, and the infamous little Gasparilla is also said to have landed here on a number of occasions (see below Boca Grande · Gasparilla Island).
   In 1885 Punta Gorda was granted its charter, and by 1904 it was the terminus of the Florida Southern Railway. From Long Dock ships sail to Key West (see entry), Havana in Cuba and New Orleans.

History

Sights

Town centre
In the last few years the area around Marion Avenue in the old town centre has been undergoing restoration. On the bank of Peace River the old pier has been replaced by "Fishermen's Village", a modern complex with boutiques and souvenir shops, restaurants, apartments and leisure facilities as well as a marina.

County Museum
In the Charlotte County Museum on Retta Esplanade the natural history exhibits, such as fossils, remains of mammals, etc., are well worth seeing.

★Ponce de León Park
A visit is recommended to Ponce de León Park at the west end of Marion Avenue. This park remembers the landing of the famous Spaniard of that name in 1513 and a second Spanish expedition which followed in 1521.
The park has nature-trails, a boat-ramp and picnic areas.

Surroundings

Port Charlotte
Until the 1960s the area north-west of Punta Gorda, between Peace River and Myakka River, was still open grazing land. Today Port Charlotte is one of seven large projects undertaken by the General Development Corporation in Florida. This experimental town is designed for 80,000 inhabitants. Some 40 miles/60km of natural river bank together with 165 miles/264km of waterways, most of which flow directly into the bay, make Port Charlotte a sought-after place to live and to holiday, especially for water sports enthusiasts.

Port Charlotte Beach
The beach, which is open to the public from 6am to 9pm each day, lies at the south-west end of Harbor Boulevard.

Boat trips
An excursion by boat to the offshore islands of Useppa Island, Cabbage Key and Cayo Costa is to be recommended. There are also interesting boat trips to be made on the waterways in the close vicinity, such as those arranged by Babcock Wilderness Adventures or Charlotte Harbor Florida Water Safaris.

Boco Grande · Gasparilla Island   J 11

Location
Boca Grande lies at the end of the CR 771 on the semi-uninhabited Gasparilla Island, a coral isle which guards the entrance to Charlotte Harbor some way inland.

Sights
Boco Grande retains much of its original charm. The old railroad station has been refurbished in its original style and small shops, bars and offices have been set up there. From the lighthouse, erected in 1926, there is a fine view of the Boca Grande Pass and its busy boat traffic.

★Beach
Boca Grande's main attraction is the superb shell-beach. Keen anglers will also find fish in abundance, such as tarpon (*megalops antlanticus*).

History, Name of the island
It is not clear whether the island was named after a Spanish priest named Gaspár, who worked as a missionary among the Indians on the Gulf Coast in the 16th c., or after the pirate José Gaspár (1756–1821), whose ships terrorised the coast and around whom a number of legends have been woven.

Gasparilla. the pirate
A member of the Spanish navy by the name of Gasparilla, a man relatively small in stature, initially carved out a career for himself and was presented at the Spanish court. He later fell out of favour and was forced to flee Spain in the late 18th c. He took control of a ship by force and from then on, as a pirate captain, made the waters of Florida an unsafe place to be. His lair is

thought to have been on Gasparilla Island. It is said that of the crews and passengers of the ships he captured only pretty young women were allowed to live and were kept prisoner on Captiva Island. When Florida became part of the United States in 1821 the US Navy took decisive action against the pirates along the Gulf Coast. Gasparilla, finding himself in a situation from which there was no escape, threw himself into the sea.

Towards the end of the 19th c. phosphates mined in Central Florida were exported from Gasparilla Island. After 1915 members of the "Upper Ten Thousand" from the north, keen on sport and including the Dupont family, discovered the rich fishing grounds off Gasparilla Island, and built themselves houses on the island in which to spend the winter.

Developments since the 19th c.

Redington Beach

See Pinellas Suncoast and St Petersburg.

St Augustine

C 13

St John's County
Altitude: 0–10ft/0–3m
Population: 13,000

On the Atlantic coast of north-east Florida lies St Augustine, the oldest town in North America, founded by Europeans and continually inhabited ever since. Its Spanish legacy, something which it has jealously and consciously guarded ever since, has made it one of the main tourist attractions in the "Sunshine State". Narrow lanes, houses built in the Spanish style with their typical inner courtyards, balconies and wrought-iron screens all add to the Spanish feel and atmosphere.

Location

After the discovery of Florida by Ponce de León in 1531 Spain made several unsuccessful attempts to colonise the new territory. It was 1565 before French Huguenots succeeded in founding Fort Caroline at the mouth of St John's River, something which the Spanish regarded as an affront. In September of the same year the Spanish Admiral Pedro Menéndez de Aviles established the town of San Augustin on an easily defended little peninsula, water and impassable swampland formed a natural defensive boundary. The town quickly developed to become the administrative seat controlling some thirty Spanish military bases and mission stations in Florida, in spite of being permanently dependent for supplies on other Spanish territories because the swampy ground was entirely unsuited to any degree of self-sufficiency. In the 16th and 17th c. St Augustine was many times plundered by freebooters such as Sir Francis Drake in 1586. When English settlers moved further south in the 17th c. the Spaniards built the Castillo de San Marcos in St Augustine. British troops several times laid siege to St Augustine, until in 1763 the stroke of a pen made the whole of Florida British in exchange for the recently conquered island of Cuba. During the American War of Independence St Augustine became an asylum for British Loyalists, until Florida was again returned to Spain in 1783. Enticed by generous land-titles Americans now sought to acquire properties and land left behind by the the British Loyalists. When the USA took possession of Florida in 1821 St Augustine became largely impoverished. Many American speculators, who had streamed to St Augustine in their thousands, fell victim to yellow fever in 1821. During the wars against the Seminole Indians St Augustine was an American military post. Although the town was difficult to reach its morbid charm attracted numerous famous visitors during the 19th c. During the American Civil War St Augustine supported the Confederates. However, when in 1862 a platoon of

History

233

Fountain of Youth, Old Jail, Our Lady de la Leche

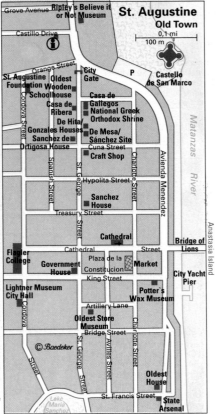

St. Augustine Old Town

0.1 mi

100 m

Unionist troops arrived and demanded the town's surrender the small Confederate garrison left under cover of darkness and the town surrendered without a struggle.

Henry Flagler (see Famous People) and his Florida East Coast Railroad proved to be extremely important factors in the town's development. Winter tourists were now able to travel south quickly and in comfort, and fruit and vegetables grown in Florida could be transported speedily to markets in the north. 1883 saw the completion of the first rail link with neighbouring Jacksonville, and in that same winter Henry Flagler visited St Augustine. Impressed by the Spanish atmosphere of the town, the warm climate and the obvious potential of the region, he built two large hotels and bought a third. For many years these buildings proved to be outstanding examples of the Mediterranean style of building to be found along Florida's East Coast.

By the end of the 19th c. St Augustine had become the "in" resort as far as the influential classes from the North East and the Middle West of the United States were concerned. Flagler, co-founder of the Standard Oil Company (Esso) bought up the existing railroads in the region and made them the nucleus of his ambitious project, the "Florida East Coast Railroad" (FEC), which finally reached Miami in 1896.

In 1887 and 1894 fires devastated a part of the Spanish Old Town. In addition many old buildings and the remains of the town's fortifications were bulldozed to make way for new buildings needed in a time of rapid industrial expansion. Since the Second World War, however, much has been done in an attempt to preserve historical buildings and to go at least some way towards restoring the old Spanish Colonial appearance of the town.

Today St Augustine relies mainly on tourism, although the processing of agricultural produce, fishing, boat-building and the aircraft industry all make an important contribution to its economy. Also the Florida East Coast Railroad still has its headquarters here, although no passenger trains have left St Augustine for a number of years.

★★ Old Town of St Augustine

Visitor Information Center	In the Visitor Information Centre (10 Castillo Drive, tel. 825–1000; open: daily 8.30am–5.30pm) a small exhibition and a half-hour multi-media show give an insight into the town's history and suggest places of interest to visit.
St Augustine Sightseeing Trains	The sights of St Augustine can be seen by taking a ride in one of the "Sightseeing Trains", which depart daily between 8.30am and 5pm from 170 San Marco Ave., tel. 829–6545.

In front of the entrance to the Castillo de San Marcos horse-drawn carriages offer leisurely rides lasting about one hour through the Spanish Old Town (Avenida Menendez, tel. 829–2818; daily 8.30am–5pm.

Carriage Tours

Built between 1672 and 1695, the Castillo de San Marcos has dominated the townscape for the past three hundred years. This fortress, now under a protection order, is one of the oldest in the USA and was once an important base used by the Spaniards in safeguarding the shipping route from Havana to Spain and the Spanish claim to Florida. The coquina limestone (soft, and composed of crushed and fossilised shells) used in the construction of the star-shaped fortress with walls up to 13ft/4m thick and four massive bulwarks was quarried on the offshore Anastasia Island. In order to provide even better defences earthworks were laid from the fort as far as the San Sebastian River in the 18th c. Still clearly visible is the "Cubo Line", a wooden wall erected above the entrenchments in 1808 and made almost impregnable by the planting of yucco gloriosa trees with their sharp, bayonet-shaped leaves.

★Castillo de San Marcos

The fortress withstood all sieges imposed by freebooters and Anglo-American troops in the 17th and 18th c. In 1821, after Florida was ceded to the United States, the Americans took over the Castillo and modernised it. In 1825 it was temporarily re-named Fort Marion. The artillery equipment in front of the fort dates from 1842.

Two drawbridges lead to the main entrance and thence to a spacious inner courtyard. From here the visitor will enter the garrison's quarters and the store-rooms with their massive vaulted roofs designed to withstand cannon-balls. These rooms now house exhibitions describing the fort's history (open: daily 8.45am–4.45pm in winter; 8.45am–8pm in summer). Steps lead up to the cannon-floor which once contained more than 60 cannon. From here there is a fine view to be had of the Old Town.

Castello de San Marcos

235

St Augustine

St George Street

The main street in the Spanish Old Town is the narrow St George Street, now barred to traffic, once known as Calle Real and entered through a reconstructed town gate. Some 50 houses and workshops have been renovated or newly built.

★Wooden Schoolhouse

Built more than 200 years ago from red cedar and cypress wood, this little schoolhouse in St George Street is said to be the oldest building of its kind in the USA. The teacher lives above the school-house, with the kitchen detached. Open: daily 9am–5pm.

★★San Agustin Antiquo (Spanish Quarter Museum)

In some of the houses on St George Street staff dressed in contemporary costume act out scenes from everyday life during the Spanish Colonial Period (first half of the 18th c.).

Entrance to the museum is through Triay House on 29th Street (open: 9am–5pm), which serves as a visitor centre. Casa de Gallegos, at 21 St George St., built of "tabby", a building brick made from mussel shells and chalk, is a typical example of how a settler would have lived about 1750.

More modest is Casa Gomez at 23 St George St. Gomez, a simple soldier, set up shop here in an attempt to supplement his meagre pay.

The neighbouring smithy shows how blacksmiths worked in the 18th c.

Casa Gonzales and Casa de Hita are typical of the Spanish Colonial style as used in Florida. 18th c. weaving techniques are demonstrated.

Casa de Mesa/Sanchez originally consisted of only two rooms. During the Second Spanish Period (1783–1821) it was considerably extended and another storey added.

Opposite it stands the Francisco Pellicer Kitchen (candles are made here now) and Casa de Burgo/Pellicer, a reconstructed semi-detached house, or duplex, in late 18th c. style. It contains a museum shop.

St Photios

In the reconstructed Cas Avero of 1749 at 41 St George St, a small Greek Orthodox Church was consecrated in 1982 and dedicated to the first Greeks who landed in St Augustine in 1768, and to their descendants. There is a small museum depicting Greek culture and their emigration to America.

Casa Peña, Peck House

Probably built before 1690 for the Spanish chamberlain, this house at 143 St George St./Treasury St. (open: Mon.–Sat. 10am–4pm) was purchased in 1832 by Dr Peck of Connecticut. It is now furnished in the Ante-Bellum (pre-Civil War) style.

Treasury Street

Treasury Street, less than 6½ft/2m wide in places, is the narrowest street in the town.

★Plaza de la Constitución

This typical open plaza close to the sea, the main square of the Spanish Colonial town, was laid out in 1598 as part of a plan drawn up by the Spanish government. The slave market was also held here. The memorial in the centre was erected by the Spaniards in 1813.

The old 1824 market hall on its east side, facing Matanzas Bay, has been reconstructed.

At the west end of the square stand the former Spanish Government Buildings.

Bridge of Lions

At the bottom of Cathedral Street is the Bridge of Lions to St Augustine Beach, built in 1927. The western exit from this bridge is guarded by two stone lions.

Cathedral

In the north of the Plaza stands the Cathedral, which has undergone a number of changes during its life. Its records date back to 1594. The present building was erected in the late 18th c. and reconstructed in 1887 after a devastating fire.

Trinity Episcopal Church

Opposite it stands Trinity Episcopal Church, Florida's first Protestant church built in 1825.

More than 150 life-sized effigies of famous historical figures are on display in Potter's Wax Museum at the eastern end of King Street. Open: daily 9am–8pm June to Labor Day; 9am–5pm rest of year.

Potter's Wax Museum

From Municipal Yacht Pier south of the Bridge of Lions there are boat trips into Matanzas Bay.

Municipal Yacht Pier

Avenida Menendez, which runs along the shore, leads to St Francis Street, once the southern boundary of the town. A visit to the Oldest House Museum (14 St Francis St., guided tours daily 9am–4.30pm) is to be recommended. The house wall is decorated by the same four flags which have flown over the town at one time or another – the Spanish, the British, that of the Confederate States and the Stars and Stripes of the United States of America.

★Oldest House, Casa Gonzáles-Alvarez

Also known as Casa Gonzáles-Alvarez, this is one of the oldest houses built in the USA by Europeans, the coquina (shells in limestone) walls of the ground floor having been built in 1702. The first occupant was a soldier in the artillery named Gonzáles y Hernandez. The first modifications to the building were made during the English Period (1763–83), when the British major and paymaster Peavett lived here. The life of his wife Mary provided Eugenia Price with the material for her novel "Maria".

In 1790 a Spaniard by the name of Alvarez purchased the house. His family lived in it until 1882. After a number of changes of ownership it came into the possession of the Historical Society in 1918 and was made into a museum. The rooms are now again furnished as they would have been during the Spanish and British Colonial Periods. There is a small exhibition on the town's 400-year history, and the library contains several hundred old books and documents.

On the other side of the street are the headquarters of the Florida National Guard. Re-built in 1922 after a fire, the building was originally a Franciscan priory. Later it served as a barracks for both Spanish and British troops.

National Guard

The oldest house in St Augustine

237

St Augustine

St Francis Inn	One block further west the visitor will find St Francis Inn, which was built in 1791 and has been taking in guests since 1836.
Prince Murat House	On the corner of St George St. and Bridge St. stands Prince Murat House, built in 1791. For a time the nephew of Napoleon I, married to a great-niece of George Washington, lived here before settling near Tallahassee (see entry).
Sisters of St Joseph Convent	Opposite stands the Sisters of St Joseph Convent. In 1874 nuns from Le Puy in France established a school here to educate the children of freed slaves.
Aviles Street, Casa Ximenez-Fatio	Bridge Street leads to the charming and narrow Aviles Street, which for some time has been the centre of the small artists' quarter of St Augustine. Casa Ximenez-Fatio, built of local coquina limestone in 1798 at 20 Aviles St., was converted into a guest-house in 1855.
Oldest Store Museum	Just round the corner, in Artillery Lane, will be found the nostalgic Oldest Store Museum, once St Augustine's general store. It is now a shop-museum, displaying a vast assortment of goods, ranging from corsets to dolls, crockery and material and various agricultural implements and vehicles. It is quite incredible what the good folk of St Augustine needed in the 19th c.! Open: Mon.–Sat. 9am–5pm, Sun. noon–5pm.
★Lightner Museum	From here King Street leads west out of the actual Spanish Colonial town, past St John's County Court (formerly the Cordova Hotel) and to the Lightner Museum (75 King St.; open: daily 9am–5pm), housed in the former Alcazar Grand Hotel built by Flagler. The town council also sits in this impressive building. In 1948 Otto C. Lightner, a Chicago publisher, converted the empty hotel into a museum to house his private collections. Its three storeys contain mainly exhibits from America's "Golden Age". Particularly impressive are the glass items, such as crystal vases and lustres, pieces by Tiffany, etc. The hotel is also interesting architecturally; it once had a fine casino (now an antiques emporium) and what was at the time the largest heated indoor swimming pool anywhere in the United States. The steam-baths and male gymnasium are still available for use.
Zorayda Castle	On the other side of Granada Street lies Zorayda Castle (83 King St.; open: daily 9am–5.30pm), a Moorish palace built in 1883 by a successful architect and almost certainly based on the Alhambra in Spain. The visitor can imagine the style in which the Moorish rulers in Spain were able to live.
Flagler College	Opposite stands the private Flagler College (formerly the Ponce de León Hotel), which opened in 1883 as America's most exclusive hotel. The Great Depression brought about its demise. During the Second World War it housed equipment belonging to the American Coast Guard. Attempts after the war to revive Flagler's old hotel failed. In 1967 it became a college teaching the humanities. Guided tours by arrangement (tel. 829–6481).
Flagler Memorial Presbyterian Church	Flagler Memorial Presbyterian Church (corner of Valencia St. and Sevilla St.; open: Mon.–Sat. 9am–4.30pm), was built within a twelve-month period in 1890 by Flagler as a memorial to his daughter Jennie who died in child-birth. Flagler's wife, his daughter Jennie and her baby are buried in the church, the architecture of which, with its massive dome, is strongly reminiscent of St Mark's in Venice.
Ancient City Baptist Church	The Ancient City Baptist Church, at the corner of Sevilla St. and Carrera St., was built in 1895. Flagler gave the Baptist community the money to build it, having already built his own house nearby in 1892.
Museum Theater	In the Museum Theater (5 Cordova St./Tolomato Lane; open: daily 9am–5pm) an interesting film is shown every hour on the history of the town and life during the Spanish Colonial Period.

The former "Ponce de León Hotel" (now Flagler College)

In Ripley's Believe It or Not! Museum diagonally opposite the Visitor Centre (19 San Marco Ave.; open: 9am–6.30pm, 9pm between mid June and Labor Day) there are all kinds of strange exhibits to amuse and astound the visitor.

Ripley's Believe It or Not Museum

Admiral Menéndez landed on this spot in September 1565. This is probably where mass was first celebrated on what is now USA soil. There is a 207ft/63m-high cross in memory of the founding of St Augustine. The little Mission of Nombre de Dios (San Marco Ave./Ocean St.; open: daily 9am–6pm) was the first Franciscan mission station, and it is thought that it was here where the first Florida Indians were christened.

Mission of Nombre de Dios, ★Shrine of Our Lady of La Leche

The little chapel of Our Lady of La Leche is the oldest shrine to the Virgin Mary in the USA. A diorama simulates the history of St Augustine. On September 8th every year there is a festival commemorating the founding of the town.

Further north lies a fairly large park which remembers Ponce de Léon and his fruitless search for the Fountain of Youth. It is assumed that he landed here in 1513. In the fountain building maidens dressed in historical costume ladle water from the "Fountain of Youth". Adjoining is a planetarium containing *inter alia* a globe showing the routes taken by the early explorers. Nearby is an Indian cemetery.

★Fountain of Youth

Some 1¼ miles/2km south of the Bridge of Lions (see above), on Highway A1A, will be found Florida's oldest alligator farm, now a major tourist attraction. There are alligator shows or performances with snakes every hour, and there is much to be learned about Florida's reptiles and their role in nature. There is also a small zoo, with monkeys, racoons, parrots, etc., and a nature trail. Open: June–Aug. daily 9am–6pm, Sept.–May daily 9am–5pm.

Alligator Farm

Opposite Alligator Farm, in the restored 1875 two-storied house of the lighthouse keeper, is the Lighthouse Museum of St Augustine (open: daily

Lighthouse Museum

10am–5pm, closed Easter). Taking a ship through the St Augustine inlet was at one time a hazardous task, because the sandbanks were continually lashed by tides and storms. The lighthouse, a landmark on the coast since 1874, is still functional and is not open to the public.

★Cross and Sword Theater

About ½ mile/1km south on the A1A stands the Cross and Sword Theater, where the symphonic drama by the Pulitzer prize-winner Paul Greene about the founding of St Augustine is performed every year between mid-June and the end of August. Information: Cross and Sword Theatre, P.O. Box 1965, St Augustine, FL 32085; tel. 471–1965.

Surroundings

★Fort Matanzas National Monument

Some 14 miles/22km south of St Augustine will be found Fort Matanzas, a national monument. It covers the southern side of Anastasia Island as well as Rattlesnake Island, a small island in the Matanzas River with the actual small fortress named Fort Matanzas, a Spanish outpost built to protect the southern entrance to St Augustine harbour.

Anastasia Island

On Anastasia Island, which is reached along Highway A1A, there is a small Information Centre and a pretty bathing beach, together with an interesting nature trail.

Rattlesnake Island

The only way to get to Rattlesnake Island and the fort is by the free ferry run by the National Park Service (Wed.–Mon. 8.30am–5.30pm).

Matanzas

The Spanish name "Matanzas" means roughly slaughter or bloodbath. In 1565 there was a clash between the Spanish colonists in St Augustine under Pedro Menéndez de Avilés and the French Huguenots under Jean Ribault, who had settled some 38 miles/60km further north in Fort Caroline at the mouth of the St John's River. The Spanish regarded the French settlers as intruders, since French freebooters were endangering the passage of Spanish ships in the Caribbean and off the coast of Florida. Moreover, in the eyes of the strictly Catholic Spanish the Huguenots were nothing but wretched heretics. In an attempt to forestall a Spanish attack Ribault sailed south with his force but ran into a fierce hurricane off Anastasia Island, while Menéndez and his soldiers reached Fort Caroline by the land route and – favoured by heavy rain – captured and destroyed it. Two to three hundred shipwrecked Frenchmen were able to scramble ashore on Anastasia Island, but some days later, semi-starved, they had no alternative but to surrender to the Spanish. Short of supplies themselves, the Spaniards slaughtered the captured "heretics" there and then.

In 1569 the Spaniards built a small look-out post on Rattlesnake Island, strategically the most important point south of St Augustine. After British men-of-war had blockaded the approaches to St Augustine in vain, the Spanish decided to safeguard the approach along the Matanzas River by building a small fort on this island. One shot from a cannon was then sufficient to defend the passage.

When Florida was ceded by treaty to England in 1763 Fort Matanzas remained one of the key defensive positions. After the end of the 18th c. St Augustine and the little fort lost their importance. Although Matanzas Inlet was admittedly used by blockade runners during the Civil War it was nevertheless allowed to deteriorate still further. The fort has now been restored, and since 1924 it has been under a protection order because of its historical importance.

★Marineland of Florida

About 19 miles/30km south of St Augustine, on Highway A1A, can be found Marineland of Florida, on a narrow island on the far side of Matanzas Inlet directly on the Atlantic coast. Marineland was founded in 1938, the very first oceanarium. Its main attractions include performances by dolphins

St Augustine: Dolphins in Marineland

several times a day in the Dolphin Stadium and in the Circular Oceanarium and Top Deck. Through large windows visitors can watch dolphins, sharks, stingrays, barracudas and giant turtles being fed several times a day by divers. A 3-D film "Sea Dream" is shown in the Aquarius Cinema. Other highlights include sea-lions being trained and the penguins being fed in Whitney park. From June to Labor Day "The Great American Dive" (high-diving displays) take place. Open: daily 9am–5.30pm.

Some 3 miles/5km further south on Highway A1A the visitor will find a particularly charming stretch of coastline. The breakers constantly crashing in from the Atlantic have washed away the sand along a 2 mile/3km length of beach to reveal the underlying coquina limestone of compacted mussel shells, coral and sand, of which the Castillo de San Marcos was built in the 18th c. The breakers and sharp rocks make bathing extremely dangerous. However, at low tide it is possible to observe wading birds as they seek food in the numerous narrow channels and ponds. ★Washington Oaks Gardens State Park

The west of the island, on the Matanzas River, is carpeted with well cared-for gardens. Among old evergreen oaks and palm trees bloom azaleas, camelias and roses.

Washington Oaks Gardens was once part of a Spanish country estate. In 1844 a relative of President Washington married a daughter of the Spanish owner and until 1856 lived on the "Bella Vista" plantation. As well as lemon groves there are many typical native plants. In the holiday home built in the 1930s will be found an information centre and a museum. Open: daily 8am–6pm.

South of the little holiday resort of Flagler Beach (pop. 4000) lies the Flagler Beach State Recreational Area, with dunes and a beautiful bathing beach and very popular with campers. Pelicans can often be seen here, and in the summer months turtles lay their eggs on the beach. ★Flagler Beach

St John's River   B–D 12

St John's is the only river of any size in Florida which flows from south to
north. Rich in fish and watered by the (geologically-speaking) recent but
already heavily karstic range of hills along its banks, it flows initially north-
west from Ocala (see entry) and then north from Palatka (see entry). As the
result of accretions formed by the Atlantic Ocean – sand embankments,
beaches, spits of land – the mouth of the river is continually being pushed
ever further north. At its mouth near Jacksonville French Huguenots under
Jean Ribault settled in 1562 and founded Fort Caroline, but the latter was
soon destroyed by the Spaniards (see St Augustine, Surroundings, Matanzas). As the Florida peninsula was developed further St John's River
became an important through-route. New settlers in paddle-steamers
pushed further and further inland and struggled against all the odds to
support themselves and their families.

St Petersburg   G 10

Pinellas County
Altitude: 0–46ft/0–14m
Population: 240,000

Location

Famous for its many days of sunshine St Petersburg, often affectionately
called "St Pete", lies on the Pinellas peninsula on the central Gulf Coast of
Florida between Tampa Bay and Boca Ciega Bay.

Off the west coast stretches a chain of long, narrow islands, reaching as
far as Honeymoon Island (see Pinellas Suncoast). Wide beaches and numerous marinas are features of this section of the coast, making it a
favourite with holidaymakers but not to the extent that it becomes as
crowded as the well-known beaches on the Atlantic Coast.

Because of its many days of sunshine – even in winter the average daily
temperature can reach 63°F/17°C – it is a popular place for old people to
retire to, as well as a holiday resort.

More than 6 miles/10km long, the white sands of St Petersburg Beach on
the flat offshore island of Long Key make it one of the best-known parts of
the Pinella Suncoast, a paradise for swimmers and water-sports enthusiasts alike. "St Pete Beach" is linked to the mainland by two causeways.
Gulfshore Boulevard is lined with holiday apartments, motels and hotels,
the "flagship" being the palatial, pink-washed "Don Cesar Hotel", now a
protected building.

Along that side of St Petersburg which faces the sea will be found large
numbers of parks, beaches and marinas, especially on Tampa Bay and
Boca Ciega Bay. There are some very exclusive residences built on several
small islands in Boca Ciega Bay.

The high season is from January to April, it being at its busiest during the
"Spring Break". Ships from all over the world anchor in St Petersburg
harbour. The St Petersburg/Tampa region now ranks tenth among all
American holiday resorts. In contrast to neighbouring Tampa, which has
become an important business centre, St Petersburg remained until the
1970s primarily a town inhabited by retired people and those seeking a
relaxing break, a place of detached houses and plenty of open spaces.

Today St Petersburg boasts many leading schools and colleges as well as
being home to companies engaged in the aeronautical and space industries. In the last thirty years or so the population has become much younger, and during the spring break at the colleges and universities thousands
of students stream to the beaches west of St Petersburg.

History

St Petersburg was founded in 1876. In 1875 General F. C. Williams bought a
1750 acre/700ha piece of land on Pinellas peninsula with the aim of building
a town linked to the railroad. In co-operation with the Russian Peter

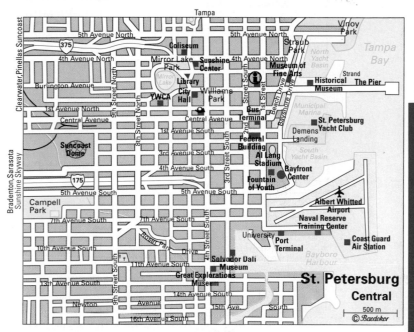

St. Petersburg Central

500 m
© Baedeker

Demens, who had already succeeded in extending his railroad line as far as the peninsula, St Petersburg – named after Demen's home town in Russia – grew up here. In 1885 the railroad line was completed.

In the 1890s an article about St Petersburg appeared in a medical journal, praising the extraordinarily healthy climate above all else. This resulted in a heavy influx of older people desirous of spending their twilight years in the Florida sunshine. Since then St Petersburg has become the fourth largest town in Florida.

New Year's Day 1915 saw the birth of organised commercial flight in America. The pilot Tony Jannus crossed Tampa Bay in his flying-boat and landed in Tampa. His first passenger was A. Phiel, the mayor. The Tony Jannus Memorial Monument on the pier was erected in memory of this event.

St Petersburg has entered the Guinness Book of Records as a result of its record number of hours of sunshine; between 1967 and 1969 the sun shone here every day. From 1910 to 1986 the St Petersburg newspaper "Evening Independent" was distributed free on every day on which the sun failed to shine. This did not exactly bankrupt the paper – in the 76 years of its existence it had to be issued free on only 295 occasions.

Sunshine

Sights

The sights of St Petersburg are concentrated mainly along Tampa Bay.

Note

The Salvador Dali Museum in Poynter Park on Bayboro Harbour (1000 3rd St. South; open: Tues.–Sat. 9.30am–5.30pm, Sun. and Mon. noon–5.30pm)

★★Salvador Dali Museum

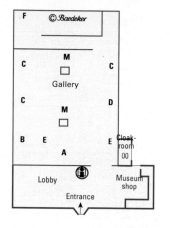

Salvador Dalí Museum

St. Petersburg

A   Early works (1914–27)

B   Transitional period (1928)

C   Surrealism (1929–41)

D   Classical period (from 1943)

E   Special exhibitions

F   Chez d'œuvres (1954–70)

M   Miniatures

houses what is undoubtedly the most comprehensive collection of works by this Catalan artist who died in 1989. These pictures were assembled over a period of some forty years by the textile designer Reynolds Morse and his wife. The Morses were close friends of Dali's wife Gala. The collection later came into the possession of the town of St Petersburg, which in 1982 was able to open its own Dali Museum based on the most modern teaching principles. Works on display include over 90 oil paintings, 100 drawings and water-colours, prints and statues dating from 1914 to 1980. These include such masterpieces as "The Ecumenical Council", "The Steadfastness of Memory" ("Melting Clocks") and "The Burning Giraffe".

Library

Adjacent to the museum is a library with some 2500 publications about Dali and Surrealism.

Boyd Hill Nature Park Lake Maggiore

A visit is recommended to Boyd Hill Nature Park situated to the south-west on the west bank of Lake Maggiore (1101 Country Club Way South; open: Apr.–Oct. daily 9am–8pm, rest of the year daily 9am–5pm, guided tours available). Six different nature trails on the 216 acre/87ha park provide information about the various eco-systems found in Florida. There is also a small museum. Powerboat races are held several times a year on Lake Maggiore.

Great Explorations

Great Explorations (1120 4th St. South; open: Mon.–Sat. 10am–5pm, Sun. noon–5pm) is a show with many "hands-on" exhibits which children in particular are very keen on. They can crawl through a 110ft/33m-long dark labyrinth, test their reactions or try to crack the combination of a safe.

Bayfront Center Theater Arena

The Bayfront Center Theater Arena (400 First St. South, information tel. (813) 892–5798) is beautifully situated on Tampa Bay and was completely renovated a few years ago. The Florida Orchestra plays here and sporting events are held as well as pop-concerts and theatrical and operatic performances.

★★The Pier

The Pier at 800 2nd. Ave. North East in downtown St Petersburg extends more than 2400ft/732m into Tampa Bay and is one of the longest of its kind in Florida. It is a popular meeting place for tourists and locals alike and there is always something going on. In 1988, the year of the town's centenary celebrations, the building symbolising St Petersburg was re-opened. This five-storey complex – shaped like an inverted pyramid – contains large numbers of shops and boutiques, art galleries, stalls and restaurants.

St Petersburg pier

There is also entertainment in the evenings, and a fine view of the town can be enjoyed from an observation platform.

Near the pier (335 2nd. Ave. North East; open: Mon.–Sat. 10am–5pm, Sun. 1–5pm, closed Jan.) the St Petersburg Historical Museum holds permanent and temporary exhibitions devoted to the history of the town and to regional studies of Florida, including a review of the history of painting in the state and of the original Red Indian inhabitants of the region. A guided tour of the St Petersburg town centre also starts from here.

St Petersburg Historical Museum

There are three large marinas on Bayfront – Bayfront Center Yacht Basin, Central Yacht Basin and North Yacht Basin. Hundreds of competitive and "weekend" sailors tie up their expensive boats here.

Yacht marina

Housed in a classical villa at 225 Beach Drive, 2nd Ave. North East (open: Tues.–Sat. 10am–4.30pm, Sun. 1–4.30pm) this museum displays masterpieces by European and American painters from the 17th to the 20th c., the collection of French Impressionists – Fragonard, Monet, Renoir, Cézanne – being of particular interest. In addition to the museum's own collections of Far East and Pre-Columbian art there are pictures on loan from other museums as well as objects and photographs of historical interest. Guided tours are available.

★Museum of Fine Arts

To the north of the town centre lies a charming botanical garden known as the Sunken Gardens (1825 4th St. North; open: daily 9am–5.30pm, tel. (813) 896–3186). Laid out in the 1930s and covering an area of some 5 acres/2ha, the gardens are covered in lush tropical and subtropical vegetation. Cages house exotic animals, some of which are native to Florida. There are daily peformances by talking parrots.

★Florida's Sunken Gardens

In Grace Turner House, a typical Florida bungalow, are exhibited various nineteenth century objects as well as a child's room with toys and a doll's house.

Grace Turner House

245

Also of interest is the mighty Banyan Tree, native to India, which is thought to be about 90 years old and already measures nearly 66ft/20m in diameter.

Banyan Tree

In Campbell Park, also in the west of the town centre, this stadium was completed in 1992 and it is planned to hold a number of top-class events here in the near future.

Pinellas Sportsplex Stadium

In the highly instructive Science Center of Pinellas County (7701 22nd Ave. North; open: Mon.–Fri. 10am–5pm) children, young people and adults can all learn something new about natural history and technology. Visitors can carry out experiments themselves, "play" with computers or study plants and animals.

Science Center

A Planetarium and Observatory have been installed in St Petersburg Junior College on 69th St. There are demonstrations on Friday evenings from September to April.

Planetarium

About 4 miles/6·5km north of the town centre lies Weedon Island, in Tampa Bay. This marsh and swamp area has been designated a nature reserve. There are signs of Pre-Columbian culture in the shape of burial mounds.

Weedon Island

Every day except Sun. from Jan.–May there are twelve greyhound races here at Derby Lane, 10490 Gandy Blvd. For information tel. (813) 576–1361.

Greyhound Racing

St Petersburg Beach

The "Don Cesar" Beach Hotel, built in 1928 at 3400 Gulf Blvd. at a cost of 1½ million dollars, today ranks as the symbol of St Petersburg Beach. It was extremely popular up to the time of the Second World War. After the war it became less so and had to be put to various other uses, such as an administrative centre. In 1973, after extensive refurbishment, it was re-opened as the Grand Hotel. Today the pink-fronted Don Cesar resort offers luxury accommodation. Old-time glamour is reflected in the 277 rooms and suites, where an overnight stay costs between US \$200 and 700, and it boasts all kinds of sport and leisure facilities, with superbly-run cafés, bars and restaurants guaranteeing a perfect holiday.

★Don Cesar Resort

At the Port Royal Sunken Treasure Museum (5505 Gulf Blvd.; open: daily until 9pm) the age of pirates comes alive again. The visitor can experience for himself the history of the seafaring town of Port Royal on Jamaica (now Kingston).

Port Royal Sunken Treasure Museum

Between May and October from St Petersburg Beach Causeway (3400 Pasadena Ave. South, tel. 367–7804, 1–800–533–2288) there are two-hour trips around Boca Ciega Bay, when dolphins can also be watched. There are also three-hour dinner cruises in the evening, with live music.

Captain Anderson Cruises

Dolphin Village and Corey Landings (4601 and 7400 Gulf Blvd.) and Silas' Bayside Market (5505 Gulf Blvd.) are two shopping centres where visitors can buy souvenirs as well as any items they may have forgotten to bring with them.

Dolphin Village and Corey Landings Silas' Bayside Market

In the south of Long Key lies Pass-A-Grill, a charming public beach.

Pas-A-Grille Beach

★Fort De Soto Park

Access to Fort De Soto Park, south of St Petersburg Beach, is by way of Pinellas Bayway (toll payable) and Tierra Verde Island. Covering some

Location

◀ *St Pete Beach with the long celebrated "Don Cesar Resort"*

900 acres/364ha, the park extends over five islands in Tampa Bay. It is named after the Spanish conqueror Hernando De Soto, who landed here in 1539. Today this nature reserve is a favourite place for holidays with the population of Tampa/St Petersburg. Miles of beaches, two jetties for fishing, nature-trails, cycle-paths, picnic and camp-sites all attract large numbers of visitors all the year round.

Fort De Soto

At the south-west tip of Mullet Key, the largest of these islands, lies the historic Fort De Soto, built in 1898 during the Spanish-American War. Its cannons were intended to safeguard the entrance to Tampa Bay, but in the event they were never used, because the war was over before the fort was completed.

★★Sunshine Skyway

Masterpiece of engineering

A ride across the "Sunshine Skyway" (I–275/US 19; toll payable), a 13 mile/20km-long "Highway on Stilts" elegantly suspended across the entrance to Tampa Bay is an essential for every visitor. Its centrepiece is a 4¼ mile/6·8km-long high bridge – the central section of which is a suspension bridge supported on two giant pylons – which allows the passage of giant ocean-going vessels.

The old bridge was rammed by a freighter in 1980 and partially collapsed, taking several vehicles into the water with it. More than 30 people lost their lives. Parts of the old bridge are now favourite spots with anglers.

Salt Springs

See Ocala National Forest

San Agustin

See St Augustine

Sanford

See Orlando

Sanibel and Captiva Islands   J 11

Lee County
Altitude: 0–6½ft/0–2m. Population: 6000

★★Topography

Sanibel Island and Captiva Island, joined by a bridge across the narrow Blind Pass, are the most southerly of the Barrier Islands on the Gulf Coast of Florida. More than 18 miles/30km of entrancing beaches – known worldwide for the vast amount of shell remains found there – as well as little mangrove islands and fens with numerous species of animals (more than 200 different types of bird have been counted) make Sanibel and Captiva appear as true island paradises.

Until 1963 they could be reached only by ferry, but now a causeway (toll payable) links them with the mainland near Fort Myers (see entry). In spite of the resultant increase in traffic the two islands have retained their unique character.

Sanibel Island

History

Sanibel Island has seen human habitation for many centuries, even if only sporadically. In the 18th and 19th c. pirates used it as a lair. Later some

Sanibel and Captiva Islands

Anglo-American "crackers" came and cultivated the land. In 1921 and 1926 it was struck by fierce whirlwinds, and floods led to the fields being ruined by salt deposits. Most of the residents gave up and left. The few who remained founded the tourist industry here as it is today, by building small cottages and motels as well as more luxurious resorts. Because of the limited accommodation it is now necessary to book in advance during the high season from December to April as well as in the summer months. Since 1974 Sanibel has been an independent community.

Very strict building regulations have prevented the island from becoming too built-up and over-populated. Palm trees and Australian pine still dominate the landscape.

The situation today

There are a very limited number of car parks on the island, so the bicycle is the most popular mode of transport. There are some 20 miles/30km of cycle paths running alongside the main roads as well as several places where cycles and mopeds can be hired.

There are a number of small shopping centres on the main street, Periwinkle Way, as well as some very exclusive shops. Bailey's General Store, at 2477 Periwinkle Way is almost an institution; it has served the needs of the islanders since 1899, having been extended several times over the years.

Held annually in early March since 1937 and lasting four days, the Sanibel Shell Fair attracts thousands of visitors. Stunning shell collections from all over the USA are on display.

Sanibel Shell Fair

The landmark and symbol of Sanibel Island is the lighthouse built in 1884 at Point Ybel, the southern tip of the 14 mile/22km-long island. Close by are the two houses for the lighthouse-keepers; built on piles they are in the style typical of the late 19th and early 20th c.

Point Ybel

Below the lighthouse stretches a beautiful beach frequented by families with children and shell-hunters.

★Lighthouse Park

Sanibel and Captiva Islands

★ Gulfside Park

On the other side of Casa Ybel Road will be found Gulfside Park, a beach as yet unspoilt with few of the usual trappings. Bathing is at your own risk, however.

Bowman's Beach

Bowman's Beach, at the north-west end of Sanibel Island, caters for naturists.

★ "Ding" Darling National Wildlife Refuge

Some 5000 acres/2023ha, or one-third of the total area of the island, is a nature reserve known as "Ding" Darling National Wildlife Refuge. Named after the well-known caricaturist J. N. "Ding" Darling, this area of mangroves and marshland on Pine Island Sound is a resting place in winter for countless migrating birds. Visitors can easily get to this nature reserve. Motorists driving along the 5 mile/8km "Scenic Drive" will be able to enjoy a piece of the original Florida in peace. Anyone who so wishes can explore the jungle along wooden trails or climb an observation tower. Pink spoonbill, silver heron – almost extinct through being hunted for their magnificent feathers – and grey heron, as well as ibis can be observed at close quarters without the need for binoculars. The dirty brown waterways "teem" with alligators.

Visitor Center
★ Canoe trips

At the entrance to the nature reserve the Visitor Center (open: daily 9am–5pm mid Nov. to mid Apr.; Mon.–Sat. 9am–4pm rest of year) will provide information about the importance of this eco-system by means of various exhibitions and audio-visual programmes. The best way to gain an authentic Florida experience, however, is by means of a canoe tour through the mangroves. Boats can be hired at the Visitor Center.

Island Historical Museum

The Island Historical Museum is housed in a typical "cracker" house at 850 Dunlop Road (open: Thur.–Sat. 10am–4pm in winter; Thur. and Sat. 10am–4pm rest of year). As the name suggests, it provides information on the history of the island which has been populated by a few Anglo-Americans since the middle of the 19th c.

An alligator in "Ding" Darling Wildlife Refuge

Captiva Island

Captiva Island is not a separate administrative entity. Only 5 miles/8km long and little over half a mile wide, it is seriously threatened by erosion in spite of being protected by a belt of mangroves. It therefore prefers to remain under county administration, because the thousand or so inhabitants could not afford to bear the enormous cost of coastal protection.

According to legend, it was on Captiva Island that the pirate José Gaspár ("Gasparilla" – see Punta Gorda, Boca Grande · Gasparilla Island) is said to have incarcerated his female prisoners in the late 18th and early 19th c.

History

The first Anglo-American settlers laid out a lemon plantation here in the 19th c., and a few trees still remain. It was here, too, that two hurricanes this century rendered the ground completely unsuitable for further agricultural use.

In 1938 the island's first hotel was opened under the shade of numerous newly-planted palm trees.

Captiva is now much more built-up and has some good fish restaurants. Unfortunately some sections of the beach are open to hotel guests only.

The northern tip of the island is taken up by the well-known "South Seas Plantation Resort", a luxurious holiday and leisure resort with several tennis courts, a golf-course and marinas.

South Seas Plantation

In a secluded position on the east coast lies the house built on piles which was once the home of J. N. "Ding" Darling. To ensure privacy it can be reached only across a drawbridge.

"Ding" Darling House

Turner Beach in the south of the island is open to the public. Many visitors come here to look for shells or to admire and take pictures of the sunset.

★ Turner Beach

Boat trips lasting several hours to the islands in Pine Island Sound, dinner cruises and deep-sea fishing trips all depart from various marinas.

★ Island Cruises

Santa Rosa Island

See Fort Walton Beach, Gulf Island National Seashore and Pensacola

Sarasota

H 10

Sarasota County
Altitude: 0–30ft/0–9m
Population: 52,000

Sarasota lies on the southern edge of the Tampa/St Petersburg conurbations. Large numbers of people settled here in the 1980s. The superb white beaches on the offshore islands of Lido Key and Siesta Key and on Longboat Key north to Bradenton, a mild subtropical climate all the year round, a relaxed southern lifestyle combined with excellent holiday and leisure facilities are all factors which attract an ever-inreasing number of holidaymakers, both short and long-term, as well as many retired people. The first golf-course was laid out as long ago as 1886; today there are more than two dozen within easy reach of the town. Luxurious houses have dotted Sarasota Bay since the beginning of this century. In the last twenty years or so some exclusive apartment buildings and tall office blocks have been erected. The bay itself is a paradise for wind-surfers and weekend sailors.

Location

The quality of the buildings reflects the fact that Sarasota is a "rich" town – income per capita is the highest in the United States. Many well-known architects have made their name here.

Homes of the affluent

Town of culture

Sarasota can thank the circus magnate and art-collector John Ringling (see below) for its reputation as a "Town of the Arts". The art museum he gifted to the town is one of the "Sunshine State's" major attractions. Since 1959 Sarasota has had its own resident opera company and its own orchestra. The Asolo State Theatre has made a name for itself far and wide. The Van Wezel Performing Arts Hall receives frequent visits from outstanding interpreters of modern and classical music

History

The first white settlers arrived here in 1842. A large number of Scottish immigrants followed them in the 1880s, including J. Hamilton Gillespie, who laid out the first golf course and thus made the sport popular in America. In 1910 Sarasota was still a sleepy fishing village. A little later tourists from the East Coast of the USA "discovered" Sarasota Bay.

John Ringling

The town's history is closely linked with the name of John Ringling. Born in Wisconsin, it was in the 1880s that John and his four brothers realised their circus dream; he started off as a clown, but later concerned himself more with the commercial side of the enterprise. His fortune was earned mainly from oil and real estate. In 1907 the Ringling brothers took over the Barnum and Bailey Circus, making theirs the "Greatest Show on Earth".

After becoming one of the richest men in the world, John Ringling came to Sarasota for the first time in 1911. Ringling soon realised the development possibilities of Sarasota and its surroundings and bought up large tracts of land, including St Armands Key and the southern end of Longboat Key, with the intention of turning Sarasota into an exclusive resort for his influential friends from the East Coast.

Ritz-Carlton

On Longboat Key a start was made on building the luxurious Ritz-Carlton Hotel. After the end of the First World War John and Mable Ringling travelled throughout Europe and bought up works of art relatively cheaply, including some ancient statues and works by Rubens, Titian and Tintoretto. The Ringling residence "Ca'd'Zan", the architecture of which is reminiscent of that of the Doge's Palace in Vienna, was built on Sarasota Bay.

The mid 1920s was a boom time for Sarasota. The New York Giants came here for spring training. Ringling's circus had its winter quarters here, and parties were thrown every time it arrived or left. The circus still spends the winter in Sarasota County. At the end of the 1920s the world economic crisis hit Sarasota also, and Ringling's ambitious plans remained largely unfulfilled. Nevertheless he succeeded in opening his School of Arts and Design and his Museum of Art in 1931. John Ringling, the benefactor of Sarasota but by now weighed down by considerable financial problems, died in 1936.

Downtown Sarasota

The old town centre, built in the Mediterranean style in the 1920s, has undergone a revival in recent years. Even in Ringling's time Palm Avenue was popular with shoppers and strollers alike, and the atmosphere of that period is still noticeable in some of the shops. Various art galleries, antique dealers and jewellery shops emphasise Sarasota's reputation as a wealthy town.

*Town centre
Palm Avenue*

The shopping centre known as Kress International Plaza at the western end of Main Street is interesting. Built in the 1930s in the Art Deco style, it today houses sundry boutiques, bars, a "Food Court" and a permanent exhibition of work by local artists.

*★Kress
International
Plaza*

Another landmark is Edwards Theater (Pineapple Ave./First St.), whose stage was trodden by stars of the 1920s and 1930s. It closed in the early 1970s. It is now home to the Sarasota Opera Association.

Edwards Theater

The status of Bayfront was also enhanced. The Van Wezel Performing Arts Hall at 777 North Tamiami Trail, a modern concert hall built in an unusual shell-like design, was designed in the offices of the Frank Lloyd Wright Foundation. From October to April guest theatrical performances, dance events and concerts are held here; for information tel. 953–3366.
    On the other side of a small canal lies the modern Marie Selby Library, at 1001 Blvd. of the Arts. Completed in 1988, the peach-coloured building complex of Sarasota Bay (offices and shops) is an architecturally dominant feature by the waterside. At the end of Main Street the Municipal Marina and Island Park have been built directly on the bay. Boat excursions leave from here.

Bayfront

★★John and Mable Ringling Museum of Art

The town's chief attraction is the museum complex on the 69 acres/28ha former Ringling estate, about 3 miles/5km north of the town centre (5401 Bayshore Road; open: daily 10am–5.30pm, Thur. to 10pm), which the circus king made over to the state of Florida in 1936. In addition to the beautifully cared-for gardens, with some fine views over Sarasota Bay, the Museum of Art, the Circus Collection, Ringling's own residence Ca'd'Zan as well as the Asolo Theater are all open to visitors. The John and Mable Ringling Museum of Art, built between 1927 and 1930 in the Renaissance style, houses a magnificent collection of European masters of the 16th, 17th and 18th c., including important works by Cranach, Rubens and Van Dyke. The Baroque Collection contains some 750 paintings, prints and statues. The charming inner courtyard of the museum is adorned with replicas of famous statues, including "David" by Michelangelo.

*Museum
complex*

The adjoining wing built on in 1966 houses the contemporary collections. The museum also owns an important collection of ancient Cypriot art.

Adjoining wing

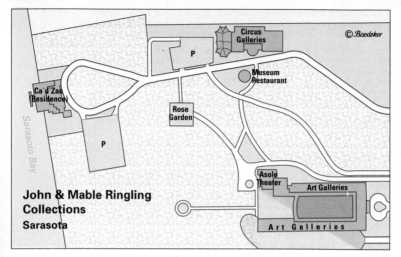

John & Mable Ringling Collections Sarasota

★Asolo Theater   The Asolo Theater is in a separate building. In 1950 the museum purchased the whole interior of the Baroque Theatre in Asolo (Italy) and faithfully re-installed it here in Florida. From 1960 until the completion of the new Asolo Center for the Performing Arts in 1989 it was home to the Asolo State Theater; for programme information tel. 351–8000.

Circus Gallery   Various exhibits in the circus gallery are reminders of its halcyon days. In addition to vintage circus vehicles, costumes and posters there is also a pretty miniature circus to delight the eye.

★Ca'd'Zan   Ca'd'Zan, lying directly on Sarasota Bay, was the palatial winter residence of John and Mable Ringling. "John's House", as the 30-room villa became known, was built in 1926 in the style of a Venetian Renaissance palace. It is still one of most beautiful examples of the pseudo-historical architecture so admired by rich Americans during the 1920s. The old bricks and tiles for the roof and 100ft/30m high tower were imported from Barcelona. The windows are of Venetian glass. From the 900sq.yd/750sq.m terrace thirteen marble steps lead down to the water where Mable Ringling's Venetian gondola was berthed.

Further Sights

Bellm's Cars and Music of Yesterday   Close by the visitor will find the unusual Bellm's Cars and Music of Yesterday Museum (5500 North Tamiani Trail/US 41; open: Mon.–Sat. 8.30am–6pm, Sun. 9.30am–6pm), with more than 100 lovingly restored vintage cars as well as over 2000 music-boxes and other mechanical musical instruments of the 18th c. The collection also includes some very old fruit machines. Some of these were in use back at the turn of the century.

Sarasota Jungle Gardens   Sarasota Jungle Gardens to the south of the town (3701 Bayshore Road; open: daily 9am–5pm) are botanical and zoological gardens with lush tropical or subtropical vegetation and exotic animals. Five times a day macaws and cockatoos perform in the "Jungle Bird Circus", as do snakes and alligators in the "Reptile Show". In the "Gardens of Christ" eight dioramas show scenes from the life of Jesus.

South of the town centre the Marie Selby Botanical Gardens (811 South Palm Ave.; open: daily 10am–5pm) cover an area of 10 acres/4ha on Sarasota Bay. Here the visitor can study tropical plants grouped under various headings. Selby Gardens is internationally famous for its orchid collection and its research laboratories. Since 1975 botanists from here have made many expeditions to tropical rain-forests and built up one of the most comprehensive collections of epiphytes (plants growing on another). These include many rare species threatened with extinction.

★Marie Selby Botanical Gardens

The gardens also contain the former residence of the Selby family as well as the Christy Payne Mansion – now a Museum of Botany and Art – both typical examples of the elegant architecture of the southern states of the USA.

In the Mote Marine Science Aquarium on City Island (1600 City Island Park; open: daily 10am–5pm) the visitor can study marine animals and plants from Sarasota Bay and elsewhere in the Gulf of Mexico. Of particular interest are the shark-ponds as well as the various research projects and the shell exhibition.

Mote Marine Science Aquarium

Ringling Causeway links St Armands Key and Lido Key with the mainland. St Armands, named after the first settler Charles St Armand, was purchased in the 1920s by John Ringling with the object of building elegant shops and villas among the mangroves. Today St Armands Circle is famous for its exquisite shops, restaurants and night-life. Since 1988 its inner ring has served to commemorate famous circus artistes (Circus Ring of Fame). Between the shops and dwellings there are pretty inner courtyards, terraces and pergolas to delight the eye, as well as lush tropical gardens. Lido Beach is Sarasota's most popular beach, miles long and well equipped with picnic and play-areas such as those at South Lido Beach, as well as swimming pools. The more secluded North Lido Beach is a favourite spot with amateur bird-watchers.

★St Armands Key, Lido Key, Lido Beach

On the Lido of Sarasota

Sebring

Longboat Key	See Bradenton
★ Siesta Key	Siesta Key, a sandy island south of Lido Key, has long been an artists' colony. The white sand of Crescent Beach makes it one of the most beautiful in the world; there are plenty of holiday apartments.

From Point of the Rocks the enthusiast can indulge in some interesting snorkelling and diving. In 1907 two entrepreneurs developed Siesta Key and started an advertising campaign to attract holidaymakers to the "most beautiful spot on earth". Today sizeable areas of the island are taken up by holiday accommodation and villas.

A number of the older houses to the north, hidden in lush gardens and under palm trees, are built in typical "Sarasota style", designed by the architects Ralph Twitchell and Paul Rudolph, who changed the face of Sarasota in the 1920s.

Surroundings

★ Myakka River State Park	Myakka River State Park lies almost 19 miles/30km east of Sarasota off the SR 72 (13207 SR 72; for information tel. 924–1027). Its total area of 30,000 acres/12,140ha makes it the largest park of its kind in the "Sunshine State".

It is also one of the major wild life reserves in the United States. This largely intact eco-system on the Myakka River varies between open countryside, a clear view across areas of water and swampland with thickly wooded copses or hammocks, clumps of pine-trees and palmetto prairie. The park is renowned for its many deer, wild turkeys, alligators and water-fowl. Frequently eagles, herons and sand-cranes can be observed.

The 7500 acre/3035ha "Wilderness Preserve", the very core of the nature reserve, can be reached only by means of a long walk or by boat (permit required). At the park entrance a small Interpretive Center will provide information about the reserve. Park rangers offer guided tours and campfire programmes as well as bird-watching for beginners (winter months only). In all there are 40 miles/64km of paths criss-crossing the park. The Myakka River Trail is part of the Florida Trail which is being constructed.

Tours and excursions	Myakka Wildlife and Nature Tours offer one-hour boat trips as well as a tour by tram, and rents out boats, canoes and bicycles on Upper Myakka Lake (Boat Basin). There are camp-sites, backpacking facilities and some simple log-cabins.
Osprey, Historic Spanish Point	Some 10 miles/16km south of the town centre, in Osprey, the visitor will find Historic Spanish Point (500 Tamiami Trail, US 41; open: Tues.–Sat. 9am–4pm, Sun. noon–4pm), a 30 acre/12ha park on Little Sarasota Bay with four Indian mounds or fortresses dating from *c.* 2000 B.C. which were scientifically examined in the 1960s, and a "homestead", or parcel of land sold to settlers by the State in accordance with the Federal Homestead Act. In 1867 a family settled here and named the place "Spanish Point" after the Spanish traders and fishermen who were based on the coast nearby. In 1910 the land was bought by the influential Mrs Potter Palmer, the famous widow of a Chicago hotelier who also became well-known for her work in support of women's rights. She built her winter villa "The Oaks" here, and later became owner of a considerable amount of land in the area, including a ranch on the Myakka River. The arrival of this famous widow was a stroke of luck for Sarasota, since she brought the town welcome publicity and put it into the headlines. Her villa has since been pulled down, and new houses have been built on a part of the land. There still exists a small cemetery dating from the pioneering period as well as a local history exhibition.

Sebring   G 12

Highlands County
Altitude: 131ft/40m. Population: 10,000

In the hills of Central Florida, about 87 miles/140km east of Tampa (see entry), lies Sebring, well-known to motor racing enthusiasts. This little township on Lake Jackson is surrounded by pine forests, fields of vegetables, citrus groves and a few sizeable cattle farms.

In the 1980s the old, brick-built centre around Circle Park, Main Street and Commerce Avenue was lovingly restored.

Its relatively "high" position means that Sebring is less humid than on the coast, and the numerous lakes and rivers in the surrounding countryside help to produce a more balanced climate.

Sebring is a relatively young town, having been founded in 1911. First of all the "Circle" (town centre) was laid out together with a park area and City Pier on the banks of Lake Jackson. Later it was extended along Lakeshore Drive. In 1912 Plant's railroad, the "Atlantic Coast Line", reached the new town. By the 1920s Sebring already boasted nine largish hotels and a considerable number of winter residences owned by well-to-do families from the north-east of the USA.

In 1921 Highlands County was made independent of the neighbouring De Soto County, and Sebring became the adminstrative town. In the mid 1920s the region around Sebring was affected by the land boom, and by 1926 the town's population had risen to 7000.

The opening of Highlands Hammock State Park, which soon became one of the region's chief tourist attractions, gave Sebring a further boost.

During the Second World War an aircraft base was built nearby where B 17 bomber pilots were trained. After the end of the war the town purchased the land and now, as well as a motor racing circuit, it contains a small airfield and an industrial site.

The construction of the US 27, Florida's major north–south motorway, brought further economic benefits in its wake.

Sebring International Raceway

Sights

City Pier	City Pier is prettily situated and, especially in the evenings, there is a fine view from it over Lake Jackson.
Cultural Center	On City Pier stands the Cultural Center Complex with a library, theatre and the Highlands Museum of Art. Temporary exhibitions are held from time to time.
Roaring Twenties	There is a pretty street market in the town centre. The stall-holders dress in the 1920s style.
Kenilworth Lodge	Kenilworth Lodge, built in 1916 on Lake Jackson near to the town centre and once a Grand Hotel, has also been restored.
Lake Jackson	Lake Jackson, very popular in summer with water-sports enthusiasts, is ringed by Lakeview Drive. Along the lake there are several beautiful and well cared-for bathing beaches with facilities for sailing, water-skiing and parascending.

Sebring International Raceway

Motor race-track	Sebring International Raceway, 4 miles/6·5km in length, is laid out on the former military airfield. At the end of March every year since 1950 the "12 Hours of Sebring Endurance Race" has been held here. After Indianapolis and Daytona this is the third most important motor race held in the USA and attracts thousands of onlookers.
For some years now autumn races have been held in October and these are also very popular.

★★Highlands Hammock State Park

Location	Highlands Hammock State Park (open: daily 8am–sunset) lies 4½ miles/7km west of Sebring on the CR 634. Florida's oldest State Park, it was placed under a protection order in 1931. Here the visitor can enjoy almost unspoiled "hammock" flora – hardwood trees and palms growing on raised ridges, and nearby cypress swamps and pine forests. Many trees in the park, especially the oaks, are several hundreds of years old. Deer, racoons, alligators and birds of all kinds (including the white-headed eagle) are denizens of this park. There are plenty of nature trails and log-paths.
Guided tours	"Tram Tours" with skilled and knowledgeable couriers run to even the more remote parts of the park from Tues.–Sun. Accompanied walks: Mon. 10am, and Thur. evening (Oct.–Apr. only). Camp-fire programmes, slide-shows.
Interpretive Center	The park's Interpretive Center will provide information about the flora and fauna. Bicycles can be hired from the Ranger Station for a small fee.
Information	Highlands Hammock State Park, 5931 Hammock Road, Sebring, FL 33872; tel. (813) 385–0011.

Space Coast   D–F 13/14

Location	The middle section of the Atlantic coast of Florida between Daytona in the north and Fort Pierce in the south (see entries) is widely known as "Space Coast", after the US space centre on Merritt Island/Cape Canaveral (see entry). More and more tourists are attracted to the wide beaches and unspoilt marshes and swamps, especially as it is not far to the attractions to be found in and around Orlando (see entry). As there is always a good breeze blowing, Space Coast is very popular with sailors and wind-surfers; in fact, the best wind-surfers in the USA train here.

Details of the major sights, nature reserves and beaches along Space Coast can be found under the following individual headings: Cape Canaveral, Cocoa, Daytona, Fort Pierce, Melbourne, New Smyrna Beach, Titusville and Vero Beach.

Sights, bathing beaches

Starke

C 11

Bradford County
Altitude: 160ft/49m
Population: 6000

About halfway between Jacksonville and Gainesville (see entries) lies Starke, the chief town of Bradford County. Here, in North Florida, the visitor will still find the large forests of pine trees from which the "crackers" obtained turpentine from the middle of the 18th c. onwards. Nowadays titanium is mined in considerable quantities around Starke, and the region is also known for its cultivation of strawberries.

Location

Surroundings

Keystone Heights, a few miles south of Starke, is a charming stretch of countryside composed of limestone hills and lakes.

Keystone Heights

Mike Roess Gold Head Branch State Park, almost 20 miles/32km south-east of Starke, covers over 1500 acres/600ha rich in wild life. This beautifully scenic area with its lakes and ponds, a wildly-romantic gorge and remains of an old mill can be explored by canoe, bicycle or on foot. Those wishing to stay longer can make use of a spacious camp-site and simple holiday cabins.

★Mike Roess
Gold Head Branch
State Park

Stuart

H 15

Martin County
Altitude: 0–13ft/0–4m
Population: 12,000

The fishing port of Stuart lies in a sheltered position on the St Lucie River on the Intracoastal Waterway not far from the Atlantic coast. St Lucie Inlet between Hutchinson Island and Jupiter Island off the coast provides a narrow entrance to the harbour.

Location

Once merely a small fishing port, it has now developed to become the main base for Florida's fleet of charter boats. Thousands of amateur fishermen sail out to sea from here into the Gulf Stream, especially to try and track down the unusual "sailfish" (*istiophorus americanus*), a basking shark so named because of its strikingly large dorsal fin. The local Sailfish Club organises seven large competitions every year.

It was not until the end of the 19th c., when Flagler's Florida East Coast Railway opened up the region, that new settlers established large plantations. Stuart, originally named Potsdam, became the administrative centre of the newly-created Martin County in 1914. Today citrus groves, fields of flowers and vegetables and apartment blocks predominate.

In recent years stud farms have been established in the nearby townships of Palm City and Indiantown, breeding thoroughbred horses. Fort Myers, on the Gold Coast, can be reached by way of the St Lucie Canal, a part of the Okeechobee Waterway.

At the end of the 1980s a start was made on redeveloping an area of the old town covering eighteen street blocks along the St Lucie River and

259

building new shops and restaurants. A delightful promenade along the banks of the St Lucie has already been completed.

Sights

Gilbert's Bar
House of Refuge
Museum

In 1875 the Life Saving Service (the forerunner of the US Coast Guard) built nine houses to provide accommodation for survivors from ships wrecked off the east coast of Florida. Gilbert's Bar House of Refuge on Hutchinson Island (MacArthur Blvd.; open: Tues.–Sun. 1–4.15pm) is the only one to have survived. Having been closed down in 1945, it now functions as a museum on the history of the sea rescue service. Adjoining it are an aquarium and a turtle-breeding station.

Elliott Museum

Nearly 1¼ miles/2km further north, Elliott Museum (825 Ocean Blvd.; open: daily 1–4pm) is worth a visit. It was set up in memory of the prodigious American inventor Sterling Elliott who constructed the first addressograph and held 211 patents. In the south wing will be found a chemist's, a hairdresser's, a smithy, a clock and watchmaker's workshop as well as some small shops selling tea and herbs, cigarettes and tobacco and shooting and fishing gear, together with an ice-cream parlour furnished in 19th c. style. Indian exhibits and a shell-collection in the north wing are very interesting. Passing through a typical general store and post-office the visitor will come to the living rooms containing varied exhibits, such as a Victorian drawing-room furnished in late 19th c. style. Elliott's Oldtimers (vintage bicycles and carriages) are on display in the east wing.

★St Lucie Inlet
State Park

St Lucie State Park, at the northern end of Jupiter Island, can be reached only by boat. A pathway of planks leads between two typical coastal "hammocks" to a superb beach where turtles lay their eggs in summer. There are nature trails and a ranger station. Off the coast lies a 4½ mile/7km-long reef, very popular with divers (tel. 744–7603). Boat trips: Island Princess Cruises, 55 North East Ocean Blvd., tel. 225–2100.

Indian River
Plantation

Indian River Plantation, once a pineapple plantation between the Atlantic and Indian River, has recently been made into a quiet holiday resort with a hotel, luxurious apartments, golf-courses and tennis-courts and a private marina where boats can be chartered for deep-sea fishing.

South Hutchinson
Island

South Hutchinson Island, renowned for its beautiful beaches, stretches northwards as far as Fort Pierce. Until a few years ago Hutchinson Island was an unspoilt island with thick mangrove forests. Now it is scarred with large numbers of holiday homes, faceless hotels and apartment buildings. In the centre of the island stand the two complexes of the St Lucie Nuclear Power Plant. In summer giant turtles, threatened with extinction, come on to the beach to lay their eggs.

Save Our
Beaches

Under a "Save Our Beaches Program" local citizens worried about the effect that uncontrolled tourism is having upon their beaches have, with assistance from the local authorities, been buying up sections of the beaches with the aim of preserving them and also ensuring free access for themselves.

Suwannee River

See Live Oak

Tallahassee   B 7

Leon County
Altitude: 190ft/58m
Population: 127,000

Tallahassee (from the Indian for "old fields"), Florida's tranquil capital, lies in the north-west of the state at the base of the "panhandle" only 19 miles/30km from the Gulf Coast. It takes in several small hills and is surrounded by large pine forests and numerous lakes. The administrative centre of the "Sunshine State" has managed to retain something of the charm of the Old South, and its inhabitants are especially proud of the many well-preserved and prettily restored 19th c. buildings. Mighty old oaks, thickly overgrown with moss, make their mark on the sprawling town with its well-nurtured parks. Its landmark, the new State Capitol, still towers above all other buildings.

Location

The present town of Tallahassee was founded in 1824. There was an Indian settlement here before the first Europeans arrived. The Spaniard Panfilo de Narvaez came here in 1528, and Hernando de Santo and his force spent the winter here in 1539. Probably from 1633 to 1704 the Spanish mission settlement of San Luis de Talimali existed west of the present town centre, and at the end of the 17th c. there was also a small Spanish military base here.

History

The San Luis Franciscan mission was at the time the major Spanish settlement in the Apalachee region and had more than 1400 inhabitants. Conflicts between the rival colonial powers of Spain, France and Great Britain led to the Apalachee region being invaded by the British Governor of South Carolina in the early 18th c., when a number of Spanish towns were destroyed. The Apalachee Indians, some of whom had already become Christians, were either killed in the fighting or were taken prisoner by the British troops. Some managed to flee to Pensacola or to St Augustine, from where they emigrated to Cuba.

In the 1730s other Indian tribes, mainly the Seminoles, settled here but were later driven out especially during the Seminole Wars. Increased numbers of white settlers then moved into the Tallahassee region where they grew cotton and sugar beet on the plantations. A devastating fire in 1843 and a yellow-fever epidemic had an adverse effect on the young town's development. At that time the population was about 3000. Since the 1940s the enormous influx of people into Florida has also involved Tallahassee.

Today Tallahassee is predominantly an administrative centre and college town. In addition to the many government offices the main employers in

Economy

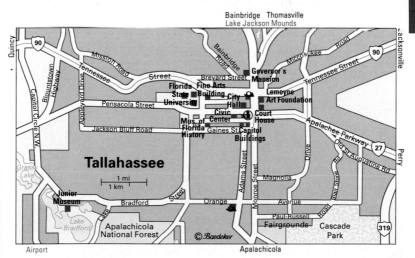

the town are Florida State University (founded in 1857, 23,000 students), Florida Agricultural and Mechanical University (FAMU, founded in 1887 primarily as a school for coloured people, now with 5000 students) and Community College (3000 students). It is anticipated that the population will be more than 200,000 by the year 2000. Even now the skyline of the little capital is beginning to change, and new industrial sites and housing estates are developing.

Sights

★ Old State Capitol

On the highest hill in the town stands the Old State Capitol built in 1839 (400 South Monroe St./Apalachee Parkway), with its dazzling white front and the typical red and white striped awnings above the windows. Some time ago the building was restored in the "turn of the century" style. The Governor's Room and the Chambers of the Supreme Court, the Senate and the House of Representatives are all open to visitors. There is a very informative exhibition on the history of Florida (open: Mon.–Fri. 9am–4.30pm, Sat. 10am–4.30pm, Sun. and public holidays noon–4.30pm).

★ New State Capitol

The New State Capitol was opened in 1978 in S. Adams Street. It is a symbol of the very dynamic economic development experienced by the "Sunshine State" within a few decades. In the course of a tour of the Chambers of the Senate and House of Representatives the visitor will be provided with details of how the state government works. The Grand Seal of the State of Florida is displayed in the entrance hall. Guided tours: Mon.–Fri. 9am–noon and 1–4pm, Sat., Sun., public holidays 11am–noon and 1–3pm. Viewing platform.

Florida's Vietnam Era Veterans' Memorial

On a small lawn opposite the Old Capitol a memorial was erected in 1985 to the Florida victims and veterans of the Vietnam War. A giant US flag flies over it.

The old and new Capitol in Tallahassee

At the back, on Apalachee Parkway, stands the pleasant little 1841 building which belonged to the Union Bank, once the major bank used by the Florida plantation owners (open: Mon.–Sat. 10am–1pm, Sun. 1–4.30pm).

North of the Capitol complex two blocks of old Tallahassee houses have been restored. Paved streets, some restaurants, bars, boutiques and Gallie's Hall, a late 19th c. town theatre, make Adam's Street Commons a popular meeting place.

West of the Capitol stands the Supreme Court Building, built in 1948 in Neo-Classical style.

Nearby, at 500 South Bronough St., is the R. A. Gray Building, erected in 1976. In addition to the state archives and a library it houses the excellent Museum of Florida History (open: Mon.–Fri. 9am–4.30pm, Sat. 10am–4.30pm, Sun. and public holidays noon–4.30pm). Particularly impressive is the almost 10ft/3m high skeleton of a mastodon found in Florida.

Behind Gray Building towers the massive 1981 Civic Center, with an auditorium seating 14,000.

Every day between 7am and 6pm this vintage tram or street-car leaves from the Civic Center on a tour of the town centre. It drops and picks up at thirteen stops, with the aim of helping to reduce the parking and traffic problems in the government quarter of town.

Passing through Bronough Street the visitor will find the charming East Park Avenue with its beautiful old trees and several historical buildings. On the corner stands the post-office, and diagonally opposite it "The Columns" (100 North Duval St.), the town's oldest preserved building. Built in 1830 by the then president of the Bank of Florida, it now houses the offices of the Tallahassee Chamber of Commerce.

A few yards further on stands the First Presbyterian Church, built in brick in 1838 in the Neo-Classical style and in which the populace sought refuge when the Seminole Indians attacked the town in 1838–39. It is the town's oldest church. Until the Civil War the gallery – now rebuilt – was reserved for slaves.

Between Calhoun Street and Gadsden Street, east of South Monroe Street, will be found some interesting buildings, mostly dating from before the

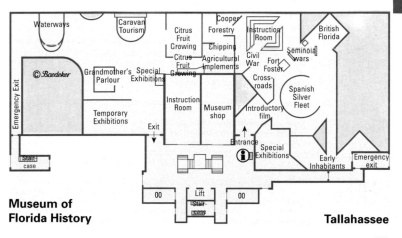

Museum of Florida History

Tallahassee

Tallahassee

Downtown Tallahassee

American Civil War and with the typical verandas and porches supported on pillars. Some examples are Knott House (*c.* 1840), Wood House (1905), Murphy House (1836), Shine-Chittenden House (*c.* 1840) and Lewis House (19th c.).

Calhoun Street

A stroll along Calhoun Street, Tallahassee's prime boulevard built in the 19th c., will be found most rewarding.

Brokaw-McDougall House

Brokaw-McDougall House (329 North Meridian St.), built in 1856 in typical Neo-Classical style, serves as a conference centre for the Florida government. There are some very beautiful gardens.

DeSoto Archaeological and Historic Site

When a new building estate was about to be built in 1986–87 on a hill east of the town centre (Goodbody Lane/Lafayette St.) the contractors stumbled almost by chance on the remains of the camp of De Soto, who spent the winter here in 1539. There is a small exhibition of items found there in the restored hunting-lodge of the governor J. W. Martin (1925–29).

San Luis Archaeological and Historical Site

Some 2½ miles/4km west of the town centre (2020 Mission Road) the remains of an Apalachee Indian settlement and of the 17th c. San Luis Spanish mission station have been uncovered.

Before the Civil War the manor house of a large plantation stood here. Later Emile Dubois cultivated vines on the land. However, the present house, built in the typical Southern States style, dates only from the 1930s (open: Mon.–Fri. 9am–4.30pm, Sat. 10am–4.30pm, Sun. noon–4.30pm).

Tallahassee Junior Museum

Tallahassee Junior Museum, near the airport at 3945 Museum Drive north of Lake Bradford, shows what life on the land must have been like in the 19th c. Some old buildings have been moved here and used to construct Big Bend Farm. The elegant Maison Bellevue was once the home of Cathérine Murat, widow of a nephew of Napoleon I. After the Battle of Waterloo he emigrated to America and in 1825 bought a plantation east of Tallahassee and settled there. The open-air museum also has some nature trails and a small animal park (open: Mon.–Sat. 9am–5pm, Sun. 12.30–5pm).

Tallahassee is well known for its "canopy roads". This term applies to roads over which old oak trees have spread to form a "canopy". Particularly pretty examples are Micusukee Road, Centerville Road (County Road 151), Meridian Road, Old Bainbridge Road (County Road 157) and St Augustine Road.

Canopy roads

Surroundings

Nearly 6 miles/10km north-west of Tallahassee, at the southern end of Lake Jackson which is so popular with anglers, lies a field of Indian "mounds". It is assumed that from about 1200 to 1500 this was either the residence of an Indian chief or a cult centre of some kind. At least one of these mounds was a burial site. The high quality of the grave-goods indicates close links with other Pre-Columbian cultures in the south-east of the United States.
    Access to this site is by way of the US 27 North Crowder Road. Open: daily 8am–sunset.

★ Lake Jackson Indian Mounds (State Archaeological Site)

East of the town on the US 90 (6505 Mahan Drive) lies one of the "Sunshine State's" four major vineyards. Wine has been produced here since 1982 on land which once formed part of the estates of the French Marquis de Lafayette. He was given them in 1824 in recognition of his services in connection with American independence. Open for visits and wine-tasting: Mon.–Sat. 10am–6pm, Sun. noon–6pm.

Lafayette Vineyards and Winery

From Tallahassee to the Gulf Coast

There is an interesting trip to be made to the Gulf Coast south of Tallahassee. Woodville Highway (SR 363) first of all leads to the Natural Bridge Historic Site, about 6 miles/10km east of Woodville on the SR 354, where St Marks River flows through a cavern some 160ft/50m long, forming a natural bridge. Here the people remember a battle in 1865 during the American Civil War, when the defenders of Tallahassee won the day against the Union troops; on the first week-end in March the "Battlefield Re-enactment" is performed here.

★ Natural Bridge Battlefield Historic Site

About 19 miles/30km south, near the township of St Marks and at the confluence of the Wakulla and St Marks Rivers, is where the Spanish fort of San Marcos de Apalachee was built in 1679 to defend the mission stations and settlements in this area. Shortly afterwards pirates overran and destroyed the first wooden fort. In 1739 a start was made on constructing a stone replacement. In 1758 San Marcos was struck by a fierce hurricane, and when the English occupied the fort in 1763 it was only half finished. In 1787 the Spaniards returned. In May 1800 the fort was occupied by W. A. Bowles, a discharged British officer who had joined up with the Indians, and 400 Indians. Bowles proclaimed himself king of Florida, but his reign lasted only five weeks before the fort was again taken by the Spanish. In 1818 Andrew Jackson occupied Fort San Marcos. After Florida became part of the United States the fort was abandoned. It was 1857–58 before anyone thought of it again and built a hospital here for yellow-fever victims from the US Navy. From 1861–65 the Confederates held the fort in order to blockade the mouth of St Marks River. A small museum now stands on the foundations of the former naval hospital (open: Thur.–Mon. 9am–5pm).

★ San Marcos de Apalachee State Park

The town of St Marks lies on the edge of St Marks National Wildlife Refuge, 100sq.miles/259sq.km of marshland with marsh-cypress trees at the confluence of the St Marks and Aucilla Rivers. "Bayous" (marshy river off-shoots), large ponds of both fresh and brackish water, drier pine forests

★ St Marks National Wildlife Refuge

and copses of hardwood trees, oaks and palmettos characterise the landscape. Its denizens include large numbers of water-fowl and alligators as well as deer, white-headed eagles, osprey and numerous migratory birds. There is a Visitor Center (open: Mon.–Fri. 8am–4.30pm, Sat., Sun. 10am–5pm) about 3 miles/5km south of the US 95 on the CR 59.

St Marks
Lighthouse

At the end of the CR 59 (7 miles/11km) stands the lighthouse built in 1831. There is a viewing platform and also the Mounds Hill Interpretive Trail, from which animals can be observed in their natural habitat.

★ Wakulla Springs

It is well worth making an excursion to Wakulla Springs, Florida's most powerful limestone springs – in 1973 a record flow of 11,930galls/54,280 litres of water per second was recorded. So far only a 385yd/350m length of the linked cave-system has been explored.

In Edward Ball Wakulla Springs State Park, which covers an area of only 4½sq.miles/12sq.km, a small piece of the original Florida has been preserved. It was here, too, that the early Tarzan films with Johnny Weismuller and other jungle films were shot.

In the course of a half-hour boat trip on the Wakulla River the visitor may well see more alligators and turtles than he will on a trip through the Everglades (see entry). Often the very unusual anhingas can be seen sitting on tree-stumps and drying their plumage after diving for fish.

From a glass-bottomed boat the cave-entrance can be clearly seen 115ft/35m down in the clear spring water. Visitors can swim in the relatively cool water in a fenced-off area.

Wakulla Springs Lodge, built in 1937 for the financier and naturalist Edward Ball and which has been under a protection order for a number of years, is worth a visit. It is charmingly furnished in 1930s style. In the entrance hall lies "Old Joe", an alligator about 200 years old who lived in Wakulla Springs until he was shot by an unknown hunter in 1966.

From Tallahassee into South Georgia

The drive north from Tallahassee passes through old "Plantation America".

Alfred B. Maclay
Gardens

Leave Tallahassee on the Thomasville Road (SR 61/US 319), which has been improved almost to freeway standards. After crossing the I-10 the road passes the Alfred B. Maclay Gardens (3540 Thomasville Road; open: daily 8am–dusk), a charming park by Lake Hall, with a nature trail and a small bathing beach by the lakeside. On a hill stands Maclay House, furnished in 1920s style, which was originally the winter residence of a wealthy New York financier. Beautiful camelias bloom in December.

Pebble Hill
Plantation

About 19 miles/30km north of Tallahassee Pebble Hill Plantation (on the US 319), laid out in the 1820s, is open to visitors, who can obtain an insight into the aristocratic life-style enjoyed by the plantation owners of the Old South. The estate later became the winter residence of a rich family from Cleveland, Ohio. The spacious house is open Tues.–Sat. 10am–4pm, Sun. 1–4pm.

Thomasville
(Georgia)

It is a further 35 miles/56km to Thomasville (pop. 20,000), in the state of Georgia. A number of beautiful 19th c, buildings have been preserved. At that time this town on the border with Florida was renowned for its pleasant climate and boasted several elegant hotels. American presidents have stayed here to hunt quail and play golf.

The "Historic District" has been lovingly restored. Typical of the Old South at the turn of the century are villas built in the Victorian style, such as Lapham Patterson House, 626 North Dawson St. and Hardy-Brian House, 312 North Broad St., and some pretty shops in the old Main Street (Broad/Jackson St.). Also worthy of note is the Thomas County Historical Museum in North Dawson St. The local Chamber of Commerce at 401 South Broad St. arranges "plantation tours" from Monday to Friday.

The best route back to Tallahassee is the Florida State Road 155/Meridian Road, one of the "canopy roads" (see above). 22 miles/35km north of Tallahassee, will be found the Susina Plantation near the town of Cairo. Typical architecture will be found in the ante-bellum manor house, built in the Neo-Classical style in 1841 and now a pretty guest-house.

Susina Plantation

Tamiami Trail

F–K 10–15

Laid in the first quarter of this century and measuring 260 miles/420km in length, the Tamiami Trail was the first road linking Tampa and Miami (see entries). The US 41 now follows it for part of its length.

The first part of the old trail is between Tampa and Naples near the coast. Great difficulties were encountered in constructing the section through the northern part of the Everglades. Surveying and measuring was done in 1915 from Indian canoes, but in 1918 building work came to a standstill after some 30 miles/50km had been completed, between Naples and the lumber camp at Carnestown. It seemed impossible to proceed further through the "bottomless swamp", and local taxpayers were not prepared to see any more of their money wasted on what seemed to be a pointless project.

History

In 1923 twenty-six men with a thirst for adventure risked all in a spectacular attempt to complete the route. Driving seven Model T Fords with thick rope wrapped round the wheels, they set out from Carnestown in the direction of Miami. They followed Indian trails, driving across relatively dry hammocks and higher ground as well as over punishing marshland. After

The smallest post-office in the USA . . .   *. . . warning notice on the Tamiami Trail*

eleven days they reached Miami. Work on the road was re-started, this time with financial assistance from the state of Florida. Using lots of dynamite, a drainage system was laid, and the hardcore and subsoil thrown up was used for the foundations of the new road. The workers often laboured waist-deep in water, plagued by mosquitoes and snakes. It took a month to build just one mile of road. In 1928 a ceremony was held declaring the Tamiami Trail finally open. It now took only two days to drive from Tampa to Miami.

Sights

The major sights and places to visit along the Tamiami Trail will be found under the following individual entries: Big Cypress National Preserve, Bradenton, Everglades National Park, Fort Myers, Miccosukee Indian Village, Miami, Naples, Punta Gorda, Sarasota, Tampa and Venice.

Tampa   F/G 10/11

Hillsborough County
Altitude: 0–56ft/0–17m
Population: 280,000 (Metropolitan Area: 2,000,000)

Enjoying a sheltered position on a bay in the Gulf of Mexico, Tampa is the financial and economic centre of West Florida and the heart of a metropolitan area with a total population of some two million. Whereas it was the famous beaches of St Petersburg (see entry), just 19 miles/30km on the far side of Old Tampa Bay, which attracted so many tourists and retired people to the Pinellas Suncoast (see entry), the industrial port of Tampa with its modern airport frequently served merely as a gateway to the beaches and other attractions. In fact this city, charmingly situated on Tampa Bay with its three large bridges, has much of its own to offer. The city centre is admittedly dominated by modern office-blocks, but nearby will be found histor-

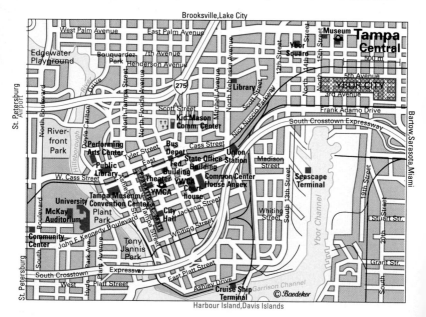

ical quarters such as Ybor City or Old Hyde Park, together with several museums and world-famous attractions like Busch Gardens.

The maps drawn up by the Spanish conquerors showed Indian settlements around Tampa Bay. However, the Spanish paid little regard to this area in the course of their colonisation of Florida and their search for its wealth; they concentrated more on the Atlantic coast and the north. In 1824 the Americans built Fort Brooke at the mouth of the Hillsborough River, in an attempt to control the activities of the Seminole Indians who had immigrated here from the north. After the Second Seminole War Tampa began to expand, becoming an administrative centre and soon boasting a court building and a bank. Trade with Cuba flourished, but the American Civil War led to a period of economic stagnation. It was not until Henry B. Plant pushed his "South Florida Railroad" through to Tampa in 1885 that new commercial enterprises became possible. Plant tried to outdo his rival Flagler, who had opened up the east coast of Florida to tourism by means of his railroad and his Grand Hotels. With the opening of the luxury Tampa Bay Hotel in 1891 this became the fashionable place to spend the winter. In 1886 the Cuban cigar manufacturer Vincente Martinez Ybor moved his factories from Cuba and Key West to Tampa. Several thousand workers now came to Tampa, and the Spanish-speaking factory employees lived mainly in the quarter that became known as "Ybor City". The Cuban revolutionary José Marti also sought refuge here, and from Tampa he organised his campaign to free Cuba from Spanish colonial rule. Some three million cigars are still produced every working day in Tampa. There is now far less demand for the hand-made variety than there used to be, and the tobacco comes mainly from Puerto Rico and Honduras rather than from Cuba. The mining of phosphate in the countryside behind Tampa in the 1880s and 1890s led to an economic boom for the city and its port. In 1898 Colonel – later President – Theodore Roosevelt established his headquarters in Tampa Bay Hotel, where his largely volunteer "roughriders" trained in the hotel grounds in readiness for the Spanish-American War. The 30,000 or so American troops posted to Cuba were kitted-out in Tampa.

When the automobile became available to the masses in the 1920s Tampa enjoyed a building boom. New suburbs grew up, and it became fashionable to spend the winter months on Tampa Bay. Today it is a major financial and industrial city. The harbour is one of the best natural harbours in the world and is a starting-out point for cruises in the Gulf of Mexico. At one time citrus fruits, cattle and phosphates were shipped from here. Now the "shrimp fleet" plays an important role. Some 50 million tonnes of goods are handled every year. In addition to the many industrial concerns and two large breweries, the MacDill Air Force Base to the south-east of the town makes an important contribution to the local economy. Tampa is also the seat of two universities; the private University of Tampa (2000 students) was founded in 1931, and 10 miles/16km north of the city lies the campus of the University of Southern Florida, founded in 1956, with some 28,000 students.

The Tampa Gasparilla Festival recalls the legendary pirate José Gaspar, who plagued the Florida coasts in the early 19th c. First held in 1904, the highlight of the many events, processions and firework displays which last the whole of February is the "Gasparilla Invasion and Parade". Some 700 city dignitaries dressed as pirates aboard the pirate ship "José Gaspar" invade and "take" the town. The festival ends with the "Gasparilla Sidewalk Arts Festival" near Hillsborough River in downtown Tampa.

Downtown Tampa

The heart of Tampa's city centre at the mouth of Hillsborough River is Franklin Street Mall, a very popular pedestrian zone between Cass Street and Whiting Street, with plenty of shops, attractive bars and cafés, fountains and trees. The 1970s and 1980s saw the building of high-rise office

History

Gasparilla Festival

Franklin Street
Mall

269

The skyline of Tampa

blocks, reflecting the economic development of this industrial city and port. However, there are still old buildings to be found with friendly Art Deco fronts as well as cobbled streets and old railway lines.

Tampa Theater

In the midst of modern glass and steel monsters the freshly-restored Tampa Theater at 711 Franklin Street Mall shines forth in all its old splendour. It was opened in 1926 as a cinema, and now gives theatrical performances, concerts and film-shows.

Tampa Museum of Art

West of the city centre by Hillsborough River, near Curtis Nixon Hall (an old conference centre), lies Tampa Museum of Art (601 Doyle Carlton Drive; open: Tues.–Sat. 10am–5pm, Wed. to 9pm, Sun. 1–5pm). Its collections of Greek and Roman antiquities number among the best in America. Touring exhibitions, modern paintings.

Tampa Bay Performing Arts Center

Opened in 1987, Tampa Bay Performing Arts Center near Hillsborough River (1010 North McInnes Place) combines three theatres under one roof, with seats for 300 to 2400 spectators (plays, opera, musicals, concerts).

Tampa Bay Center

Tampa Bay Center, at 3300 West Buffalo Ave. (SR 574), has 160 shops, making it one of Tampa's largest shopping centres.

Harbour Island

Location

South of the city centre, separated from the mainland only by the narrow Garrison Channel, lies Harbour Island. The Peoplemover, a high-speed railway built on stilts, means that it takes only two minutes to cross from the city centre to the island. Covering 180 acres/73ha, the island has been re-developed in recent years and now boasts expensive apartment complexes, some on the water's edge with their own landing-stages, as well as a number of office-blocks. Among its attractions are the Harbour Island Market, at 601 South Harbour Island Blvd., and a new Congress Centre.

Harbour Island Market came into being in its present form in the 1980s as part of an attempt to make Tampa's waterfront more attractive. Today it is a lively waterside shopping-centre, with numerous boutiques, fast-food stalls and popular restaurants. From Parker's Lighthouse Restaurant there is a beautiful view of the city skyline. Behind it towers the twelve-storey Wyndham Harbour Island Hotel. A "Waterwalk" provides a pleasant stroll with a good view of the downtown skyscrapers.

The Florida Aquarium in the north-eastern corner of the island is also worth a visit.

West of Harbour Island lies Davis Island, an artificial island named after the man who planned it, D. P. Davis, who created one of the city's most exclusive residential quarters here in the 1920s. Many of the elegant residences and villas still remain.

In the south of the island lies Peter O'Knight Airport. Seaplanes fly from the adjoining Seaplane Basin. At the southern tip of the island is Davis Island Yacht Club.

West of Hillsborough River the minaret-like towers of the former Tampa Bay Hotel on Kennedy Boulevard stand out against the skyline. In 1890 the railway tycoon Henry B. Plant, with a bottomless purse at his disposal, went on a buying spree to Europe and the Orient. The furniture, fittings and works of art he bought for the hotel filled 80 coaches. From 1891 to 1929 the building, constructed on the lines of a Moorish palace, served as a hotel. Today it is the home of the University of Tampa.

The south wing of the former hotel houses the Henry B. Plant Museum (401 West Kennedy Blvd.; open: Tues.–Sat. 10am–4pm). Its exhibits include furniture and works of art from the late 19th and early 20th c. and original items from the old Tampa Bay Hotel.

To the south-west lies Hyde Park (between Swann Ave. and Bayshore Blvd.), Tampa's best-maintained old residential quarter with many Victorian buildings still reflecting late 19th c. elegance. Today Hyde Park is where Tampa's "yuppies" like to live.

In Old Hyde Park Village (712 South Oregon Ave./Swann Ave.) there are some sixty fashion shops and others selling high-quality goods and designer clothes, galleries and fine restaurants. A successful attempt has been made to re-create a late Victorian atmosphere, and there are still some magnificent Victorian buildings to be seen along the edge of the park. From May to October jazz concerts are held on the last Wednesday of every month.

University Square Mall (2200 East Fowler Ave.), in the north-east of the city on the edge of the campus of the University of Southern Florida, is Tampa's largest shopping centre, with branches of five large department stores and more than 130 shops and restaurants.

6 miles/10km long, Bayshore Boulevard on the west side of Hillsborough Bay offers an interesting view of the centre of Tampa and is very popular with strollers, joggers, cyclists and roller-skaters.

Along the west bank of Hillsborough River stretches the charming Lowry Park (7525 North Blvd./Sligh Ave.; open: daily 9.30am–5pm, pleasure park until sunset). It is a zoological garden with the accent on local fauna; there is a sea-cow (manatee) research station, together with a fairyland and pleasure park, with camel and elephant rides.

★Ybor City   F 10

Tampa's Cubo-Spanish history lives on in the old Latin quarter known as Ybor City (between 12th St. and 22nd St., as well as Palm Ave. and 7th Ave.,

Margin notes

★Harbour Island Market

Davis Island

★University of Tampa (formerly Tampa Bay Hotel)

Henry B. Plant Museum

Hyde Park

Old Hyde Park Village

University Square Mall

Bayshore Boulevard

Lowry Park

Location

Attractive architecture in Ybor City

north-east of the city centre). After years of neglect, during which whole blocks of historic old houses were pulled down, this quarter has now enjoyed a revival. The cityscape is made up of old wooden and brick-built buildings, wrought-iron balconies, arcades and street cafés renowned for their Cuban food and dark Cuban coffee. Information boards give details of various historical events.

In 1886 V. M. Ybor moved his cigarette factory to Tampa at a time when the city was stagnating and had only 700 inhabitants. With him came thousands of Cuban workers who rolled by hand the famous Cuban cigars from Cuban tobacco while somebody read to them from newspapers and story-books. Only two street-blocks away, on 15th Street, a second factory opened at the same time, known as the "Sanchez y Haya Cigar Factory". During Ybor City's heyday there were more than fifty cigar-makers, employing a total of some 40,000 workers. From this period, too, date the five clubs which still exist and which at that time played a very important role in safeguarding the welfare of the workers. Established in 1892, they provided food and medical assistance to workers who had fallen on hard times, formed bookshops and gave English lessons.

★Ybor City
State Museum

A good starting-out point for a tour of Ybor City is the State Museum (open: Tues.–Sat. 9am–noon and 1–5pm) housed in a former Cuban bakery (information from Ybor City Visitor Information Center, 1800 East 9th Ave.; open: Tues.–Sat. 11am–4pm). Adjacent to it is "Preservation Park" with six renovated old houses once inhabited by cigar-makers.

Tour

The visitor will then pass the splendid building of the Cuban Club (El Circulo Cubano, 9th Ave./13th St.) and also the Centro Espanol (7th Ave./15th St.). and the Italian Club (L'Unione Italiana, 7th Ave./18th St.).

7th Avenue was once the main business street in Ybor City. Here, too, will be found the Ritz Theater at 1503 7th Ave.: built in 1917, its entrance hall is magnificently decorated with Art Deco motifs. The historic Columbia Restaurant at 2117 7th Ave. was opened in 1905; cigar-workers used to meet in its "snug".

One whole block between 13th/14th St. and 8th/9th Ave. is taken up by the brick buildings of the former Ybor Cigar Factory. At the time it was one of the biggest factories of its kind in the world, with more than 1000 workers. Now restored and coverted into a small mall, the buildings house various shops and restaurants. In the "Tampa Rico Cigar Company" on the first floor visitors can watch cigars being rolled by hand. From the steps leading down from the east entrance onto 14th Street José Marti harangued the workers on the question of the liberation of Cuba.

★Ybor Square

★★Busch Gardens · The Dark Continent

F 11

One of Tampa's major attractions is Busch Gardens in the north-east of the city, a combination of zoo and leisure-park (Busch Blvd.; SR 580/40th St.; open: daily 9.30am–6pm. later in the holiday season). There is also a branch of the Anheuser-Busch Brewery.

Busch Gardens is now a family leisure-park which concentrates on themes connected with "The Dark Continent". There is entertainment to suit every taste. Animals, an exotic atmosphere, live-shows in several theatres, roller coasters and other exciting rides complete the programme. The zoological gardens have made a name for themselves for the work they do in connection with endangered species. They are particularly proud of their success in breeding rare black rhinos. They also have a family of koalas here which they hope will breed. Under a wider programme Busch Gardens are co-operating with Peking Zoo in seeking to rear pandas. The zoo also has an impressive herd of 21 Asian elephants.

At the end of the tour visitors can sample the products of the Anheuser-Busch Brewery in the "Bird Garden".

Busch Gardens: Elephants . . .   *. . . and the Looping Ride*

273

In 1959 the park first opened its doors to visitors to the Anheuser-Busch Brewery, providing a tour of the brewery with free beer, restaurants, tropical parks and exotic birds, a parrot-show and large African animals. From this humble beginning it has grown to become the greatest attraction on the Gulf Coast of Florida. In 1966 it was extended for the first time with the construction of the Safari Monorail. In the 1970s further attractions and roller-coasters were added, and the zoo has been constantly enlarged.

Today other leisure-parks in the USA form part of the Busch empire, such as the Sea World parks in Orlando (see entry), San Diego (California), San Antonio (Texas) and Aurora (Ohio), as well as Cypress Gardens in Winter Haven (see entry).

The individual areas of the park are the following:

Morocco	The Morocco Palace Theatre presents various shows, such as a Broadway Show and ice-revues, while outside may be found snake-charmers and various artistes and gymnasts.
Nairobi	Near Nairobi Train Station the elephant enclosure (rides available) and the centre where young animals are raised are both very popular.
Crown Colony	Crown Colony is the starting-place for the "Skyride" gondola trip to Congo or to the monorail. The latest attraction is a flight simulator.
Serengeti Plain	The theme-parks seek to remind visitors of conditions in Africa at the beginning of this century. Most of the larger animals – gazelles, kudu, antelopes, giraffes, zebras, chimpanzees – can be seen on the "Serengeti Plain". They can be observed either from gondolas or from the modern monorail. An even more enjoyable and relaxing tour can be made in a nostalgic old steam train.
Timbuktu, Congo, Stanleyville	In the "Timbuktu", "Congo" and "Stanleyville" theme areas there are various roller-coasters and adventure rides. A rather wet ride can be had going over artificial waterfalls in hollowed-out tree-trunks at "Stanley Falls", taking "Wild Water Trips" through the "Congo River Rapids" or riding on the "Tanganyika Tidal Wave". Some rare white Bengal tigers can be seen on Claw Island.
Festhaus	Here German-type brass-band music can be enjoyed.
Bird Gardens	The oldest part of the park will be found near the brewery. Here some 2000 exotic and rare birds can be observed flying free in a generous enclosure. The visitor can also watch birds in "Eagle Canyon" and on "Flamingo Island".

Other Sights

Adventure Island	Nearly 1¼ miles/2km north-east lies Tampa's large water-park, Adventure Island (4500 Bougainvillea Ave.; open: Mar.–Oct. Mon.–Fri. 10am–5pm, Sat./Sun. 9.30am–6pm, extended hours in summer). The fun-pool, with several waterchutes and a pool with artificial waves, is also very popular.
Museum of Science and Industry	The modern Museum of Science (4801 East Fowler Ave., near the campus of the University of South Florida; open: Mon.–Fri. 9am–4.30pm, Sat./Sun. 9am–9pm) has won much praise for its unusual architecture and is recognised as one of the best technical and natural history museums in America. Particularly interesting is the department devoted to weather and climate, where the visitor can experience the force of a hurricane with wind-speeds of 75mph/120kph.
Seminole Cultural Center (Bobby's Seminole Indian Village)	On the eastern edge of the city, north of the Interstate 4 Highway, lies the Seminole Cultural Center (5221 North Orient Road; open: Mon.–Sat. 9am–5pm, Sun. noon–5pm), which provides background on the history and culture of the Seminoles. Indian handicrafts are on display in the adjoining Seminole village with its typical "chickees" (open wooden huts). There are also performances involving alligators and snakes.

Surroundings

A very popular excursion indeed is that which goes from Tampa to St Petersburg (see entry) and then further along Sunshine Skyway (see St Petersburg). When returning along the US 41 (see Tamiami Trail) the visitor will probably wish to stop in Ruskin or Apollo Beach, with its restaurants by the water's edge on Tampa Bay providing charming views of the Tampa skyline and of St Petersburg (see entry).

Sunshine Skyway, Ruskin, Apollo Beach

A further excursion along the US 301 to the north-east of Tampa passes through 22 miles/35km of delightful orange groves and green meadows. Here in Hillsborough River State Park will be found some unspoilt country, with dark water flowing sluggishly into the river and lush vegetation on its banks. The river is spanned by two foot-bridges and there are walks along the banks as well as a nature-trail. Canoe-trips along the river are also very popular.

★Hillsborough River State Park

In the State Park lies Fort Foster, dating from the time of the Seminole Wars. It was vacated in 1832 because of its unfavourable position, and has recently been reconstructed. Between 9am and 4pm at week-ends and on public holidays a popular programme of "Living History" is performed.

Fort Foster

A few miles further to the north-east lies the town of Zephyrhills (108ft/33m above sea-level, pop. 9000), the site of the Phoenix 12 Hills Parachute Center. Every day between October and May many parachute-jumpers can be watched as they float down. Colourful sporting events are held on Thanksgiving Day and during the Christmas and Easter holidays.

Zephyrhills

Tarpon Springs

See Pinellas Suncoast

Titusville

E 13

Orange County
Altitude: 0–20ft/0–6m
Population. 40,000

Titusville is situated on the Indian River in the Space Coast (see entry) hinterland. Its development from a small fishing port to a rapidly growing industrial town and the administrative centre of Orange County is due in no small measure to events on nearby Cape Canaveral (see entry) and Merritt Island, where the US space centre was built after the Second World War and from where space flights are now made. Many of the technicians and scientists employed with NASA and the US Air Force live in Titusville. It is also a good setting-out point both for journeys to see the space centre at Cape Canaveral (see entry) and also for excursions into Merritt Island National Wildlife Refuge and to the superb Playalinda Beach near Canaveral National Seashore (see Cape Canaveral). The many attractions in the Orlando region are also within easy reach.

Location

In the US Astronaut Hall of Fame on the NASA Parkway visitors can marvel at the various exhibits and memorabilia illustrating space flight in recent years, especially those linked with the Mercury flight programme. Audio-visual teaching aids demonstrate the part that space flight has played and continues to play in technical advances worldwide. In Space Camp children and young people can see how astronauts are trained and experience the effects of weightlessness and what it is like in a space-flight simulator. As this is always very popular it is best to book in advance. Information: US Astronaut Hall of Fame, 6225 Vector Blvd., Titusville, Florida, 32780–8040; tel. 269–6100.

US Astronaut Hall of Fame, US Space Camp

Venice   H 11

Sarasota County
Altitude: 0–20ft/0–6m
Population: 17,000

The town of Venice lies on the Gulf Coast south of Sarasota. Once an enchanting little fishing port, it enjoyed a huge boom in the 1920s when a large housing estate for retired people sprung up almost overnight. However, the 1929 Wall Street crash soon brought an abrupt end to this boom. It was 1962 before the town flourished again, when the Ringling Bros. and Barnum and Bailey circus moved its winter quarters here from Sarasota (see entry). Today Venice is a popular holiday resort, with three beautiful beaches, a number of marinas and some good fishing.

Sights

★Ringling Bros. and Barnum and Bailey Circus Winter Quarters

Since 1960 this famous circus company has had its winter quarters near the road to the local airport.
Every year around Christmas or the New Year the company puts on sparkling, often breathtaking performances by circus artistes or spectacular animal dressage events.

★Oskar Scherer State Recreation Area

The Oskar Scherer State Recreation Area, some 6 miles/10km to the north near Osprey (see Sarasota) is a small holiday resort in the marsh and beach region of the Gulf Coast where visitors can paddle canoes, fish and swim. Amateur bird-watchers come here to see the rare Florida scrub jay. In the winter white-headed eagles frequently fly round the park. Depending on the tides, South Creek can be excellent for short canoe trips. There is an interesting nature trail, and camp-fire programmes are arranged by the park ranger. In addition there is a small freshwater lake for bathers, and canoes and bicycles can be rented.

Warm Mineral Springs

The Warm Mineral Springs are situated about 14 miles/23km south-east of Venice. These springs gush out large amounts of thermal water with a high mineral content. A bath-house and various other facilities enable the springs to function as a spa.

Cyclorama

A "Cyclorama" has been built near Warm Mineral Springs, where anyone who is interested can watch audio-visual demonstrations of scenes from the life of Ponce de León (see Famous People).

Englewood

The little town of Englewood lies nearly 10 miles/16km south of Venice, with the beautiful Port Charlotte Beach nearby. Further to the south is the spot where the Spaniard de Narváez came ashore in 1528.

Vero Beach   G 14

Indian River County
Altitude: 0–23ft/0–7m
Population: 18,000

Vero Beach, on the Atlantic coast (see Spacecoast) north of Fort Pierce (see entry), is the chief town in the citrus fruit-growing region of Indian River County. The little town is also a quiet holiday resort; its charming streets lined with tropical trees and plants and the miles of beaches on the offshore islands prove attractive to visitors all the year round. It also offers golf-courses, plenty of tennis-courts and opportunities for deep-sea fishing.

Location

Some 19 miles/30km further north along the A1A this recreation area on the offshore sandy island between the Atlantic Ocean and Indian River is ideal for water-sports enthusiasts. In summer large turtles lay their eggs on this stretch of beach.

★ Sebastian Inlet State Recreation Area

Treasures salvaged from Spanish galleons sunk off the coast in 1715 are displayed in the McLarty Treasure Museum (open: Wed.–Sun. 10am–4.30pm). There is also a small ethnographic exhibition.

McLarty Treasure Museum

In February or March every year the Los Angeles Dodgers come to train in the Holman Stadium, Dodgertown (4000 Walker Ave.; tel. 569–4900 for information).

Baseball Spring Training

Wakulla Springs

See Tallahassee

Walt Disney World

F 12

Orange and Oscela Counties

By air:
Orlando International Airport, 20 miles/32km north-west; from here there are airport buses to Walt Disney World and its hotels.

Getting there

By coach:
Greyhound Coaches to Orlando. From many hotels along International Drive in Orlando or Irlo Bronson Memorial Highway (US 192) coaches run to Walt Disney World entrances to Magic Kingdom, EPCOT Center and Disney/MGM Studios.

By rail:
Amtrak to Orlando.

Highways:
Walt Disney World is easily reached by the I–4 and US 192.

The giant parking lots (fee payable) at the entrances to Magic Kingdom, the EPCOT Center and the Disney/MGM Studios will give some idea of how many people visit Walt Disney World every day. In order to be able to find your vehicle easily when you return it is best to note the number of the park and name of the area or simply the time of arrival.

General tips
When to go

Walt Disney World has more than 23 million visitors each year, with between 140,000 and 150,000 a day at peak times. Dense crowds can be expected especially during the summer months, around Thanksgiving Day (end of November), at Christmas and Easter and during the spring break from colleges and universities. At those times expect to have to join queues at some of the attractions. Magic Kingdom and the EPCOT Center attract most visitors between Monday and Friday, while Disney/MGM Studios are at their busiest from Wednesday to Friday. Guests staying at the Disney Hotel are allowed into Magic Kingdom one hour before it officially opens.

Magic Kingdom: daily 9am–6pm |
EPCOT Center: daily 9am–8pm
Disney/MGM Studios Theme Park: Sun.–Fri. 9am–9pm, Sat. 9am–10pm
   The above may stay open later in the high season and during special events.

Walt Disney World Resort Information, west of the I-4, P.O. Box 10040, Lake Buena Vista, FL 32830–1000; tel. (407) 824–4321.

Information

An extra charge is made for each theme park, although the relatively high admission charges do include free use of all the attractions, the monorail, ships, roundabouts and entrance to the various shows including the cinemas. It will probably work out cheaper to buy a "Four Day All Three Parks Passport" or a "PLUS Super Pass", which is valid for five days and allows unlimited visits to Typhoon Lagoon, River Country, Discovery Island and Pleasure Island. These special passes valid for several days also permit free travel on all railways and buses operating between the three theme parks of Magic Kingdom, EPCOT Center and Disney/MGM Studios.

Admission fees

A monorail system runs between Magic Kingdom, EPCOT Center, the Transportation and Ticket Center at the main entrance as well as some hotels and holiday complexes (including "Disney's Contemporary Resort", where it passes right through the hotel lobby), "Disney''s Polynesian Resort" and "Disney's Grand Floridinian Beach Resort".

Monorail System

Buses serve all points in Walt Disney World along routes marked with different colours.

Buses

There are various cafetarias and fast-food stands, as well as good restaurants (early reservations essential), together with stalls serving ice-creams, drinks, sweets and fruit.

Refreshments

Special signs – "Kodak Photo Spots" – mark the best places from which to take photographs. Cameras and video equipment can be rented from special shops, such as Camera Centers, Mainstreet/Town Square in Magic Kingdom, Space Ship Earth in the EPCOT Centre, Kodak Center in Disney/MGM Studios.

Photography

The opening of Walt Disney World near Orlando on October 1st 1971 marked the start of a new era for Central Florida. Whereas previously its main visitors had been people seeking peace and relaxation, the region now became what is probably the world's largest fairground. After the colossal success enjoyed by Disneyland which had been opened in Anaheim in California in 1955, Walt Disney looked in 1963 for somewhere to realise his dream of a perfect and clean leisure park. He found ideal conditions here in Central Florida; white stretches of open countryside not too far away from the holiday centres on the Florida coast, with good approach roads and a climate which meant it could remain open all the year round.

History

In 1964 the first steps were taken to purchase more than 27,500 acres/11,129ha of former swampland and bush. At that time the price was about five cents per square metre. It was the end of 1965 before it became known that the Walt Disney Corporation was behind this deal, and that it intended to construct a gigantic leisure park and amusement centre as well as a futuristic town (the EPCOT Center). Walt Disney died in 1966 before he could see his dream realised.
   The first building phase was completed in 1971, namely "Magic Kingdom" with about 50 attractions and covering an area of about 100 acres/40ha.
   Eleven years later the futuristic "EPCOT Center", with "Future World" and "World Showcase" opened its doors. Further buildings, attractions

◀ *Walt Disney World: by horse-drawn tram to Cinderella's Castle*

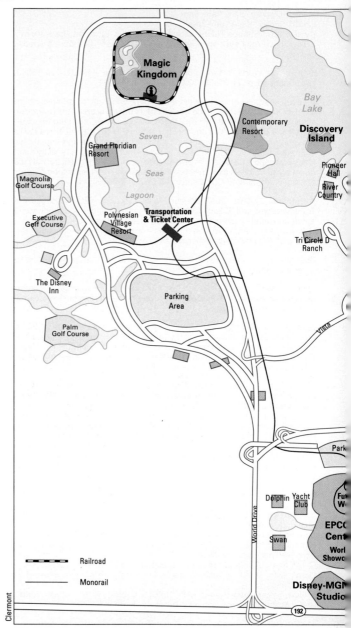

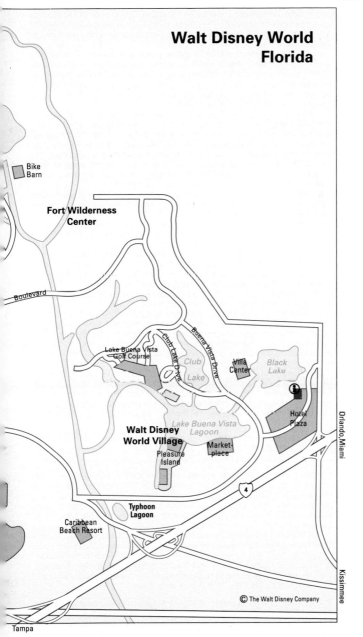

Walt Disney World
Florida

Bike Barn

Fort Wilderness Center

Boulevard

Lake Buena Vista Golf Course

Club Lake Drive

Buena Vista Drive

Club Lake

Villa Center

Black Lake

Lake Buena Vista Lagoon

Walt Disney World Village

Hotel Plaza

Pleasure Island

Market-place

Typhoon Lagoon

Caribbean Beach Resort

Orlando,Miami

Kissimmee

Tampa

© The Walt Disney Company

and holiday complexes continue to be added. The Disney/MGM Studios have been open since 1989. The Disney success story persuaded Universal Studios to set up film studios and amusements near Orlando (see entry) in the autumn of 1990.

Around the kingdom of Mickey Mouse grew up a "Vacation Kingdom", with sundry holiday centres, hotels and camp-sites. In the meantime some 12,000 hotel rooms, a small shopping centre, a conference centre, an amusement centre with a busy night-life, a small zoo, two aquaparks, several golf-courses and tennis courts and other leisure facilities too numerous to mention have all come into being.

A further holiday complex is at present taking shape south-west of EPCOT Center. In November 1990 "Disney's Yacht and Beach Club Resort" was opened on Stormalong Bay, a short distance from "International Gateway", the new entrance to "World Showcase". It boasts more than 1100 rooms, a beach of white sand, its own adventure-pool and boats for rental. The charming Fin-de-Siècle summer houses on the coast of New England served as the model for this complex. Guests can travel by water-taxi from here to the Disney/MGM Studio theme park.

In 1991 "Disney's Broadwalk" was completed, together with two further hotel complexes. This amusement area, based on those in Atlantic City and on Coney Island, covers 30 acres/12ha. Further hotel and holiday complexes are either in course of construction or in the planning stage.

The modern holiday complex known as "Port Orleans/Dixie Landing" was also completed in 1991. It is in the style of the old plantation houses or the French Quarter of New Orleans and attempts to revive the romance of the Old South and the Mississippi. Winding paths and a picturesque waterway are intended to simulate a trip along the Mississippi. Flat-bottomed boats sail to Disney Island and Pleasure Island.

By the end of this century there will be some 20,000 hotel rooms available here, and a fourth large theme park is planned.

To date about a quarter of the land bought up by the Walt Disney Company has been built on. It is currently planned that nearly 7500 acres/3000ha should be preserved as a nature reserve, and the rest will be kept in reserve for future projects. At present Walt Disney World employs more than 30,000 mainly young people of various nationalities who are constantly striving to make the "Empire of the Mouse" function perfectly.

Walt Disney World is an "ideal world" for youngsters and adults of all age groups, a gigantic and perfect "illusion machine", clean, without problems, and endless amusements (provided the queues are not too long). A giant underground labyrinth deals with all the necessary supply networks and waste removal – to have overflowing waste-bins all over the place would conflict with Walt Disney's philosophy!

★★ Magic Kingdom

Tips

It is always best to arrive as early as possible. Even if there are only short queues at the various attractions a visit to this 100 acre/40ha amusement park will still take about six hours. From the main entrance near the Transportation and Ticket Center large ferries, modelled on the old Mississippi steam-boats, carry visitors to the Magic Kingdom by way of the Seven Seas Lagoon.

The Walt Disney World Steam Railroad encompasses the "Kingdom". Until Disney World's latest water-slide, known as "Splash Mountain", was opened in 1993 this railway operated as "Goofy's Back-Track Express" between Main Street Station and Duckburg Station in Micky's Starland. Visitors are advised to travel to Duckburg Station as early as possible and then commence their tour of the park from there.

Symbol

The symbol and focal point of Magic Kingdom is Cinderella's Castle. Around it are grouped seven areas on differing themes with 45 attractions and rides as well as countless small souvenir shops and restaurants.

© The Walt Disney Company

Mickey Mouse and Co. appear everywhere, much to the delight of the children. Every day at 3pm the great Disney Hit-parade with all the well-known figures from Disney films parades through Main Street to Frontierland. A large live show is then held in front of Cinderella's Castle.

Disney Figures, Disney Hit-parade, Disneymania

Immediately behind the railway station is the start of Main Street; built in the style of the late 19th c. it boasts numerous shops and restaurants as well as Penny Arcade, with slot machines and a casino. On the right "The Walt Disney Story" gives background information about Walt Disney himself. Classic Disney strips from the silent film days are continuously shown in the Walt Disney Cinema. Visitors can ride along Main Street to the Castle in restored old vehicles, including motor-coaches, horse-drawn wagons and a fire-engine. Seats should be reserved as early as possible for the "live" Wild West Show "Diamond Horseshoe Jamboree" held near Disneyana Collectibles in Frontierland.

Main Street, USA

On the left will be found "Adventureland". Its highlights include "Pirates of the Caribbean" and "Jungle Cruise", an expedition along a river through a primeval forest with wild animals and natives.

Adventureland

The theme of Frontierland relates to the days of the pioneers and the Wild West. Its main attraction is a trip on the "Big Thunder Mountain Railroad" and also the "County Bear Jamboree". A raft takes visitors to "Tom Sawyer's Island".

Frontierland

Liberty Square brings colonial history to life. In the "Hall of Presidents" various American presidents put in an appearance. It is also possible to travel on a paddle-steamer or to visit the "Haunted Mansion".

Liberty Square

Here the visitor will meet all the fantasy characters from Walt Disney's famous films, including Snow White, Peter Pan, Captain Nemo in his submarine voyaging "20,000 Leagues Under the Sea". The cable-railway known as "Skyway" leads high above Fantasyland to "Future World".

Fantasyland

Walt Disney World

Tomorrowland

The "Space Mountain" roller coaster in "Tomorrowland" will test the strongest nerves. Other attractions here include "Starjets", "Mission to Mars", "Wedway People Mover" and "Grand Prix Raceway". A new addition is "Dreamflight", which describes the history of flight and explains supersonic flight.

Micky's Starland

"Micky's Starland" (formerly "Micky's Birthdayland") stands against a backcloth of the world-famous Walt Disney comic figures. Performances of "Micky's Magical TV World" are well worth watching.

★★ EPCOT Center

EPCOT – Experimental Prototype Community of Tomorrow – is the somewhat more technical counterpart of Magic Kingdom. The attractions on this 262 acre/105ha site relate to technology past and future. Visitors can travel round the world, while the "Future World" exhibition claims to forecast future discoveries in science and technology and to enter the world of the 21st c. "World Showcase" presents a permanent world exhibition. On a 1¼ mile/2km-long promenade along World Showcase Lagoon eleven different countries are at present represented by exhibitions of their architecture and culture, shops selling wares typical of the country concerned, restaurants in which visitors can try various national culinary delicacies, together with amusements of all kinds.

Tip

To avoid unnecessarily long waits at the attractions near the entrance to "Future World", such as "Spaceship Earth", visitors are recommended to start their tour here in the morning, after having armed themselves with informative material from the World Key Information System in Spaceship Earth and, if necessary, booked seats for their evening meal in one of the thirteen restaurants, because these are generally fully booked by early afternoon.

World Showcase

There are various learning programmes arranged for English-speaking children and young people. Visitors over sixteen years of age can take part in guided tours lasting two, three or four hours through the "World Showcase" exhibition, which will give them a look behind the scenes together with detailed information on various aspects of culture, architecture and horticulture; an additional charge is made for these tours, and further information can be obtained and bookings made by telephoning 407/345–5860.

Disney Learning Programs, Gardens of the World, Hidden Treasures of World Showcase

Much can be learned about Mexico and Central America during a small boat-trip on the "River of Time".
    The North European state of Norway offers an adventurous voyage on a Viking ship through the "maelstrom".
    The Circle Vision 360 cinema illustrates the Wonders of China.
    There is also a German "Biergarten" with a permanent "Oktoberfest" atmosphere.

Italy has its Venetian gondolas and St Mark's Square, together with performances of the Commedia dell'Arte, while "The American Adventure" portrays the history of America.
    Other exhibitions relate to Japan, Morocco, France, Great Britain and Canada.

In the near future there will be exhibitions dealing with the former Soviet Union (now the Confederation of Independent States) and Switzerland. Towering above the Swiss Village will be a "Matterhorn" from which a roller coaster will roar down, just like the one in Disneyland in California. The highlights of every evening are the enormous firework and laser displays along the World Showcase Lagoon, known as the "IllumiNations", accompanied by classical music.

IllumiNations

Mickey Mouse outside the film studios

The World Showcase

★Future World

Concept

"Future World" concerns itself with scientific discoveries and achievements. The main attractions include "Spaceship Earth", a 177ft/54m-high
sphere which is the symbol of EPCOT and which portrays developments in
human communications from Stone Age cave-drawings to satellite technology (presented by AT & T), "Communicore" (computer), behind that
"Universe of Energy" (sponsored by Exxon), "Wonders of Life" (sponsor
Metropolitan Life), "Horizons" (sponsor General Electric) with a journey
into the 21st c., "World of Motion" (sponsor General Motors) which looks
back over the development of transport, "World of Imagination" (sponsor
Kodak) with "Captain Eo", a 3-D musical with Michael Jackson in the Magic
Eyes Theater, "The Land" (sponsor Kraft) and "The Living Seas" (sponsor
United Technologies Co.), a giant marine aquarium with more than 80
different species of fish, including sharks, and aquatic mammals, including
manatees and dolphins.

A pavilion at present in course of construction will shortly offer a new
adventure trip in which modern systems and special effects will simulate a
journey into outer space and the cosmos.

★Disney/MGM Studios

Opened in 1989, the latest theme park is known as Disney/MGM Studios, a
genuine television and film studio with regular productions together with
an amusement park. With luck the visitor may be able to watch a TV show
being recorded. Included in the price is a Backstage Studio Tour, lasting
one and a half hours. The latest attraction is an adventure film based on the
Disney box-office hit "Honey, I've shrunk the kids"; the visitor enters an
overgrown back-yard with a miniature Liliputian world and sees everything
as a tiny child would. Children in particular have great fun in this adventure
playground with its climbing-frames and slides.

EPCOT Center: Spaceship Earth

Catastrophe
Canyon

**Disney-MGM
Studios**

Theme Park

The Backlot

Earffel Tower
Water tower

Let's make
a Deal
(Soundstage I)
Production
Center
Soundstage II
Soundstage III
The Great
Movie Ride

Star Tours

The Monster
Sound Show
Superstar
Television

Here come
the Muppets
Backstage
Studio Tour
The Magic of
Disney Animation

Indiana Jones
Epic Stunt
Spectacular

Hollywood
Boulevard

Crossroads
of the World

Entrance Plaza

Parking

© The Walt Disney Company

Almost a second Hollywood has thus grown up here in Florida, with the famous Hollywood and Sunset Boulevard as well as Mann's Chinese Theater crossed by "The Great Movie Ride", one of the amusement complex's major attractions.

The most popular American TV shows can be seen on Superstar Television, while extraordinary sound-effects are produced in the "Monster Sound Show". In "Sound Works" members of the audience can appear with Roger Rabbit. The exciting Indiana Jones Stunt Spectacular can be watched in the "Backlot Annex" and "Star Tours" offers a thrilling space adventure with the aid of highly-developed flight-simulation techniques, the whole based on the successful George Lucas film "Star Wars".

Second Hollywood

Discovery Island

On ten acres/four hectares of land between Disney's Contemporary Resort and Fort Wilderness Resort & Campground lies Discovery Island. There is a small zoological garden here, and it is on this island that scarlet ibis have their largest breeding colony in the United States.

Ferries transport visitors to the island from Magic Kingdom and various Disney resorts. It is open to visitors from 10am to dusk.

Location

River Country

The River Country leisure complex is a superb pool in natural surroundings near Bay Lake, where visitors can relax after the somewhat exhausting time spent in the theme parks. There are trams from the River Country car park, boats from Magic Kingdom or buses from the Ticket and Transportation Center.

Open: daily 10am–6pm; in summer there is a reduced admission charge after 3pm.

Typhoon Lagoon

Near Disney Village Market Place will be found Typhoon Lagoon, a second adventure pool under palm trees. It has eight water-chutes or flumes, a large pool covering an area of 9600sq.yd/8000sq.m, with artificial waves and breakers, "Shark Reef", a man-made salt-water reef for snorkelling and diving (snorkels and wet-suits can be hired) and white-water canoeing along the winding Castaway Creek. The bathing-pool and play area at Ketchakiddie Creek was built in a novel way for children. Open: daily 10am–5pm, longer in summer.

Disney Village Marketplace

To serve the various Disney World holiday complexes a small shopping centre with restaurants and boutiques, some quite high-class, has opened up near Buena Vista Lagoon. There are also shops selling sports items and souvenirs (open: daily 10am–10pm). During the summer season a number of events are held on the Dock Stage in Captain's Tower. Small motor-boats and pedalos can be rented at the marina. Disney Village Marketplace is linked by footbridge to the restaurant and amusement complex on Pleasure Island.

Pleasure Island

A glittering "Sylvester Party" is held every evening on Pleasure Island, with fireworks, dancing and confetti. It lasts until the early hours and takes place on the cobbled streets and in the six night-clubs; anyone under 18 must be accompanied by an adult and there is an admission fee in the evening. The latest films are continually being shown in the ten cinemas.

Winter Haven   F 12

Polk County
Altitude: 170ft/52m
Population: 25,000

See Map pp. 290/91

Winter Haven, founded in Central Florida in 1883, is the second largest town in Polk County, a region known mainly for its cultivation of citrus fruit. Winter Haven is also the place where visitors to the nearby Cypress Gardens (see below) usually choose to spend the night.

The town is also known as "City of the Lakes" and there are plenty of places in the vicinity in which to spend a holiday. Florida's other sights and attractions are all within easy reach.

Florida Citrus Festival and Polk County Fair

In February Winter Haven hosts the quite colourful Florida Citrus Festival, together with an exhibition and a large programme of entertainment.

★Cypress Gardens

Location

The wonderful Cypress Gardens, a combination of botanical gardens and leisure park, stretch some 4 miles/6km south-west of Winter Haven along the SR 540. It was here that the world's first water-skiing spectacular was held in the 1940s (see below).

A peacock in flowers in Cypress Gardens

American water-ski pyramid

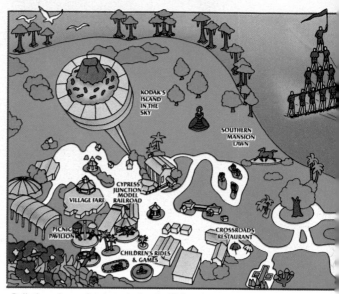

Opening times	Daily 9am–6pm, often later during the high season.
History	Opened in 1936, Cypress Gardens were the first tourist attraction in Central Florida. The furniture-maker Richard D. Pope, who was particularly keen on plants, boats and running, had spent a part of his youth in Winter Haven and made his name as an organiser of regattas on the local lakes. In the 1930s he laid out some botanical gardens on swampland near lake Eloise.

The world-famous water-ski show, still one of the park's main attractions, came into being almost by chance during the Second World War. Having seen a newspaper report about it some soldiers stationed nearby came here in 1943 to see the show described in the report. Caught somewhat unawares, Pope's children and some of their friends were quickly assembled and they put on the first show. It received such acclaim that the next weekend several hundred interested people wanted to see it, and from this improvised beginning "The Greatest American Show on Earth" quickly came into being.

After the Second World War Hollywood film moguls discovered Cypress Gardens and films such as "On an Island with You" or "Easy to Love" were shot here. The opening of Disney World nearby produced a fresh flood of visitors to Cypress Gardens.

Since 1989 the Gardens and Sea World have belonged to the Busch Entertainment Group.

Attractions	There are more than 8000 species of plants from all over the world to be seen on the 227 acre/90ha site. Arrangements of gardenias, roses, bougainvillaeas, hibiscus and chrysanthemums ("mum flowers") are a delight to the eye. At some especially picturesque points, such as Gazebo Hill, pose "Southern Belles", young ladies dressed in the costume of the Old South.

There is a fine view of the whole complex to be had from "Island in the Sky", a viewing tower 154ft/47m high. The model town "Southern Cross-

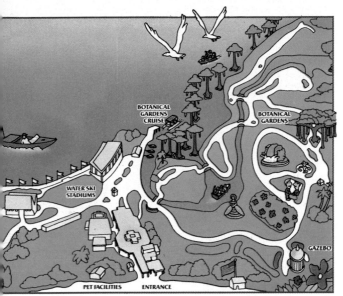

roads" commemorates the period before the American Civil War. Small shops and restaurants give it a Colonial atmosphere. Various revues are performed in the "Cypress Theater". There is a giant model railway lay-out in "Cypress Junction".

Other attractions include a bird and alligator show, the star of which is Barney, a macaw which drives a jeep, as well as "Animal Forest", a small zoo, and the "Fly Free" bird-house with many exotic birds. Numerous wild birds nest here too, such as silver, grey and green herons and sea eagles. Children will enjoy "Critter Encounter", a zoo where they can stroke the animals. Electric boats (J. C. Pontoon Lake Cruises) take visitors along artificial canals.

Every November the displays of beautifully coloured chrysanthemums at the Mum Festival attract a lot of visitors.

Mum Festival

Developments in water-skiing are displayed in the Water Ski Museum (799 Overlook Drive South East; open: Mon.–Fri. 10am–5pm). Famous figures in this sport are commemorated in the adjoining Hall of Fame.

Water Ski Museum and Hall of Fame

Surroundings

Almost 21 miles/34km north (I–4/US 27) lies Baseball City, with its large Baseball Stadium and various training facilities. Baseball games are played here all the year round. The adjoining amusement park (previously known as "Boardwalk and Baseball" or "Circus, Circus") is closed at present.

Baseball City

On the way to Tampa a small detour leads to the town of Mulberry (21 miles/34km south-west on the US 60). For a long time Mulberry was the phosphate-mining centre of the region. Ten million years ago Florida as we know it today was covered by an ocean. In the sediment left by this ocean

Mulberry Phosphate Museum

various phosphates (marine animal excrement, organic remains) were deposited, later to be covered by massive layers of sand and clay. In the Mulberry Phosphate Museum (SR 37; open: Tues.–Sat. 10am–4.30pm) there is much of interest to be learned about phosphate mining. There is also a comprehensive collection of fossils.

Grenelefe

About 19 miles/30km north-east of Winter Haven lies Grenelefe Resort, which boasts one of America's most beautiful golf courses.

Haines City

At a major road junction 10 miles/16km north-east of Winter Haven lies the little town of Haines City (160ft/49m above sea-level, pop. 12,000). This lively little place at the foot of "The Ridge" is in the very heart of the countryside where most of Florida's lemon plantations are to be found. In recent years electronics and tourism have also played quite an important part in the region's economy.

Zephyrhills

See Tampa

In the kingdom of Walt Disney ▶

Practical Information

Accommodation

See Camping, Hotels and Motels, Youth Hostels

Air Travel

Most visitors to Florida travelling from Europe go by air, entering the Sunshine State at Miami, Fort Lauderdale, Orlando or Tampa.

Airports

International airports

Miami Airport is a major international destination which in 1990 handled around 24 million passengers. It has daily scheduled flights from all the major European airports.

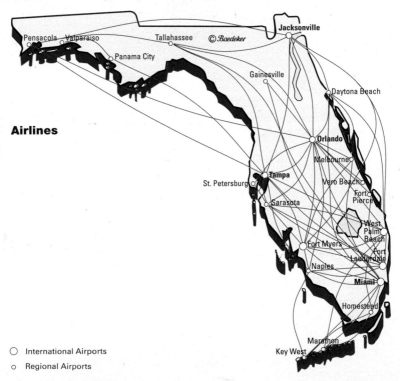

Airlines

○ International Airports

o Regional Airports

En route to Florida

Fort Lauderdale, Orlando and Tampa are Florida's other main airports for international flights, and especially charter services. Fort Myers and Tallahassee have also recently become easy to get to from Europe by air.

Florida has regional and local airports with good connections into America's domestic airline network. They also handle a great deal of private and commercial traffic.

Regional and local airports

The kind of services the American airports offer are well up to international standards. On arrival, however, you may have a long wait to recover your luggage and get through immigration controls, especially at Miami.

Waiting times

Airlines

All the major US airlines, such as American Airlines, Delta Air Lines, United Airlines and USAir, fly into Florida's main airports. Some of them also have international services, with good connections to European destinations.

US airlines

European airlines with scheduled services to Miami include Air France, British Airways, KLM and Lufthansa, and there are several flights a day from London's Gatwick and Heathrow. Charter flights and package tours also operate in and out of Miami, Fort Lauderdale, Orlando and Tampa.

European airlines

Air fares on the trans-Atlantic routes and inside America are in a state of considerable confusion and it pays to check for any special fare deals before booking. There are very good rates for young people, students and senior citizens. The most expensive time to travel is at weekends, in peak holiday periods, and at holiday weekends. Transatlantic passengers on American airlines can take advantage of cheaper rates for round trips and excursions. Information about these can be had from reputable travel agents and the airlines themselves.

Air fares

Alcohol

Private pilots

Pilot's licence,
flight permit

Holders of a pilot's licence and the British radio-operator permit can rent planes in Florida provided they can pass a test. Ask locally for further information.

Alcohol

Warning

Alcohol may not be sold to anyone under 21. Spirits can normally only be bought in licensed liquor stores. Alcoholic beverages may not be sold before 1pm on a Sunday. Consumption of alcohol is forbidden in public recreational areas such as on the beach or in State Parks.

Drinking and driving is severely punished, and there is a ban on carrying open, or empty, cans or bottles that are holding, or have held, alcohol anywhere in a car, including the boot (or trunk, as it is called in the States).

Amusement Parks

Florida has many amusement parks. They differ in size, and descriptions of the largest can be found in the A to Z section of the guide under the heading of the particular place or attraction where they are located.

Art Galleries

Many notable galleries exist in larger places and the traditional tourist centres such as Miami, Miami Beach, Coral Gables, Coconut Grove, Key West, Fort Lauderdale, Palm Beach, St Augustine, Fernandina Beach, Naples, Fort Myers, Sarasota and Tampa.

Banks

See Currency

Bathing Beaches

Florida is justly famous for the crystal clear waters and fine sands of its bays and beaches. They may get more crowded, especially at weekends, near the big hotels and residential areas, but it is also relatively easy to get away from it all by boat to the remoter spots for a good swim. Many hotels have their own swimming pools, often filled with freshwater.

Ocean breakers

The Atlantic coast of Florida is always likely to have a very high swell with some strong breakers.

Naturism

See entry

Waterskiing

Waterski enthusiasts can hire boats and equipment at many of the beach hotels and bigger tourist centres.

Snorkelling

The relatively shallow lagoons between the islands and offshore reefs are particularly good for snorkelling, and are full of all kinds of wonderfully colourful corals, fish and shellfish. Pollution and over-fishing have led to the creation of marine sanctuaries around some of the islands to protect the sealife from further destruction.

Because the water is so clear the conditions for underwater photography and filming are excellent.

When out snorkelling it is easy to forget that the combination of saltwater and tropical sun can soon result in serious sunburn, so it is sensible to wear a cotton T-shirt or shirt. Beware of touching anything strange with bare hands – it could be a stinging jellyfish – and wear strong rubber gloves if necessary. Do not put your hands in hollows in the coral. When walking along the water's edge beware of hidden sting-rays (see Facts and Figures, Flora and Fauna). *(margin: Dangers)*

In many places collecting sea creatures is forbidden. In any case this is necessary to avoid upsetting the delicate natural balance of the marine environment.

See entry. *(margin: Diving)*

Florida's best beaches

Florida has over 1000 miles/1600km of beaches, and the best of them have been opened up for tourism.

The Gulf Coast undoubtedly has the best bathing beaches. Many of these have fine quartz sand, particularly along the Gulf Island Seashore in the north, on the Pinellas Suncoast, and around Sarasota, Fort Myers and Naples. *(margin: Gulf Coast)*

The Atlantic Coast has mainly firm to hard beaches, especially in the north between Daytona, where you can drive a car on the sands, and the Georgia *(margin: Atlantic Coast)*

On Vanderbilt Beach near Naples

State Border. The beaches on the Gold Coast between Palm Beach and Miami have been eaten away by erosion in recent decades, and around Palm Beach, Fort Lauderdale, Miami Beach, etc. measures have had to be taken to prevent further loss of sand.

Florida Keys

The beaches around the Florida Keys are relatively few and far between, and quite small, too, but they provide a good base for some excellent snorkelling.

The following list gives some of the best beaches.

Amelia Island	Amelia Island Plantation, Fernandina Beach
Bradenton	Bradenton Beach
Crystal Beach	Crystal Beach Wayside Park
Dania	John U. Lloyd Beach State Recreation Area
Englewood	Port Charlotte Beach
Florida Keys	Bahia Honda State Recreation Area and Key West beaches
Fort Lauderdale	Fort Lauderdale Beach Area
Fort Myers	Fort Myers Beach
Fort Walton	Fort Walton Beach Area
Gulf Islands	Gulf Islands National Seashore, Fort Walton Beach, Fort Pickens Recreation Area
Longboat Key	Beer Can Beach
Miami Beach	Beaches along Ocean Drive, in front of the Fontainebleau Hilton, at Litmus Park and Pier Park (southern tip of Miami Beach)
Miami	Key Biscayne beaches
Naples	Delnor Wiggins Pass State Recreation Area, Vanderbilt Beach
Palm Beach	Palm Beach Area
Panama City	Panama City Beach Area
Pensacola	Gulf Islands National Seashore beaches
Pinellas Suncoast	Caladesi Island State Park, Clearwater's beaches, St Petersburg Beach, Dunedin, Indian Rocks Beach, Madeira Beach
Sanibel Island	All the beaches on Sanibel Island, but especially Bowman's Beach
Sarasota	A number of Sarasota's beaches, including Siesta Beach, which has particularly fine sand
Space Coast	New Smyrna beaches, Cocoa Beach and Melbourne Beach
Venice	Venice Beach

Boating

Florida will appeal to anyone who enjoys boating, sailing or canoeing. The Atlantic and Gulf Coasts, not to mention the lakes and inland waterways, provide plenty of scope for all kinds of waterborne activities. As the map of Florida's main waterways and canoeing routes shows, you can sail round the state on the Intracoastal Waterway or cross it on the Okeechobee Waterway. And there is plenty of adventure to be had, negotiating mangroves, swamps, coral islands, complete with crystal-clear waters and sleepy lagoons, and encountering the rich wildlife of birds, beasts and insects along the way.

The local tourist information centres (see Information, Chambers of Commerce) and national and state parks (see entry) can supply information on the navigability of particular parts of the route, and supply current lists of reputable boat rental agencies.

Boat Trips

Boat trips in Florida range from exploring the Everglades by airboat to cruising down the St John's River, dining and being entertained on a Mississippi steamboat. Many of the tourist resorts offer all kinds of excur-

Waterways

CANOEING STRETCHES
1 Perdido River
2 Coldwater Creek
3 Sweetwater/Juniper Creeks
4 Blackwater River
5 Yellow River
6 Shoal River
7 Holmes Creek
8 Econfina Creek
9 Chipola River
10 Ochlockonee River (Oberlauf)
11 Ochlockonee River (Unterlauf)
12 Sopchoppy River
13 Wakulla River
14 Wacissa River
15 Aucilla River
16 Withlacoochee River (Nord)
17 Suwannee River
18 St. Mary's River
19 Santa Fe River
20 Pellicen Creek
21 Bulow Creek
22 Tomoka River
23 Spruce Creek
24 Wekiva River
25 Econlockhatchee River
26 Withlacoochee River (Süd)
27 Pithlachascotee River

CANOEING STRETCHES
(continued)
28 Alafia River
29 Little Manatee River
30 Upper Manatee River
31 Peace River
32 Loxahatchee River
33 Hickey's Creek
34 Estero River
35 Blackwater/Royal Palm Hammock Creek

BOATING STRETCHES
36 Okeechobee Waterway
37 Fort Pierce - Miami
38 Miami - Key West
39 Port Canaveral Lock & Canal
40 Fernandina - Fort Pierce
41 St. John's River
42 Cross-Florida Barge Channel
43 Anclote - Fort Myers
44 Bay Section, Anclote - Carabelle
45 Apalachicola, Chattahoochee & Flint Rivers
46 Apalachicola, Chattahoochee & Flint Rivers
47 Carrabelle - Pensacola

sions, especially on the Intracoastal Waterway, around Miami and along the Pinellas Suncoast.

Houseboats

Houseboats can be rented on the St John's River and in the Everglades. Again, information can be had from the local tourist information centres. Some of these information points are listed below:

DeLand
(St John's River)

Hontoon Landing Marina, 2317 River Ridge Rd., Deland; tel. (904) 734–24 24, 1–800–458–24 74 (freephone throughout the USA), 1–800–248–24 74 (freephone in Florida only)

Go Vacation Houseboat Rentals, 2280 Hontoon Dr., Deland; tel. (904) 736–94 22, 1–800–262–34 54 (freephone in Florida only)

Sanford
(St John's River)

Sanford Boat Rentals, 4370 Carraway Place, Sanford, FL 32771; tel. (407) 321–5906, 1–800–237–5105 (freephone in Florida only)

Everglades

Tel. 1–800–325–35 35 (freephone)

Sailing

There are plenty of marinas all round the Florida peninsula where boats can be rented for a sailing trip. The most popular areas for sailing are the waters between Miami and the Bahamas, around the Florida Keys, and some parts of the Gulf Coast. For more detailed information contact the local tourist information service (see Information).

Canoeing

Canoeing trips are possible on many of Florida's inland waterways, but it is essential to make the proper preparations. Above all, take precautions for dealing with the insects and the various hazards that can be met with in the wild. It is also easy to get lost in the maze of waterways, so tell the canoe rental people, or the park authorities if in one of the parks, your destination and planned route.

Information

Department of Natural Resources, Division of Recreation & Parks, 3900 Commonwealth Blvd., Tallahassee, FL 32399–3000; tel (904) 487–3671. They can supply maps and descriptions of Florida's canoe trails, plus other useful items of reference. These include Recreational Trail System (Canoe Trail Maps), the Canoe Liveries & Outfitters Directory, and a leaflet entitled Canoe Resources.

Canoe Rentals (a selection)

Arcadia

Canoe Outpost, Rt. 7, Box 301, Arcadia, FL 33821; tel. (813) 494–12 15
Canoe Safari Inc., P.O. Box 1787, Arcadia, FL 33821; tel. (813) 494–78 65

Key Largo

America Outdoors, US 1, Mile Marker 97 1/2. Rt. 1, P.O. Box 38A; tel. (305) 852–80 54

Little Manatee
River

Little Manatee Canoe Outpost, 18001 US 301 S., Wimauma, FL 335987; tel. (813) 634–22 28

Live Oak
Suwannee River

The Spirit of the Suwannee (Campground), US 129 North, Rt. 1, P.O. Box 98, Live Oak, FL 32060; tel. (904) 364–16 83

Chipola River Canoe Trails, Curtis & Anna Harcus, P.O. Box 621, Marianna, FL 32446; tel. (904) 482–49 48   Marianna

Adventures Unlimited, Tomahawk Landing (SR 87), Rt. 6, P.O. Box 283, Milton, FL 32570; tel. (904) 623–61 97, (904) 626–16 69   Milton
Blackwater Canoe Rental, Rt. 16, P.O. Box 72, Milton, FL 32570
Bob's Canoes, ST 191, Route & P.O. Box 34, Milton, FL 32570

Canoe Outpost, P.O. Box 188, SR 476, Nobleton, FL 33554; tel. (904) 796–43 43   Nobleton

Oklawaha Outposts (SR 316), Rt. 1, P.O. Box 1462, Ft. McCoy, FL 32637; tel. (904) 236–46 06   Ocala National Forest

Katie's Wekiva River Landing Inc., 190 Katie's Cove (FL 32771)   Sanford

Business Hours

See Opening Times

Bus Travel

Greyhound and Trailways both generally provide a comfortable way to travel in buses fitted with all the usual facilities. They have connections between all Florida's main towns and cities and tourist centres, with major bus terminals in Daytona, Fort Lauderdale, Jacksonville, Key West, Miami, Orlando, Sarasota, Tallahasse, Tampa and West Palm Beach.   Greyhound/ Trailways

Greyhound's Ameripass, valid for 4, 7, 15 or 30 days, can also be used for travel round Florida, but can only be purchased outside the USA.   Greyhound Ameripass

Information in the UK can be obtained from: Information
Greyhound World Travel Ltd., Sussex House, London Road, East Grinstead, West Sussex RH19 1LD; tel. (0342) 317317
The address to contact in the States for more detailed information is:
Greyhound/Trailways, P.O. Box 660362, Dallas, TX 75266–0362; tel. (214) 419–39 05; fax (214) 715–70 29.

Camping

Florida has over 200 campsites. Most of them have good facilities and it is also possible to rent mobile homes and chalets at some of them. Camp sites are very busy in the peak holiday season and at holiday weekends, so it is extremely advisable to reserve a site well in advance.

Camping on anywhere but official sites is forbidden in the United States. Permits to camp elsewhere must be obtained from the authorities at the place in question.   Ban on off-site camping

Florida Campground Association, 1638 N. Plaza Drive, Tallahassee, FL 32308–5364; tel. (904) 656–88 78   Information

The local Chamber of Commerce or Division of Tourism can also supply information on camping.

Campground Directory	Every year the Florida Campground Association (see above) also publishes the Florida Campground Directory, which is obtainable free of charge.
Reservations, information	Freephone in Florida: 1–800–FLA–CAMP

Canoeing

See Boating

Car Rental

Rates	Anyone wanting to explore Florida for themselves can hire a car, and there are plenty of car rental firms offering cars at quite low rates, especially by the week. However, don't be misled by the cheap basic rate. Make sure that full insurance cover is included (third party, comprehensive, etc.), since proper insurance can be quite expensive.
Guarantee	Car rental firms will only hire out cars against some kind of guarantee. In many cases you can only get a car on presentation of a credit card.
Driving licence, age limit	Drivers must be over 21 and be able to produce a valid national or international driver's licence.

Car Rental Firms (selection)

All reputable car rental firms have a freephone service, and can take bookings on these 800 numbers. They can be found in the local telephone directory. The following list gives the Florida numbers for the major car rental agencies. Almost all of them also have offices at the international airports, as well as in the larger hotels, holiday resorts and downtown areas.

Alamo	Bookings: tel. 1–800–327–9633 (freephone)
Avis	Bookings: tel. 1–800–331–1212 (freephone)
Budget	Bookings: tel. 1–800–527–0700 (freephone)
Dollar	Bookings: tel. 1–800–822–1181 (in Florida); 800–800–400 (in US) (freephone)
Hertz	Bookings: tel. 1–800–654–3131 (freephone)
National	Bookings: tel. 1–800–CAR–RENT (freephone)
Thrifty	Bookings: tel. 1–800–367–2277 (freephone)
Value	Bookings: tel. 1–800–327–2501 (freephone)

Chemists

Drugstores	American drugstores differ from the usual European chemists in that they are more like a small general store, and dispensing medicines on prescription represents only a small part of their business.

Every hotel room will have a copy of the Yellow Pages in which you can find the address and telephone number of the nearest drugstore.

Yellow Pages

Outside normal opening hours there is no special chemist emergency service. In an emergency you have to go to the nearest hospital. These are open 24 hours a day and have a dispensary on the premises.

Emergency service

Drugstores and pharmacies are usually open 9am–6pm. Some of them also stay open until 9pm and later.

Opening times

Clothing

Casual wear is the order of the day in Florida. As a rule all that is needed is comfortable summer clothing, preferably in easy-to-wear natural fibres. It can become quite chilly in the winter (November to March) so it is sensible to take something warmer as well, such as a jacket or a sweater. Casual resort attire is acceptable in the evening.

Visitors are expected to dress more formally on many of the cruises and in the better restaurants and hotels. When booking a table it is wise to check up on the dress code. Remember to pack beach wear (there is no sunbathing in the nude in Florida), a light raincoat and protection against the sun.

Consulates

See Diplomatic Representation

Crime

See Safety and Crime

Cruises

Many visitors to Florida take a cruise to the Bahamas or the West Indies. Miami handles well over 3 million passengers a year and claims to be "the Cruise Capital of the World".

Cruise Ports

Port of Miami, on the Atlantic at Biscayne Bay, and home port for nine cruise lines. Port of call for many foreign cruise ships.

Miami

Atlantic port between Miami and Fort Lauderdale, home base and port of call for 15 cruise lines.

Port Everglades

Port of Palm Beach, on the Atlantic, home base and port of call for four cruise lines.

Palm Beach

On the Atlantic, about 47 miles/75km east of Orlando. Home port for two cruise lines and port of call for many other vessels.

Port Canaveral

Port Tampa
On Tampa Bay in the Gulf of Mexico and port of call for Holland America Line and Regency Cruises.

Currency

US dollar
The unit of currency in the States is the US dollar. Banknotes (dollar bills) are in denominations of $1, $2, $5, $10, $20, $50 and $100, and as they are all the same shape and colour they should be kept separately.

There are 100 cents to the dollar, and the coins in circulation are 1 cent (or penny), 5 cents (nickel), 10 cents (dime), 25 cents (quarter), very occasionally 50 cents (half-dollar), and 1 dollar.

The dollar rate can be very variable against most foreign currencies. It is best to change money before leaving home and make sure you have enough small change (coins and small bills) since the rate of exchange is better in Europe than in America.

Currency regulations
Generally speaking there is no limit on the amount of foreign or US currency that can be taken in or out of America, but to take in more than $10,000 a customs declaration form must be filled in before arrival and handed in on entry.

There are banks at the international airports which will exchange currency for US dollars, and usually it is no problem exchanging money at banks in tourist resorts. It is best to avoid doing so in hotels since they offer a lower rate of exchange than the banks.

Traveller's cheques
The safest course is to buy American Express or traveller's cheques before departure. These are readily cashed by banks, hotels and restaurants on production of a passport. Keep a record of them with the receipt. These should be retained separately so that they can be produced if the cheques are lost or stolen which will facilitate immediate replacement by an office of the issuing authority.

Credit cards
Hotel and restaurants are quite prepared for bills to be charged to credit cards, as are stores for larger purchases. The best known – and hence most acceptable – are American Express, Mastercard (Eurocard), Visa, Diner's Club and Carte Blanche. Charge cards can also be used to pay for air travel. When renting a car a credit card is essential – cash is not welcome.

Banks
Florida has a very well organised banking system. There are many branches of the principal American banks and local money institutions, and virtually any major shopping centre will have at least one bank. Since tourism is so well catered for there will usually be no problem getting banks to change sterling.

Opening times
Banks are usually open from 8.30am to 3 or 3.30pm and on Fridays until 6pm. The only banks open at weekends and on public holidays are at the international airports.

Customs Regulations

Customs regulations governing entry into the USA and re-entry into Europe are currently under review so it is advisable to check before departure with the nearest US consulate or the appropriate customs authorities on what regulations are actually in force.

Entry into the USA
On arrival a customs declaration and a form for the entry permit must be completed.

Items that may be taken in duty-free are those for personal use, i.e. clothing, toilet articles, jewellery, cameras and camcorders, film, binoculars, portable typewriters, radios, TV sets, and cassette-players, sporting equipment, motor vehicles (for up to 1 year); adults may take in 1 quart of wine or spirits, 200 cigarettes or 100 cigars or 3 lbs of tobacco, plus presents up to the value of $100, including, for adults, up to 1 gallon of wines or spirits and 100 cigars.

The duty-free allowance on return to a European Union country directly from the States includes all the personal items taken out (see above), 200 cigarettes or 100 cigarillos or 50 cigars or 250g tobacco, 1 litre of spirits over 22% alcohol or 2 litres spirits below 22% or 2 litres sparkling wine, plus 2 litres wine, 250g coffee or 100g instant coffee, 100g tea or 40g instant tea, 50g perfume, 0.25 litres toilet water (tobacco and alcohol only if aged over 17, coffee if over 15).

Re-entry to
the EU

Diplomatic Representation

The nearest Consulates are:

845 Third Avenue, New York; tel. (212) 752–8400
225 Peachtree Street, N.E. Atlanta, Georgia; tel. (404) 524–5856

United Kingdom

1251 Avenue of the Americas, New York; tel. (212) 586–2400

Canada

636 5th Avenue, New York; tel. (212) 245–4000

Australia

Suite 530, 630 5th Avenue, New York; tel. (212) 586–0060

New Zealand

Disabled Access

See Help for the Disabled

Diving

Florida's waters have always been considered a diver's paradise. The turquoise sea is still amazingly clear, particularly around the less inhabited islands, many of them protected in whole or in part by coral reefs, those especially sensitive and wonderfully colourful underwater gardens built up over the years by millions of tiny calcereous organisms. There are the shipwrecks, too, some of them Spanish treasure galleons, resting on the seabed and attracting treasure seekers from all over the world.

The rapid rate of marine pollution, destruction by holiday developments of the mangroves which serve as nurseries for many of the sea creatures, and thoughtless action of many scuba-divers and sporting fishermen have also led to what is clearly a drastic reduction of the myriad forms of undersea life that only a few decades ago were still to be found in Florida's waters. In some places the seabed and coastal waters have been designated marine sanctuaries and diving made subject to strict regulation. Divers may only enter the water at specifically marked places, and in some cases only follow prescribed trails in a group. Many places have a ban on hunting or taking sea creatures, and particularly endangered habitats are either out of bounds or may only be visited with special permission.

Nature
conservation

Dangerous marine life	It is worth remembering that there are several more poisonous sea creatures in tropical than in temperate waters. Fire corals, sea anemones, and jellyfish (including the Portuguese man of war) can give a very nasty sting; sea urchin spines are poisonous and break off easily; scorpion and stone fish have venom in their fins, and moray eels, rays, barracudas, and sharks can also threaten danger. This means that before diving in unfamiliar waters it is best to find out all about them, and what the situation is regarding underwater hunting – harpoon guns are banned in many places.
Scuba diving	Florida has well-equipped diving centres, which are particularly popular with tourists who arrive by air. Visitors with their own aqualung may have to get an adaptor to use cylinders with a different kind of connection. As a rule proof of ability has to provided when renting this kind of equipment.
Diving areas	The best area for diving is around the Florida Keys. There are good diving facilities on Big Pine Key and Cudjoe Key, at Islamorada, on Key Largo, Key West and Looe Key and at Tavernier. Particularly interesting areas for diving are to be found in Key Biscayne National Park, Key Largo Coral Reef Preserve, John Pennekamp Underwater Park and around the small coral islands between Marathon and Key West. There is some good diving off the Gulf Island National Seashore, on the Gulf Coast of the Panhandle, and Destin, Fort Walton Beach, Panama City and Pensacola all have diving facilities. Diving is also possible in some of the inland pools and lakes where places such as Live Oak and High Springs also offer diving facilities.
Underwater hotel	The world's first underwater hotel is just outside Key Largo: Jules Undersea Lodge, Shoreland Dr., Key Largo, FL 33037, tel. (305) 451–2353.

Driving Licence

See Motoring

Electricity

110 volts AC	In Florida, as in the rest of the United States, the electricity supply is at 110 volts (60Hz) AC. Visitors from Europe should get a plug adaptor in advance if they want to use their own electrical appliances, since plugs are the standard two-flat-prong American type. Adaptors can also be bought in Florida in the Appliances department of an appropriate store.

Emergencies

Dial 911	For police, fire, or a medical emergency dial 911.
1–800–336–HELP	The 1–800–336–HELP number is an all-America helpline.
Highway emergency phones	There are emergency phones along some highways.

Events

Some local tourist information services (see Information) can provide a list of the month's events. The newspapers, especially the Sunday, also publish a "What's On" for the region.

Some of the Main Events

Brooksville, Raid Festival; DeLand, Manatee Festival; Fort Myers, Rodeo; **January** Key Biscayne, Art Festival; Lake Worth, Gulfstream Polo; Miami Beach, Art Deco Weekend; Orlando, Scottish Highland Games; Palm Beach, Polo Season; Tarpon Springs, Greek Epiphany.

Coconut Grove, Art Festival; Crystal River, Manatee Festival; Daytona, **February** Speed Weeks (motor racing, including the Daytona 500); Fort Myers, Edison Pageant of Light; Hollywood, Florida Derby; Islamorada, Sportfishing Festival; Key West, Old Island Days; Kissimmee, Silver Spurs Rodeo; Lake City, Battle of Olustee Re-enactment; Miami, Film Festival; Miami Beach, Festival of the Arts, International Boat Show; Palm Beach, horse shows, horse racing, Flagler's birthday; Tampa, Gasparilla Festival; Winter Haven, Citrus Festival.

Arcadia, Rodeo; Boynton Beach, Boynton's Gala; Daytona, motor racing; **March** Fort Myers Beach, Shrimp Festival; Gainesville, Gatornationals; Jacksonville, Delius Festival; Key Biscayne, Tennis Championship; Miami, Little Havana Carnival; Naples, Florida Days Festival; New Port Richey, Chasco Fiesta; New Smyrna Beach, Images & Arts Festival; Palatka, Azalea Festival; Pensacola, Mardi Gras; Port Canaveral, Seafood Festival; Sanibel, Shell Fair; Sebring, 12-hour motor race; St Petersburg, Ocean Racing, International Folk Fair, Renaissance Festival, Festival of States; Tallahassee, Spring Time; Tampa, Florida State Fair, Strawberry Festival; Titusville, Valiant Air Command Air Show; Winter Park, Bach Festival.

Boca Raton, Addison Mizner Festival; Clearwater, Fun'n Sun Festival; **April** Deerfield Beach, Cracker Day; Gainesville, Spring Arts Festival; Hialeah, River Cities Festival; Jacksonville Beach, Beaches Festival; Key Largo, Indian Key Festival; Key West, Conch Republic Festival; Lakeland, Orange Cup Regatta; Lake Wales, Black Hills Passion Plays; Miami, Grand Prix motor racing; St Augustine, Easter Festival with Blessing of the Fleet; Sarasota, Sailor Circus.

Fernandina Beach, Isle of Eight Flags Shrimp Festival; Jensen Beach, **May** Sailfish Powerboat Championship; Panama City, Spring Festival of the Arts; Pensacola, Festival of the Five Flags; Pompano, Seafood Festival; West Palm Beach, SunFest.

Coconut Grove, Miami – Bahamas Goombay Festival; Fort Walton Beach, **June** Billy Bowlegs Festival; Miami, Miami/Budweiser Hydroplane Regatta; St Augustine, Spanish Night Watch, Greek Landing; Sarasota, Music Festival.

Key West, Hemingway Festival. **July**

Boca Raton, Boca Festival. **August**

Coconut Grove, Miami Boat Show; DeLand, DeLand – St John's River **September** Festival; Jacksonville, Riverside Art Festival; Miami, Festival; St Augustine, Anniversary of the Founding.

Cedar Key, Seafood Festival; Clearwater, Jazz Holidays; Cocoa Beach, **October** Space Coast Art Festival; Destin, Seafood Festival, Deep Sea Rodeo; Key West, Fantasy Festival; Kissimmee, State Air Fair; Lake City, North Florida Air Show; Miami, Bayfront Park, October Festival; Naples, Swamp Buggy Festival; Orlando, Pioneer Days; Perry, Forest Festival; St Petersburg Beach, Beach Festival; Venice, Venetian Sun Fiesta.

Apalachicola, Seafood & Oyster Festival; Jensen Beach, Pineapple Festival; **November** Key Largo, Island Jubilee; Marathon, Key Colony Beach Sailfish

Tournament; Orlando, Light Up; Pensacola, Gulf Coast Art Festival, Blue Angel Air Show.

December   Fort Lauderdale Winterfest, Boat Parade, Rodeo; Miami, Orange Bowl Festival; Miccosukee Village, Indian Arts Festival; Palm Beach, Polo Season (until April); St Augustine, British Night Watch, Christmas Regatta; St. Petersburg, Florida Tournament of Bands; Walt Disney World, Christmas Parade.

Filling Stations

See Motoring

Filming and Photography

Florida is ideal for filming and photography. Film is readily available, and is often sold in drugstores or supermarkets at discount prices. It always shows the DIN or ASA light rating. Processing is up to European standards, and there is no shortage of places to get film developed, some of them offering ready-same-day services.

Fishing

Local tourist services often keep a full range of brochures showing the best places for fishing in their locality.

Big Game Fishing

Big game fishing for trophy fish such as marlin, shark, sailfish and wahoo is a very popular sport in the waters around Florida. Boats, complete with crew, can be charted at many of the resorts, with tackle and bait provided. Deep-sea fishermen often favour the waters between Florida and the Bahamas where there have been many record catches. There are strict rules governing the times when fishing is allowed.

Fishing off the Beach

Fishing off the beach calls for heavy tackle similar to that used for deep-sea fishing, since it requires weights in excess of 100–150g and rods to match. To get a cast far enough out involves using a line that is at least 490ft/150m long, and there can be the same kinds of fish, with a big bite, to contend with.

Freshwater Angling

Opportunities for the freshwater angler vary considerably according to the district, so it is difficult to make generalisations. The best course is simply to find what the local situation is and to get a visitor's licence.

Food and Drink

Breakfast   The best place for breakfast is a coffee shop – most hotels have them – or one of the many fast-food outlets. An American breakfast usually consists of a glass of fruit juice – orange, grapefruit or pineapple – coffee, eggs, done in various ways, bacon, and *grits* or fried potatoes, with toast, butter and jam (jelly). Many breakfast buffets also serve milk and cornflakes, possibly freshly made muesli, fresh fruit and various kinds of yoghourt.

Lunch usually consists of something light, such as a burger, a salad, or a sandwich. The main meal in the evening can be much more substantial, with meat and fish dishes and all kinds of vegetables and other accompaniments on the menu. — Lunch and dinner

As Florida produces so much of its own beef it comes as no surprise to find that the top meat dishes are T-bone steak, porterhouse steak, sirloin steak and prime rib, and the ubiquitous hamburger. Chicken and pork dishes are very popular too, especially cooked in the southern style. — Meat dishes

Florida is famous for its seafood ranging from shellfish such as crab, shrimp, mussels, crawfish and oysters, to saltwater fish including yellowtail and red snapper. Stone crabs are a particular delicacy in the south of the peninsula, as is conch, a kind of shellfish found around the Keys and delicious in conch chowder. — Fish dishes

Besides traditionally American versions of steak, chicken and salad there is also plenty of good food which has been introduced by Florida's large ethnic communities. Besides Italian specialities, including the inevitable pizza, there are Greek dishes such as keftedes and moussaka, Mexican tacos and tortillas, Cuban-hispanic paella and picadillo, and food from the Caribbean and Far East. Kosher cooking is very well represented too. — Ethnic eating

As well as ice cream and yoghourt and various kinds of cheese cake, a favourite dessert is Key Lime pie, a real Florida speciality, creamy and flavoured with the juice of the local limes. — Desserts

Florida has fresh fruit and vegetables all year round. Its citrus fruit is particularly good, but so are the local salad vegetables, tomatoes, avocados, etc. — Fruit, vegetables

Thanks to Florida's many Cuban exiles, another local speciality is café cubano, an espresso-type strong, sweet coffee. — Coffee

Although Florida produces some wine of its own, most restaurants only have Californian and foreign wines. — Wine

Beer from the big breweries in Tampa and Jacksonville is sold everywhere in Florida. Like most American beer it tends to be more of a lager than the stronger beers found in Europe. — Beer

Locally produced orange, grapefruit and pineapple juice can be obtained throughout Florida. Cola type drinks are also very popular as thirst-quenchers. — Juice, soft drinks

Getting to Florida

Most people travel to Florida by air. Their principal destination is Miami, which has several daily flights from London's Heathrow and Gatwick, but there are also non-stop flights to Tampa and Orlando. During the holiday season there are plenty of charter flights as well. — By Air
Miami is also the main port of entry for visitors to Florida from Central and South America and the Caribbean.

Golf

Special fares	Some American airlines, such as USAir, offer special cheap air travel packages with discounts on internal flights to other American cities or combined air tickets covering trips elsewhere in the States and excursions to the Bahamas or the West Indies. It is certainly worth while finding out as much as possible about these before making a booking.
By Sea	The port of Miami handles more cruise passengers than anywhere else in the world and is where many of them start or finish their cruises in the Caribbean and around Central and South America.
Fly & Sail	Many of Florida's visitors arrive by sea and depart by air, and vice versa.
By Rail	In the past many vacationers who have fled the cold winters of the north-eastern states have made the trip to Florida's sunnier climes by rail. They still continue to do so, albeit on a smaller scale, and Amtrak has attractive bargain programmes for Florida, with a range of fares and packages, for travellers coming, for example, from Boston, Philadelphia, Chicago and New York.
By Road	The main routes into Florida by road are the Interstate 95 down the east coast, Interstate 75, which links up with the Florida Turnpike, and, from the west, Interstate 10. (See also Bus Travel.)

Golf

The Sunshine State is a mecca for golfers, where the stars of the golfing world can be seen playing on such famous courses as the Seminole Golf Club in Palm Beach, right on the ocean. There are other superb courses on Amelia Island, at Boca Raton, Bredenton, Fort Walton Beach, Jacksonville, Naples, Sarasota and around Orlando, etc.

Golf takes up a larger area in Florida than in any other state, and 1990 saw the opening of the thousandth golf course.

Many of these are public golf courses, and some of the private clubs also allow members of golf clubs from elsewhere to play on their courses. Various hotels and resort complexes which have their own golf course or access to neighbouring Golf and Country Clubs offer worthwhile flat-rate packages.

Information	Florida State Golf Association, P.O. Box 21177, Sarasota, FL 33583 Florida Golf Foundation Inc., 5500 Watkins Rd., Haines City, FL 33844; tel. (813) 439–27 65
Golf Guide	Florida State Golf Association publishes an annually updated Golf Guide listing over a thousand private and public golf courses.

Help for the Disabled

Florida building regulations cater specifically for disabled access, and this applies to all public buildings, transportation facilities, such as airports and cruise terminals, and hotels, restaurants, etc. The many attractions also have special services for the physically handicapped. There are plenty of additional parking spaces for the disabled everywhere.

Highways

Florida has an excellent network of highways and expressways. These fast dual carriageways, allowing the free flow of traffic, are the best way to get

Distances

Kilometres	Cape Canaveral	Clearwater	Daytona Beach	Fort Lauderdale	Fort Myers	Ft. Walton Beach	Jacksonville	Key West	Kissimmee	Miami	Miami Beach	Ocala	Orlando	Panama City	Pensacola	Sarasota	St Augustine	St Petersburg	Tallahassee	Tampa	West Palm Beach
Cape Canaveral		229	104	266	304	693	245	546	82	298	301	189	74	608	757	269	186	226	461	195	198
Clearwater	229		257	398	200	609	346	660	129	442	445	165	170	523	673	72	297	32	378	32	370
Daytona Beach	104	257		371	331	629	143	658	113	411	408	122	86	531	691	298	85	254	376	222	302
Fort Lauderdale	266	398	371		213	955	512	288	306	40	37	442	334	859	1021	325	449	374	712	376	69
Fort Myers	304	200	331	213		814	456	438	235	232	238	314	245	717	878	114	402	176	570	198	198
Ft. Walton Beach	693	609	629	955	814		514	1214	642	992	992	506	619	101	64	701	554	632	253	629	888
Jacksonville	245	346	143	512	456	514		798	257	552	549	152	214	418	576	384	62	334	261	304	443
Key West	546	660	658	288	438	1214	798		568	248	261	699	594	1118	1280	552	737	606	971	621	357
Kissimmee	82	129	113	306	235	642	257	568		346	349	125	28	544	724	185	184	150	410	121	257
Miami	298	442	411	40	232	992	552	248	346		13	477	371	896	1058	346	492	401	747	398	109
Miami Beach	301	445	408	37	238	992	549	261	349	13		478	371	896	1058	349	484	394	749	400	106
Ocala	189	165	122	442	314	506	152	699	125	477	478		115	419	581	232	133	184	272	154	373
Orlando	74	170	86	334	245	619	214	594	28	371	371	115		534	696	211	156	168	387	136	266
Panama City	608	523	531	859	717	101	418	1118	544	896	896	419	534		165	605	468	547	155	531	790
Pensacola	757	673	691	1021	878	64	576	1280	724	1058	1058	581	696	165		766	619	696	317	693	952
Sarasota	269	72	298	325	114	701	384	552	185	346	349	232	211	605	766		365	62	456	86	301
St Augustine	186	297	85	449	402	554	62	737	184	492	484	133	156	468	619	365		316	312	286	380
St Petersburg	226	32	254	374	176	632	334	606	150	401	394	184	168	547	696	62	316		400	32	320
Tallahassee	461	378	376	712	570	253	261	971	410	747	749	272	387	155	317	456	312	400		384	643
Tampa	195	32	222	376	198	629	304	621	121	398	400	154	136	531	693	86	286	32	384		312
W. Palm Beach	198	370	302	69	198	888	443	357	257	109	106	373	266	790	952	301	380	320	643	312	

to the main holiday resorts for motorists heading south. They also provide speedy east–west routes between places on the Atlantic coast and those on the Gulf.

Intercity Turnpikes (toll highways)

Tolls are charged for some highways and expressways, known in the States as turnpikes, and for certain bridges, causeways and tunnels. To avoid a long wait at the toll booth it is best to have some small change ready so that where an "Exact Fare" notice is seen it is unnecessary for a driver to stop but merely to throw the correct amount into the basket.

Tolls

From Downtown Miami to the Airport; 9 miles/15km.

Airport Expressway

Bee Line Connector: from Interstate Highway I–4 to County Highway Co 436 (Semoran Boulevard); 10 miles/16km
Bee Line Expressway: from Orlando Airport Plaza to State Highway FL 520; 22 miles/36km
Bee Line East: from State Highway FL 520 to Cape Canaveral; 20 miles/33km

Bee Line

From Downtown Miami to the Palmetto Expressway; 9 miles/15km

Dolphin Expressway

Everglades Parkway (Alligator Alley): from Naples to Andytown; 78 miles/126km

Everglades Parkway

Interstate Highway I–75 from the state border to Miami; 260 miles/419km
Homestead Extension from Miramar to Florida City; 47 miles/76km.

Florida's Turnpike

Holland East–West Expressway	Through southern Orlando; 13½ miles/22km
J. Turner Butler Expressway	From Jacksonville to Jacksonville Beach, FL 115; 10 miles/16km
Sawgrass Expressway	Expressway from Interstate Highway I–75 Interstate Highway I–95; 23 miles/37km
S Crosstown Expressway	Through southern Tampa: 17½ miles/28km
Speed limit	The speed limit on intercity dual carriageways is usually 55mph/88kph, but on some stretches where there is little traffic it can be 65mph/105kph. Look out for the speed limit signs, since American highway patrols take speeding over the limit very seriously.
Emergency telephones	Some highways have emergency telephones at regular intervals. There are call boxes situated along some highways. Otherwise the help-line to call, throughout America, is 1–800–336–HELP.
Police	Dial 911 for Highway Patrol.

Hiking

See Walking, Hiking and Cycling

Hitch-hiking

See Motoring

Holiday Apartments

During the past couple of decades blocks of holiday apartments and condominiums have sprung up all over Florida. These can range from the de luxe version, complete with its own mooring, to a plainly furnished highrise apartment with a view of the sea. These are mostly small furnished flats, with a few rooms, that work out particularly cheaply for more than three or four people travelling together. They have fully fitted kitchens but have the disadvantage compared with hotels of requiring more than a one-night stay, usually a minimum of two to five nights. Annually updated lists of these are kept by the local and regional tourist offices (see Information).

Hotels

Florida has an immense range of overnight accommodation. The number of rooms available in hotels, motels and resorts runs into hundreds of thousands, with new ones opening every year. These are often by the beach and provide top quality accommodation at relatively high rates. Cheaper alternatives are of course always available, from very simple motels and tourist hotels to places with a less favourable location and which are a long way from the beach or the tourist attractions.

Hotels are mostly located downtown or at the beach. The bigger hotels operate a shuttle service to fetch guests from the nearest airport, and some of them have shopping malls with hairdressing and beauty salons, airline, car rental, and travel agencies and sightseeing operators, and possibly also restaurants, snack bars and coffee shops.

Hotels

Resorts in the Florida sense are luxurious holiday centres with all kinds of leisure and sporting facilities. Often run along the lines of a very upmarket holiday camp, this type of hotel complex has its own beach, tennis courts, golf courses, horseback riding, etc., provides very good entertainment, and is generally extremely expensive.

Resorts

Motels are clearly for the motorist, so they are usually located on the highway with free car parking outside the room, and sometimes their own swimming pool and sports facilities, depending on what category they fall into. At times, however, the standard of service leaves quite a lot to be desired.

Motels

Hotel and motel prices are for the room, not according to the number of occupants, and for a double room with bath range from $40–$60 for budget accommodation to $120 and upwards for the most expensive. State and resort taxes are also added to the bill, accounting for up to 15% of the total. There is no extra to pay for children staying in the same room as their parents, but there is a $5 to $20 supplement for additional adults.

   Breakfast is rarely included in the price. Many hotels charge extra for garaging.

Prices

Many hotels, and especially the bigger and grander ones, have one or more restaurants, with prices varying according to the nature of the hotel.

   The larger hotels also have coffee shops, snack bars, small shops, beauty and hairdressing salons, and car rental and airline agencies.

Amenities

As a rule keys are not left at reception but are kept by the guest. All hotels have safes for valuables either in the rooms or at reception.

   (See also Safety and Crime.)

Keys and safes

Hotel and motel bills can be paid by credit card, traveller's cheque, or cash.

Payment

See Holiday Apartments

Condominiums

Accommodation should be booked as far in advance as possible, especially in high season. Most hotels have "800" numbers for making a reservation over the phone free of charge. Rooms can also be booked on arrival at international airports. These have a whole range of agencies which can take flight reservations and book excursions and rental cars as well. In Greater Miami the Greater Miami Reservation System operates a free-phone daily between 8am and 8pm; tel. (305) 866–03 66 or 800–356–83 92. Accommodation Guides can be obtained from local tourist information services (mostly Chambers of Commerce, see Information).

Room reservation

The big American hotel chains such as Days Inn, Hilton, Holiday Inn, Howard Johnson, Ramada and TraveLodge, are all well represented in Florida, often in some of the most attractive locations. Hotel vouchers are available and rooms can be booked in advance through travel agencies.

Hotel and motel chains

Best Western, tel. 800–528–12 34
Choice Hotel, tel. 800–4–CHOICE
Days Inn, tel. 800–325–25 25
Econo Lodge, tel. 800–4–CHOICE
Four Seasons, tel. 800–322–34 42
Hilton, tel. 800–HILTONS

Freephone reservations for some hotel and motel chains

Hotels

Holiday Inn, tel. 800–HOLIDAY
Hyatt, tel. 800–233–12 34
Inter-Continental, tel. 800–327–02 00
Marriott, tel. 800–228–92 90
Quality Inn, tel. 800–4–CHOICE
Radisson, tel. 800–333–33 33
Ramada, tel. 800–228–28 28
Ritz-Carlton, tel. 800–241–33 33
Sheraton, tel. 800–325–35 35
Stouffer, tel. 800–468–35 71
TraveLodge, tel. 800–255–30 50
Trusthouse Forte, tel. 800-225–58 43

Hotels, Resorts (Selection; hotels with good facilities)

Amelia Island	Amelia Island Plantation, 3000 First Coast Hwy.; tel. (800) 874–68 78, 534 r. Ritz-Carlton, Amelia Island, 4750 Amelia Island Pkwy.; tel. (094) 277–11 00, 449 r.
Boca Raton	Boca Raton Resort & Club, 501 E Camino Real; tel. (407) 395–30 00, 963 r.
Clearwater Beach	Radisson Suite Resort, 1201 Gulf Blvd.; tel. (813) 596–11 00, 220 r. Sheraton Sand Key Resort, 1160 Gulf Blvd.; tel. (813) 595–16 11, 390 r.
Coral Gables	Colonnade, 180 Aragon Ave.; tel. (305) 441–26 00, 157 r.
Crystal River	Best Western Plantation Inn & Golf Resort, West Fort Island Trail; tel. (904) 795–42 11, 136 r.
Daytona Beach	Best Western Aku Tiki Inn, 2225 S Atlantic Ave.; tel. (904) 252–96 31, 132 r. Howard Johnson Hotel & Conference Center, 600 N Atlantic Ave.; tel. (904) 255–44 71, 323 r. Treasure Island Inn, 2025 S Atlantic Ave.; tel. (904) 255–83 71, 232 r.
Fort Lauderdale	Bahia Mar Resort & Yachting Center, 801 Seabreeze Blvd.; tel. (305) 764–22 33, 298 r. Bonaventure, 250 Racquet Club Rd.; tel. (305) 389–33 00, 504 r. Pier 66 Resort & Marina, 2301 SE 17th St., Causeway; tel. (305) 525–66 66, 388 r.
Fort Myers	Sanibel Harbour Resort & Spa, 17260 South Harbour Pointe Drive; tel. (813) 466–40 00, 340 r.
Islamorada	Cheeca Lodge, on Oceanside Hwy.; tel. (305) 664–46 51, 203 r. Pelican Cove Resort, on Old Overseas Hwy.; tel. (305) 664–44 35, 63 r.
Jacksonville Beach	Lodge at Ponte Vedra Beach, about 8 miles to the south, on the A1A; tel. (904) 273–95 00, 66 r. Ponte Vedra Inn & Club, 200 Ponte Vedra Blvd.; tel. (904) 285–11 11, 202 r.
Jupiter	Jupiter Bay Resort & Tennis Club, 353 US 1 S; tel. (407) 744–02 10, 155 r.
Key Biscayne	Sheraton Royal Biscayne Beach Resort & Racquet Club, 555 Ocean Dr.; tel. (305) 361–57 75, 194 r. Sonesta Beach, 350 Ocean Dr.; tel. (305) 361–20 21, 292 r. Marriott Biscayne Bay Hotel & Marina, B, 1633 N Bayshore Dr.; tel. (305) 374–39 00, 605 r.
Key Largo	Sheraton Key Largo Resort, 97000 South Overseas Hwy.; tel. (305) 852–55 53, 200 r.

Curry Mansion Inn, 511 Caroline St.; tel. (305) 294–53 49, 15 r.　　　　Key West
Galleon Resort & Marina, 617 Front St.; tel. (305) 296–77 11, 96 r.
Hyatt, 601 Front St.; tel. (305) 296–99 00, 120 r.
Little Palm Island, Little Torch Key 33042; tel. (305) 872–25 24, 28 r.
Marquesa, 600 Fleming St.; tel. (305) 292–19 19, 15 r.
Ocean Key House, Duval St.; tel. (305) 296–77 01, 100 r.
Pier House, 1 Duval St.; tel. (305) 296–46 00, 142 r.

Hyatt Orlando, 6375 Irlo Bronson Memorial Hwy.; tel. (407) 396–12 34,　　Kissimmee
　924 r.

Chalet Suzanne, 4 miles to the north on US 17 A, at intersection US 27;　　Lake Wales
　tel. (813) 676–60 11, 30 r.
River Ranch, 24700 SR 60 E, 25 miles to the east; tel. (813) 692–13 21, 130 r.

Colony Beach & Tennis Resort, 1620 Gulf of Mexico Dr.; tel. (813) 383–64 64,　Longboat Key
　235 r.
Harbour Villa Club at the Buccaneer, 615 Dream Island Rd.;
　tel. (813) 383–95 44, 30 r.
The Resort at Longboat Key Club, 301 Gulf of Mexico Dr.;
　tel. (813) 383–88 21, 229 r.

Hawk's Cay Resort & Marina, 8 miles to the north on Overseas Hwy.;　　Marathon
tel. (305) 743–70 00, 178 r.

Eagle's Nest Beach Resort, 410 S Collier Blvd.; tel. (813) 394–51 67, 96 r.　Marco Island
Marco Island, Hilton Beach Resort, 560 S Collier Blvd.; tel. (813) 394–50 00,
　298 r.

Hilton, to the east via Melbourne Causeway; tel. (407) 777–50 00, 118 r.　　Melbourne

Doral Resort & Country Club, 4400 NW 87th Ave.; tel. (305) 592–20 00, 651 r.　Miami
Grand Bay, 2669 S Bayshore Dr.; tel. (305) 858–96 00, 181 r.
Inter-Continental, 100 Chopin Plaza; tel. (800) 327–30 05, 644 r.
Mayfair House, 3000 Florida Ave.; tel. (305) 441–00 00, 181 r.
Miami Lakes Inn, Athletic Club & Golf Resort, 18 miles to the north-west;
　tel. (305) 821–11 50, 308 r.
Turnberry Isle Resort & Club, about 9 miles to the north;
　tel. (305) 932–62 00, 342 r.

Alexander, 5225 Collins Ave.; tel. (305) 865–65 00, 160 r.　　Miami Beach
Doral Ocean Beach Resort, 4833 Collins Ave.; tel. (305) 532–36 00, 420 r.
Fontainebleau Hilton Resort & Spa, 4441 Collins Ave.; tel. (305) 538–20 00,
　206 r.
Ramada Resort Deauville, 6701 Collins Ave.; tel. (305) 865–85 11, 544 r.
Seville Beach, 2901 Collins Ave.; tel. (305) 532–25 11, 327 r.
Sheraton Bal Harbour Resort, 9701 Collins Ave.; tel. (305) 865–75 11, 663 r.

Edgewater Beach, 1901 Gulf Shore Blvd. North; tel. (813) 262–65 11, 124 r.　Naples
Park Shore Resort Hotel, 600 Neapolitan Way; tel. (813) 263–22 22, 118 r.
Registry, 475 Seagate Dr.; tel. (813) 597–32 32, 474 r.
Ritz-Carlton, 280 Vanderbilt Beach Rd.; tel. (813) 598–33 00, 463 r.

Delta Orlando Resort, 5715 Major Blvd.; tel. (407) 351–33 40, 800 r.　　Orlando
Peabody Orlando, 9801 International Dr.; tel. (407) 352–40 00, 891 r.
Penta, 5445 Forbes Place; tel. (407) 240–10 00, 300 r.
Stouffer Orlando, 6677 Sea Harbor Dr.; tel. (407) 351–55 55, 780 r.

The Breakers, 1 S County Rd.; tel. (407) 655–66 11, 528 r.　　Palm Beach
Chesterfield Hotel Deluxe, 363 Cocoanut Row; tel. (407) 659–58 00, 58 r.
Colony, 155 Hammon Ave.; tel. (407) 655–54 30, 111 r.

The Ocean Grand, 2800 S Ocean Blvd.; tel. (407) 582–28 00, 212 r.
Ritz-Carlton, Palm Beach, 100 S Ocean Blvd., Manalapan 33462;
tel. (407) 533–60 00, 270 r.

Pensacola | New World Inn, 600 S Palofax Street; tel. (904) 432–41 11, 16 r.

Pompano Beach | Palm-Aire Spa Resort & Country Club, 2601 Palm-Aire Dr. North;
tel. (305) 972–33 00, 191 r.

St Augustine | Ponce de León Golf & Conference Resort, 4000 N US 1; tel. (904) 824–28 21,
194 r.

St Petersburg Beach | Don CeSar Resort, 3400 Gulf Blvd.; tel. (813) 360–18 81, 277 r.
Sandpiper Resort Inn, 6000 Gulf Blvd.; tel. (813) 360–55 51, 159 r.
TradeWinds, 5500 Gulf Blvd.; tel. (813) 367–64 61, 381 r.

Stuart | Indian River Plantation Resort & Marina, 555 NE Ocean Blvd.;
tel. (407) 225–37 00, 320 r.

Tallahassee | Governor's Inn, 209 S Adams St.; tel. (904) 681–68 55, 40 r.

Tampa | Hyatt Regency Westshore, 6200 Courtney Campbell Causeway;
tel. (813) 874–12 34, 445 r.
Wyndham Harbour Island, 725 S Harbour Is. Blvd.; tel. (813) 229–50 00,
300 r.
Saddlebrook, Wesley Chapel; tel. (813) 973–11 11, 530 r.

Tavares | Mission Inn Golf & Tennis Resort, 10400 CR 48, Howey-in-the-Hills;
tel. (904) 324–31 01, 176 r.

Walt Disney World | Buena Vista Palace, 1900 Buena Vista Dr.; tel. (407) 827–2727, 1028 r.
Disney's Grand Floridian Beach Resort, 4401 Grand Floridian Way;
tel. (407) 824–30 00, 906 r.
Disney's Yacht Club Resort, 1700 Epcot Resort Blvd.; tel. (407) 934–80 00,
635 r.
Walt Disney World Swan, 1200 Epcot Resort South Blvd.;
tel. (407) 934–30 00, 758 r.

West Palm Beach | PGA National Resort, 400 Ave. of the Champions; tel. (407) 627–20 00, 335 r.
Palm Beach Polo & Country Club, 13198 Forest Hill Blvd.;
tel. (407) 798–70 00, 105 r.

Hurricanes

See Practical Information, Radio, also Facts and Figures, Climate

Information

Offices in the United Kingdom | United States Travel Service, 22 Sackville Street, London W1X 2EA;
tel. (0171) 495 44 66
Florida Division of Tourism in Europe, 18–24 Westbourne Grove, London
W2 5RH; tel. (0171) 727 16 61

Information Services in Florida

Travel Phone | Travel Phone USA gives out all kinds of tourist information;
tel. 1–800–255–30 50 (freephone).

State of Florida Department of Commerce, Division of Tourism,
107 W. Gaines Street, Collins Building, Tallahassee, FL 32399–2000;
tel. (904) 488–75 98, fax (904) 487–14 07

The Florida Keys & Key West, P.O. Box 114–7, Key West, FL 33041;
tel. (305) 296–38 11

Key Largo Chamber of Commerce, 105950 Overseas Hwy., Key Largo,
FL 33037; tel. (305) 451–14 14

Lower Keys Chamber of Commerce, Mile Marker 31, Overseas Hwy., P.O.
Box 511, Big Pine Key, FL 33043, tel. (305) 872–24 11. Free information
service: tel. 1–800–872–37 22

Monroe County Tourist Development Council, P.O. Box 866, Key West,
FL 33041–0866; tel. (305) 296–228

Key West Welcome Center, 3840 N. Roosevelt Blvd., Key West, FL 33040;
tel. (305) 296–44 44. Free information service: tel. 1–800–284–44 82

Greater Key West Chamber of Commerce, 402 Wall St., Key West, FL 33040;
tel. (305) 294–25 87

Greater Miami Convention & Visitors Bureau, 701 Brickell Ave., Suite 2700,
Miami, FL 33131; tel. 539–30 00

Greater Miami Chamber of Commerce, 1601 Biscayne Blvd., Miami,
FL 33145; tel. (305) 350–77 00

Miami Beach Chamber of Commerce, 1920 Meridian Ave., Miami Beach,
FL 33139; tel. (305) 672–12 70

Coconut Grove Chamber of Commerce, 2820 McFarlane Rd., Coconut
Grove, FL 33133; tel. (305) 444–72 70

Tropical Everglades Visitor Association, 160 US Hwy. 1, Florida City,
FL 33034; tel. (305) 254–91 80

Broward County Hotel & Motel Association, 1212 NE 4th Ave., Fort Lauderdale, FL 33304; tel. (305) 462–04 09

The Greater Fort Lauderdale Convention & Visitors Bureau, 200 E Las Olas
Blvd., Suite 1500, Fort Lauderdale, FL 33301; tel. (305) 765–44 66

Greater Fort Lauderdale Chamber of Commerce, 512 NE 3rd Ave., Fort
Lauderdale, FL 33301; tel. (305) 462–60 00

Greater Hollywood Chamber of Commerce, 4000 Hollywood Blvd., Suite
265–S, Hollywood, FL 33021; tel. (305) 985–40 00

Greater Pompano Beach Chamber of Commerce, 2200 E Atlantic Blvd.,
Pompano Beach Chamber of Commerce, 2200 E Atlantic Blvd., Pompano
Beach, FL 33062; tel. (305) 941–29 40

Palm Beach County Convention & Visitors Bureau, 1555 Palm Beach Lakes
Blvd, Suite 204, West Palm Beach, FL 33401; tel. (407) 471–39 95

Palm Beach Chamber of Commerce, 45 Coconut Row, Palm Beach,
FL 33480; tel. (407) 655–32 82

Chamber of Commerce of The Palm Beaches, 401 N Flagler Dr., West Palm
Beach, FL 33401; tel. (407) 833–55 82

Kissimmee/Osceola County Chamber of Commerce, 320 E Monument
Ave., Kissimmee, FL 32741; tel. (407) 847–-31 74

Kissimmee – St Cloud Convention & Visitors Bureau, P.O. Box 422007,
Kissimmee, FL 34742–2007; tel. (407) 847–50 00

Lakeland Area Chamber of Commerce & Visitors Bureau, P.O. Box 3607,
Lakeland, FL 33802–3607; tel. (813) 688–85 51

Orlando/Orange County Convention & Visitors Bureau, 7208 Sand Lake
Road, Suite 300, Orlando, FL 32819; tel. (407) 363–58 00

Seminole County Tourist Development Council, 1939 Booth Circle, Longwood, FL 32750; tel. (407) 834–33 04

The Walt Disney World Village Hotel Association, P.O. Box 10000, Lake
Buena Vista, FL 32830; tel. (407) 828–34 81

Information

West Orange Chamber of Commerce, 1450 Hwy. 50, Winter Garden, FL 32787; tel. (407) 656–13 04

Winter Haven Area Chamber of Commerce, 401 Ave. NNW, Winter Haven, FL 33881; tel. (813) 293–21 38

Winter Park Chamber of Commerce, 150 N New York Ave., Winter Park, FL 32789; tel. (407) 644–82 81

Central east coast,
Cape Canaveral,
Daytona

Cocoa Beach Area Chamber of Commerce, 400 Fortenberry Rd., Merritt Island, FL 32952; tel. (407) 459–22 00

Melbourne Palm Bay Area Chamber of Commerce, 1005 E Strawbridge Ave., Melbourne. FL 32901; tel. (407) 724–54 00

Destination Daytona Convention & Visitors Bureau, 126 E Orange Ave., P.O. Box 910, Daytona Beach, FL 32115; tel. (904) 255–04 15

Florida's Space Coast Office of Tourism, 2725 St John's St., Melbourne, FL 32940; tel. (407) 633–21 10

Stuart/Martin County Chamber of Commerce, 1650 South Kanner Hwy., Stuart, FL 34994; tel. (407) 287–10 88

Titusville Area Chamber of Commerce, P.O. Drawer 2767, Titusville, FL 32781–2767; tel. (407) 267–30 36

Central west coast, Tampa,
St Petersburg

Manatee County Convention & Visitors Bureau, 1111 3rd Ave. West, Suite 180, Bradenton, FL 34205; tel (813) 892–78 92

Pinellas County Tourist Development Council, Florida Suncoast Dome, Suite A, St Petersburg, FL 33705; tel. (813) 892–78 92

Discover Sarasota, 655 N Tamiani Trail, Sarasota, FL 34236; tel. (813) 957–18 77

Tampa/Hillsborough Convention & Visitors Association, 111 Madison St., Suite 1010, Tampa, FL 33602; tel. (813) 826–83 58

South-west coast
Fort Myers

The Chamber of South West Florida, 1365 Hendry St., Fort Myers, FL 33902; tel. (813) 334–11 33

Lee County Convention & Visitors Bureau, P.O. Box 2445, Fort Myers, FL 33902; tel. (813) 335–26 31

Marco Island Chamber of Commerce, 1102 N Collier Blvd., C–2, Marco Island, FL 33937; tel. (813) 394–75 49

Naples Area Chamber of Commerce, 3620 Tamiami Trail N, Naples, FL 33942; tel. (813) 261–61 41

North-west
Florida,
Tallahassee,
Panama City,
Pensacola

Okaloosa County Tourist Development Council, P.O. Box 609, Fort Walton Beach, FL 32549–0609; tel. (904) 651–71 31

Leon County Tourist Development Council, Leon County Courthouse, Tallahassee, FL 32302; tel. (904) 488–39 90

Panama City Beach Convention & Visitors Bureau, P.O. Box 9473, 12015 Front Beach Road, Panama City Beach, FL 32417; tel. (904) 233–65 03

Pensacola Convention & Visitors Information Center, 1401 E Gregory St., Pensacola, FL 32501; tel. (904) 434–12 34

South Walton Tourist Development Council, P.O. Box 1248, Santo Rosa Beach, FL 32459; tel. (904) 267–12 16

Tallahassee Area Convention & Visitors Bureau, 200 W College Ave., Tallahassee, FL 32302; tel. (904) 651–71 60

North-east
Florida,
Amelia Island,
Jacksonville,
St Augustine

Alachua County Visitors & Convention Bureau, 10 SW 2nd Ave., Suite 220, Gainesville, FL 32601; tel. (904) 374–52 60

Amelia Island/Fernandina Beach/Yulee Chamber of Commerce, 102 Centre St., Fernandino Beach, FL 32034; tel. (904) 261–32 48

Jacksonville Chamber of Commerce, P.O. Box 329, Jacksonville, FL 32201; tel. (904) 353–03 00

Jacksonville & The Beaches Convention & Visitors Bureau, 6 E Bay St., Suite 200, Jacksonville, FL 32202; tel. (904) 353–97 36

St Augustine & St John's County Chamber of Commerce, 1 Riberia St., St Augustine, FL 32084; tel. (904) 829–56 81

Inoculations

Inoculation certificates are only required for travellers arriving from parts of the world where there have been outbreaks of notifiable diseases. It is as well to check up with the appropriate consulate on the latest regulations before departure.

Insurance

It is essential to take out short-term health and accident insurance when visiting the United States, since the costs of medical treatment are high; it is also desirable to have baggage insurance, and (particularly with a package holiday) cancellation insurance. Arrangements can be made through a travel agent or insurance company; many companies organising package holidays now include insurance as part of the package.

Within the United States foreign visitors can effect insurance through American International Underwriters, 11226 Connecticut Avenue, NW, Suite 414, Washington D.C. 20036 (UK address: 120 Fenchurch Street, London WC3M 5BP).

Jai Alai

Jai Alai, pronounced "hi li", is a fast and furious ball game, combining speed and athletic prowess like no other sport, which is played in a stadium called a Fronton where spectators bet on the result. Thirteen games a night take place on a concrete court, 31ft/9.50m by 164ft/50m, surrounded on three sides by a wall, with the spectators behind protective fencing on the fourth side.

A version of the Basque game of pelota, Jai Alai in the United States is mainly a spectator sport in Florida, New York and California. Using a 28 in./70cm long type of curved racket called a cesta to gain speed and spin, the first player hurls the pelota, the hard rubber ball, against the opposite wall where it must hit above a marked line. Like tennis, the ball is only allowed to bounce once, but is then kept in play by being hit against the side and back walls of the court, or "cancha", reaching speeds of up to 186mph/300kph. The first player, or team in a doubles match, to reach seven points wins. The skill of the players, mostly professionals, combined with the gambling fever on all sides, make Jai Alai a very exciting and popular spectacle, for locals and visitors alike.

Big Bend Jai Alai, Exit 24, Chattahoochee; tel. 442–41 11
Dania Jai Alai, 301 E Dania Beach Blvd., Dania; tel. 927–28 41
Daytona Beach Jai Alai, 1900 Volusia Ave., Daytona Beach; tel. 255–92 22
Fort Pierce Jai Alai, 1750 S King's Hwy., Ft. Pierce; tel. 464–75 00
Melbourne Jai Alai, I–95, Eau Gallie Blvd., Melbourne; tel. 259–98 00
Miami Jai Alai, 3500 NW 37th Ave., Miami; tel. 633–64 00
Ocala Jai Alai, SR 318, Orange Lake; tel. 591–23 45
Orlando-Seminole Jai Alai, 6405 S US 17/92, Fern Park; tel. 339–62 21
Palm Beach Jai Alai, 1415 W 45th St., West Palm Beach; tel. 844–24 44
Tampa Jai Alai, 5125 S Dale Mabry, Tampa; tel. 831–14 11

Some of Florida's Jai Alai Frontons

Language

It has been said of the English and Americans that nothing divides us as much as our common language. Some of the more common differences are listed below. In Florida you will also hear a good deal of Spanish, thanks to the influx of refugees and other Hispanics, mainly from Cuba.

American English	English English
aisle	gangway
baggage	luggage
bathroom	toilet (private)
bill	dollar note
billfold	wallet
check	bill (restaurant)
collect call	reverse charges
comforter	eiderdown
daylight saving time	summer time
elevator	lift
erasor	rubber
eyeglasses	spectacles
fall	autumn
faucet	tap
fender	bumper
first floor	ground floor
flashlight	torch
gas, gasoline	petrol
hood	car bonnet
icebox	fridge
pants	trousers
pavement	road surface
purse, pocketbook	handbag
rest room	public toilet
round trip ticket	return ticket
second floor	first floor
sidewalk	pavement
stand in line	queue
store	shop
subway	underground train
suspenders	braces
trailer	caravan
trunk	car boot
two weeks	fortnight
underpass	subway
wrench	spanner
zip code	post code

Medical Care

Doctors, dentists, hospitals

In terms of provision, Florida has a fine network of medical care, and there are plenty of good doctors, dentists and hospitals. The problem for European visitors can be how to pay for them. A stay in hospital is usually very expensive, so it is most advisable to take out the level of temporary health insurance that will cover such an eventuality.

Medicines

Medicines are also easy to obtain in Florida. Any visitor needing regular medication should take a copy of their prescription with them so that an American doctor can renew it if necessary.

Health insurance

If you already have health and accident insurance check in advance on what kind of cover it affords in Florida. In most cases it pays to take out special insurance for the duration of the trip.

You would also be well advised to take out accident insurance to cover your time in Florida.

Accident insurance

Money

See Currency

Motoring

American Automobile Association (AAA)
Head office: 1000 AAA Drive, Heathrow, Florida, 32746–5063;
    tel. (407) 444–70 00
Branches: AAA East Florida Division, 4300 Biscayne Blvd., Miami 33137;
    tel. (305) 573 56 11
AAA East Florida, Colonial Shopping Center, 590 Primrose Dr., Orlando
    32803; tel. (407) 894 33 33

AAA

Anyone who breaks down driving a rented car (see Car Rental) should first contact the car rental people. The American Automobile Association can also provide assistance.

Breakdown assistance

Some highways have emergency telephones. Otherwise, the 1–800–336–HELP number is an all America helpline.

Emergency telephones

Dial 911 for Highway Patrol.

Police

Driver's Safety and Hitch-hiking

Hitch-hiking is not actually forbidden in the United States but it is illegal in Florida on highways and slip roads, and along the Florida Keys. Anyone who tries it runs the risk of being robbed, mugged, or worse, and it is very much frowned on by the police.
    Drivers are strongly advised not to pick up hitch-hikers. They should also keep a watchful eye out for pedestrians.

Hitch-hiking

Car drivers should check beforehand to make sure the car is safe and fit to drive. If it is a rented car any faults should be noted down in writing.
    When out driving make sure you know precisely how to get to your destination. If you want to ask the way pull up at a filling station or in front of a shop.
    If another road-user indicates something is wrong with your car, do not stop. Drive to the nearest filling station or a well-lit, easy to see parking spot and try and get help from there.
    If you do break down, stay put, with doors and windows locked, tie a handkerchief or scarf to the doorhandle or aerial and raise the bonnet.
    Keep doors and windows locked when driving and particularly when parked. That applies to stopping at traffic lights in towns as well.
    If you see anyone by the side of the road who seems in need of assistance do not stop but inform the Highway Patrol by calling 911 from the next public telephone.
    Always give way to police and emergency vehicles. They will be using sirens and flashing red and blue lights to make their presence known.
    If another vehicle runs into the side or back of the car do not stop immediately but try and get to the nearest well-lit parking lot of a store or filling station to call up the Highway Patrol.

Safety tips for drivers

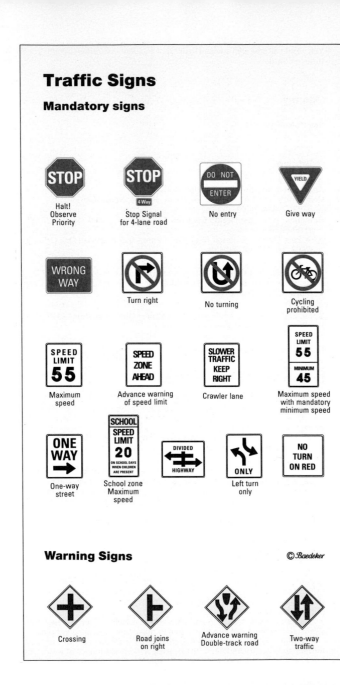

Traffic Signs

Mandatory signs

STOP
Halt!
Observe
Priority

STOP 4 Way
Stop Signal
for 4-lane road

DO NOT ENTER
No entry

YIELD
Give way

WRONG WAY

Turn right

No turning

Cycling
prohibited

SPEED LIMIT **55**
Maximum
speed

SPEED ZONE AHEAD
Advance warning
of speed limit

SLOWER TRAFFIC KEEP RIGHT
Crawler lane

SPEED LIMIT **55** MINIMUM **45**
Maximum speed
with mandatory
minimum speed

ONE WAY →
One-way
street

SCHOOL SPEED LIMIT **20** ON SCHOOL DAYS WHEN CHILDREN ARE PRESENT
School zone
Maximum
speed

DIVIDED HIGHWAY
ONLY
Left turn
only

NO TURN ON RED

Warning Signs

© *Baedeker*

Crossing

Road joins
on right

Advance warning
Double-track road

Two-way
traffic

Road narrows

Level-crossing

No overtaking zone

NARROW BRIDGE

Bends

Double curve beginning to right

Bends

STOP AHEAD

Give way ahead

School children

School area

Pedestrians

Dangerous descent

Slippery road

Maximum height

Heavy traffic

Beware of Alligators

Beware of deer

Cattle

Roadworks

Advance warning traffic warden

Maximum speed on Motorway exit

Warning Signs

© *Baedeker*

Rest area

Hospital

Camping site

Caravan site

Motoring

Never leave anything of value in the car.

Only park the car in a place that is well-lit and easy to see.

If stopping to get cash from a cash dispenser only use those that are safely located. Put the money away immediately and do not stop to count it.

Never leave your car unattended with the motor running (see also Safety and Crime).

Driving Licence

Anyone wanting to drive in Florida must be able to produce their own valid driving licence, and it is advisable to have an international driving licence as well, particularly if the visitor is from a non-English speaking country.

Filling Stations

There are plenty of filling stations in towns and on highway sliproads and intersections but they are not so easy to find in places that are more off the beaten track. Filling stations and repair shops are also fewer along the big intercity highways.

Traffic Laws

Each American state has its own traffic laws in addition to the federal legislation. These do not differ substantially from those that apply in Europe. Be sure to observe them, otherwise the police will not hesitate to take action.

Speed limits

Anyone breaking the speed limit will have the police to reckon with. In built-up areas the speed limit is between 20mph/32kph and 30mph/48kph, but it can be down to only 15mph/24kph near schools, hospitals and old people's homes. On single carriageways outside built-up areas the limit is usually 45mph/72kph, but if there could be wild animals crossing then at night it will only be 35kph/56kph. The speed limit on dual carriageway highways and expressways is 55mph/88kph, and it can be up to 65mph/104mph on less busy, out of the way stretches (see also Highways).

School buses

All traffic in both directions must come to a halt if a yellow schoolbus signals it is stopping to drop off or pick up schoolchildren. If the bus stops on a carriageway that is separated from the oncoming traffic by a green strip or a barrier only the traffic proceeding in the same direction as the bus has to stop.

Right turn on red

You are allowed to turn right on a red light provided you have first come to a complete stop and given way to any cross-traffic or pedestrians.

Dipped headlights

Dipped headlights must be used at dawn and dusk, when visibility is less than 328yd/300m, and on long straight roads with oncoming traffic such as the Tamiami Trail in the Everglades.

No Parking

Parking is not allowed on expressways outside built-up areas or on many busy urban roads. If you do have to stop, you must pull up onto the verge.

U-turns

You are not allowed to make U-turns on roads where this is indicated by a "No Turns" sign.

Unbroken lines

Unbroken yellow and white double lines indicate no overtaking. The same applies to single white lines on the driver's side. Many roads have turning lanes which can only be entered at the finish of the unbroken lines.

1 km = 0,62 mi
1 mi = 1,61 km

© Baedeker

State Parks

Traffic signs
See pages 322/323 for the major traffic signs.

Motorways

See Highways

Museums

The main museums are covered in the A to Z section of this guide under the headings for the separate places. For opening times it is advisable to check beforehand with the local information service (see Information). Many museums are closed on Mondays and some of them on Sunday mornings or another day of the week.

The cost of admission can be quite high. Some museums have concessions for children, schoolchildren and senior citizens.

National and State Parks and Forests

Florida has a great many natural conservation areas. These usually take the form of National and State Parks, Forests, Monuments, Historic or Archaeological Sites, and Recreational Areas, with restrictions governing land use and certain rules that visitors have to observe. They are wardened by park rangers and anyone wanting to explore them for themselves can only do so with the permission of the park ranger or under his or her supervision. Such conservation areas are usually well signed. Many of them also charge quite high admission. See maps pages 325, 327.

Naturism

Naturism is banned on Florida's beaches, and anyone picked up by the police will have to pay a large fine. A certain amount of tolerance is exercised in some parts of Miami Beach and Key West.

Newspapers and Periodicals

News-stands, drugstores and vending machines between them sell a wide range of newspapers and periodicals. The Sunday editions of the American dailies include supplements with full "what's on" listings and all the TV and radio programmes.

Florida's leading daily is the Miami Herald, and there are a number of other well-known local papers.

Opening Times

Shops,
shopping malls
Most shops are open Monday to Friday from 10am to 6pm; shopping malls which stay open until 9pm are also open on Saturdays. Some stores and malls open on Sundays, when they close at 6pm.

National Parks, Protected Forests
Game Reserves
Florida Trail

National Parks
Protected Forests
Game Reserves

GAME RESERVES

1 La Floresta Perdida
2 St. Regis
3 Blackwater
4 Eglin
5 Point Washington
6 Gaskin
7 G.U. Parker
8 Edward Ball
9 Apalachee
10 Robert Brent
11 Joe Budd
12 Ochlockonee River
13 Talquin
14 Apalachicola
15 Aucilla
16 Tide Swamp
17 Steinhatchee
18 Gulf Hammock
19 Fort McCoy
20 Citrus
21 Croom
22 Richloam
23 Green Swamp
24 Hillsborough
25 Cypress Creek
26 Osceola
27 Lake Butler
28 Raiford Tract
29 Nassau
30 Camp Blanding
31 Guana River
32 Hudson
33 Lochloosa
34 Ocala
35 Relay Tract
36 Tomoka
37 Farmton
38 Bull Creek
39 Three Lakes
40 Avon Park
41 J.W. Corbett
42 Holey Land
43 Brown's Farm
44 Everglades
45 Cecil Webb
46 Lykes Brothers
47 Rotenberger
48 Big Cypress
49 Crocodile Lake
50 Lignumvitae Key
51 Key Deer
52 Great White Heron
53 J.N. "Ding" Darling
54 Merritt Island
55 Canaveral Seashore

Banks are open Monday to Friday from 10am to 3pm, but with the later closing hour on Thursdays or Fridays of 6pm. | Banks

Post offices are open from 9am to 6pm Monday to Friday and from 8am to noon on Saturdays. Some of the smaller offices may also close for lunch. | Post Offices

Police

In America there is a difference between the city police, who deal with local crime and traffic violations in their areas, and the Highway Patrol, or State Troopers as they are also called, who look after highway safety and observance of the traffic laws out of town.

Post

The US Mail, America's postal service, only deals with letters and packages. Unlike most European countries, telephone and telegram services are provided by private companies. | US Mail

The postage rate for inland letters is 29 cents for the first ounce (28g) and 23 cents for each additional ounce. Post cards cost 14 cents. Airmail letters | Postage rates to Europe go for 50 cents for the first half ounce (14g) and 45 cents for each ounce thereafter. The rate for postcards and for airmail letter forms is 40 cents.

Post Offices   Post offices can be identified by the American flag outside. They are open Monday to Friday from 9am to 5pm or 6pm and Saturdays from 8am to noon. In the big cities there are post offices that stay open 24 hours a day. Postage stamps can also be bought in hotels, drugstores and various other locations, including air, sea and bus terminals.

Post Restante   Letters and packages sent as post restante should be marked "General Delivery" and sent to the main post office. They will only be kept for up to one month.

Letter boxes   American "mail drop" letter boxes are blue with the words "US Mail" in white.

Public Holidays

America has relatively few national public holidays. Even then, apart from Thanksgiving, Easter Sunday, Christmas and New Year's Day, some of the shops stay open, but banks, schools, public offices and some restaurants do close. There is no public holiday on Easter Monday or Boxing Day. Florida also has some local holidays such as Mardi Gras and Confederate Memorial Day. (See also Events.)

New Year's Day	January 1st
Martin Luther King Day	Third Monday in January
Washington's Birthday	Third Monday in February
Mardi Gras	Local Carnival, in parts of the Panhandle
Good Friday and Easter Sunday	March/April
Confederate Memorial Day	April 26th
Memorial Day	Last Monday in May
Independence Day	July 4th
Labor Day	First Monday in September
Columbus Day	Second Monday in October
Veterans' Day	November 11th
Thanksgiving Day	Fourth Thursday in November
Christmas Day	December 25th

Public Transport

City buses   All the larger towns and cities have a good local bus service.

Miami Metrorail   Miami has its own Metrorail rapid transit system. The "City Mover" runs through the centre of the city, linking all the main downtown destinations. There is also a commuter service with connections to the southern suburbs.

Tri-Rail   Tri-Rail operates regular daily rail services between Miami and Palm Beach (see Rail Travel).

Radio

Florida's airwaves are crammed with a great jumble of local and regional radio stations, mostly broadcasting canned pop and country and western music interspersed with commercials, traffic and weather updates and news headlines, plus the occasional phone-in.

Some of them are aimed at listeners of a particular ethnic origin (Haiti, Cuba, etc.) or one of Florida's many religious groupings, while others just broadcast news, sport or classical music.

Radio station WAQI Miami on AM channel 710 broadcasts 24 hours a day giving the latest traffic update.

Traffic news

The NOAA Weather Radio Network broadcasts on three frequencies with the latest news on what is happening to Florida's weather. It keeps listeners in the picture about conditions over Florida, the Gulf of Mexico, the West Atlantic and the Caribbean, and is the first station for information when a hurricane is in the offing.

Weather report, Hurricane warning service

The list below shows the frequencies that give the best reception of the NOAA weather reports for the following places:

Jacksonville, Melbourne, Miami, Panama City, Tampa	162.550 MHz
Clewiston, Daytona Beach, Key West, Pensacola, Tallahassee	162.400 MHz
Fort Myers/Cape Coral, Gainesville, Orlando, West Palm Beach	162.475 MHz

Rail Travel

Although the history of tourism in Florida and the whole development of the Sunshine State is inextricably linked with the coming of the railroad, travel by train nowadays is nothing like it was in the days when grand locomotives with equally grand names brought sunseekers in crowds from the north. Today only two intercity trains bring holidaymakers from the big northern cities to America's southeastern resorts.

Amtrak

In Florida, as in the rest of America, Amtrak, the National Railroad Passenger Corporation, provides the rail passenger service and sets the timetable, but the track and the rolling stock are still owned by the various railroad companies.

Amtrak offers a variety of fare packages, such as its Rail Pass, at bargain rates. It also has a special Florida Rail Pass which covers travel on Amtrak services for a specific period with no limit on the number of stopovers.

Amtrak, 60 Massachusetts Ave., NE, Washington, D.C. 20002;
tel. (202) 906–30 00, fax (202) 906–22 11
Amtrak Hot Line: tel. 1–800–USA–RAIL

Information

In Florida Amtrak operates out of the following stations: Jacksonville, Palatka, DeLand, Sanford, Winter Park, Orlando, Kissimmee, Lakeland, Tampa, Clearwater (bus shuttle), St Petersburg (bus shuttle), Waldo (Gainesville), Ocala, West Palm Beach, Delray Beach, Deerfield Beach, Fort Lauderdale, Hollywood, Miami.

Amtrak stations in Florida

A regular motorail service operates in the peak holiday season (Christmas to Easter) carrying cars between Washington D.C. and Sanford, Florida.

Motorail

Tri-Rail

Tri-Rail operates cheap and frequent daily services Monday to Saturday over a 68 miles/110km-stretch of line linking Miami International Airport

Restaurants

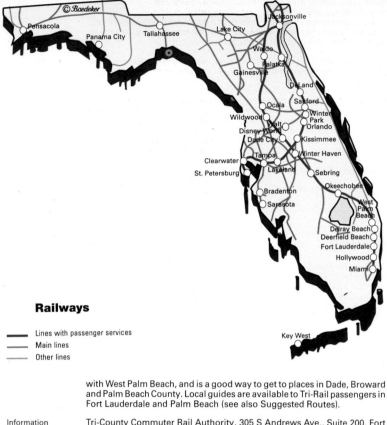

© Baedeker

Pensacola
Panama City
Tallahassee
Lake City
Jacksonville
Walde
Palatka
Gainesville
DeLand
Ocala
Sanford
Wildwood
Winter Park
Walt Disney World
Orlando
Dade City
Kissimmee
Tampa
Winter Haven
Clearwater
Lakeland
St. Petersburg
Sebring
Okeechobee
Bradenton
Sarasota
West Palm Beach
Delray Beach
Deerfield Beach
Fort Lauderdale
Hollywood
Miami
Key West

Railways

▬▬▬ Lines with passenger services

───── Main lines

───── Other lines

with West Palm Beach, and is a good way to get to places in Dade, Broward and Palm Beach County. Local guides are available to Tri-Rail passengers in Fort Lauderdale and Palm Beach (see also Suggested Routes).

Information   Tri-County Commuter Rail Authority, 305 S Andrews Ave., Suite 200, Fort Lauderdale, FL 33301; Tri-Rail Hot Line: 1–800–TRI–RAIL

Seminole Gulf

The Seminole Gulf Passenger Service operates excursion trains at least once a day during the holiday season between Naples, Fort Myers, Punta Gorda, Fort Ogden and Arcadia. Sections of the line also have "Brunch" and "Dinner" trains.

Information   Seminole Gulf Passenger Service, Metro Mall Station, Fort Myers FL; tel. (813) 275–84 87

Restaurants

Florida has an unusually large number of restaurants. They also range over many different types of food. Visitors can get all the traditional American dishes and sample the local seafood, as well as enjoying Tex-Mex, Greek, Italian and gourmet French cuisine, not to mention German, Swiss, Austrian, Korean, Vietnamese, Chinese, Thai, Japanese, Brazilian, Argentinian and Arabic fare. There are also more and more kosher and vegetarian eating places. Florida's many good seafood restaurants are particularly highly recommended, with a wide range of local specialities to choose from. As a drink with the meal, take the opportunity of sampling some of Florida's very respectable local wines, and be sure to try some delicious Key Lime Pie for dessert

Prices vary considerably. It is possible to eat relatively cheaply in one of the many fast-food outlets franchised by chains such as Denny's, Taco Bell, Pizza Hut, MacDonald's, Burger King, and Kentucky Fried Chicken. Better, if much more expensive, eating places are to be found in all the main tourist centres – the historic downtown areas, by the marinas, and close to the big resorts and grand hotels. Many places will take credit cards and American Express traveller's cheques as well as cash.

Prices

In the more expensive restaurants it is advisable to make a reservation in advance, especially on holiday weekends and at the height of the season, and it is usual to wait to be shown to a table.

See entry

Tipping

Mealtimes

Breakfast is served between 7 and 10am, and tends to be rather on the hearty side, with cereal and bacon and eggs.

Breakfast

Brunch is very popular on Sundays and holidays. A combination of breakfast and lunch, it is usually served from 11am onwards and consists of a big buffet with a good choice of dishes.

Brunch

Generally lunch, which is quite a light meal, is served between noon and 2pm.

Lunch

Dinner is the main meal of the day and is served between 6 and 10pm. Some eating places lay on "Dinner Shows" for the entertainment of their diners.

Dinner

A Selection of Restaurants (higher price category; see also Hotels)

Enzo's (Italian), 1130 S US 17/Longwood; tel. (407) 834–98 72
Kobé (Japanese), 468 W Semoran Blvd.; tel. (407) 862–28 88

Altamonte Springs

The Grill, in the Ritz-Carlton Hotel, 4750 Amelia Island Parkway; tel. (904) 277–11 00

Amelia Island

Chez Marcel (French), 1 S Ocean Blvd.; tel. (407) 362–99 11
J.T.'s, 301 Yamato Rd.; tel. (407) 241–93 66
Joe Muer (esp. seafood), 6450 N Federal Hwy.; tel. (407) 997–66 88
La Vieille Maison (French), 770 E Palmetto Park Rd.; tel. (407) 391–67 01
Seafood Connection, 6998 Federal Hwy.; tel. (407) 997–54 40

Boca Raton

Mr. C's (fish), 850 Lafayette St.; tel. (813) 549–18 18

Cape Coral

Captain's Table (fish), west end of the pier; tel. (904) 543–54 41

Cedar Key

Bentley's, 2516 McMullen Booth Road, Northwoods Shopping Plaza; tel. (813) 797–11 77
Black Swan, 13707 58th St. N; tel. (813) 535–79 26

Clearwater

Restaurants

Seafood Broiler (seafood), 28253 US 19 N; tel. (813) 799–37 30
Heilman's (esp. fish dishes), Clearwater Beach, 447 Mandalay Ave.; tel. (813) 442–41 44
Julie's (seafood), 351 S Gulfview Blvd.; tel. (813) 441–25 48

Cocoa Beach — Jack Baker's (seafood), 2200 S Orlando Ave.; tel. (407) 783–13 50

Coral Gables — Aragón, in the Colonnade Hotel, 180 Aragon Ave.; tel (305) 441–26 00
Charade, 2900 Ponce de León Blvd.; tel. (305) 448–60 77
Thai Orchid, 317 Miracle Mile; tel. (305) 443–63 64

Daytona Beach — Hungarian Village (Hungarian), 424 S Ridgewood Ave.; tel. (904) 253–57 12
Prime Sirloin (esp. seafood), 2595 Volusia Ave.; tel. (904) 257–67 67

Destin — Caporelli's (Italian), 104 US 98 E; tel. (904) 654–19 00
Louisiana Lagniappe, 775 Gulfshore Dr.; tel. (904) 837–08 81

Fort Lauderdale — Café de Genève (Swiss), 1519 Andrews Blvd.; tel. (305) 522–89 28
Casa Vecchia (Italian), 209 N Birch Rd.; tel. (305) 463–75 75
Down Under, 3000 E Oakland Park Blvd.; tel. (305) 564–69 84
La Coquille (French), 1619 E Sunrise Blvd.; tel. (305) 467–30 30
Old Florida (seafood), 1414 NE 26th St.; tel. (305) 566–10 44

Fort Myers — Peter's La Cuisine, 2224 Bay St.; tel. (813) 332–22 28
Veranda, 2122 2nd St.;/Broadway; tel. (813) 332–20 65

Ft. Myers Beach — Fisherman's Wharf, 1821 Estero Blvd.; tel. (813) 49 94

Ft. Walton Beach — The Landing, 225 Miracle Strip Parkway SW; tel. (904) 244–71 34
The Sound (esp. seafood), 108 US 98 W; tel. (904) 243–77 72

Islamorada — Coral Grill, Overseas Hwy., MM 83.5; tel. (305) 664–48 03
Plantation Yacht Harbour, 87000 Overseas Hwy.; tel. (305) 852–23 81

Jacksonville — Alhambra, 12000 Beach Blvd.; tel. (904) 641–12 12
L & N Seafood, 2 Independent Drive; tel. (904) 358–77 37
Patti's, 7300 Beach Blvd.; tel. (904) 725–16 62

Jacksonville Beach — King Wu (Chinese), 1323 S 3rd St.; tel. (904) 246–05 67
Point of View (esp. seafood), 2600 Beach Blvd.; tel. (904) 249–04 00

Jupiter — Backstage, 1061 E Indiantown Rd.; tel. (407) 747–95 33
Charley's Crab, 1000 N Federal Hwy.; tel. (407) 744–47 10

Key Largo — Italian Fisherman, 10400 Overseas Hwy., MM 104; tel. (305) 451–44 71

Key West — A & B Lobster House, 700 Front St.; tel. (305) 294–25 36
Half Shell Raw Bar (seafood), 231 Margaret St.; tel. (305) 294–74 96
Logun's Lobster House, 1420 Simonton St.; tel. (305) 294–15 00
Martha's, 2591 S Roosevelt Blvd.; tel. (305) 294–34 66

Kissimmee — Chef's Pantry, 809 N Main St.; tel. (407) 847–24 33
Murphy's Lobster House, 4736 W Irlo Bronson Hwy.; tel. (407) 396–04 01

Lake Wales — Chalet Suzanne; tel. (813) 676–60 11
Malcolm's, 253 Stuart Ave.; tel. (813) 676–82 42

Longboat Key — Euphemia Haye, 5540 Gulf of Mexico Dr.; tel. (813) 383–36 33
La Scala, 5350 Gulf of Mexico Dr.; tel. (813) 383–37 44
Moore's Stone Crab, 800 Broadway; tel. (813) 383–17 48

Perry's, 6900 Overseas Hwy., MM 51; tel. (305) 743–31 08   Marathon

Bavarian Inn (German), 961 Winterberry Dr.; tel. (813) 394–72 33   Marco Island
Café de Marco, 244 Royal Palm St.; tel. (813) 394–62 62
Snook Inn, 1215 Bald Eagle Dr.; tel. (813) 394–33 13

Nick's Steakhouse, 903 Oak St.; tel. (407) 723–66 59   Melbourne

Casa Juancho (Spanish), 2436 SW 8th St.; tel. (305) 642–24 52   Miami
Grand Café, 2669 S Bayshore Dr.; tel. (305) 858–96 00
Kaleidoscope, 3112 Commodore Plaza; tel. (305) 446–55 10
Wah Shing (Chinese), 9503 S Dixie Hwy.; tel. (305) 666–98 79

Café Chauveron, 9561 E Bay Harbor Dr.; tel. (305) 866–87 79   Miami Beach
Forge, 432 Arthur Godfrey Ave.; tel. (305) 538–85 33
Tiramisú (Italian), 500 Ocean Dr.; tel. (305) 532–45 36

Chardonnay, 2331 Tamiami Trail; tel. (813) 261–17 44   Naples
Merriman's Wharf (fish dishes), 1200 5th Ave. South; tel. (813) 261–18 11

Caruso's, 8986 International Dr.; tel. (407) 363–71 10   Orlando
Le Coq au Vin (French), 4800 S Orange Ave.; tel. (407) 851–69 80
Siam Orchid (Thai), 7575 Republican Dr.; tel. (407) 351–08 21

Julian's, 88 S Atlantic Ave.; tel. (904) 677–67 67   Ormond Beach

Café L'Europe (French), 150 Worth Ave.; tel. (407) 655–40 20   Palm Beach
Charley's Crab, 456 South Ocean Blvd.; tel. (407) 659–15 00
Providencia, 251 Royal Palm Way; tel. (407) 655–26 00

Blue Dolphin, 3101 W 23rd St.; tel. (904) 763–50 25   Panama City
Treasure Ship, PC Beach, 3605 S Thomas Dr.; tel. (904) 234–88 81

Jamie's, 424 E Zaragoza St.; tel. (904) 434–29 11   Pensacola
Jubilee Oyster Bar, 400 Quiet Water Beach; tel. (904) 934–31 08
Skopelos (Greek), 670 Scenic Hwy.; tel. (904) 432–65 65

Barnacle Bill's (fish dishes), 14 Castillo Dr.; tel. (904) 824–36 63   St Augustine
Raintree, 102 San Marco Ave.; tel. (904) 829–59 53

Basta's (Italian), 1625 4th St.; tel. (813) 894–78 80   St Petersburg
St Pete Fish House, 1080 Pasadena Ave.; tel. (813) 345–46 70

Le Pompano, 19325 Gulf Blvd.; tel. (813) 596–03 33   St Pete Beach
Wine Cellar, 17307 Gulf Blvd.; tel. (813) 393–34 91

Iggy & Paul's, Periwinkle Way; tel. (813) 472–13 56   Sanibel
Nutmeg House, 2761 W Gulf Dr.; tel. (813) 472–11 41

Café of the Arts, 5230 N Tamiami Trail; tel. (813) 351–43 04   Sarasota
Coasters (esp. seafood), 1500 Stickney Point Rd.; tel. (813) 923–48 48
Marina Jack, Island Park Pier; tel. (813) 365–42 32

Summerhouse, 6101 Midnight Pass Rd; tel. (813) 349–11 00   Siesta Key

Rayz, on Roosevelt Bridge; tel. (407) 286–35 00   Stuart

Café di Lorenzo (Italian), 1003 N Monroe St.; tel. (904) 224–17 83   Tallahassee
Chez Pierre, 115 N Adams St.; tel. (904) 222–09 36

| | Mill Bakery, 2136 N Monroe St.; tel. (904) 386–28 67 |
| | Morrison's (Southern cooking), 2415 N Monroe Street; tel. (904) 385–34 71 |

Tampa
Bern's, 1208 South Howard Ave.; tel. (813) 251–24 21
Harbour View Room, 725 S Harbour Island; tel. (813) 229–50 00
RG's, 110 N Franklin St.; tel. (813) 229–55 36
Spanish Park (Cuban), 2517 E 7th Ave.; tel. (813) 248–61 38

Tarpon Springs
Pappas' Riverside (Greek, seafood), 10 W Dodecanes Blvd.;
tel. (813) 937–51 01

Titusville
Sand Point Inn, 801 Marina Dr.; tel. (407) 269–10 12

Venice
Flying Bridge, 482 Blackpoint Rd.; tel. (813) 966–74 31

Vero Beach
Black Pearl, 1409 Ocean Dr.; tel. (407) 2334–44 26

West Palm Beach
Café du Parc (French), 612 N Federal Hwy.; tel. (407) 845–05 29
Cocoanut, 1201 US 1; tel. (407) 694–69 00
Parker's Lighthouse (esp. seafood), 2401 PGA Blvd.; tel. (407) 627–00 00
Picadilly, 1447 10th St.; tel. (407) 842–09 77

Winter Haven
Christy's, Ave. K/3rd St. SW; tel. (813) 293–00 69

Winter Park
Jordan's Grove, 1300 S Orlando Ave.; tel. (407) 628–00 20
Park Plaza Gardens, 319 Park Ave.; tel. (407) 645–24 75

Safety and Crime

Crime and criminals
Since the days of Al Capone, and more recently through Miami Vice, Florida, or rather Miami, has had a reputation for attracting the criminal element that operates on the darker side of American life. The social contrasts are particularly marked in Miami where jet setters and millionaires live side by side with impoverished refugees from Cuba and Haiti, and affluent yuppies dance the night away in the flashing neon of discos, while around the corner pitiful old people huddle in night shelters. Pimps, warlords and drug barons cruise around in their chauffeur-driven limousines past poverty-stricken blacks and hispanics who have to fight one another over the most poorly paid of jobs.

Warning
When in Florida be on your guard. Take all the necessary precautions. Muggings are not just something that happen in the big cities. They can also occur in the less densely populated areas, especially after dark. In an emergency ring the police immediately on 911.

Drug trafficking
Drug trafficking creates massive problems for the law enforcement agencies. Its long coastline and the nearness of the drug producers in Central and South America have turned Florida, and particularly Miami, into a dangerous major centre for the drug dealers and their trafficking in drugs.

Safety precautions
Avoid certain places at night, including parking lots, traffic terminals, public transport, and badly lit parts of town. If returning late at night take a cab. If at all possible, do not go out alone after dark.
Try not to look and behave like a tourist. Be discreet with your camera. Do not take candid shots in problematic places. Remember that there is nothing picturesque about poverty for the people who have to suffer it.
Never carry valuables or large amounts of cash; deposit them in a safe.

Avoid wearing conspicuous jewellery. Necklaces are a particularly attractive target for thieves.

Carry your belongings in a sturdy bag fastened round your waist rather than in a handbag or a shoulder bag.

At airports, bus or train terminals do not let anyone, however helpful they may appear, carry your bags to the taxi or hotel room for you, and do not divulge information about yourself to strangers or casual acquaintances.

If you think someone is following you tell the police as soon as you get to the nearest safe place.

Personal
safety tips

Keep a watch on your luggage at all times, but especially at airports, railway stations, car rental halls and on public transport.

Carry travellers' cheques rather than cash.

Use whatever hotel security facilities are available to you. Never leave any valuables in your room. Keep the door of your hotel room locked whether you are in the room or not, and do not open it to strangers. Take the key with you when you leave the room. Never keep the key with you if you leave the hotel with the intention of walking in the street – leave it with reception.

Always carry a note of the hotel name, address, and telephone number in case you get cut off from the rest of your party for any reason.

Children should always be accompanied by an adult.

If you are going out in a group agree on a place to meet (hotel reception, information booth, etc.) in case you get separated.

See Motoring

Safety tips
for motorists

Sailing

See Boating

Shopping

Typical Florida souvenirs include the locally grown citrus fruit; it is possible to get the larger fruit stands to pack any quantity of oranges and grapefruit and ship them back to Europe. Juices, jams and honey also make good souvenirs.

Souvenirs

The lovely seashells, mainly found on the Gulf Coast, are also popular as souvenirs. The big theme parks provide their own souvenirs and there is a whole range to choose from – Mickey Mouse T-shirts, sweatshirts and caps from Kennedy Space Center, cuddly dolphins from Sea World, Marineland or Seaquarium, movie memorabilia from Universal and MGM Studios, to name but a few. Indian handicrafts are another favourite with visitors to Florida. These come mainly from the villages along the Tamiami Trail.

All of Florida's towns and tourist resorts have an amazing variety of places to shop. Any place of any size will have at least one shopping mall, marketplace, galleria, flea market and discount store. The local tourist information services (usually Chambers of Commerce, see Information) will be able to supply the necessary details.

Places to shop

For the ultimate in shopping in Florida visit some of its prestige malls and places such as Worth Avenue in Palm Beach, Las Olas Boulevard in Fort Lauderdale, the Mayfair Shopping Center in Coconut Grove, a southern suburb of Miami, and, on the rather less expensive side, Miami Beach's Española Way, Ocean Drive and Bal Harbour Shopping Center, Miami's

Exclusive
boutiques

Clothing sizes							
Men suits	Europa USA	46 36	48 38	50 40	52 42	54 44	56 46	58 48
Ladies clothes	Europa USA	36 6	38 8	40 10	42 12	44 14	46 16	48 18
Men shirts	Europa USA	36 14	37 $14^1/_2$	38 15	39 $15^1/_2$	40 16	41 $16^1/_2$	42 17
Ladies stockings	Europa USA	0 8	1 $8^1/_2$	2 9	3 $9^1/_2$	4 10	5 $10^1/_2$	6 11
Men shoes	Europa USA	39 $6^1/_2$7	40 $7^1/_2$	41 $8^1/_2$	42 9	43 10	44 $10^1/_2$	45 11
Ladies shoes	Europa USA	35 5	36 $5^1/_2$	37 6	38 7	39 $7^1/_2$	40 $8^1/_2$	41 9

Bayside Marketplace, Orlando's Church Street Station district, Tampa's Harbour Island, Sarasota's St Armand's Circle, Pensacola's Palafox District and, lastly, St George Street in St Augustine.

Sightseeing

There are various ways of getting to Florida's main attractions. Bus operators, boating agencies and private pilots all offer their services, and some places can be reached by train. Hotel and motel reception desks and local tourist information services can supply brochures detailing the different excursion programmes.

Bus Travel   See entry

Rail Travel   See entry

Souvenirs

See Shopping

Smoking

No Smoking is gradually becoming the order of the day in America. Several airlines have already banned smoking and many public buildings have done the same. A great many restaurants are largely no smoking, with smokers confined to a small corner.

Sport

When it comes to sport, Florida has more to offer than any other state of the Union. It regularly attracts the world's best golfers, tennis and polo players, and is home to some of the top sailors, divers and windsurfers. Daytona and Sebring are famous for their auto races, Jacksonville for its dragster racing and Naples for its swamp buggy events – all this and the big horse shows and race days, not to mention greyhound racing.

Needless to say, most popular of all are the water sports – fishing, swimming, snorkelling, boating, sailing, and diving. Ball games include golf, Jai Alai, tennis, baseball, football and polo; these all have a great following.

Popular sports

A growing number of people have also recently taken up exploring Florida on foot, by trailbike (see Walking, Hiking and Cycling) and canoe. Florida's Department of Transportation in Tallahassee publishes various trail guides for cyclists and the Department of Natural Resources can provide more detailed information on routes for canoeing (see Boating).

Listings for sports events can be found in the daily papers or obtained from local tourist information services.

Sporting calendar

Taxis

Taxis, or cabs as they're called in the States, are usually quite easy to find in cities and tourist centres, and they can be hailed in the street.

Charges $2 for the first mile and $1.50 per mile thereafter. Waiting time costs 20 cents a minute. Since the distances covered in cities and beach resorts may be quite considerable some fares can be very expensive. The fare from Miami International Airport to Miami Beach, for example, will be at least $50, and that's not including a tip of 15 to 20%.

Fares

Tennis

Florida is the Promised Land so far as tennis is concerned. Many of Europe's top tennis players have worked on furthering their careers here, and the parents of aspiring young champions also send their youngsters to train here. TV-viewing tennis fans are also familiar with the tournaments at Amelia Island, Boca Raton and Key Biscayne.

Anyone who likes a game of tennis will be able to play in Florida virtually all year round, often on their hotel's own tennis courts, and there is always the chance of being able to watch top ranked players. Good travel agencies will be able to advise which hotels have their own courts and when the big tournaments are on.

Telephone

Public pay phones take nickels (5 cents), dimes (10 cents) and quarters (25 cents).

Public pay phones

Florida is divided into four three-digit area codes: 305 (the south-east and Greater Miami), 813 (west coast, Tampa/St Petersburg), 407 (Central Florida, Orlando, Palm Beach) and 904 (North Florida, Tallahassee).

Area Code

To make a local call dial 1 followed by the subscriber's number.

Local calls

To call long-distance in the USA dial 1 followed by the area code and the subscriber's number.

Calls within the USA

International calls	To make an international call on a private phone dial 011 followed by the code of the country then the area code, leaving off the first 0, and the subscriber's number. If using a pay phone dial 0 or 01 to get the operator who will give you further instructions.
International dialling codes	From the United Kingdom to the States dial 00 1 then the area code (without the 0) and the rest of the number.

From Florida the international dialling codes are:

Australia	011 61 plus area code, minus the first 0, and number
New Zealand	011 64, etc.
Republic of Ireland	011 353, etc.
South Africa	011 27, etc.
United Kingdom	011 44, etc.

Free telephone information	This can be obtained from the telephone directory of the phone company in question.
Rates	A three-minute call to Europe costs between 80 cents and $1.30, depending on the time of day. It is only worth trying to make an international call from a pay phone if it will take 25 cent pieces. Hotel phone calls are expensive and it is better to use a private phone or reverse the charges, i.e. make a collect call.
Cheap rate	The rate is slightly cheaper between 5 and 11pm, but the cheapest rate is between 11pm and 8am and at weekends.
Telecard	Many pay phones will only take telecards. Anyone wanting to use his or her own telephone charge card must give the number to the Europa Direct Service operator and the call will then be booked to their own phone bill.
AT&T Card	AT&T offers a similar, but cheaper, service with their own telecard. This can be obtained by anyone with an American bank account or holding a Diners or Visa credit card. The call will then be handled by the AT&T operator and put on the monthly credit card account.
Collect calls	To make a collect call ask the operator to get the number and see if the person at the other end will accept the call, thus reversing the charge.
Telegrams/cables	America has very few cable offices. Most telegrams are sent by phone. Check in the local phonebook for the number of a cable company, e.g. Western Union. In hotels telegrams can be phoned in to the operator or the receptionist. The cost, which will be quite considerable, will then be put on the hotel bill.

Television

American television has a great many channels. Programmes begin at 6am and go on well into the night, liberally sprinkled with commercial breaks on everything except the educational Public Service channel.

Theatre and Concerts

Florida's more affluent towns and cities enjoy a rich cultural life, due largely to patronage by their wealthier citizens. This has led to the endowment of theatres, concert halls, etc. The same applies to anywhere with a college or university since these will also have their own cultural facilities. This is particularly the case in Miami, Miami Beach, Boca Raton, Fort Lauderdale, Palm Beach, Jacksonville, Fort Myers, St Petersburg, Tampa and Tallahassee.

To find out what is on at theatres and concert halls look in the daily paper or ask at the local tourist information centre (see Information).

Programme information

Time

Most of Florida observes Eastern Standard Time, i.e. 5 hours behind Greenwich Mean Time.

Eastern Time

Florida's Panhandle observes Central Standard Time, an hour behind the rest of Florida and thus 6 hours behind Greenwich Mean Time.

Central Time

Summer Time, or Daylight Saving Time as it is called in America, when the clocks are put forward by one hour, is from the first Sunday in April to the last Sunday in October.

Summer Time

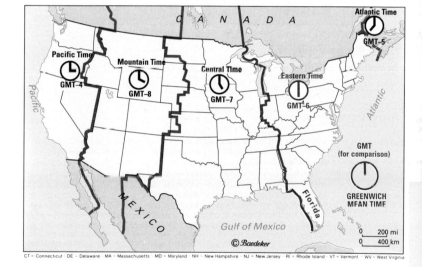

 CT = Connecticut · DE = Delaware · MA = Massachusetts · MD = Maryland · NH = New Hampshire · NJ = New Jersey · RI = Rhode Island · VT = Vermont · WV = West Virginia

Tipping

Unlike Europe, a service charge is seldom included in the bill in America, and has to be given separately. The people who work in hotels and restaurants are often badly paid and have to earn most of their income from tips.

Hotel porters expect a tip of 50 cents per item of luggage carried to or from the hotel room. The tip for hotel maids is usually $2 per day. Receptionists

Hotels

do not expect to be tipped unless it is for something special. Pool attendants get $1 per day per person. It is usual to tip the porter $1 for getting a taxi. For "Valet Parking", when the car is parked for you at a hotel or restaurant, you should give $1 for parking the car and $1 when it is returned.

Restaurants
The usual tip – which is left on the table – is 15–20% of the bill before sales tax. In the better class of restaurant the wine waiter and the head waiter will also expect a tip.

Taxi
Taxi drivers get 20% of the amount shown on the meter and on short trips sometimes a little extra.

Hairdresser/
barber
Barbers and hairdressers expect a tip of 15–20%.

Shoeshine
The usual tip for a shoeshine is 50 cents to $1.

Traffic Regulations

See Motoring

Traffic Signs

See Motoring

Travel Documents

Passport
Visitors to Florida, and indeed to the rest of America, must hold a passport which is valid for at least six months beyond their date of departure from the United States.

Visas
Although most people wanting to enter the United States require a visa, under legislation enacted in 1989 and extended in 1991 citizens of the United Kingdom, and other EU countries, can enter America without a visa if they are travelling on business, as a tourist, or in transit. Before arrival in America, however, they will have to fill in form I–94W which can be obtained from airlines, etc., or from immigration officials. Anyone who already has a B–1 or B–2 visa in their passport does not need to fill in the form. A visa is still required for anyone wanting to stay longer than 90 days, and for students, journalists, exchange visitors, government officials on official duty, prominent American citizens, and air crew. If a visa is necessary apply to your US embassy or consulate.

Return ticket
Anyone entering the United States must have a return ticket, or one for further travel beyond America.

Walking, Hiking and Cycling

To cater for the needs of environmentally friendly tourism, and thus avoid further deterioration of the state's ecology and natural habitats, Florida has set up a network of trails for hikers and cyclists. Besides the Florida Trail, which runs the length of the state, there are trails of varying lengths – often on raised boardwalks in the swamplands – in national and state parks, recreational areas and shorelands. These make it possible to explore the countryside in relative safety and enjoy some breath-taking views.

See A to Z, Florida Trail   Florida Trail

See entry   National and
                                                              State Parks, etc.

The national and state parks and forests have their own visitor centres and   Information
information bureaus. Various park rangers also lead guided tours of their   and guides
areas.

Florida Trail Association, P.O. Box 13708, Gainesville, FL 32604;   Trail Association
tel. (904) 378–8823, 1–800–343–1882 (Florida only)

Weather Services

So far as its weather is concerned, Florida has a record of the sort of cold fronts, areas of low pressure, tropical storms, etc. that can bring tornadoes and sometimes hurricanes sweeping over the country (see Facts and Figures, Climate).
  The hurricane season is between May and November, and more particularly from mid-August to mid-October. The National Hurricane Center in Miami uses data from satellite and aircraft to monitor weather patterns over the Gulf of Mexico and the Caribbean as well as Florida, and their information is passed on to the NOAA weather service which operates a very good warning system.

Newscasts on radio and television (see entries) include weather reports   Weather reports
and forecasts at regular intervals.

See Radio   NOAA Weather
                                                              Radio Network

When to Go

See Facts and Figures, Climate

Wine

Florida has a number of vineyards and wineries. These are mostly around Tallahassee and in the western part of the peninsula.

Young People's Accommodation

Youth hostels in Florida are few and far between, but for young people they do offer relatively cheap accommodation. To qualify you need to have an international youth hostel card or be a member of the American Youth Hostels Association.

Youth Hostels

Miami Beach

Miami Beach AYH Hostel (200 beds), 1438 Washington Avenue, Miami Beach, FL 33139; tel. (407) 534–29 88, fax (305) 673–03 46

Orlando

Orlando International AYH Hostel at Plantation Manor (90 beds), 227 N Eola Dr., Orlando, FL 32801; tel. (407) 843–88 88, fax (407) 841–88 67

Women's Community Club (women only, 10 beds), 107 E Hillcrest St., Orlando, FL 32801; tel. (407) 425–25 02

Panama City

Myrtlewood Lodge Home Hostel (14 beds); tel. (904) 785–62 26 (also exact address information)

St Augustine

St Augustine AYH Hostel (24 beds), 32 Treasury St., St Augustine, FL 32084; tel. (904) 829–61 63

YMCA, YWCA

All of Florida's big cities have YMCA and YWCA hostels for young men and women respectively, but most of them tend to be fully booked and they can be quite expensive.

Information

In the USA:
YMCA/YWCA Central Office, 291 Broadway, New York NR 10010
In the United Kingdom:
National Council of YMCAs, 640 Forest Rd., Walthamstow, London E17 3DZ; tel. (0181) 520 5599

Index

125 illustrations, 26 maps and plans, 3 drawings, 2 block diagrams, 1 large map at end of book

Original German text: Inge Scherm, Annette Bickel, Helmut Linde, Dr Christina Melk-Haen, J. and P. Seeberger, Reinhard Zakrzewski, Dagmar Zimmermann

Editorial work: Baedeker, Stuttgart
English language edition: Alec Court
General direction: Dr Peter Baumgarten, Baedeker Stuttgart

Cartography: Christoph Gallus, Hohberg-Niederschopfheim; Gert Oberländer, Munich; The Walt Disney Company, Frankfurt am Main; Sea World, Orlando; Busch Entertainment Corporation, Tampa; H. M. Gousha, New York (general map)

Source of Illustrations: Amtrak (1), Cabos (4), Deutscher Wetterdienst (1), Florida Department of Tourism (6), Florida State Archives (10), Herzof HC Consulting (2), Historia (1), Lang (5), Linde (31), Orlando Chamber of Commerce (1), Pinellas Sun Coast Chamber of Commerce (4), Randall G. Prophet (1), Scherm (48), Strüber (1), Tampa Convention & Visitors Bureau (2), USAir (1), Walt Disney Company (4)

English translation: Julie Bullock, David Cocking, Brenda Ferris, Crispin Warren

2nd English edition 1995

© Baedeker Stuttgart
Original German edition 1995

Published in the United States by:
Macmillan Travel
A Simon & Schuster Macmillan Company
1633 Broadway
New York, NY 10019–6785

Macmillan is a registered trademark of Macmillan, Inc.

Distributed in the United Kingdom by the Publishing Division of the Automobile Association, Fanum House, Basingstoke, Hampshire RG21 2EA

Licensed user:
Mairs Geographischer Verlag GmbH & Co., Ostfildern-Kemnat bei Stuttgart

The name *Baedeker* is a registered trademark

A CIP catalogue record of this book is available from the British Library

Printed in Italy by G. Canale & C.S.p.A – Borgaro T.se –Turin

ISBN 0–02–860681–7 US and Canada

Library of Congress Catalog Card Number: 92–083959